Students with Acquired Brain Injury

Students with Acquired Brain Injury

The School's Response

edited by

Ann Glang, Ph.D.
Teaching Research Division
Western Oregon State College
Eugene, Oregon

George H.S. Singer, Ph.D.
University of California
Santa Barbara

Bonnie Todis, Ph.D.
Teaching Research Division
Western Oregon State College
Eugene, Oregon

·P·A·U·L·H·
BROOKES
PUBLISHING Cº

Baltimore • London • Toronto • Sydney

Paul H. Brookes Publishing Co.
Post Office Box 10624
Baltimore, Maryland 21285-0624

Typeset by A.W. Bennett, Inc., Hartland, Vermont.
Manufactured in the United States by
Thomson-Shore, Dexter, Michigan.

All case examples in this book describe real events. Parents, students, and educators have given their permission to the authors to publish their stories in the hope that their experiences might benefit others. Names and other identifying information have been changed to protect the privacy of these individuals.

Library of Congress Cataloging-in-Publication Data
Students with acquired brain injury : the school's response /
    edited by Ann Glang, George H.S. Singer & Bonnie Todis.
        p.   cm.
    Includes bibliographical references and index.
    ISBN 1-55766-285-1
    1. Brain-damaged children—Education—United States.
    2. Brain-damaged children—Rehabilitation—United States.
    I. Glang, Ann.   II. Singer, George H.S.   III. Todis, Bonnie.
    LC4596.S88   1997
    371.92—DC21   97-2177
                                                        CIP

British Library Cataloguing in Publication data are available
from the British Library.

Contents

Section I   Understanding and Defining the Context

Section II   Planning and Carrying Out Instruction

About the Editors

Ann Glang, Ph.D., Associate Research Professor, Teaching Research Division, Western Oregon State College, 99 West 10th Avenue, Suite 370, Eugene, Oregon 97401

Dr. Glang is an associate research professor at Teaching Research–Eugene, a division of Western Oregon State College. She is a certified special education teacher and formerly worked as an educational and behavioral consultant in a rehabilitation unit specializing in treating adolescents and adults with brain injuries. Since 1987, her research interests have focused on a variety of areas related to service provision for children with traumatic brain injury, including support services for families, school consultation, social reintegration, and instructional interventions. With Dr. Singer and Dr. Janet M. Williams, Dr. Glang co-edited an earlier volume on pediatric brain injury published by Paul H. Brookes Publishing Co.: *Children with Acquired Brain Injury: Educating and Supporting Families.*

George H.S. Singer, Ph.D., Professor, Graduate School of Education, University of California at Santa Barbara, 2321 Phelps Hall, Santa Barbara, California 93106

Dr. Singer is a professor at the Graduate School of Education at the University of California at Santa Barbara. He is the editor of six volumes on children with disabilities and their families and has conducted qualitative and treatment research with parents of children with acquired brain injury. He is interested in ways of improving practices and policies in schools and other community organizations in order to better serve children with disabilities and their families.

Bonnie Todis, Ph.D., Associate Research Professor, Teaching Research Division, Western Oregon State College, 99 West 10th Avenue, Suite 370, Eugene, Oregon 97401

Dr. Todis is an associate research professor at Teaching Research–Eugene, a division of Western Oregon State College. In research projects at Teaching Research as well as previously at Oregon Research Institute and the University of Oregon, Dr. Todis has used qualitative methodology to explore a number of issues in special education. These issues include views on aging of older adults with cognitive disabilities, users' perspectives on assistive technology, resilience factors for youth with disabilities who have been incarcerated, barriers to self-determination for adolescents with disabilities, and an ongoing longitudinal investigation of educational issues for students with acquired brain injury and their educators and parents.

About the Contributors

Jan Blacher, Ph.D., Professor, University of California–Riverside, School of Education, Sproul Hall, Riverside, California 92521-0128

Dr. Blacher is a professor in the School of Education at the University of California–Riverside. She has directed the University of California–Riverside Families Project since 1982, a longitudinal study of the impact of children with severe disabilities on their families. She also serves on the Professional Advisory Boards of the May Institute and Bancroft, two organizations that serve individuals with acquired brain injury.

Thomas M. Boyd, Ph.D., ABPP, Clinical Neuropsychologist, Sacred Heart Medical Center, 1255 Hilyard Street, Eugene, Oregon 97401

Dr. Boyd did his undergraduate work at the University of Virginia and his graduate study at the University of New Mexico. He has worked with individuals with brain injuries since 1982. His areas of clinical and research interest include executive functions and everyday skills.

Elizabeth A. Cooley, Ph.D., Director, Special Education Projects, WestEd/Far West Laboratory, 730 Harrison Street, San Francisco, California 94107

Dr. Cooley is the director of Special Education Projects and a senior research associate at WestEd/Far West Laboratory. Since the mid-1980s, Dr. Cooley has developed, implemented, evaluated, and disseminated programs for students with disabilities and their families and the professionals who serve them, with a particular emphasis on children with traumatic brain injury. In addition to her federally funded work, she serves as a consultant, trainer, and evaluator for several other state and local programs.

Ann V. Deaton, Ph.D., Director, Psychology/Neuropsychology Services, Children's Hospital, 2924 Brook Road, Richmond, Virginia 23220-1298

Dr. Deaton is the director of psychological services at a specialized children's hospital where she works with children who have chronic medical conditions and catastrophic injuries. She has published numerous articles and chapters on the social, behavioral, and emotional effects of traumatic brain injury.

Mary Ann Fabry, B.A., Researcher, Teaching Research Division, 99 West 10th Avenue, Suite 370, Eugene, Oregon 97401

Ms. Fabry has been a data collector since the early 1990s; during 4 of these years she has gathered data on students with acquired brain injury. She is completing an interdisciplinary master's degree at the University of Oregon at Eugene in sociology, history, and counseling psychology. As a mother of a child born with disabilities, she has had personal motivation that has guided her along the research path.

Timothy J. Feeney, Ph.D., Assistant Professor of Special Education, The Sage Colleges, 45 Ferry Street, Troy, New York 12180

Dr. Feeney teaches graduate courses in special education. In addition, he is the coordinator of the Sage Statewide Neurobehavioral Resource Project, a program designed to serve people with traumatic brain injury and severe challenging behaviors in community settings. Since the mid-1980s, Dr. Feeney has worked with individuals who demonstrate challenging behaviors in schools, hospitals, rehabilitation centers, and community settings.

Tracey E. Hall, Ph.D., M.A., Assistant Professor of Special Education, Pennsylvania State University, 231 Cedar Building, University Park, Pennsylvania 16802

Prior to earning her doctoral degree, Dr. Hall taught special education in resource and self-contained classrooms for students with mild and moderate disabilities. In addition, Dr. Hall was a school district administrator for special education and Chapter 1 programs. She has served as a consultant for elementary through high school settings in explicit instruction, classroom discipline programs, curriculum-based measurement, and the inclusion of students with disabilities in general education classrooms. In addition to teaching, she has provided supervision for practicum students and trained doctoral students in supervising student teachers using effective teaching practices. Her areas of research interest include instructional design, curriculum modification in general education classrooms for the inclusion of students with disabilities, alternative assessment procedures, and formative evaluation practices.

Bonnie R. Kraemer, M.A., Diagnostic Education Specialist, Diagnostic Center, Southern California, 4339 State University Drive, Los Angeles, California 90032

Ms. Kraemer is a diagnostic education specialist at the Diagnostic Center, Southern California. She is also a doctoral student in special education at the University of California–Riverside. She is a frequent presenter on the topic of inclusive education and on topics related to educating students with severe disabilities. Her previous work experience includes working with adults who have severe disabilities in vocational and instructional settings as well as working at the University of California–Los Angeles's Neuropsychiatric Institute.

Robert T. Kurlychek, Ph.D., Clinical Neuropsychologist, Neuropsychology Associates, 132 East Broadway, Suite 700, Eugene, Oregon 97401

Dr. Kurlychek holds a doctoral degree from the University of Oregon and a diplomate in clinical neuropsychology from the American Board of Professional Psychology. He maintains an independent practice in Eugene and Albany, Oregon.

Ellen Lehr, Ph.D., Pediatric Psychologist, 19105 36 Avenue West, Suite 206, Lynnwood, Washington 98036

Dr. Lehr has worked with children and adolescents with acquired brain injury since the early 1980s in a variety of settings, including trauma care, acute and postacute rehabilitation programs, and schools. She is the author of the book *Psychological Management of Traumatic Brain Injuries in Children and Adolescents* published by Aspen Publishers, Inc., in 1990.

Kathleen A. Madigan, Ed.D., Assistant Dean, University of Oregon, College of Education, Education 102, Eugene, Oregon 97403

Dr. Madigan has been a teacher in general and special education environments since the mid-1970s. Since the early 1980s, she has been involved in designing instructional programs to improve memory and learning rates for individuals with acquired brain injury and other disabilities. She is the former regional vice president and program director for a postacute rehabilitation facility for individuals with acquired brain injury.

Sue Pearson, M.A., Iowa Consultant for Students with Brain Injury, Iowa Department of Education, Bureau of Special Education, and the University of Iowa, Iowa City, Iowa 52242-1011

Trained in special education with a special interest in orthopedic disabilities and learning disabilities, Ms. Pearson is the coordinator of educational services for students with brain injuries in Iowa. This position is a joint project between the Iowa Department of Education, Bureau of Special Education, and the Iowa University Affiliated Program. She provides technical assistance and support to Iowa's 15 Area Education Agency Brain Injury Teams as they build networks with medical services providers, educators, and families to assist students with school reentry following brain injury. Pearson is co-editor of the book *Signs and Strategies for Educating Students with Brain Injuries: A Practical Guide for Teachers and Schools* published by HDI Publishers in 1995 and has assisted in the production of two videotapes on school reentry and family adjustment following brain injury.

Ronald C. Savage, Ed.D., Director of Behavioral Health Systems, May Institute, 220 Norwood Park South, Suite 204, Norwood, Massachusetts 02062

Dr. Savage has worked with children, adolescents, and young adults with neurological disabilities since the 1970s. Dr. Savage is the director of Behavioral Health Systems at the May Institute. He has taught at the elementary and secondary school level as a classroom teacher and as a special educator. In 1990, Dr. Savage spearheaded the campaign to include the diagnosis of "traumatic brain injury" in PL 101-476, the Individuals with Disabilities Education Act. Dr. Savage has published numerous articles, chapters, manuals, and books about children, adolescents, and adults with traumatic brain injuries and other neurological disabilities; and he has spoken at many conferences, training seminars, and grand rounds presentations.

Joanne Singer, Ph.D., Researcher/Principal Investigator, University of California at Santa Barbara, Graduate School of Education, Santa Barbara, California 93106

Dr. Singer is the co-director of the Partners in Care Project with University of California at Santa Barbara and of the Neonatal Intensive Care Unit at Santa Barbara Cottage Hospital. She previously was an assistant professor at the Hood Center for Family Support at the Dartmouth Medical School and a behavioral and learning specialist for children with serious behavioral disorders and children with developmental disabilities. Her research has focused on promoting family-centered care in health care settings for children with special health care needs.

Sally Morgan Smith, Ph.D., M.S.Ed., Principal Transitional Alternative Program, North Kansas City Missouri Public Schools, 3100 NE 46th Street, Kansas City, Missouri 64117

Dr. Smith is the principal of a Transitional Alternative Program (TAP) for students with disabilities. Previously, she served on the Kansas Traumatic Brain Injury Project. For several years she was the transition coordinator at Leander High School in Texas.

Janet S. Tyler, Ph.D., Director, Kansas State Board of Education's Traumatic Brain Injury Project, Department of Special Education, University of Kansas Medical Center, 4001 H.C. Miller Building, 3901 Rainbow Boulevard, Kansas City, Kansas 66160-7335

Dr. Tyler is the director of the Kansas State Board of Education's Traumatic Brain Injury Project, a program designed to deliver inservice and preservice training and technical assistance in the area of traumatic brain injury to educational personnel. Dr. Tyler is also an adjunct faculty member in the Department of Special Education at the University of Kansas. She has published several articles on educational programming for students with traumatic brain injury and has presented at numerous international, national, and state-level special education and traumatic brain injury conferences.

Judith Voss, M.A., Project Coordinator, Teaching Research–Eugene, Western Oregon State College, 99 West 10th Avenue, Suite 370, Eugene, Oregon 97401

Ms. Voss is a doctoral candidate in special education and rehabilitation at the University of Oregon with an emphasis in building community and facilitating social relationships between diverse people. She works with children and adolescents in a variety of educational and recreational settings and is the parent of a teenage daughter with special needs.

Barbara R. Walker, Ph.D., Psychologist, Peace Health Medical Group/Behavioral Medicine, 175 West B. Street, Building D, Springfield, Oregon 97477

Since the early 1980s, Dr. Walker has worked in the area of parent–professional communication and collaboration. In addition to parenting a child with a disability, she has worked professionally to develop training programs to foster family-centered planning for children with disabilities. Most recently, this work was conducted at Oregon Research Institute and Teaching Research–Eugene. She is currently working full time as a counseling psychologist with a special interest in working with families who have a child who has disabilities as well as a consultant and trainer for various projects focusing on team building.

N. William Walker, Ed.D., Professor, Psychology Department, James Madison University, Harrisonburg, Virginia 22807

Dr. Walker is currently a professor in the Psychology Department at James Madison University (JMU). Before coming to JMU he was the national director of Neuro-Rehabilitation Services for a major rehabilitation hospital corporation and before that the director of pediatric neuropsychology at a major trauma center.

Mark Ylvisaker, Ph.D., Assistant Professor, College of Saint Rose, 432 Western Avenue, Albany, New York, 12203

Dr. Ylvisaker has worked with children and adolescents with acquired brain injury since the mid-1970s, in both rehabilitation and school settings. He is the author of a large number of publications on the subject, consults for several projects and programs, and is a frequent presenter at national and international conferences.

Preface

TEACHERS, ADMINISTRATORS, AND other school-based professionals play a crucial role for school-age children with brain injuries. In partnership with the child's family, they are the primary providers of each student's rehabilitation and educational program, and, as such, they are charged with preparing the child or adolescent for adult life.

Children and youth are unlikely to achieve optimal outcomes without the support, efforts, and commitment of a knowledgeable team of educators. Parents and educators consistently report that understanding the unique characteristics of these students is critical to serving them effectively. Although having a solid understanding of the causes and effects of brain injury is important, educators also need practical information about how to work with this challenging group of students.

The purpose of this volume is to provide a resource for educators that 1) is grounded in the experiences of students and their families and educators; 2) focuses on educational issues that occur in a range of typical school settings; and 3) describes, in detail, approaches that have been effective in improving the school experiences of students with brain injury. Because there is already much research and information on effective rehabilitation practices and on how to help students successfully make the transition from medical to school settings, contributors to this volume were asked to address issues that face students and educators in the months and years after students leave hospitals and rehabilitation facilities during their remaining school years. The interventions discussed here, therefore, span the school continuum and include approaches that can be implemented in a variety of school settings, from self-contained classrooms and one-to-one instruction to fully inclusive programs. The emphasis throughout this volume is on specific data-based intervention strategies that have proven effectiveness with students with acquired brain injury (ABI).

Section I, the first three chapters of this volume, provides an overview of ABI in children and youth. In these chapters, the authors describe the unique impact this growing population of students has had on the public school system. Perhaps most important, the chapters illustrate how parents, students, and educators experience the complex challenges of coping with the effects of ABI in educational settings. Although some previous research has highlighted the different perspectives of each of these groups, particularly during hospitalization and recovery, the examination of how each of these perspectives evolves once the student returns to school and how each individual with his or her differing views interacts around educational issues is only beginning to be recognized. Understanding the interaction of these perspectives provides the critical foundation for planning and implementing effective educational programs. More important, ignoring the importance of this interaction can doom even the best laid intervention plans to failure.

The chapters in Section II describe effective instructional planning, implementation, and monitoring for students who have experienced ABI. The steps in providing well-considered instruction are presented as an ongoing process, beginning with school reentry and continuing through the youth's transition to post–high school life.

Section III describes intervention approaches to help educators and students manage the social and behavioral challenges associated with ABI. The chapters include student-, peer-, educator-, and environment-centered strategies to help the student have a successful school experience, and they present empirically validated approaches to address what are often very difficult problems for educators.

Section IV presents specific information on creating effective professional development programs for educators serving students with ABI. This section includes strategies for forging collaborative parent–professional relationships as well as information on developing preservice and in-service training programs in ABI. The final chapter in Section IV presents frequently asked questions about students with ABI and offers practical solutions to common problems encountered by educators.

We have chosen to use the term *acquired* brain injury as opposed to the more common *traumatic* brain injury throughout this volume. The reason for this is practical. Although the cause of some injuries may be internal (e.g., brain tumor, encephalitis, anoxia), the effects are often quite similar to injuries resulting from external, traumatic events; and the strategies that educators can use to help students are the same.

We hope that through reading this book, educators who work with students with ABI will find that the problems identified in this volume by their colleagues resonate with their own experiences and that they will find the suggested approaches described in sufficient detail that they can be used to address the unique challenges faced by their students with ABI. In addition, we hope that educators will share their experiences using these and other strategies with colleagues to contribute to the growth of effective, school-based approaches to supporting students with ABI.

To the TBI Inservice team members who have worked to improve the quality of education provided to students with ABI and to the many students, family members, and educators who have allowed us to observe in their homes, schoolyards, and classrooms and have taught us about the realities of serving students with ABI

Students with
Acquired Brain Injury

Understanding and Defining the Context

All of us who live and work with children with acquired brain injury look for guidance as we learn about the challenges these children must face and how we can cope with the challenges they present. Our children need education to provide them with knowledge of their strengths, to help them compensate for their limitations, and to prepare them for the real world outside of their family, but their difficulties often are barriers to learning. Providing information to educators about our children's unique needs enables educators to design programs and make accommodations that minimize our children's frustrations and maximize their progress. Section One provides an overview of ABI and its effects and gives a much-needed map to help in charting a course of action.

Mary Grace Perry, mother of a daughter with ABI

chapter one

An Overview of Educationally Relevant Effects, Assessment, and School Reentry

Bonnie R. Kraemer and Jan Blacher

BRAIN INJURIES ARE a leading cause of death and disability in industrialized Western countries. The statistics are overwhelming. Estimates suggest that in the United States there are close to 1 million cases of brain injury requiring hospitalization each year (Berrol & Rosenthal, 1986). The number of brain injuries may be as high as 3 million per year if one does not limit the count to incidents of hospitalization or severe injury. At least 10% of individuals who survive a significant brain injury are likely to have residual impairments that endure over time (Kingston, 1985). In addition, the majority of individuals who experience a brain injury are likely to experience at least some transient cognitive, communicative, motor, or sensory impairment (Bigler, 1987a). Although the medical and rehabilitation fields have made remarkable inroads, it is surprising how little attention special educators have given to this issue.

This chapter addresses educationally relevant effects, assessment, and school reentry issues for children with acquired brain injury (ABI). The etiology and incidence of this multifaceted disabil-

Partial support for the preparation of this chapter was provided by Grant #HD 21324 from the National Institute of Child Health and Human Development, Jan Blacher, Principal Investigator.

ity, possible risk factors, and developmental considerations are high-lighted. Discussion includes both medical and educational models of ABI classification, as well as the complex constellation of cognitive, language, motor, memory, behavioral, and psychosocial effects manifested by many children with brain injuries. This chapter concludes with a brief overview of school reentry issues as they affect the family.

ETIOLOGY OF ABI

ABI results from a structural change within the soft tissue of the central nervous system above the spinal cord. The structural change can occur from two major events: 1) external events, such as closed or open brain trauma or 2) internal events, such as cerebral vascular accidents or tumors. Special imaging techniques, such as CT (computed tomography) scans, MRI (magnetic resonance imaging) scans, and EEGs (computerized electroencephalograms), have helped in the localization of brain injury, although it is still difficult to detect many microscopic lesions (Harrington, 1987).

External Events

The most frequent and pervasive type of ABI for school-age children is traumatic brain injury (TBI), defined as closed or open brain trauma. Closed brain trauma can occur either when a moving object strikes a child's head causing a sudden movement of brain tissue or when a child's moving head and body are suddenly slowed or stopped by a stationary object. This movement of brain tissue can cause localized injury through bruising, which occurs at the site underlying the area of impact or at the surface directly across from the site of impact (Harrington, 1987).

The major feature of most closed brain traumas is the wide-spread damage that occurs throughout the brain from the rotational forces acting on the child's brain tissue during an injurious act. The diffuse impact comes from neuronal shearing (Savage & Wolcott, 1994). The rapid acceleration and subsequent deceleration that accompany high-velocity impact cause the twisting of brain tissue and stretching of neuronal fibers that interconnect different brain regions (Bigler, 1987b; Johnson, 1992). This phenomenon is referred to as *diffuse axonal injury* (Harrington, 1987). It is this interruption of efficient communication through the nerve cells that causes the problems of closed brain trauma. Thus, "there is clear neuropathological evidence to suggest that the predominant pattern of injury in cerebral trauma is of a diffuse, nonspecific nature" (Bigler, 1987b, p. 462). This has significant implications for educators and rehabilitation professionals because results of the injury are typically widespread and affect many areas of functioning (e.g., memory, attention, perception, social skills, motor skills).

Open brain trauma (i.e., penetrating tissue wounds) occurs when a foreign object enters the brain, tearing a path in the tissue. Depending on the type of object and the force with which it enters the child's brain, it may cause a precise, localized path, or it may produce diffuse fragments causing damage throughout the brain (Harrington, 1987).

Risk Factors   Although ABI can result from both internal and external causes, most risk factors are related to external events and result in traumatic injury to the brain. Researchers have attempted to identify antecedent risk factors associated with childhood TBI. Although the conclusions are mixed, those studies that do report significant risk factors indicate the importance of considering premorbid characteristics of both the child and family. According to Goldstein and Levin (1987), investigations of the personality characteristics of children with TBI suggest that they may not represent a random sample. For instance, Craft, Shaw, and Cartlidge (1972) found a higher incidence of teacher-reported, preexisting behavior problems in children with TBI versus their classmates. Moreover, it has been hypothesized that features including impulsivity and hyperactivity may lead to risk-taking behaviors that result in TBI. Postinjury effects, then, may reflect, in part, premorbid characteristics, rather than being the direct result of brain trauma (Rutter, 1981). However, this is not definitive, as a 23-year follow-up study of children with TBI identified severity of the original TBI as the primary predictor of long-term outcome (Klonoff, Clark, & Klonoff, 1993).

There has been conflicting evidence in the literature concerning whether children who sustain brain injuries are at greater risk for a second injury (Goldstein & Levin, 1987). Studies by Jamison and Kaye (1974) and Partington (1960) did not find greater frequency of previous trauma in their sample of individuals with TBI. However, other investigations suggest the opposite trend. Annegers, Grabow, Kurland, and Laws (1980) found that the risk for a second TBI was age related. They found that expected incidence rates doubled after a brain injury sustained in children under 14 years of age and tripled for adolescents and adults ages 15–24. These authors postulate that some individuals develop behavioral patterns that in turn predispose them to additional injuries.

Age and Gender   The causes of TBI vary as a function of age and gender. Falls constitute a major source of TBI in children younger than 5 years old (Annegers, 1983), with a peak incidence rate typically reported at age 2. As children get older (5–14 years of age), the role of recreational injuries and injuries related to sports increases. In addition, both pedestrian–motor vehicle and bicycle accidents are common during this time period (Goldstein & Levin, 1987). Motor vehicle injuries are extremely prevalent in individuals 15 years old and older, with the number of severe injuries from car accidents experienced by 15- to 19-year-old adolescents equal to that of all the previous 14 years combined (Savage, 1991). Indeed, approximately 1 in every 181 adolescents experiences TBI. This rate is 2½ times higher than for children ages birth to 14 (Savage & Wolcott, 1994).

As is consistent with adults with TBI, boys are more likely than girls to sustain TBI, with an average reported ratio of 2:1 (Annegers, 1983). Boys also tend to have more severe TBI, with a mortality ratio estimated to be as high as 4:1 for boys and girls, respectively (Moyes, 1980). There are several difficulties with all of these estimates, however. For example, there is wide variation in occurrence depending on factors such as the source of the injury (car accident versus fall) or the geographic region of the country (urban versus rural) (Savage & Wolcott, 1994). Moreover, there might be some kind of gender versus source interaction (e.g., boys may be more likely to be injured on motorcycles than girls, but boy infants would not be more likely to be injured in car accidents than girl infants).

Internal Events

Although most children experience brain injury as a result of external events, children can also experience brain injury through internal events or causes. Internal causes of brain injury consist of the following: anoxic injuries, infections in the brain, vascular accidents, brain tumors, metabolic disorders, and the ingestion of toxic substances (Savage & Wolcott, 1994).

One of the most frequent internal causes of brain injury in children is injury that results from reduced oxygen in the brain (i.e., anoxia). Oxygen is necessary for the brain to perform metabolic and energy functions, and the brain can survive only a few minutes at reduced oxygen levels (Harrington, 1987). Thus, children are at risk for brain damage any time the flow of oxygen to the brain is interrupted for more than a few minutes. Anoxia can occur as a result of near-drowning accidents, anesthetic accidents, choking, and severe blood loss. Effects of anoxia are similar to those of closed brain injury (Savage & Wolcott, 1994); that is, there are widespread effects of diffuse damage that affect multiple areas of functioning.

ABI can also occur as a result of infections in the brain. There are various forms of infection that can enter the brain. Two of the most common are meningitis and encephalitis. Meningitis, which occurs as a result of a virus, bacterium, fungus, or parasite (Harrington, 1987), is an inflammatory disease that attacks the protective tissue surrounding the brain (the meninges). Encephalitis, which is usually caused by viral invasion of neurons in the brain (Harrington, 1987), is a generalized infection of the brain. Encephalitis may cause widespread damage, such as that seen with closed brain trauma or anoxia, or more localized damage, such as that seen with penetrating tissue wounds.

Vascular accidents (e.g., strokes) are another means by which children can incur brain injury. Cerebral vascular incidents occur when blood vessels become blocked, thus restricting the flow of blood and oxygen to various parts of the brain. Such incidents typically result in specific, localized damage (Harrington, 1987). Brain damage can also occur as a result of tumors in the brain or metabolic disorders that affect the brain, such as liver and kidney disease or insulin shock (Savage & Wolcott, 1994). Children are also at an increased risk for brain injury if they ingest or inhale toxic substances, such as lead, mercury, crack cocaine, or organic solvents (e.g., gasoline, cleaning fluids, paint solvents) (Harrington, 1987). Damage due to toxic substances typically results in widespread effects and affects many functional areas.

DEVELOPMENTAL CONSIDERATIONS OF ABI

Developmental considerations are paramount when trying to understand the effects of ABI. There are several perspectives on development in this context. The first involves consideration of typical developmental periods and how growth within these periods may be affected by ABI. The second involves life course considerations during which the effects of ABI may be experienced differently by parents and siblings depending on their development or stage in the typical family life cycle. The third perspective considers developmental influences in the selection and implementation of intervention for children with ABI and their families.

Children undergo developmental changes that involve the maturation of psychological and neurological systems (Lazar & Menaldino, 1995). It follows, then, that development at any given age or period (infancy, preschool, school-age, and adolescence) will be affected by ABI. The impact ABI has on an individual varies according to the chronological age of the child (Deaton & Waaland, 1994; DePompei & Williams, 1994). There is some literature containing evidence of children having greater recovery success than do adults (Fletcher & Levin, 1988; Lehr, 1990; Levin, Ewing-Cobbs, & Benton, 1984). This recovery often has been attributed to the greater plasticity of the brain of young children and to the capacity of certain areas of the brain to take over functions for damaged areas (Lehr, 1990). However, severe ABI does have unique consequences for young children as a result of the overlay of the recovery process on typical development (Lehr, 1990, 1996). Younger children have skills that are developing rapidly and are, therefore, more susceptible to the effects of ABI (Lazar & Menaldino, 1995). Indeed, some studies contradict the notion that younger children (e.g., those younger than 7 years old) are spared major dysfunction and suggest that these children may be even more vulnerable than adolescents or adults to brain damage (Lazar & Menaldino, 1995; Waaland & Kreutzer, 1988).

Developmental and life-span considerations pertain to the family of the child with ABI as well. The impact of ABI may be experienced differently by family members depending on their age and other developmental concerns. Drawing from the more generic literature on mental retardation or developmental disabilities, one might surmise that adolescent siblings of a younger child with ABI would endure considerable impact, whereas children younger than the child with ABI may be less immediately aware of the consequences. Undeniably, studies have shown that adolescent daughters, in particular, endure additional caregiving or even housekeeping responsibilities in families in which there is a child with mental retardation requiring extensive supports (Farber, 1959; Stoneman & Berman, 1993); we would anticipate similar role acquisitions by sisters of children who have ABI. In addition, young or middle-age parents of very young children may be severely affected by the injury and experience much stress and burden as they struggle to cope with new daily care needs in addition to an already busy life (Blacher, 1994). Older parents, whose other children have been "launched" (e.g., are in college, are living on their own), may have more time to care for a child or adolescent with ABI yet will face the "dual challenge" of continued caregiving as they, themselves, age (DePompei & Williams, 1994; Lehr, 1990; Seltzer & Krauss, 1989; Seltzer & Ryff, 1994).

Finally, developmental changes of the child also influence the type of therapeutic or intervention strategies recommended for a given family (Waaland & Kreutzer, 1988). For example, parents of an infant who is either unresponsive or hypersensitive may need to focus on strategies to promote bonding and attachment to their child who recently experienced ABI. Parents of a preschool child with ABI might be involved in parent-training efforts to facilitate their child's learning of new skills or behavior management programs to learn how to mitigate disruptive behaviors. Parents of an adolescent, however, might be more concerned with their son's or daughter's vocational or psychosocial needs (e.g., peer acceptance, sexuality, making the transition into adulthood). It should be noted that these strategies for intervention are not unlike those recommended for parents of children with developmental disabilities in general (see Baker, 1989, 1996). In addition to engaging in specific interventions geared to the developmental level of the child with ABI, families may have their own continuing needs, such as the need for information about ABI, family counseling, family support, advocacy efforts, or mentoring (Blosser & DePompei, 1995; Rosenthal & Young, 1988).

CLASSIFICATION OF ABI: A MEDICAL MODEL

It is important for educators and families to have an understanding of the medical model, in addition to the educational model, of classification for ABI so that they are better able to discern the nature and severity of the injury in "medical terms." That is, recommended practices in planning for a child who has experienced ABI require frequent dialogue and ongoing communication among medical/rehabilitation professionals, educators, and family members. Thus, it is critical that all individuals understand each other in terms of the language and terminology used.

The traditional benchmark classification of ABI is an alteration in level of consciousness. Because the majority of all brain injuries do result in some alteration in level of consciousness, this provides important information in establishing the magnitude and degree of the child's ABI. It also can provide some predictive information regarding outcome (Bigler, 1987b).

The most commonly employed method of quantifying level of consciousness is the Glasgow Coma Scale (GCS) (Teasdale & Jennett, 1974). The GCS evaluates three components of wakefulness independently of one another: 1) eye opening, 2) best motor response, and 3) best verbal response (Bigler, 1987b). The severity of injury can be quantified by using the total score for these three measures: Mild ABI is a GCS score of 13–15, moderate ABI is a GCS score of 9–12, and severe ABI is a GCS score of 3–8 (Savage, 1991). Based on the criteria of the GCS, coma is defined as the absence of eye opening, an inability to obey commands, and a failure to speak recognizable words. This definition is applied to individuals with a GCS score of 8 or less (Bigler, 1987b). The GCS ratings offer some indication as to the level and degree of severity of the child's brain injury on admission to the hospital.

The GCS does not necessarily predict level of outcome, although there is a relationship between lower GCS scores and poor outcomes. For instance, Heiden, Small, Caton, Weiss, and Kurtze (1983) studied 213 individuals with a GCS score of 8 or less and found that within 1 year postinjury 52% had died. Of the 48% who survived, 19% had good recovery (able to pursue typical activities with little difficulty), 16% had moderate disability, 11% had severe disability (awake but dependent on others for personal assistance), and 2% were in a constant vegetative state. To date, most studies that have examined the relationship between GCS scores and outcome have been conducted with adults, and, thus, the relationship between GCS and outcome in children is more tentative (Savage, 1991).

Posttraumatic amnesia (PTA) also has been used as an indicator of classifying ABI and has been used as an index for the severity of the injury. PTA assumes that the child is awake and functioning and has recovered from the comatose state but has persistent, severe impairments in retaining new memories (Bigler, 1987b). Several studies have consistently demonstrated that PTA lasting longer than 1 week (very severe PTA) is associated with poor outcome and persistent mental/cognitive dysfunction (Brooks, 1983; Ewing-Cobbs & Fletcher, 1987).

Last, the development of imaging procedures such as CT and MRI scans have enabled neurologists to examine a child with ABI in terms of the anatomical dimensions of the injury (Bigler, 1987b). CT scans provide utility in locating tumors and hemorrhages in the child's brain, whereas MRI scans are useful in locating and investigating edema and/or tissue pathology (Sattler, 1992).

CLASSIFICATION OF ABI: AN EDUCATIONAL MODEL

The Education for All Handicapped Children Act of 1975, PL 94-142, defines children with disabilities as those who require specially designed instruction or related services in order to benefit from education. These services include, but are not limited to, speech-language therapy, physical and occupational therapy, adapted physical education, psychological services, school counseling, school health services, social work services, and/or parent counseling and training. Until 1990, brain injury was not a specific disability category delineated in the regulations, and, as a result, many children had to qualify for services under other preexisting categories (e.g., other health impairments, multiple disabilities). Unfortunately, a number of children were not able to receive special education services because they did not "qualify" under one of the preexisting categories.

Fortunately, when PL 94-142 was reauthorized by the Individuals with Disabilities Education Act (IDEA) of 1990, PL 101-476, a separate category for students with TBI[1] was created. This was in part a result of a Cooperative Agency Agreement that was adopted in 1985 by the National Head Injury Foundation [now known as the Brain Injury Association] and the U.S. Office of Special Education and Rehabilitative Services, Council of State Administrators of Vocational Rehabilitation, and the National Association of State Directors of Special Education (Harrington, 1990). The purpose of the agreement was to provide a framework for individuals to work together with a common goal of improving and expanding research, education, and rehabilitation services for children with TBI. As a result of this Cooperative Agency Agreement and the efforts of educators, support personnel, medical professionals, and parents, the following definition of TBI was included in PL 101-476:

> Traumatic Brain Injury means an acquired injury to the brain caused by an external physical force, resulting in total or partial functional disability or psychosocial impairment, or both, that adversely affects a child's educational performance. The term applies to open or closed head injuries resulting in impairments in one or more areas, such as cognition; language; memory; attention; reasoning; abstract thinking; judgement; problem solving; sensory, perceptual and motor abilities; psychosocial behavior; physical functions; information processing; and speech. The term does not apply to brain injuries that are congenital or degenerative or brain injuries induced by birth. (IDEA, Reg. Sec. 300.7b[12])

NEUROBEHAVIORAL EFFECTS

After a severe injury to the brain, a variety of memory, cognitive, language, motor, and behavior disturbances may occur. The type of disturbance is often dependent on the location of the injury in the brain and the degree to which that brain region is used in the processing of information and environmental stimuli (Harrington, 1987). An examination of the neurobehavioral effects of ABI can

---

[1]In order to be consistent with the language used in federal legislation, the term TBI is used throughout this section.

assist in the design of a specialized educational program for a child who has sustained ABI.

Memory

Memory impairments are probably the most common characteristic of children with ABI. In fact, Telzrow (1987) states that memory impairments are among the more lasting and pervasive neuropsychological effects of ABI. This may be attributed to the fact that so many prerequisite skills, such as processing, organization, storage, and retrieval, comprise "memory," and difficulties with any one of these skills will affect what is remembered and recalled (Rosen & Gerring, 1986).

For children with ABI, the conflict between short- and long-term memory may be a source of continual frustration. A primary difficulty experienced by the child is an inability to consolidate short-term memories. That is, a child with ABI might have difficulty storing information from the immediate environment so that it can be used and acted on some time in the future. Because of this difficulty, he or she may have poor recall of the present moment and trouble acquiring and consolidating new information—a significant hindrance to successful education. However, long-term memory, or information that was previously acquired, often remains relatively well intact. Thus, the child with ABI can have relatively good recollection of the past (e.g., former abilities; previous social status; prior goals, interests, hobbies) but poor understanding and awareness of the present and future. This often results in memory gaps, confusion, frustration, and social-emotional difficulties (Harrington, 1987).

Cognition

Most children with severe ABI display some degree of decline in intellectual functioning relative to premorbid levels. Because of the typically diffuse nature of ABI in children, "It generally is not possible to identify unique neuropsychological performance patterns of localizing significance" (Telzrow, 1987, p. 537). However, children who have experienced ABI often have difficulty with tasks that involve complex problem solving, abstract reasoning, visual-motor integration, motor planning, and sustained attention.

For educators, the implications of cognitive impairment in children with ABI are significant. That is, for a child who returns to school following a brain injury, there may be significant differences in the degree of general comprehension and problem-solving abilities exhibited. In addition, children may demonstrate regressions in achievement skills from previous levels and may be unaware of these losses (Telzrow, 1987). The acquisition of new learning also may be unusually difficult for the child (Henry, 1983).

It must be underscored that children with ABI will likely display more marked variations in intellectual abilities, with greater variability among areas of cognitive functioning, than in children without ABI (Telzrow, 1987). Thus, a single index of ability, such as IQ score, cannot capture the range of actual performance levels (Johnson, 1992; Telzrow, 1987). There is some support, however, that the tasks associated with the Wechsler Intelligence Scale for Children–Third edition (WISC–III) Performance Scale (Wechsler, 1991) are sensitive to the neuropsychological effects of brain injuries (Chadwick, Rutter, Brown, Shaffer, & Traub, 1981). These types of tasks assess areas such as nonverbal reasoning, visual organization, visual memory, visual-motor integration, and motor planning (Sattler, 1992). When compared to tasks on the Verbal Scale of the WISC–III, performance tasks rely much less on the retrieval and use of overlearned information. As a result, preserved abilities, such as general information and vocabulary, may give the impression of intact functioning, when the child actually may be incapable of reasoning and problem solving at a commensurate level (Telzrow, 1987).

According to Ewing-Cobbs and Fletcher (1987), it is unclear whether IQ scores eventually return to preinjury levels. Comparison of posttraumatic IQ scores with premorbid estimates of intellectual functioning suggests that only a partial intellectual recovery is attained by children with severe ABI. Typically, the most rapid recovery of cognitive skills occurs within the first few months following the injury (Savage, 1991), with continued observable changes over the first year (Chadwick et al., 1981). Improvement may continue through the second year at a slower rate and in some cases for several years postinjury. Over time, however, it often becomes difficult to differentiate between a child's neurological recovery and the child's ability to learn to use his or her residual abilities more effectively (Ylvisaker, Szekeres, & Hartwick, 1994).

Language

There are many difficulties in linguistic abilities that can result from ABI. For instance, some children may demonstrate the inability to retrieve a specific name of an item or person, particularly in a demanding or stressful situation. Other children may exhibit slow, poorly articulated speech and/or an inability to comprehend complex sentences. In addition, written language skills may be depressed because of underlying language impairments (Telzrow, 1987).

Motor

Motor or movement impairments often occur as a result of damage to the brain. The injury can result in spasticity that produces tightness and discomfort, sometimes leading to the shortening of muscles, which limits the full range of physical movement. Brain injury may also produce tremors. Tremors are an uncontrollable rhythmic movement of part or all of the body. Apraxia can occur as a result of damaged brain tissue, which affects the ability to carry out an organized, sequential motor movement. Ataxia, which affects gross motor coordination and movement, can also occur with ABI. Moreover, oral musculature used for speech articulation can become impaired (Harrington, 1987; Telzrow, 1991).

Behavior

The behavior of children who have sustained ABI may be dramatically different following the injury. However, the relationship between injury severity and psychosocial adjustment appears to be rather complex. A study by Brown, Chadwick, Shaffer, Rutter, and Traub (1981) compared the incidence of behavior disorders in children with mild and severe ABI with that of a group of children with orthopedic injuries. The results indicated that the rates of new psychiatric disorders arising after the injury were unchanged for children who had mild ABI or an orthopedic injury. However, nearly half of the children with severe ABI developed new psychiatric disorders. The researchers found that by 2 years postinjury, the rate of behavior disturbance was three times higher in the group with severe ABI when compared to the other two groups. Despite substantial improvement in cognitive functions, the behavior disturbances of the group with severe ABI persisted over time.

There is some evidence that the expression of behavioral effects is age related, with younger children displaying overactivity, difficulties with attention, and aggressiveness, and older children displaying more difficulty with impulse control and self-monitoring (Telzrow, 1987). Furthermore, difficulties in self-control, compliance, motivation, mood, or self-esteem may need to be addressed in children of all ages. Rosen and Gerring (1986) point out that as children emerge from coma they frequently exhibit an extreme form of self-control loss. This is often referred to as disinhibition. For instance, some children may swear often, be agitated, or be aggressive. In addition, lack of control may be manifested in inappropriate joking or in instances of uncontrollable laughter or crying. Other forms of disinhibition may appear in social exchanges or may be manifested in poor temper control. Furthermore, children with damage to their frontal lobe may demonstrate difficulty with motivation. This lack of motivation may be interpreted as a conduct disorder, when actually it may be organic in nature. (See Chapters 7 and 8 for further information on behavior.)

PSYCHOSOCIAL ISSUES

The effect ABI has on a child extends beyond cognitive and behavior realms into the area loosely known as social or psychosocial adjustment. Much like losses in cognitive areas (e.g., memory, communication), social readjustment problems require ongoing and continued monitoring, all with the assistance and direct involvement of parents. Lehr (1990) provides a thorough review of psychosocial issues from a clinical or descriptive perspective. Longitudinal, empirical research is lacking, however, on psychosocial issues as they affect both the child with ABI and his or her parents. A useful conceptualization of psychosocial impact is provided by Deaton and Waaland (1994) who outline a variety of injury-specific, child-specific, and environmental factors that can interact to produce postinjury psychosocial difficulties.

Injury-specific factors are organic effects that result in altered behavior. One clear example is precocious puberty (i.e., involving the development of secondary sex characteristics), possibly as a result of damage to the hypothalamic area of the brain. Child-specific factors depend on what the child was like before, as well as after, he or she experienced ABI. Developmental considerations, mentioned previously, are also child specific. For example, psychosocial impact will vary greatly depending on the age of the child and the severity of injury. Bergland and Thomas (1991) interviewed 12 adolescents and their primary caregivers about issues of adjustment and transition. The teenagers interviewed reported suffering greatly from loss of self-esteem and body image. The most stressful thing for their parents, however, was the amount of time and energy required to provide care and supervision. These interviews covered the adolescents' reactions, as well as the reactions of other family members (e.g., parents, siblings, close relatives), to their injuries and therefore provided a comprehensive description of each youth's postinjury psychosocial environment.

There appears to be some discrepancy between cognitive and psychosocial recovery. Cognitive gains seem to increase over time with therapy and intervention. However, gains in the areas of social adjustment are less apparent; indeed, psychosocial problems may actually get worse over time (Waaland & Kreutzer, 1988). Emotional changes in children who have newly experienced ABI may cause stress in parents and their families, especially when they overlap with behavior or cognitive changes. Some investigators indicate that 25%–50% of children with ABI manifest persistent psychiatric or behavioral effects, including inattention, hyperactivity, irritability, mood swings, and poor anger control (Klonoff & Paris, 1974; Martin, 1988). As with more general psychosocial difficulties, predictors of diagnosable psychiatric effects seem to depend on child and family adjustment experienced prior to the injury. As noted previously, certain behavior characteristics may lead to more frequent risk-taking behaviors that eventually lead to brain injury (Rutter, 1981).

ASSESSMENT

The assessment of children with ABI can be a complicated process, particularly in light of the cognitive, linguistic, motor, memory, and behavior difficulties that often ensue as a result of damage to the brain. Nevertheless, it may serve several purposes. For instance, assessment during the beginning stages of recovery can provide a baseline level of performance that permits an estimation of the degree of recovery at different time intervals (e.g., immediately following injury, 3 months postinjury, 6 months postinjury). In addition, periodic evaluations that identify a child's changing patterns of strengths and needs are useful for monitoring progress made as a result of rehabilitative efforts (Ewing-Cobbs & Fletcher, 1987). Moreover, most professionals recommend that a child's current abilities and levels of functioning be assessed just prior to school reentry (Telzrow, 1991) in order to facilitate efficacious educational programming and intervention.

Assessment of children with ABI is multifaceted and covers many evaluation domains (e.g., cognition, memory and learning, communication, information processing, attention, sensorimotor, academic achievement, social behavior) (Rosen & Gerring, 1986; Telzrow, 1991). When conducting an assessment, it is critical to obtain current information about the child's functioning across such domains as well as to gather information regarding the child's learning and social behavior prior to injury. Moreover, it is critical to supplement standardized methods of assessment with naturalistic observations of the child's behavior in routine learning and social situations. Such observations can lend important information regarding the child's attending behavior, organization and planning skills, and reactions to environmental stimuli (Rosen & Gerring,

1986). A brief overview of assessment related to children with ABI follows.

Medical History

The first step in conducting a comprehensive assessment of a child with a newly acquired brain injury is to become familiar with the child's medical history and medical information surrounding the injury. This can provide data regarding the child's postinjury status. According to Harrington (1990), it is important to gather information regarding the length and severity of coma, the length of PTA, and the type and location of brain damage. The severity and length of coma, as well as the duration of amnesia following the injury, are generally good indicators of long-term outcome (see "Classification of ABI: A Medical Model" in this chapter). In addition, the type and location of injury is important in order to distinguish a localized, focal injury that may affect only one area of functioning from a more global, diffuse one that may affect several areas.

Preinjury Abilities

When assessing a child with ABI, it is critical to obtain information regarding the child's level of functioning and behavior style prior to injury. This can help professionals to gauge behavior that is radically different from levels prior to the injury and can assist when designing educational interventions. For the most part, it is believed that a child with above-average cognitive, academic, and social abilities has the best prognosis for long-term recovery and adaptive functioning. As would be expected, a preexisting academic or behavior difficulty will often remain or even worsen after the injury (Harrington, 1990). Prior school records are one important source from which to gather information about the child's previous levels of functioning. Most school-age children are given initial assessment batteries and group achievement tests that provide comparisons with same-age peers. Thus, information regarding the child's previous academic status and abilities can often be obtained through record review. Interviews with pertinent family members and school staff can also help assessors to gain a profile of the child's strengths and needs prior to injury.

Cognition

The most frequently used assessment procedure for determining cognitive functioning is the individualized IQ test (Sattler, 1992). IQ tests are employed with children of all ages in order to determine overall intellectual functioning as well as a cognitive profile. In addition, the IQ test is the primary tool used within the educational field to determine special education eligibility and to determine appropriate educational interventions for children with exceptional learning and behavior needs. For children with ABI, however, many researchers argue that IQ testing may be an inadequate measure of cognitive behavior. According to Johnson (1992), "Reliance on the traditional global concept of IQ is of limited value since its ubiquitous nature demands extreme caution when dealing with head injured children" (p. 407). Johnson points out that although children who have sustained a brain injury typically display a lower Wechsler Performance IQ score versus Verbal IQ score, this performance impairment could be the result of a number of confounding problems including response speed, sequencing, perceptual planning, and abstract reasoning difficulties. The WISC–III may provide some utility because one can contrast child performance across a number of subtests. The results may also be used to generate hypotheses for evaluation by other measures.

Undeniably, a variety of cognitive areas must be assessed, in addition to overall general intelligence, for a child who has experienced ABI (see Chapter 4). Specifically, a cognitive assessment should include evaluation in the following domains: arousal, orientation to person and place, visual and auditory perception, attention, rate of information processing, learning and memory, executive functions (e.g., planning, problem solving), and generalization of learned skills (Ewing-Cobbs & Fletcher, 1987; Harrington, 1990; Johnson, 1992; Rosen & Gerring, 1986; Telzrow, 1991). To assist in the assessment of such areas, many authors have identified specific measures and subtests that assess these cognitive domains. (See Ewing-Cobbs and Fletcher, 1987, and Telzrow, 1991, for examples of such instruments.)

Communication

For a child with ABI, the degree of language difficulty and the type of communicative impairment is dependent on several factors, including the type of brain injury, the child's preinjury status, and the child's stage of development at age of onset. For instance, although primary language dysfunction is thought to occur as a result of left hemispheric damage, the child's chronological age and stage of development at the time of injury can play a major role. For young children, the two hemispheres of the brain are less rigidly specialized in their functions (Obrzut & Hynd, 1987); thus young children may demonstrate language difficulties even though primary localizing damage may have occurred to the right hemisphere.

Although most communication disorders involve the receptive and expressive aspects of oral communication, some involve the child's internal mediation of language (Harrington, 1990). As a result, assessment of communication skills requires an investigation of a variety of abilities, including naming speed and accuracy, word retrieval, oral fluency, and auditory comprehension (Blosser & DePompei, 1989; Ewing-Cobbs & Fletcher, 1987; Telzrow, 1987). An evaluation should include assessment in both receptive and expressive language, pragmatics (the social use of language), and motor speech dysfunction. Some instruments that may be helpful in such an assessment include the Clinical Evaluation of Language Fundamentals–Third Edition (Semel, Wiig, & Secord, 1995), the Illinois Test of Psycholinguistic Abilities (Kirk, McCarthy, & Kirk, 1968), the Peabody Picture Vocabulary Test–Revised (Dunn & Dunn, 1981), and the Test of Auditory Comprehension of Language–Revised (Carrow-Woolfolk, 1985).

Physical Abilities

Children with ABI often demonstrate complex motor difficulties as a result of significant damage to the central nervous system. Areas to be considered in psychomotor assessment include fine and gross motor skills, balance, motor planning, coordination, range of motion, spatial orientation, strength and stamina (Harrington, 1990; Telzrow, 1987). Assessments in these areas are typically conducted by trained individuals including adaptive physical education teachers, physical therapists, and/or occupational therapists.

Behavioral/Psychosocial Functioning

Behaviors that may be most difficult to understand and manage after ABI are those in the psychosocial domain. Children with ABI often have difficulties in this area long after gains have been made in other areas of functioning (Telzrow, 1987). They can experience a host of emotional problems including withdrawal, dependency, anxiety, emotional lability, poor anger control, depression, and aggression (Deaton, 1987; Fletcher, Ewing-Cobbs, Miner, Levin, & Eisenberg, 1990; Lehr, 1990). These problems may stem from a child's preexisting emotional difficulties, which remain or become exacerbated after the injury (Deaton, 1987; Telzrow, 1987), or by problems the child has in coping with and adapting to his or her new learning and living circumstances (Lehr, 1996).

Skills in the behavioral domain are typically evaluated through 1) observation of the child's behavior across multiple environments;

2) structured and unstructured interviews with the child, family, and educators; and 3) the use of adaptive behavior scales or descriptive behavior rating scales (e.g., Child Behavior Checklist [Achenbach & Edelbrock, 1986]; Vineland Adaptive Behavior Scales [Sparrow, Balla, & Cicchetti, 1984]). If a child demonstrates extreme maladaptive behavior following ABI, it is often useful to conduct a functional assessment of behavior. A functional assessment involves a thorough and descriptive examination of the stimulus events that precede a behavior (e.g., antecedents) and the consequences that occur as a result of the behavior. By performing a functional assessment of a child's maladaptive behavior, assessors can better determine the communicative intent of the behavior and the environmental contingencies that may be maintaining it (see Chapters 7 and 8).

Academic Performance

Children with ABI typically exhibit gaps in academic learning. It is important for assessors to evaluate lost skills, understand previously acquired skills (that may be regained after a short period of instruction), and take into account more severe cognitive impairments and their impact on new skill acquisition (Harrington, 1990). Standardized achievement testing (e.g., Kaufman Test of Educational Achievement [Kaufman & Kaufman, 1985]; Wechsler Individual Achievement Test [Wechsler, 1992]; Woodcock-Johnson Psychoeducational Battery–Revised [Woodcock & Johnson, 1989]) is a widely used method of assessing a child's academic performance. However, it is important to remember that scores on standardized academic measures may not accurately reflect a child's performance in actual classroom activities and tasks. Many variables exist in natural learning situations that are not as salient in artificial testing situations (e.g., cumulative fatigue, extraneous environmental stimuli, competing instructional stimuli, low/high child motivation for task). In addition, standardized achievement measures often require a child to perform rote skills in isolation and do not require the synthesis and application of abstract thinking/reasoning skills. As a result, observational, diagnostic teaching methods will often provide much utility in determining a child's academic profile, learning style, and areas of need (Harrington, 1990) (see Chapter 5).

REENTERING THE SCHOOL SYSTEM

As evidenced, children with ABI frequently demonstrate a complex constellation of neurological impairments that have a profound impact on their current adaptability as well as on their future level of functioning. However, regardless of the degree of neurological impairment incurred, important steps along the road to recovery include leaving the hospital or rehabilitation facility and moving on to a school setting. In order to facilitate this transition to the school setting, communication between rehabilitation professionals and educators is necessary (Savage, 1991; Savage & Carter, 1991). Ongoing dialogue and planning will need to occur in order to determine the most appropriate educational placement for the child with ABI and to determine the specific supports needed for the child.

Despite the specific educational placement that is determined for the child with ABI, educators and other school representatives (e.g., speech-language therapists, adaptive physical education teachers, physical therapists, occupational therapists, school psychologists) will continually need to make accommodations for the child in order to facilitate the child's success in both academic and social arenas. Educators must strive to create learning situations in which the child with ABI can successfully readjust to school, reestablish previously acquired knowledge, and begin to learn new information (Szekeres & Meserve, 1994).

Typically, a child with ABI will need some accommodations (whether they are physical, environmental, or instructional) to help him or her in one or more of the following domains: attention, orientation, information processing, sensory perception, organization and planning, memory, reasoning and problem solving, behavior, and motor skills (Rosen & Gerring, 1986). Some accommodations will be very simple (e.g., giving a child extra time to complete assignments, repeating directions, allowing the child with ABI to work with another child), whereas other accommodations may be more complex (e.g., incorporating the use of adaptive equipment such as computers and augmentative communication systems to complete assignments). The types of accommodations and teaching strategies used will, in all likelihood, be extensive and will vary as a function of the child's needs and progress. Table 1 lists educational techniques and strategies to accommodate children with ABI. (See Chapter 5 for more information on specific educational accommodations and Chapter 12 for more information on preparation of school personnel.)

The Role of Parents and Family

In many cases family members have little information about neurological effects and how they will affect learning and behavior in

Table 1.   Educational techniques and strategies to accommodate children with ABI

Attention

- Provide a quiet work environment.
- Remove unnecessary distractions from the learning environment.
- Limit background noise.
- Provide concrete visual cues to which to attend.
- Limit the amount of information on a page.
- Adjust assignments to the length of the child's attention span.
- Focus the child's attention on the most salient aspect of a lesson.
- Maintain a brisk pace between tasks.
- Maintain high success rate through selection of appropriate instructional content.
- Demonstrate/model a new task.
- Repeat instructions if necessary.
- Use short and concise instructions and assignments.
- Reinforce on-task behavior.
- Give frequent breaks.
- Break longer assignments into smaller portions.
- Give the child preferential seating (e.g., near the chalkboard and teacher).
- Set up a personalized cuing system with the child (e.g., touch the child on the shoulder, gain eye contact).
- Work with the child in a small-group setting.

Orientation (to time, place, person, and event)

- Have the child keep an appointment book and/or a daily log of activities.
- Assign a peer buddy to the child to help with making the transition between settings.
- Maintain consistent staff, room arrangement, and materials.
- Label significant objects and materials.
- Teach the child to look for permanent landmarks in various learning/living environments.
- Provide written or pictorial charts, schedules, or classroom maps that describe daily routines and routes.
- Have the child verbalize how to get to a specific place before going there.
- Allow extra time in moving from one location to another.

Information processing

- Repeat instructions and ask the child to repeat instructions.
- Tailor cuing system to student needs.
- Summarize information as it is being taught.
- Pair pictures or visual cues with oral information.
- Have the child overlearn material.
- Integrate previously learned information with new information.
- Limit the amount of information presented.
- Provide sufficient processing time for child to respond to inquiry.

Sensory

Auditory

- Give clear directions.
- Repeat instructions if necessary.
- Encourage the child to repeat information that is understood.
- Use concrete language.
- Use concrete visuals.

Visual

- Give the child preferential seating.
- Color-code printed material.
- Use enlarged texts and materials.
- Utilize slant boards to facilitate the proper angle of material presentation.

(continued)

Table 1.   *(continued)*

- Provide visual material that is free from unnecessary distractors.
- Encourage the child to utilize external guides to facilitate visual scanning (e.g., ruler).
- Provide longer viewing time.
- Place materials within the child's best visual field.
- Provide visual cues for the beginning and end of lines in narrative text.

Organization and planning
- Provide concrete advance organizers.
- Limit the number of steps in a task or activity.
- Structure the thinking process through the use of graphic organizers (e.g., time lines, flowcharts, graphs).
- Set up external organization aids (e.g., a daily notebook, assignment sheet, calendar, desk organizer).
- Select a peer buddy to help with the clarification of assignments.
- Assist the child in setting short-term goals for completing assignments.
- Provide frequent opportunities to review schedules and tasks to be completed.

Memory and learning
- Make the material to be learned meaningful and relevant.
- Develop active learning situations.
- Break instructional tasks into component parts.
- Have the child utilize visual imagery.
- Have the child use verbal rehearsal and self-talk.
- Have the child take notes or record classroom instruction on an audiotape recorder.
- Provide a printed schedule of daily activities, locations, and materials needed.
- Have the child write down key information to be remembered.
- Teach generalizable strategies.
- Model new skills.
- Use a sufficient range of examples.
- Have the child role-play or pantomime stories to be remembered.
- Use positive and negative examples to teach new skills.
- Provide sufficient practice on new skills and information.
- Sequence skills to build on previous learning.
- Maintain a high mastery criteria.
- Provide cumulative review of previously taught material.

Reasoning and problem solving
- Role-play cause-and-effect scenarios.
- Teach the structure or format of an activity or task.
- Raise questions about alternatives and consequences for behavior.
- Role-play situations that simulate situations the child may encounter.
- Demonstrate the application of problem-solving skills across daily routines.
- Provide a highly structured learning environment.
- Provide assistance with alternative solutions and courses of action.
- Provide ongoing feedback.
- Provide assistance with sequencing tasks and prioritizing objectives.
- Provide clear expectations and check for understanding.

Behavior
- Analyze the child's behavior in terms of its communicative intent.
- Ignore inappropriate behavior and reinforce appropriate behavior.
- Manipulate antecedents in the environment to facilitate appropriate behavior.
- Utilize stimulus change as a means of decreasing inappropriate behavior.
- Prepare the child for transitions or changes in routine.

(continued)

Table 1.   *(continued)*

Motor
- Structure the physical environment of the classroom to permit ease of movement by carefully planning seating and the arrangement of the furniture.
- Utilize adaptive equipment such as switches, computers, and augmentative communication devices to facilitate the child's access to his or her surroundings.
- Include ramps or level spaces to allow the child with orthopedic impairments easy access to classrooms and other school structures.

school (Mira & Tyler, 1991). In addition, there is often inadequate communication between rehabilitation professionals and education professionals regarding the child's injury, course of recovery, and cognitive and behavior profile (Blosser & DePompei, 1991). Feelings of optimism expressed by family members and rehabilitation professionals when the child leaves the hospital are frequently diminished when the child encounters new and unexpected difficulties in the school environment.

One way to facilitate a smooth and successful school reentry for children with ABI is to ensure that parents (or primary caregivers) are part of the school-reentry process. This will take extra time and consideration on the part of education professionals, who need to recognize that these families are dealing with circumstances very different from those of families who have children with other types of disabilities. In most cases, children with ABI were typically achieving students within general education classrooms who did not require any special services or assistance (DePompei & Blosser, 1994).

The impact of ABI can result in a sudden and unexpected intrusion on the family system. It is not uncommon for family members to initially display feelings of anger and injustice at what has occurred (DePompei, Zarski, & Hall, 1988; Martin, 1988). After the shock of the injury subsides, however, family members most often respond with coping behaviors consistent with previous organizational patterns within the family (DePompei & Williams, 1994). The way each family copes with the child's injury will affect the child's school-reentry process. Some families will be open and willing to interact with outside agencies and resources (e.g., education professionals), whereas others will be more closed and prefer to rely on the internal resources of the family.

Many families equate a return to school with a return to normalcy (Savage & Carter, 1991). They are not prepared for the difficulties, social as well as academic, that frequently accompany severe ABI. As a result, there are several issues that need to be discussed with parents prior to school reentry in order to ensure a successful transition for the child. First, it is critical to ascertain what the family knows about the child's educational needs. Although parents may have been told of their child's physical, emotional, or cognitive-communicative impairments, in all likelihood the discussions have centered around the impairments themselves and not the educational implications of such impairments (DePompei & Blosser, 1994). For instance, parents may have been told that their child has difficulty organizing and sequencing information but may not realize that this problem could interfere with their child's ability to organize and sequence his or her thoughts when engaged in oral and written language tasks at school. They may know that their child has visual-motor difficulties but may be unaware that their child will be unusually taxed when having to copy information from the blackboard.

A second issue that needs to be discussed with parents prior to school reentry concerns policies and procedures for admission to special education services. Because the majority of children with ABI did not require special education services prior to injury, most parents are not familiar with the procedures that go along with receiving such services (DePompei & Blosser, 1994; Ylvisaker, Hartwick, & Stevens, 1991). Education and service coordination support are critical. Parents should be given information on IDEA, the services available in their school district, and the process of acquiring those services.

Being a member of an individualized education program (IEP) team will be a new and overwhelming experience for parents. The parents of a child who has newly experienced ABI are not familiar with the assessment process involved in determining programming and class placement, nor are they familiar with the formal development of educational goals and objectives for their child. Moreover, families often assume that the services provided by the rehabilitation facility (e.g., speech-language therapy, physical therapy, occupational therapy) will continue to be provided within the school setting with the same degree of intensity and frequency that they were provided in the rehabilitation center. This can pose a potential problem in the school-reentry process because families want their child to receive the best services possible, but educators are constrained by limited professional and fiscal resources.

A third issue that may concern family members and should be discussed prior to school reentry is that of social adjustment (DePompei & Blosser, 1994). Often children will have difficulty sustaining and maintaining the friendships and relationships that existed before the injury. Peers are not aware of the behavioral manifestations that can result from ABI (e.g., disinhibition, aggression, impulsivity, withdrawal, apathy) and are unprepared to cope with such behaviors when they do arise. In addition, extracurricular activities, such as after-school sports and clubs, may not be as appropriate or accessible for a child after sustaining a brain injury. As a result, it may be more difficult for the child to meet other children his or her own age. Ideally, family members and education professionals should discuss specific strategies for facilitating friendships and relationships among the child with ABI and his or her peers *prior to* school reentry. Programs such as Tribes (Gibbs, 1987) and Circle of Friends (Forest & Lusthaus, 1989) are often useful in facilitating friendships and social relationships among children with and without disabilities. Tribes is a heterogeneous grouping of five to six students who form a social network and work together throughout the school year. The purpose is to foster positive peer support and to facilitate social growth and learning (Gibbs, 1987). Circle of Friends is a process that involves gathering a group of students together, primarily to discuss ways to increase friendships and social networks for children with disabilities (Falvey & Rosenberg, 1995). (See Chapter 9 for a description of how these processes might be implemented.)

To ensure a successful school reentry for their child, the family will need to take on many new roles. Some new roles will come naturally and with little difficulty, such as caring for the physical needs of the child, whereas others may take more time to acquire. A summary of new roles available for family members is provided in Table 2.

CONCLUSION

ABI is a complex disability that is, unfortunately, not uncommon. With brain injury accounting for approximately 16% of pediatric hospital admissions each year, it is critical that professionals understand the short-term and long-term effects of ABI on the child, as well as the repercussions for family members and school personnel (Tucker & Colson, 1992). Children who have experienced ABI typically exhibit multifaceted cognitive, language, motor, memory, and behavioral effects that have serious implications for present as well as future learning and living. Furthermore, ABI affects not just the child, but family members and rehabilitation and school professionals as well. Once the child has left the rehabilitation setting and has returned to school, the education agency becomes the primary vehicle for facilitating ongoing recovery. Interactive and dynamic teamwork among educators, rehabilitation professionals, and families will facilitate an appropriate education and recovery process for these children. In fact, it is only through such coordinated teamwork that these children will be able to reach their maximum potential.

Table 2.   New roles for family members of a child with ABI

Participants in rehabilitation

- Provide relevant history (e.g., medical, cognitive, behavioral, and emotional history of child).
- Provide background information about the family.
- Become reacquainted with the child—the child may be markedly different from before the injury.
- Be involved in the assessment process.
- Be involved in the therapy process (e.g., speech-language therapy, physical therapy, occupational therapy).
- Learn techniques to foster the development of skills in the areas of communication, motor, cognition, and behavior.
- Learn how to care for the child's increased adaptive needs and increased dependence on the family.
- Report on changes in behavior and progress, or lack of progress.

Participants in the educational program

- Become a member of the individualized education program (IEP) team.
- Provide assessment information regarding the child's strengths, needs, and preferences.
- Provide information regarding current and future expectations and aspirations for the child.
- Become well versed of the rights guaranteed by special education law to families of children with disabilities.
- Learn teaching strategies that can be used in the home to facilitate academic, social, and emotional growth.
- Become familiar with positive approaches to address challenging behaviors.

Service coordinator

- Communicate with school personnel about the child's needs.
- Facilitate communication between home and school environments.
- Facilitate communication between rehabilitation professionals and educational professionals.
- Ensure that services are provided as delineated in the IEP.
- Ensure that appropriate educational accommodations are being made for the child.

Advocate

- Network with other families of children with ABI.
- Become involved in parent–professional organizations for children with ABI.
- Pursue extracurricular activities that the child enjoys and in which he or she can be actively involved.
- Learn how to gain access to supports and services for the child (e.g., respite care, orthopedic equipment) through community resources.
- Fight for the child's school and community inclusion and acceptance.

REFERENCES

Achenbach, T.M., & Edelbrock, C.S. (1986). *Child Behavior Checklist and Youth Self-Report.* Burlington, VT: Author.

Annegers, J.F. (1983). The epidemiology of head trauma in children. In K. Shapiro (Ed.), *Pediatric head trauma* (pp. 1–10). Mt. Kisco, NY: Futura Publishing.

Annegers, J.F., Grabow, J.D., Kurland, L.T., & Laws, E.R. (1980). The incidence, causes, and secular trends of head trauma in Olmsted County, Minnesota, 1935–1974. *Neurology, 30,* 912–919.

Baker, B.L. (1989). *Parent training and developmental disabilities.* Washington, DC: American Association on Mental Retardation.

Baker, B.L. (1996). Parent training. In J.W. Jacobson & J.A. Mulick (Eds.), *Manual of diagnosis and professional practice in mental retardation* (pp. 289–299).Washington, DC: American Psychological Association.

Bergland, M.M., & Thomas, K.R. (1991). Psychosocial issues following severe head injury in adolescence: Individual and family perceptions. *Rehabilitation Counseling Bulletin, 35,* 5–21.

Berrol, S., & Rosenthal, M. (1986). From the editors. *Journal of Head Trauma Rehabilitation, 1,* 9.

Bigler, E.D. (1987a). Acquired cerebral trauma: An introduction to the special series. *Journal of Learning Disabilities, 20*(8), 454–457.

Bigler, E.D. (1987b). Neuropathology of acquired cerebral trauma. *Journal of Learning Disabilities, 20*(8), 458–473.

Blacher, J. (Ed.). (1994). *When there's no place like home: Options for children living apart from their natural families.* Baltimore: Paul H. Brookes Publishing Co.

Blosser, J.L., & DePompei, R. (1989). The head-injured student returns to school: Recognizing and treating deficits. *Topics in Language Disorders, 9*(2), 67–77.

Blosser, J.L., & DePompei, R. (1991). Preparing education professionals for meeting the needs of students with traumatic brain injury. *Journal of Head Trauma Rehabilitation, 6,* 73–82.

Blosser, J.L., & DePompei, R. (1995). Fostering effective family involvement through mentoring. *Journal of Head Trauma Rehabilitation, 10,* 46–56.

Brooks, D.N. (1983). Disorders of memory. In M. Rosenthal, E.R. Griffith, M.R. Bond, & J.D. Miller (Eds.), *Rehabilitation of the head injured adult* (pp. 185–196). Philadelphia: F.A. Davis.

Brown, G., Chadwick, O., Shaffer, D., Rutter, M., & Traub, M. (1981). A prospective study of children with head injuries: III. Psychiatric sequelae. *Psychological Medicine, 11,* 63–78.

Carrow-Woolfolk, E. (1985). *Test of Auditory Comprehension of Language–Revised.* Allen, TX: DLM Teaching Resources.

Chadwick, O., Rutter, M., Brown, G., Shaffer, D., & Traub, B. (1981). A prospective study of children with head injuries: II. Cognitive sequelae. *Psychological Medicine, 11,* 49–61.

Craft, A.W., Shaw, D.A., & Cartlidge, N.E. (1972). Head injuries in children. *British Medical Journal, 4,* 200–203.

Deaton, A.V. (1987). Behavioral change strategies for children and adolescents with severe brain injury. *Journal of Learning Disabilities, 20,* 581–589.

Deaton, A.V., & Waaland, P. (1994). Psychosocial effects of acquired brain injury. In R.C. Savage & G.F. Wolcott (Eds.), *Educational dimensions of acquired brain injury* (pp. 239–255). Austin, TX: PRO-ED.

DePompei, R., & Blosser, J.L. (1994). The family as collaborator for effective school reintegration. In R.C. Savage & G.F. Wolcott (Eds.), *Educational dimensions of acquired brain injury* (pp. 489–506). Austin, TX: PRO-ED.

DePompei, R., & Williams, J. (1994). Working with families after TBI: A family-centered approach. *Topics in Language Disorders, 15,* 68–81.

DePompei, R., Zarski, J.J., & Hall, D.E. (1988). Cognitive communicative impairments: A family focused viewpoint. *Journal of Head Trauma Rehabilitation, 3*(2), 13–22.

Dunn, L.M., & Dunn, L.M. (1981). *Peabody Picture Vocabulary Test–Revised.* Circle Pines, MN: American Guidance Service.

Education for All Handicapped Children Act of 1975, PL 94-142, 20 U.S.C. § 1400 *et seq.*

Ewing-Cobbs, L., & Fletcher, J.M. (1987). Neuropsychological assessment of head injury in children. *Journal of Learning Disabilities, 20*(9), 526–535.

Falvey, M.A., & Rosenberg, R.L. (1995). Developing and fostering friendships. In M.A. Falvey (Ed.), *Inclusive and heterogeneous schooling: Assessment, curriculum, and instruction* (pp. 267–283). Baltimore: Paul H. Brookes Publishing Co.

Farber, B. (1959). Effects of a severely mentally retarded child on family integration. *Monographs of the Society for Research in Child Development, 24,* (2, Serial No. 71).

Fletcher, J.M., Ewing-Cobbs, L., Miner, M.E., Levin, H.S., & Eisenberg, H.M. (1990). Behavioral changes after closed head injury in children. *Journal of Consulting and Clinical Psychology, 58,* 93–98.

Fletcher, J.M., & Levin, H.S. (1988). Neurobehavioral effects of brain injury in children. In D.K. Routh (Ed.), *Handbook of pediatric psychology* (pp. 258–295). New York: Guilford Press.

Forest, M., & Lusthaus, E. (1989). Promoting educational equality for all students: Circles and maps. In S. Stainback, W. Stainback, & M. Forest (Eds.), *Educating all students in the mainstream of regular education* (pp. 43–57). Baltimore: Paul H. Brookes Publishing Co.

Gibbs, J. (1987). *Tribes: A process for social development and cooperative learning.* Pleasant Hill, CA: Center for Human Development.

Goldstein, F.C., & Levin, H.S. (1987). Epidemiology of pediatric closed head injury: Incidence, clinical characteristics, and risk factors. *Journal of Learning Disabilities, 20*(9), 518–525.

Harrington, D.E. (1987). The nature of acquired brain injury. In J. Cook, S. Berrol, D. Harrington, M. Kantor, N. Knight, C. Miller, & L. Silverman (Eds.), *The ABI handbook: Serving students with acquired brain injury in higher education* (pp. 9–33). Sacramento: California Community Colleges, Disabled Students Programs and Services.

Harrington, D.E. (1990). Educational strategies. In M. Rosenthal, M. Bond, E. Griffith, & J. Miller (Eds.), *Rehabilitation of the adult and child with traumatic brain injury* (pp. 476–492). Philadelphia: F.A. Davis.

Heiden, J., Small, R., Caton, W., Weiss, M., & Kurtze, T. (1983). Severe head injury. *Journal of the American Physical Therapy Association, 63,* 4–9.

Henry, K. (1983). Cognitive rehabilitation and the head-injured child. *Journal of Children in Contemporary Society, 16,* 189–205.

Individuals with Disabilities Education Act (IDEA) of 1990, PL 101-476, 20 U.S.C.. § 1400 *et seq.*

Jamison, D.L., & Kaye, H.H. (1974). Accidental head injury in children. *Archives of Disease in Childhood, 49,* 376–381.

Johnson, D.A. (1992). Head injured children and education: A need for greater delineation and understanding. *British Journal of Educational Psychology, 62,* 404–409.

Kaufman, A.S., & Kaufman, N.L. (1985). *Kaufman Test of Educational Achievement.* Circle Pines, MN: American Guidance Service.

Kingston, W.J. (1985). Head injury. *Seminars in Neurology, 5,* 197–270.

Kirk, S.A., McCarthy, J.J., & Kirk, W.D. (1968). *The Illinois Test of Psycholinguistic Abilities.* Urbana: University of Illinois Press.

Klonoff, H., Clark, C., & Klonoff, P.S. (1993). Long-term outcome of head injuries: A 23 year follow up study of children with head injuries. *Journal of Neurology, Neurosurgery, and Psychiatry, 56,* 410–415.

Klonoff, H., & Paris, R. (1974). Immediate, short-term and residual effects of acute head injuries in children: Neuropsychological and neurological correlates. In R.M. Reitan & L.A. Davison, (Eds.), *Clinical neuropsychology: Current status and applications* (pp. 179–210). New York: Halstead Press.

Lazar, M.F., & Menaldino, S. (1995). Cognitive outcome and behavioral adjustment in children following traumatic brain injury: A developmental perspective. *Journal of Head Trauma Rehabilitation, 10,* 55–63.

Lehr, E. (1990). *Psychological management of traumatic brain injuries in children and adolescents.* Rockville, MD: Aspen Publishers, Inc.

Lehr, E. (1996). Parallel processes. Stages of recovery and stages of family accommodation to ABI. In G.H.S. Singer, A. Glang, & J.M. Williams (Eds.), *Children with acquired brain injuries: Educating and supporting families* (pp. 53–64). Baltimore: Paul H. Brookes Publishing Co.

Levin, H.S., Ewing-Cobbs, L., & Benton, A.L. (1984). Age and recovery from brain damage: A review of clinical studies. In S.W. Scheff (Ed.), *Aging and recovery of function in the central nervous system* (169–205). New York: Plenum.

Martin, D.A. (1988). Children and adolescents with traumatic brain injury: Impact on the family. *Journal of Learning Disabilities, 21,* 464–470.

Milton, S.B., Scaglione, C., Flanagan, T., Cox, J.L., & Rudnick, F.D. (1991). Functional evaluation of adolescent students with traumatic brain injury. *Journal of Head Trauma Rehabilitation, 6,* 35–46.

Mira, M.P., & Tyler, J.S. (1991). Students with traumatic brain injury: Making the transition from hospital to school. *Focus on Exceptional Children, 23*(5), 1–12.

Moyes, C.D. (1980). Epidemiology of serious head injuries in childhood. *Child Care Health Development, 6,* 1–6.

Obrzut, J.E., & Hynd, G.W. (1987). Cognitive dysfunction and psychoeducational assessment in individuals with acquired brain injury. *Journal of Learning Disabilities, 20,* 596–602.

Partington, M.W. (1960). The importance of accident-proneness in the aetiology of head injuries in childhood. *Archives of Disease in Childhood, 35,* 215–223.

Rosen, C.D., & Gerring, J.P. (1986). *Head trauma: Strategies for educational reintegration.* San Diego: College-Hill.

Rosenthal, M., & Young, T. (1988). Effective family intervention after traumatic brain injury: Theory and practice. *Journal of Head Trauma Rehabilitation, 3*(4), 42–50.

Rutter, M. (1981). Psychological sequelae of brain damage in children. *American Journal of Psychiatry, 138,* 1533–1544.

Sattler, J.M. (1992). *Assessment of children* (3rd ed.). San Diego: J.M. Sattler.

Savage, R.C. (1991). Identification, classification, and placement issues for students with traumatic brain injuries. *Journal of Head Trauma Rehabilitation, 6,* 1–9.

Savage, R.C., & Carter, R.R. (1991). Family and return to school. In J.M. Williams & T. Kay (Eds.), *Head injury: A family matter* (pp. 203–216). Baltimore: Paul H. Brookes Publishing Co.

Savage, R.C., & Wolcott, G.F. (1994). Overview of acquired brain injury. In R.C. Savage & G.F. Wolcott (Eds.), *Educational dimensions of acquired brain injury* (pp. 3–12). Austin, TX: PRO-ED.

Seltzer, M.M., & Krauss, M.W. (1989). Aging parents with adult mentally retarded children: Family risk factors and sources of support. *American Journal on Mental Retardation, 94,* 303–312.

Seltzer, M.M., & Ryff, C.D. (1994). Parenting across the lifespan: The normative and nonnormative cases. In D.L. Featherman, R. Lerner, & M. Perlmutter (Eds.), *Life-span development and behavior* (Vol. 12, pp. 1–40). Hillsdale, NJ: Lawrence Erlbaum Associates.

Semel, E., Wiig, E.H., & Secord, W.A. (1995). *Clinical evaluation of language fundamentals* (3rd ed.). San Antonio: Harcourt Brace & Company.

Sparrow, S.S., Balla, D.A., & Cicchetti, D.V. (1984). *Vineland Adaptive Behavior Scales.* Circle Pines, MN: American Guidance Service.

Stoneman, Z., & Berman, P.W. (Eds.). (1993). *The effects of mental retardation, disability, and illness on sibling relationships: Research issues and challenges.* Baltimore: Paul H. Brookes Publishing Co.

Szekeres, S.F., & Meserve, N.F. (1994). Collaborative intervention in schools after traumatic brain injury. *Topics in Language Disorders, 15,* 21–36.

Teasdale, G., & Jennett, B. (1974). Assessment of coma and impaired consciousness: A practical scale. *Lancet, 2,* 81–84.

Telzrow, C.F. (1987). Management of academic and educational problems in head injury. *Journal of Learning Disabilities, 20*(9), 536–545.

Telzrow, C.F. (1991). The school psychologist's perspective on testing students with traumatic brain injury. *Journal of Head Trauma Rehabilitation, 6,* 23–34.

Tucker, B.F., & Colson, S.E. (1992). Traumatic brain injury: An overview of school re-entry. *Intervention in School and Clinic, 4,* 198–206.

Waaland, P.K., & Kreutzer, J.S. (1988). Family response to childhood traumatic brain injury. *Journal of Head Trauma Rehabilitation, 3*(4), 51–63.

Wechsler, D. (1991). *Wechsler Intelligence Scale for Children–Third edition.* San Antonio, TX: The Psychological Corporation.

Wechsler, D. (1992). *Wechsler Individual Achievement Test.* San Antonio, TX: The Psychological Corporation.

Woodcock, R.W., & Johnson, M.B. (1989). *Woodcock-Johnson Psychoeducational Battery–Revised.* Allen, TX: DLM Teaching Resources.

Ylvisaker, M., Hartwick, P., & Stevens, M. (1991). School reentry following head injury: Managing the transition from hospital to school. *Journal of Head Trauma Rehabilitation, 6,* 10–22.

Ylvisaker, M., Szekeres, S.F., & Hartwick, P. (1994). A framework for cognitive intervention. In R.C. Savage & G.F. Wolcott (Eds.), *Educational dimensions of acquired brain injury* (pp. 35–67). Austin, TX: PRO-ED.

chapter two

Family–School–Child

A Qualitative Study of the School Experiences of Students with ABI

Bonnie Todis,
Ann Glang, and Mary Ann Fabry

LITTLE IS KNOWN about the long-term, day-to-day school experiences of students with acquired brain injury (ABI). Most of the pediatric ABI literature has focused on rehabilitation, transition from hospital to school, and assessment for placement purposes (Blosser & DePompei, 1994; Savage, 1991; Shurtleff, Massagli, Hays, Ross, & Sprunk-Greenfield, 1995; Telzrow, 1991; Ylvisaker, Feeney, Maher-Maxwell, et al., 1995; Ylvisaker, Feeney, & Mullins, 1995; Ylvisaker, Hartwick, & Stevens, 1991). Only since the mid-1980s have some researchers begun to address specific behavioral (Feeney & Ylvisaker, 1995), academic (Glang, Singer, Cooley, & Tish, 1992; Koegel & Koegel, 1986; Light et al., 1987), social (Sowers, Glang, Voss, & Cooley, 1996), and organizational (Sohlberg & Mateer, 1987, 1989) interventions for students with ABI. There is still, however, no clear holistic view of the issues students with ABI, their families, and their educators face together. Without an understanding of these issues and the context surrounding students with ABI in public schools, it is difficult to

Preparation of this chapter was supported in part by Grant #H086R30029 from the U.S. Department of Education. The views expressed in this chapter do not necessarily reflect those of the funding agency.

determine whether interventions, especially those that emerge from rehabilitation studies, will be effective in school settings.

In the course of three federally funded, ABI-focused research projects over a 5-year period, the authors have had an opportunity to gather longitudinal, qualitative data from students with ABI, their families, and their educators. The data reveal a number of factors that interact to create environments in which it is difficult for students with ABI and their educators to experience success. However, the same data reveal ways that teachers, schools, and families are overcoming challenges and implementing school programs that are highly effective for students with ABI. In this chapter, the designs of the research projects are discussed as well as the origins of the problems students with ABI encounter in schools and the approaches that work to avoid or correct them. The observations described in this chapter are from Glang and Todis (1993–1994, 1994–1995).

RESEARCH DESIGN

Between 1991 and 1996, the authors conducted three projects to improve school services to students with ABI. One project focused on promoting social inclusion, another on training teams of educators to provide consultation and in-service training in ABI to fellow educators, and the third on developing strategies to promote the independence of secondary students with ABI. In all three projects, both qualitative and quantitative data were collected. A qualitative approach was included because it allowed the authors to explore broad research questions while developing specific interventions. These questions included the following:

- What are the educational experiences of students with ABI?
- How do the perspectives of students, families, and educators interact to influence these experiences?
- What challenges do each of the parties encounter, and how do they respond to those challenges?
- What interventions and styles of interaction are effective in meeting the challenges?

Although quantitative research is well suited to verify or confirm theories or hypotheses (Bogdan & Biklin, 1982; Filstead, 1979; Reichardt & Cook, 1979), qualitative research is well suited to explore research in studies such as these in which the specific issues are not yet well defined and theories are not yet developed (Stainback & Stainback, 1984).

Participants

Most of the authors' data on the school experiences of students with ABI came from the Qualitative Longitudinal Study for which the authors collected weekly qualitative interview and observational data on six students with ABI over a 3-year period. Additional qualitative and quantitative data were collected on four students with ABI in the Building Friendships Project and 12 secondary students with ABI in Project SOS. Purposive sampling was employed in selecting participants for these studies to maximize the variation among participants and settings and thereby maximize the variation in situations available for study (Lincoln & Guba, 1985). The 22 participants were selected to sample a range of factors of interest including gender, degree and type of disability resulting from the injury, age of student, age at onset, family socioeconomic status, school size, and school setting (i.e., urban, rural, or suburban). Table 1 describes the students for whom qualitative data were available for this study.

Although this limited number of students obviously does not sample the entire range of issues and situations affecting students with ABI, the sample does permit a preliminary analysis of how a variety of factors interact to produce different outcomes for students with ABI.

Recruitment and Consent Procedures

Participating students, parents, and educators were recruited through schools. Project personnel sent information about the study and consent-to-contact forms to schools throughout western Oregon. Schools gave the information to parents of students with ABI, who then returned the signed forms to the project personnel. Project personnel then described the study more fully and obtained informed consent from parents, students, and all educators who worked with the student.

Data Collection

As Table 1 indicates, the students were followed from several months to 3 years. Field researchers trained in qualitative methodology conducted participant observations, spending time in classrooms and other school settings, interacting informally with students and teachers, and observing both the student and the surrounding activities and events. Observations lasted approximately 3 hours and were scheduled at different times in order to sample the entire school day. During the observation, the field researcher took

Table 1.   Participants with ABI in the qualitative studies of school experiences

Name	Age in years	Age at onset	Time on project	School setting	Type of injury
Amber	17	16	6 mos	Small town	MVA
David	15	6	2 mos	Small town	MVA
Eddy	13	4	3 mos	Rural	Chemical exposure
Elise	9	infant	1 yr	Rural	MVA
Frankie	8	3	1 yr	Rural	MVA
Jack	16	11	4 yrs	Small town	Bicycle—MVA
Jane	8	7	3 yrs	Small town	MVA
Joachim	15	11	3 yrs	Urban	Pedestrian—MVA
Josh	15	4	6 mos	Rural	T Cell Acute Lymphoblastic Non-Hodgekin's Lymphoma
Kathy	19	17	1 yr	Small town	MVA
Levi	17	2	7 mos	Rural	Abuse
Mandy	15	15	9 mos	Small town	MVA
Matt	15	13	6 mos	Small town	Brain tumor
Matteo	11	7	1 yr	Rural	Bicycle—MVA
Max	18	16	2 mos	Suburban	Fall
Mike	12	7	3 yrs	Rural	MVA
Reba	2	infant	3 yrs	Rural	Hit by a baseball
Sarah	9	2	1 yr	Rural	Abuse
Stacy	15	1	5 mos	Urban	Fall
Tia	18	9	2 yrs	Rural	Bicycle—MVA
Tim	10	9	3 yrs	Suburban	Fall
Todd	14	3	3 mos	Small town	Abuse

Abbreviation: MVA, motor vehicle accident.
Note: All of the names are pseudonyms.

no notes but observed both the student and the surrounding context. Following the observation, the field researcher prepared detailed notes describing the setting, activities, participants in the setting, interactions, and observer impressions. Interviews with students were conducted informally during the course of these observations.

Interviews with each student's parents and teachers were conducted at least twice per year. Additional interviews were conducted with support personnel and other professionals (e.g., physical therapists, occupational therapists, speech-language therapists) who served the student with ABI. Interviews were largely unstructured. Interviewees were asked for their impressions of the student's progress, barriers to his or her success, and effective strategies for overcoming barriers. They were also encouraged to bring up additional topics related to the student. These often included the family's and educators' views of each other and the factors other than school that the family believed affected the student's functioning. In some cases, year-end interviews were conducted as focus groups, with all the student's teachers attending. Additional informal interviews were conducted by field researchers throughout each school year to get the impressions of the educators, students, and parents. All interviews were audiotaped and transcribed verbatim.

To gain a broader perspective on each student's experience, school and medical records were also reviewed as well as the student's academic work, the student's report cards, teacher logs, newspaper accounts of the accident resulting in ABI, and other documents.

Data Analysis

The data were analyzed systematically using a computer program, The Ethnograph, for coding and retrieving test-based data (Seidel, Friese, & Leonard, 1995). Data were coded by topic area, then code categories were compared across students to identify differences and similarities and factors that might account for them. As themes and hypotheses emerged concerning factors that promote or interfere with the education of students with ABI, they were tested by seeking additional data either to confirm or to disconfirm the tentative theories. Gradually the authors formulated theory statements that explained the situations they were observing and about which they were hearing from participants. These theory statements—describing problem situations and ways that schools overcome problems related to students with ABI—were presented to parents, professionals, adults with ABI, students with ABI on the project's advisory board and on ABI in-service teams (see Chapter 13), and the participants themselves. The individuals confirmed the extent to which these theories fit with their own experiences. When they did not agree with the interpretations of the data, theories were modified to incorporate the divergent views. This process continued until all inconsistencies in the data were explained or until the theories had been revised to account for inconsistencies.

Through this intensive, long-term work with a range of students in a variety of settings, the authors have learned much about what it is like to be a student with ABI in a public school, the experience of being the teacher of such a student, and the perspectives of the student's family. The authors have been able to track the development of problem situations and, in the process, have learned how such situations might be avoided or corrected. In this chapter, three factors are described that contribute to difficult or disappointing school experiences: 1) educational climate and capacity of teachers to serve students with special needs, 2) poor communication between families and school personnel, and 3) conflicts between the school's and family's perspectives of the student with ABI. Approaches and interventions that have successfully avoided or corrected problems resulting from these factors are then described.

ISSUES THAT AFFECT
EDUCATIONAL SERVICES TO STUDENTS WITH ABI

The issues that contribute to less than adequate school services for students with ABI can be viewed as existing in three broad, overlapping, and complex domains: the systems domain involving the educational context surrounding the provision of services to students with ABI, the individual domain of educator capacity to provide appropriate academic services, and the interpersonal domain involving communication between school personnel and students with ABI and their parents.

Current Educational Context Surrounding Students with ABI

Families of students with ABI who return to school after their injuries often expect a level of support comparable to that provided in rehabilitation settings. Written information they may have received about federally mandated special education services may lead them to believe that such services will be readily available. The actual situations they may encounter, however, are a version of the original vision of a free appropriate public education for every student based on his or her individual needs that is strongly influenced by funding issues and the way special education service delivery has evolved since the mid-1970s.

Shrinking Resources   ABI is a new disability area with a rapidly increasing, diverse membership. Students with ABI and their families are entering the special education system at a time when it is beleaguered by shrinking resources, increasing numbers, and increasing pressures to provide individualized services to students in inclusive settings. The needs of students with ABI are often numerous and complex, requiring the services of a variety of specialists, therapists, and medically trained personnel. These needs may strain the physical rehabilitation resources of public school systems. Speech-language therapists, physical therapists, occupational therapists, and school nurses may be able to schedule only minutes per week with each student on their large caseloads, relying on instructional assistants (IAs) and teachers to implement their recommendations with little training or supervision.

Special Education Service Delivery   Although there is an increasing emphasis on including students with disabilities in general, or regular, education classrooms, in many schools "special education" is a program with clearly defined procedures that are organized around familiar categories of disability and around school schedules and time lines. At the secondary level in particular, special education is likely to be organized by severity of disability, with students with severe disabilities receiving training in daily living skills, social skills, and vocational skills, and students with mild disabilities receiving simplified curricula, remedial instruction in basic skills, or assistance in study skills to meet graduation requirements. According to a school psychologist with training in the area of ABI,

I'd say that is the remaining area that needs some work—the secondary level. It has been the tradition at the high school level: This is the program we're offering and you fit into the program we offer.

It is often difficult for a school to determine in which of the two special education tracks a student with ABI should be placed, especially because parents may be exerting pressure on the school to provide an individualized program designed to help the student overcome specific cognitive or behavior problems. In addition, the special education paradigm is shifting. Schools are being strongly encouraged to serve students in noncategorical, more inclusive general education settings. As educators struggle to determine how to do this for all students, students with ABI, whose needs and behaviors are new to special educators and not well understood, can represent a special challenge.

Some schools cope with this challenge by assigning a full-time, one-to-one IA to a student, especially if there are behavioral concerns or if the student is disruptive. As described in the following scenario, assigning an IA may be an appropriate approach or it may create conflict between special and general educators and between home and school.

Jack had a preinjury history of violent and delinquent behavior, and school authorities were concerned that these behaviors might be intensified after his injury. Because Jack was entering high school, his work load increased substantially over what he had been doing in middle school. Also, because of truancy, suspensions, and lack of effort prior to his injury, Jack was below average in basic reading and math skills. He was therefore assigned a full-time instructional assistant.

The IA saw her job as minimizing Jack's frustration so he could maintain appropriate behavior. If classwork was difficult for him, she did it.

Jack learned little, and some of Jack's teachers and classmates were re-
sentful that Jack got good grades without doing the work. District ad-
ministrators, however, were satisfied that Jack's behavior was under
control and that his mother's goal, to have Jack graduate with his class,
would be met.

In the schools in which the authors observed, educators were responding as well as they could to the needs of students with ABI,
given the context of school funding at that time and special education service delivery practices. The authors have seen, however, that
this context can exert pressures that drive special education services
for some students far from the vision of a free appropriate public education in the least restrictive environment as outlined and mandated
in the Individuals with Disabilities Education Act (IDEA) of 1990,
PL 101-476.

Declining resources, reliance on old models of service delivery,
and the natural resistance of large organizations to change are all factors that contribute to school contexts that have difficulty responding to the needs of students with ABI. Other factors that contribute
to this situation operate at the level of individual educational practitioners.

Educator Capacity and Instructional Approaches

The capacity of educators to meet the needs of students with ABI is
limited by lack of training in this newly identified disability area. In
addition, the work styles and instructional classroom management
practices adopted by many teachers are not conducive to developing
collaborative, structured yet flexible accommodations that many
students with ABI require.

Training in ABI   Few special or general educators receive preservice training specific to the frequency of ABI or its effects on a
student's educational performance and behavior (see Chapter 12).
Some teachers, unfamiliar with ABI, assume from the first day a student enters the classroom that he or she is unteachable or that academic goals are not a priority. This view may be unintentionally
reinforced by hospital personnel who focus on medical issues and
rehabilitation goals as the transition is made.

When Jane made the transition from the hospital back to school, a school
psychologist from the hospital conducted an in-service training in ABI
for the school staff. The school psychologist stressed that during recovery,
Jane should experience only success in academics and that material
should be presented with many repetitions so that it is "overlearned."
The school staff interpreted this to mean that Jane should not be intro-

duced to any new academic concepts that might frustrate or discourage her, so she worked at her preinjury level in math and reading for a year after she returned to school.

Ironically, the specialists whose time with the students with ABI is extremely limited are the only school personnel who are likely to have received some training in assessing and working with students with ABI. No matter how inadequate school-based rehabilitation services may be, a student's needs in the areas of physical rehabilitation may be better addressed than those in the areas of academic, cognitive, and behavioral functioning. Teachers, even special educators, often are not trained to work with students with ABI (Blosser & DePompei, 1991) and do not believe they are qualified to work with them (Glang, Todis, Sohlberg, & Reed, 1996; Lash & Scarpino, 1993). Although school-based therapists (e.g., occupational therapists, physical therapists, speech-language therapists) with training in ABI may see the student regularly, they may not believe they are qualified to answer teachers' questions about instructional and behavior management strategies (see Chapter 13).

Teacher Work Styles and Approaches to Problem Solving   Teachers typically work in isolation (Little, 1982) and respond quickly to problem situations in their classrooms from a private repertoire of intervention and correction procedures. Many general educators believe they should not be expected to expand this repertoire to include accommodations to serve students with special needs in their classrooms. They expect such students to receive remedial instruction in a special education setting or to have a special education teacher or assistant available in the classroom to work individually with the student. Some teachers are uncomfortable with providing any type of accommodation to students with learning impairments, as the following scenario of a U.S. history teacher suggests:

Jack's history teacher is upset because she thinks [the IA] is doing Jack's work. She is also upset because all of the students who get help with history in the resource room have the same notes from her class, so their answers on the tests are all similar. The IA explained that she provides them with the notes that she takes during lectures. The teacher got angry and said she wants them to take their own notes: "If they can't do the work, they don't belong in the class."

Likewise, some special educators believe that students with disabilities are best served in segregated settings in which material can be presented at a pace that allows for repetition, adequate practice, and other accommodations.

The special education teacher in Jack's school reminded the team that junior year gets hard fast, especially U.S. history class. If Jack is willing to go for a modified, rather than a typical diploma, he can take U.S. history with her in the resource room. She said that when kids start struggling, she reminds them of the modified diploma option.

Other general and special educators may initially rise to the challenge of their first student with ABI by enthusiastically participating on interdisciplinary teams to plan interventions. Unfortunately, interventions are too often based only on practices and programs with which the teachers are already familiar and that are already in place or are reactive to a particular, immediate student need. The team's task then becomes deciding where to plug the student in or determining how to get the student credit for a class rather than designing an educational program based on a careful consideration of the student's current level of academic performance and his or her long-term goals.

Mike is fully included in his middle school where all seventh graders take a one-term exploratory foreign language class. Mike enrolled in a French class but quickly became frustrated and clashed with the teacher. The teacher insisted Mike be removed from her class. The only other class available that period was exploratory Russian. Mike was even more lost in this class, and he and a friend were constantly off-task and acting out. The teacher allowed both boys to complete all assignments, including developing dialogues, in English.

Some teachers may initially be enthusiastic about trying new approaches to meet the needs of a student with ABI but may quickly become discouraged by the pattern of responding. For example, the student understands a concept one day but not the next; the student has a slow rate of acquisition, requiring many more repetitions and much more practice than other students; or the student may require close monitoring because of problems with initiation. Each of these learner characteristics is extremely difficult for one general education teacher with a classroom of 20–25 other students with whom to work. The teacher's initial enthusiasm can fade rapidly when students "fail" to respond quickly and consistently or if the teacher is not informed in advance that finding an appropriate intervention might require a lengthy process of trial and error as well as frequent modification of interventions to maximize their effectiveness. Faced with these difficulties, the teacher may conclude that the intervention is faulty; the student is inappropriately placed; or, although an appropriate intervention might eventually be found, the process requires more than he or she is able to give.

Faced with the failure of new interventions for the student with ABI, teachers often respond by either turning the student over to a special educator or by falling back on their old repertoire of interventions and lowering expectations of the student in their general education classrooms.

Monitoring   Another common situation that occurs when the student with ABI is quiet and compliant or works closely with an aide is that teachers who have large classes are not experienced in monitoring individual students and may lose track of whether an intervention is working. A school psychologist noted the following:

Teachers think they're doing a good job, but they sometimes have a hard time identifying how what they are doing is coming across to the kid. Same situation in time, the teacher thinks what they're doing is real good, but it's totally nonproductive for the kid. The kid is spacing out or not understanding what's going on.

This is a situation the authors observed in Mike's seventh-grade language arts class in which there were 35 other students:

Although the homework assignments for the whole week were on the board, the directions were very abbreviated and it was hard to tell which assignments were due on which day. In addition, many of the worksheets looked alike. Mike handled this by asking other students for help. Still, he got mixed up and failed to complete one of the worksheets and didn't follow directions on another part of the assignment. The teacher checked in with Mike three times during the class and asked, "How's it going?" Mike answered, "Fine." At the end of the period, students corrected their own papers as the teacher called on students to give the answers. Mike marked several answers wrong on the portion of the assignment he completed. When the teacher called the roll for grades, Mike reported that he got 100%. After class, the teacher reiterated to the observer, "You see, Mike does a terrific job in here. He just needs a little help getting started."

Pedagogy   In the authors' observations, the reasons classrooms were not meeting the needs of students with ABI went beyond failure to monitor or failure to make accommodations. The teaching practices routinely employed in the classrooms that were observed often were not conducive to learning for any of the students, much less those with specific academic challenges. The following is a sample of the practices observed:

- Instruction was textbook- or workbook-based and progressed at the rate of one lesson per day rather than on the basis of whether students had mastered concepts.
- Teachers lacked behavior management skills and methods of motivating students to participate in academic activities.
- Classroom activities were often fragmented and confusing, with no clear objectives. Activities such as movies or special art projects unrelated to academic subjects took up large chunks of class time.
- For students such as those with ABI who needed to leave the classroom to receive remedial instruction in special education settings, the schedules were even more fragmented.
- Lack of mastery of subject area, course content, or basic skills was viewed as the student's problem, not an instructional problem requiring a different approach.

Although masterful teachers might benefit from reassurance that the same approaches that are effective with other students are worth a try as a first level of intervention for students with ABI, this approach is not likely to be helpful with teachers who engage in the practices described here. It is also more difficult for special educators to work with teachers who are bound to programmed teachers' guides and who are not adept at designing and coordinating instruction.

Unfortunately, the capacity of special educators to address the needs of students with ABI may not be much better than those of the general educators. They may limit individualization of instruction to selection of an appropriate packaged curriculum to address a skill impairment. The student with ABI is then placed in an instructional group of students with similar skills or with similar schedules and taught a lesson at a time, just as in the general education classroom. Such an approach often fails to address the cognitive impairments of students with ABI or to provide strategies the student can use to facilitate learning in the general education classroom and in other settings. The results can be frustrating for the student with ABI, as this excerpt from field notes of an observation in a resource room illustrates:

Jack told the IA he was going to cut his self-esteem class in the resource room because he hates that class so much, but he did show up. The special education teacher directed the students to turn to page 213 in the self-esteem workbook. Bill and Doug [students with learning disabilities] were completely noncompliant. They took turns taunting the teacher and making inappropriate comments. The teacher asked why Jack did not have his book open, and he said he had no book. She told him to come to the front and get one. As she turned to get the book, Jack leapt up and performed a karate kick in her direction, not intending to strike her. When she turned, he took the book and sat down, as the class cheered. After a few minutes of insisting that the students turn to page 213 in their workbooks, it became clear that there is no page 213. Jack was totally frustrated and started exchanging verbal challenges with Bill. The teacher found the assignment in the workbook: working in pairs to identify goals and discuss how to accomplish them. Jack threw his binder on the floor and yelled, "This class is STUPID!" The IA asked Bill what his goal was and he said, "To kill the teacher."

Family–School Tensions

Disagreements between school personnel and the family of a student with ABI can quickly become extremely emotionally charged, making resolution difficult. Many such disagreements can be traced to different, sometimes polarized, views parents and teachers hold of the student and of each other.

School Views of Families   School personnel often describe families of students with ABI as functioning poorly and unable to support the school's efforts or as having unrealistic expectations for what the school can help the student accomplish. Either view marginalizes the families' perspectives and makes it difficult for families to be included in educational planning.

The "Dysfunctional" Family   The authors' analysis of teacher comments and interactions with parents suggests that some teachers identify family-centered issues as contributors to school failure among students with ABI. The family of a student with ABI, devastated by the injury, confronted with the challenge of navigating the special education system, and faced with the other day-to-day issues that all typical families face, may well appear to be losing the struggle to support the student to succeed in school. In some cases, families may have been coping with financial or other difficult issues prior to the accident. These factors may contribute to poor school attendance, apparent lack of parent interest in school matters, and student stress and behavior problems. Undoubtedly, family factors can have a negative impact on the performance of the student with ABI.

The interviews and observations revealed, however, that in some cases a teacher's or other school staff's response to family issues is to marginalize or dismiss the family as unavailable or uninterested or to blame the family in some other way for the student's lack of progress in school. In the authors' observations, school personnel often follow a pattern described by Orenstein and Budoff (1986) as "deviantizing" parents of students in special education. This pattern, according to Orenstein and Budoff, is one in which parents' complaints about the student's lack of progress are attributed to deviant and objectionable characteristics of the parents. "They [the parents] are trouble makers; they are blaming the school in order to avoid facing their own problems at home, or they are well-meaning but naive people who cannot accept their child's disability" (Orenstein & Budoff, 1986, p. 48). In the authors' experience, educators may also suggest that the parents' expectations for the child's academic performance are unrealistic, not only because of the brain injury but because the child's preinjury potential was low initially.

> The special education teacher interjected that she believes that Jane probably would have been in special education even if the accident hadn't happened. She based this on the information gleaned from the previous school records and the school's experience with the family. There was support for this suggestion from others in the room.

> In response to the ABI consultant's suggestions about behavior management, the principal said, "You know, Tim was at this school before the injury. We are very familiar with the family situation, and that's where this behavior is coming from. He wasn't a whole child to start with [before the injury]. You can see the same kind of thing in the behavior of his brother and sister."

"Mothers from Hell"   In contrast to parents who are underinvolved in their child's school program, parents who become strong advocates for their child's education, particularly if they insist on specific programs or approaches, may be thought of by school personnel as "in denial" about their child's limitations, "unrealistic," "demanding," or "motivated by guilt and grief." In the authors' experience, parents tend to become aggressive, rather than assertive, about the services they want for their child with ABI only after they believe they were marginalized by school personnel or when their polite requests and suggestions were ignored or dismissed (Orenstein & Budoff, 1986). To get what they considered appropriate services for their children, some parents of students with ABI believe they will not be heard unless they come on strong and threaten to litigate. This mother described the process and the repercussions of being an advocate for her son:

∽✁ ✁∽

I have to keep the major goal in sight. The major goal is to get the help for my son. No matter how angry I am at them. I have to keep working with them, so [I've learned to say] "I disagree with what you're saying. I believe that this is what needs to be done. If I have to get support [an attorney] to get that, then I guess I'll get that support. If I have to get documentation, I'll get that." . . . But most people wouldn't go through what we went through. We became the clanging bell. We became the parents that they could never please. [Those were] the comments. We became the parents who were suing the school district. It was out everywhere. Teachers wouldn't talk to us. Teachers who had been Max's best, his favorites.

∽✁ ✁∽

Another mother described the approach she had developed over the years in negotiating with educators for services for her daughter:

∽✁ ✁∽

I have learned, when I sit down with a group of school people, to tell them straight out, "Look, what you have to understand about me is that I'm motivated by guilt [over the circumstances of my child's injury] and therefore I'm not going to stop hounding you until I get what I think Stacy needs." Once they understand where I'm coming from, and they know I'm not going to go away, we can get down to business.

∽✁ ✁∽

The school may respond to the parents' demands in order to avoid the threat of litigation but with resentment and with negative views of the potential outcome of the program that has been forced on them, as comments from these special educators indicate:

∽✁ ✁∽

Communication between home and school still isn't good, and I'm pretty upset about it. We will never be able to do anything to please Mom. She needs a "reality check" about what Tia is really capable of and what lies ahead for her. It just isn't fair that we extend ourselves so much and that our efforts aren't appreciated.

Stacy does okay here, with a lot of support, but I don't think this is the right program for her. Schools supposedly have a say in placement decisions, but in this case we did not. There was no dialogue. We were told by Mom what the placement would be, and even though there is a more appropriate [life skills] program for her at another school, she's here, continuing to work on an academic program.

In either case, whether the family is marginalized or feared and resented, negative views of the family by school personnel can lead to blaming for the failure of the school program. Mutual finger-pointing ensues, home–school partnerships are destroyed, and the student's education suffers (see Chapter 11).

In this study of the school experiences of students with ABI, conflicts between home and school so greatly affected the students' school functioning and were so predictable that it became a major focus of the research. Although it may be helpful to encourage parents and educators to practice effective, respectful communication techniques (Walker, 1989; Walker & Singer, 1993; see also Chapter 11) such as perspective taking and reframing, these require some examination of the relevant perspectives. Therefore, the authors sought to understand the origins of this conflict and the differing perspectives that contribute to it.

Parents' Views and Expectations   Parents have seen their child relearn rapidly following an accident or acquire new learning quickly in structured, individualized learning environments. They want their child to catch up on work missed during the hospital stay and to regain functions that might have been impaired by the injury. The hope, and often the expectation, of parents is that the student will function at the same academic level as before the accident or at least at the appropriate grade level. When a student sustains an injury in high school, parents and the student often hope and expect that the student will graduate with his or her class. The mother of a boy who was injured during his junior year in high school explained,

I think you can give adults the options to do things like that [spend 6 months at home after being released from the hospital before returning to work], but for an adolescent to drop out of school would have been like a nightmare. You know, "Not graduate with my class. Not have my senior year!" You know, I mean, all of these things! And, so he said "No, no, no. I want to stay in school." But it was a fight [to get the accommodations to make this possible].

Different Views of the Student, Different Expectations   An important factor in the development of home–school conflict is a fundamental difference in the way parents and educators view the student with ABI. These different views in turn influence the expectations each group of adults has for the student's school performance and the type of educational supports that are requested and provided. When student outcomes fail to meet expectations or when the appropriateness of the expectations of one group is questioned by the other, conflicts arise and a cycle of finger-pointing and mutual blame can result.

Initial Expectations and Accommodations   When a student with ABI first returns to school, there is often an outpouring of sympathy, goodwill, and cooperation, resulting in agreement between parents and teachers regarding initial goals. The school is likely to call in a variety of resources to continue the student's rehabilitation and to make a number of accommodations in terms of scheduling and academic expectations. The student may quickly relearn previously mastered material.

This "honeymoon" situation may change when the student is no longer making rapid cognitive improvements, when he or she exhibits inappropriate behavior as a result of frustration with academic tasks, or when grades reflect that the student is not meeting criteria for success. The school may respond by providing additional special education supports: an instructional assistant to accompany the student in classes, services in a special education classroom, or both. At this point, school and family views of the student with ABI—as a learner who needs additional supports and creative accommodations but who can succeed academically—are still parallel. When the accommodations produce the desired student outcomes and the student achieves at the level of his or her and the family's expectations, home–school relations are likely to be positive.

Changing Expectations   Even if a program with appropriate supports and accommodations is mutually acceptable to all parties for a class, a semester, or a school year, changes in the student, in expectations for his or her age and grade level, and in educational programming inevitably upset the balance, requiring modification of the program or changes in expectations for the student's academic performance. As students with ABI move through the grades, they are likely to experience difficulty with new or more abstract concepts; they will encounter teachers who are not familiar with their personal histories and are unaware of the effects of ABI in general, and they may encounter limitations in the schools' ability to provide adequate resources and appropriate accommodations. They may, in fact, become aware that some former areas of ability and interest are no longer available to them and modify their expectations for academic performance and for long-term goals. Students with ABI and their families are likely, however, to continue to desire and expect educators to provide what they consider appropriate individualized accommodations to address the student's unique needs and to maximize school success.

In contrast, educators, after trying a number of placements and accommodations, are likely to more drastically alter their expectations for the academic performance and long-term outcomes of students with ABI. Several factors work together to produce what families may regard as inappropriately low expectations on the part of educators. Once the student has been back in school for a couple of years, especially if the student changes schools, expectations of school personnel for students with ABI often become similar to their expectations for other students who are identified as having developmental disabilities. Teachers are likely to expect students with ABI to have difficulty with new learning, be slow responders, be inattentive, and function below their grade level. General educators tend to respond as they do for other students with disabilities in their classes, making the same types of accommodations (see the following section) and turning over much of the responsibility for the student's academic progress to the special education staff.

The special educator's expectations for the student with ABI, especially if students with disabilities are classified by severity of disability, may be similar to those for other students in the same program. For example, individuals in self-contained programs for students with moderate to severe disabilities are not expected to pursue academic programs but to focus on adaptive skills and vocational training. Individuals who are served in programs for students with mild disabilities may receive remedial training in basic skills, but because of their unique brain injuries may not progress at the same rate as students with other types of learning disabilities. Such incongruities may contribute to the special education teacher's low expectations.

It is important to note that lowering expectations itself is regarded by many general and special educators as an appropriate accommodation for students with a range of cognitive abilities in public schools. In fact, teachers who come into conflict with parents over expectations for their children with disabilities may see parents' higher expectations as being cruelly unrealistic and demanding of the child.

A special education teacher described her relief that the mother of a high school girl has agreed to some modifications in her daughter's program:

Mom sees now that hard things are going to have to be faced. Always before we were hampered from trying things because we were given the clear instructions, "We don't want any planned failures," meaning "Don't try things just to find out what skills she doesn't have and what she needs to learn." But when we would ask, "Well, what can Tia do?" the answer was "Everything." So we'd try things and, no, she couldn't do everything."

The parents' view often continues to be that the student has challenges resulting from the brain injury that may require accommodations beyond the typical special education program in order for the student to reach his or her academic potential. Meanwhile, the school's view of the student with ABI evolves into an understanding of what the student's abilities and limitations are and how these can be addressed within the existing special education delivery system. Not only is the conflict often emotionally charged because part of the disagreement is over whose view of the student is accurate, it is also of great practical importance because expectations help determine what kinds of programming, supports, and accommodations will be available. Tia's mother described her frustration with the outcome of an individualized education program (IEP) meeting for her daughter with ABI:

The IEP was disconcerting. What I heard at the IEP meeting was a litany of Tia's present levels of functioning described as "unable to, unable to, unable to." What made it especially hard to hear this was that she was able to do many of these things in the past. There is no neurological reason why she shouldn't be able to do the things they say she can't do. The things they say she is "unable to do" include counting and making change, reading a newspaper, doing math, using a calculator, figuring out the steps in a math problem.

It's just part of the process that has been going on since she got to high school. It feels like they are making her a disabled person instead of a person who has some disabilities. They are training her to see herself as someone who can't do things instead of someone who needs to develop some skills.

〜 〜

Making Accommodations

In the authors' experience, when school personnel understand the unique challenges of students with ABI, they try to provide accommodations that will help students succeed. Unfortunately, in the school context of inadequate resources and training, large classes, private work styles, and shifting service delivery paradigms, it is extremely difficult for school staff to design and monitor accommodations that will address the needs of a student with ABI across a number of subject areas and settings. The behavioral effects of ABI also contribute to the problem. If the student exhibits behavioral outbursts, behavior management is almost certain to become the focus of the school program. The school will exert tighter controls, in the form of more restricted placement or closer supervision. Academic and social accommodations, which, ironically, might help deescalate the problem behavior, are put on hold until the behavior is under control.

Some common approaches to academic accommodations for students with ABI are described here:

The Full-Time IA   One common accommodation, especially for students who have behavioral outbursts or whose schedules are academically challenging, is assigning an IA to work one to one with the student in all classes. Although this is an expensive accommodation, some districts regard it as a bargain compared with the alternatives: potential law suits resulting from injuries caused by the behavior of the student with ABI or from the parents of the student claiming that appropriate accommodations were not made to help the student succeed.

The primary problem the authors have observed with this accommodation is that the IAs lack the training and support needed to adapt materials and present them in a way that allows the student with ABI to independently complete coursework and master curriculum content. Instead, too often the joint focus of the IA and the student with ABI becomes simply getting through the course with a passing grade. Other accommodations (e.g., shorter assignments, longer preparation time, simplified materials) are seldom provided because the view of both special and general educators is likely to be that because the IA has been provided, at great expense, other accommodations should not be necessary. In order to ensure that the student keeps up with the rest of the class, the IA may adopt such measures as reading the assignment aloud to the student, taking notes on lectures, writing out answers dictated by the student, managing materials, or typing and editing the final drafts of a student's paper. Any or all of these supports may be appropriate if they are used to help the student master course material and if they are gradually faded so that the student functions as independently as possible. Unfortunately, independent functioning and acquiring specific knowledge and skills may not have been clearly identified as goals for the student with ABI. The IA may therefore see his or her role as getting the student successfully through the class by turning in completed assignments.

Classroom teachers have two typical responses to IAs working with students with ABI in their classrooms. They may regard the pair as separate from the class and therefore believe that they themselves are not responsible for the student's performance, or they may resent giving high grades for work turned in under the student's name but in the IA's handwriting and clearly produced by the IA. Jack's math teacher expressed her frustration with the accommodations made for all the students in her basic math class:

Jack shouldn't have passed his math final [but he got a B]. Most of the kids in that class didn't pass. They are dependent on the calculator and just punch away until they find the answer. They do not understand math and make very little effort. Why should they? The school just passes them on anyway. They really don't know anything about math, and we're just making them more dependent. I don't know how they will be able to get jobs or live once they leave high school, their skills are so bad. Jack's skills, for example, are not good at all. If he didn't have the aide he would not be able to do anything. He had 4 hours on this final and couldn't finish it. Even then I'm not sure how much help he had from his aide. I think a lot. There's not a chance he could have done any of it without the aide.

This type of accommodation can also be frustrating for parents:

After Tia's [brain] injury at age 11, she worked hard, with support from her mother, to regain her reading skills. Starting high school, Tia was reading at about the fifth-grade level. Tia enrolled in classes to earn a reg-

ular diploma and was assigned a full-time IA. Because the coursework was very demanding for Tia, and because she tended to fall behind on assignments, the IA read most of the assignments aloud to her. Tia's mother was unhappy because Tia's reading skills declined to about a third-grade level after 3 years of high school.

Assigning a full-time IA to a student with ABI can also be frustrating for special education staff, especially if they believe they were forced by parents to provide this expensive accommodation:

One of the IAs jumped in at this point [during observation] and added that she doesn't think Tia should get to participate in a new program for students with ABI because Tia has a full-time IA. "She already gets more attention than any of the other kids we work with, and that isn't right because the other kids have needs, too."

The team discussed the possibility of giving David a full-time IA. The school already has three IAs for special ed. Two of them would work well with David, but the principal said he was reluctant to assign one of them to David. The principal explained, "I had to go to the school board to fight to get them to provide assistance to all special ed. kids. I feel obligated to use them the way I told the board they would be used." The special education teacher agreed that reassigning one of the IAs would cause hardship elsewhere.

Grading and Assignment Accommodations   If the student makes an effort, appears to be on task, is cooperative, and does not have a behavior problem, the general education classroom teacher may assume the student is doing fine and does not need academic accommodations. Unfortunately, compliant behavior can mask problems with initiation, memory, and comprehension. Even if the teacher recognizes this, he or she may want to reward the student's effort and attitude by making grading accommodations. Teachers' grading practices are extremely individualized, even idiosyncratic, and in most school cultures there are no schoolwide guidelines for how grades should be assigned. In fact, grading practices are all but sacrosanct (see Little, 1982). The following are grading and other accommodations made by some of Mike's teachers during his sixth-grade year to reflect how much they appreciate his good attitude:

Mike's work was not up to grade level, but I intend to give a pass on a pass/no pass system because of his efforts.

I graded on ability and initiative. If he completed the modified assignment, that was an "A."

I gave Mike a "B" on an adjusted grading system that I use for Mike. He is very slow on the guitar, he can't really read notes, and has little rhythm, but I gave him a "B." Mike tries.

Mike was a little slower, so if he had homework he'd just take it home and hand it in the next time. He was real good. Some modifications that I did, I let him redo his tests and assignments he kind of messed up on.

I always modified the tests. He was doing maybe 30%–50% of the work that the other kids in class were doing.

Rather than being gratified by their child's good grades, some parents are frustrated by these grading accommodations that reflect low expectations for their child's academic functioning. They see their child as being moved along through the "system" without acquiring basic skills and the basic knowledge they need to be independent adults.

Mike's mother was upset because Mike's average for assignments in science class was a "B," but he got an "F" on the final. (Mike refused to go to the library with the other students in special education to get help during the test and insisted on completing it himself in the classroom.) The science teacher explained that the "B" for daily work reflected Mike's good attitude and effort. He told her, "I have kids fail tests all the time and yet they do okay if they do their assignments and get their lab reports in and participate. A lot of kids don't do well on tests." Mike's mother was still unhappy, "They grade him on effort until he gets to the test, then it's on knowledge, but of course he doesn't have the knowledge and he doesn't know why because he's been getting okay grades on the daily work. Why isn't someone tracking what he actually knows and understands, then figuring out how to help him express what he knows on tests? An "F" on the final means to me that he didn't learn anything, he's not understanding concepts, and he's going to need this stuff in high school."

Toward the end of the conversation, Jane's mom asked her to go to the computer to show how she does the math program. Jane was able to add combinations of three- and four-digit numbers without hesitation. Her mom said with a tone of disgust, "She only does single digits at school. That's all they ask her to do."

Behavioral issues can also be complicated by well-intentioned, but poorly planned, accommodations:

> The staff realized that Mike desperately wanted to interact with other students. They therefore did not intervene when Mike and his friend Tom were disruptive in class. In fact, as an accommodation for Mike's social isolation, the school staff scheduled Mike and Tom for the same classes whenever possible and let them sit together.
>
> Unfortunately, Mike had trouble recognizing when his behavior was getting out of control and sometimes continued to act out, with encouragement from Tom, until the teacher was forced to take disciplinary action to protect other students.

Accommodations that Reflect Low Expectations   If special education support is not available to help make accommodations for the student with ABI, the response of many classroom teachers is to pull accommodations out of their repertoire. It can be extremely challenging for a teacher to come up with an appropriate activity for a student who functions several grade levels below the rest of the class. Although the student may receive remedial instruction in some areas in a special education resource room, scheduling problems may require that classroom teachers "do something" with the student with ABI while the rest of the class is engaged in an academic activity. Often the alternative activities teachers provide reflect their lower expectations for the student with ABI rather than strategies to overcome ABI-related problems that would make it possible for the student to progress academically. For example, although Jane had studied for the spelling test and could spell many of the words, her classroom teacher, Linda, made modifications that reflected her low expectations:

❧ ❧

"Well, she did fine," Linda said as she handed [the observer] the paper. There were only one or two letters for each of the spelling words. For instance: "math" had "ma," "homework" had "h." There were a few words that had nothing. Linda explained that she had asked Jane to write only the first letter of each word during these tests. "That way I know she's at least listening."

❧ ❧

Other members of the school staff may be aware of what they consider to be inappropriate accommodations for the student with

ABI; but because classrooms tend to be private domains, they will probably be extremely reluctant to question the teacher's practices. The special education teacher commented,

ᦟ ᦟ

Tim's behavior is deteriorating. He listens to his teacher okay, but his teacher doesn't really make him do anything. He lets him spend a lot of time with the custodian. I don't know how his teacher is going to grade him this year.

ᦟ ᦟ

The custodian said,

ᦟ ᦟ

I ask[ed] Tim's teacher about it because it seems to me that Tim should be in class studying with the other students instead of walking around with me. I don't mind, but I don't understand why he lets Tim spend so much time out of class. He said that Tim wasn't really involved in what is going on in class and that it would be better for him to do something else.

ᦟ ᦟ

History of Conflicting Expectations and Accommodations   Over a number of years, the war of differing expectations and disagreements over appropriate accommodations can lead to entrenched positions and a focus on proving that the other side is at fault, rather than on seeking a more productive approach. The conflict often focuses on the adequacy and nature of the educational program, the competence of the school staff and on the character and emotional stability of the parent, usually the mother.

Summary

Federal policy mandates procedures that would appear well suited to meet the needs of students with ABI. At the local level, however, funding constraints, time pressures, school schedules, and other factors limit educators' abilities to implement these procedures. Districts have responded by streamlining special education procedures so that the maximum number of students can be served at the lowest cost. Too often this means placing students in preexisting special education programs rather than designing programs to meet their individual needs. Thus the context surrounding special education service delivery does not support individualized programming to meet students' needs.

Schools perceive students with ABI as different from students with other types of disabilities. The programs and resources that are set up for other students with disabilities are not appropriate or sufficient to meet the needs—behavioral, academic, organizational, and social—of the one or few students with ABI that the school services.

Because ABI is a low-incidence disability, schools look for solutions that address the needs of that student rather than increasing the capacity of the existing program to work on a more individual basis with all students with special needs. These include accommodations such as one-to-one aides; impromptu, rather than systematic, adjustments in expectations that are inconsistent across teachers; pursuit of magic bullet solutions like cutting-edge technology; and the search for a program to take over and solve the problem for that student. Such approaches reflect a goal of getting the student through the program so the program can return to normal, rather than adapting programs to meet the needs of a wider diversity of student needs.

The capacity of many general and special education teachers at the present time is not adequate to understand the needs of students with ABI and to adapt instruction and make other accommodations to address their unique learning impairments. Preservice training of special educators usually does not include information about ABI and is even less likely to include practical experience in planning instruction and behavior management strategies for this group of students. General educators are even less likely to have training and experience with students with ABI.

The authors found, furthermore, that although students with ABI often respond favorably to systematic, well-organized, well-paced instruction and to clear behavior expectations and consequences (Rosenshine & Stevens, 1986), few teachers—in either general or special education—have mastered these instructional and behavior management principles. In short, the present capacity of the typical public school system is likely to be inadequate to meet the challenges presented by a student with ABI.

Given the current context and capacity issues, it is not surprising that family–school tensions emerged as a third theme in the authors' qualitative research. A major source of family–school tensions is disagreement over appropriate academic expectations. Parents are likely to press for services that they see as restoring skills and abilities their child has lost as a result of the injury. They would like the school to develop a "whatever it takes" attitude. The school, however, frequently adopts a "what can you expect?" attitude, employing lowered expectations for the student with ABI as a primary accommodation for his or her disability. Tensions resulting from the conflict these two views produce can in turn contribute to further problems in delivering academic services to students with ABI, as home–school communication deteriorates and finger-pointing and "blame-storming" take over parent–teacher meetings.

WHAT WORKS?

Although the authors' observations reveal that the programs of many students with ABI are plagued with the problems and frustrations outlined previously, they also reveal that some schools are able to work creatively within their very real constraints to provide individualized, appropriate educational services. When school programs are regarded as successful by schools, parents, and students, they usually are based on the process outlined in IDEA for planning and implementing the education of students with disabilities. This is encouraging, as it indicates that the process for providing services is already in place and accessible to all school districts that are willing to follow the spirit, as well as the letter, of the law. In Project SOS, the authors have worked in schools serving students with ABI to learn how school personnel build on IDEA to respond creatively to the needs of students with ABI. What has emerged is a process for developing a student-centered, goal-based educational program that addresses the perspectives of teachers, students, and parents. The following case study, taken from field notes of an observation in the resource room, outlines the positive effects of this approach on Jack, a student with ABI whose sophomore year was a rocky one:

> Jack's behavior deteriorated throughout Monday morning. In first period, he threw books and papers around and muttered a threat to the teacher when he turned in his assignment. In the next class, typing, he was jumpy and agitated. When the teacher repeatedly asked him if he had work to do, he eventually replied, with arms folded across his chest, "I have thinking to do." Between classes, Jack's IA tried to find out what was wrong. She asked him about his weekend and he replied, "This was a weekend of misery." During a test in third period English class, Jack put forth little effort as he worked through the test with the IA. In the resource room during fourth period, as Mrs. Fry presented a lesson on "Handling Put-Downs," Jack's attitude swung between contempt for her and the material and total indifference. When Mrs. Fry tried to intervene to direct Jack's group, Jack yelled insults at her: "Why don't you

just stay away and leave us alone? We don't want you here!" His face reflected anger and disdain.

Jack's high school program was centered around one goal that was important to both Jack and his family: graduating with his class with a regular diploma. The school saw its role as providing the necessary supports to permit Jack to reach this goal. Because he had angry outbursts and was quite low functioning in academics, Jack was assigned a one-to-one IA to accompany him to all of his general education classes. She took notes for him, provided prompts during class to keep him focused on the assigned activity, made sure he completed all assignments, and helped him take tests. When Jack became frustrated or angry, the IA helped him organize his thoughts and think through his options, including potential consequences. Gradually Jack became able to recognize when he was becoming upset and learned strategies to calm himself or solve the problem without an angry outburst.

The constant support provided by the IA allowed Jack to pass his classes and to maintain acceptable behavioral control in the school setting. However, Jack's school team believed that he shouldn't merely be "passed along" and that he needed to become more independent if he were to be successful after high school. They enlisted the assistance of an ABI consultant and drew together a team of teachers to work with Jack and his family to modify his educational program.

A making action plans, or MAPs, meeting was held with Jack, his IA, the special education teacher, and the ABI consultant to determine Jack's goals and to come up with strategies for helping him to reach them. Jack and the team identified four key goals: find an after-school job, obtain a driver's license, prepare for college, and complete the requirements for a regular high school diploma. The team then worked with Jack to prioritize his goals. Jack's short-term objectives focused on improving his reading and spelling skills and increasing his independence throughout his school day.

Jack's team implemented a variety of strategies to assist him in reaching these objectives. First, the consultant provided training for the IA in techniques to improve Jack's reading and spelling skills and provided materials for tracking his performance over time. Second, the IA and consultant planned and implemented several strategies to foster Jack's independence (e.g., offer assistance only when needed, use peers when possible to assist with note taking and assignments). Jack and the IA purchased a watch and notebook so that Jack could keep track of where he needed to be throughout the day. Third, the IA met individually with Jack's teachers to discuss reasonable expectations for each of his classes. Finally, the IA communicated frequently via notes and telephone calls with Jack's special education teacher and his mother about his progress.

At the end of the year, Jack had made progress toward each of his long-term goals. He had successfully completed all of his junior requirements and would graduate with his class if he passed three core classes in his senior year. He had passed his driver's license exam and had an after-school job that would be extended into full time during the summer months. His spelling and reading skills had improved so that he was able to read and complete many of his assignments on his own. And Jack was much more independent in class. For example, he took his own notes in history class and filled out his own weight-lifting chart in gym class. Teachers described him as being more confident, having better social skills, and getting along well with peers. Jack's mother described him as being very responsible—setting his own goals and then doing what was necessary to achieve them.

Features of successful approaches, such as the one implemented for Jack, specifically address the problem areas that have been outlined in the previous section:

- They overcome the limitations of the current context of categorical, program-driven special education service delivery by providing a student-centered, goal-based educational plan.
- They build the capacity of educators to meet students' individual needs through training and ongoing support.
- They foster respectful communication between home and school.
- They rely on team-identified goals and ongoing home–school communication to promote agreement on appropriate expectations.
- Once expectations are agreed upon, accommodations are systematically developed that are consistent with expectations for the student and with his or her long- and short-term goals.

The remainder of the chapter describes how schools implement this approach.

Student-Centered, Goal-Based Programming

The successful programs for students with ABI that the authors have examined begin by identifying students' strengths, challenges, long- and short-term goals, barriers to reaching those goals, and strategies for overcoming the barriers. Teams find that to plan such programs, using MAPs or a similar process borrowed from person-centered planning (Pearpoint, Forest, & Snow, 1992; Salisbury, Gallucci, Palombaro, & Peck, 1995; Vandercook & York, 1990) is helpful in several ways. The process keeps the discussion positive and includes the opinions and perspectives of all players—student, family, and educators. The positive effects of giving students with developmental disabilities choices and control in planning their school programs have been well documented (Bannermann, Sheldon, Sherman, & Harchik, 1990; Harchik, Sherman, & Bannerman, 1993; Shevin & Klein, 1984). The benefits include positive effects on behavior and motivation (Feeney & Ylvisaker, 1995) and enhanced educational outcomes (Wehmeyer & Lawrence, 1995). For students with ABI who have lost control over so much of their lives as a result of their injury, it is particularly critical to involve them in planning their own programs.

Once goals are identified, progress toward goals must be assessed frequently, and honestly, and program changes made accordingly. In some cases, a student may modify his or her goals or time line for reaching those goals based on progress toward intermediate goals.

> *Jack confirmed that attending a Bible college is still one of his goals. His mother said she's concerned that if he goes to college "he won't learn how to do anything" that will help him earn a living. Jack turned to his mother and explained that he doesn't intend to go to college right after high school; but he wants to find out how to prepare so he will be ready when he does want to go. He finished by saying, "I might not go until I'm 26 or older." His mom seemed to accept this.*

Building the student's program on personal, meaningful goals changes the context of special education service delivery from program driven to student driven. Such an approach requires flexibility and communication among school personnel, which in turn depends on administrative support:

> *David's middle school releases students after lunch on Fridays so that staff members can meet to discuss general programming and to problem-solve issues involving individual students. Because David's behavior was a problem not just at school but also at home and in the community, family members and community agency representatives were also invited to the Friday meeting. At the end of the meeting, the team had an action plan to tackle several factors contributing to David's problem behavior. They agreed to review progress or modify the plan the following week.*

Although drastically changing the approach to special education service delivery initially may seem overwhelming to educators who are used to a programmatic approach, educators such as this special education teacher quickly see the rewards of individualization and frequent monitoring:

Usually you have an annual review once a year. They were telling us that with a kid with ABI, that doesn't cut the mustard. And, in the beginning I was kind of like, "Oh, God, you mean we have to have an IEP meeting every 6 weeks?" Then, now that we've done it, I realize that we couldn't have done her program if we hadn't done that.

Perhaps the most important benefit of a program based on student goals is the motivation it provides for the students to continue to confront challenges as they work their way through school:

> *Before the MAPs meeting, the IA's approach to working with Amber was power based: "Do it because I said so." Now that Amber has identified some goals, the IA will try a different prompting style. When it is time for Amber to consult her memory book, the IA will remind her, "In order to get into the independent living program, you need to be able to use a schedule."*

Building Capacity of Educators to Serve Students with ABI

Providing information about the effects of ABI increases teacher capacity to recognize aspects of current programs that are barriers to student success and to provide appropriate accommodations:

> *The ABI consultant presented a short in-service training to the staff at David's school on the impact ABI has on behavior. The staff learned, among other things, that negative consequences for problem behavior may not be effective for a student with cognitive impairments like David's. They decided to look instead at antecedents: What precedes his problem episodes? Their action plan included having David check in every morning before class: Did he have a place to sleep the previous night? Did he have all his school materials? Had he eaten breakfast? Did he have his glasses? Was he carrying cigarettes, drugs, or other items that would get him in trouble? Was he feuding with any other students? Problems in any of these areas were addressed before he went to class, greatly reducing the frequency of hassles with teachers and frustrated outbursts from David.*

In addition to information about ABI, consultation on specific strategies and interventions is also critical, especially when services to the student are delivered primarily by instructional assistants or by general education teachers who may not have a repertoire of skills in remedial instruction:

Jack's IA requested assistance in designing effective ways to help him improve his reading and spelling skills. A high school junior, he was reading at the fifth-grade level and spelling at the third-grade level. Jack believed he could find a much better job after high school if he could spell and read better.

Following an assessment of Jack's abilities, the ABI consultant shared instructional materials and techniques with the IA. They discussed and role-played procedures for presenting the materials and went over progress monitoring forms to keep track of Jack's instructional gains. Following the training, the IA implemented the techniques with Jack. The consultant gave her feedback on her teaching and offered suggestions for tailoring the instruction to Jack's performance. From that point on, the IA periodically videotaped her lessons and reviewed and critiqued the tape independently. This video feedback proved to be a powerful learning tool for her. As a result of this experience, both the IA and Jack felt more positive about their tutoring time. Jack learned to spell and read better, and the IA learned strategies she could use with other students.

Although preservice training and general community awareness of ABI issues is needed, in-service training and consultation on individual students will have to fill the gap. One important finding that emerged from the authors' qualitative analysis of teacher responses to in-service training in several schools is that teachers are not necessarily the best judges of whether they need in-service training in ABI. As one consultant remarked, teachers often "don't know that they don't know" what the issues are when they have a student with ABI in the classroom. Responses of teachers following such presentations indicate the changes in awareness they experience from even a brief training:

During a discussion about Amber's problems in getting to class on time, the IA suggested she was "lazy" and Amber became defensive. The ABI consultant gave a brief, impromptu lecture on executive functions, including impulsivity control, organization, and planning, giving examples of each in a school context. Several educators in the group made comments such as, "That makes so much sense!" "I never heard that before!" and "I thought Amber was just being lazy. Now I get what's happening." The consultant reflected afterward, "This was a group that would have said, 'No, thanks' if I had asked if they needed information on executive function. I think sometimes they don't know that they don't know."

A teacher raised her hand and asked the ABI consultant, "Did you say he had this [brain injury] when he was 6? Eight years ago? You mean you can get a blow on the head like that and never recover from it? He's not going to get any better? Man, I don't have David in my class, but I wonder how many other kids in my classes had [brain] injuries way back."

Such responses indicate that it is advantageous for the entire staff to attend at least a minimum of in-service training in ABI so that awareness of the student's needs is schoolwide. The authors, however, have also learned that specific consultation and suggestions from "experts" are rarely implemented if school personnel have not asked for them or have otherwise indicated that they are not ready to receive them (see Chapter 13):

The ABI consultant offered a behavior management program to reduce the number of fights Tim got into on the playground by rewarding him for playing appropriately. The principal listened politely and said, "We actually have something different in mind, since we're not sure Tim is trainable. We're going to have a parent volunteer follow him around and when he starts bugging other kids, she'll tell him to stop it."

A variety of such experiences have taught us that the point of consultation and in-service training should be to increase the capacity of school staff to solve their own problems in ways that are consistent with their own school culture and give them a feeling of ownership of the outcome.

The outcome of the principal's playground intervention for Tim was extremely positive. The parent volunteer noted, as the ABI consultant had, that many of the fights Tim got into resulted from his being taunted and harassed by other students. Six weeks later the special education teacher reported to the consultant,

He was getting set up a lot by the other kids. We've let them know that we're on to them and he's not getting in fights anymore. You know, he's really pretty bright. Sometimes I'll make a joke and he's the only kid who gets it. I'm really enjoying him a lot.

Communication to Minimize Family–School Tensions

Because negative patterns of communication based on a history of perceived wrongs on both sides are incredibly difficult to reverse (Orenstein & Budoff, 1986), respectful, clear communication should be established from the beginning of each family–school relationship. As described previously, training professionals to view this type of communication as part of their professional responsibility has been somewhat effective. ABI consultants trained to reframe negative views of individual parents and to take the parent perspective (Walker & Singer, 1993) have noted positive effects of these approaches on their relationships with family members:

I know Jack's family. They're very suspicious and their belief is that the system is out to get you. You know, they'll take your kids [away] or they'll just do whatever. So I've tried to really work on the communication. Just before Christmas I dropped Jack off at home, and I said "I want to come and say hi to your mom." I went in and just wished her a Merry Christmas and talked with her a little bit. The next day I brought over a bowl of fruit. And later Jack told me, "You know, my mom was in a really bad mood before you came over, just really yelling at us. And you got her to laugh! Everything was fine after you left. She said, 'I really like her.'" [Jack's mom] called me "magical" because of all the changes in Jack. I thought that was nice.

Parents who develop similar communication styles also noted the benefits:

I think the thing that helped us is, I didn't go in there angry. I just said, "I'm not happy that this isn't happening. What do we need to do?" And I think that was real important. I think they responded better to that kind of "I'm not happy about this" [approach], but I wasn't screaming and yelling. Well, I think the fact that I'm a teacher [helped], and I've been on the other end of screaming and yelling, and I know what's most effective with me and I tried to be that way with this position.

Professionals who communicate respectfully with parents and who view them as partners are better able to avoid the tendency of some school personnel to identify family problems as barriers to providing an effective educational program. Some school teams with whom the authors have worked demonstrate that they are able to recognize the problems families face and the contribution of these problems to the student's challenges but still find ways to support the student and family.

Jack's English teacher explained the school's view of Jack's difficult family situation:

I think in their own private way, [the family] is very grateful for what we're doing for their son. It goes back to the love that this faculty has for these kids . . . .We take seriously the saying that it takes a whole village to raise a child. Some families need the village more than others.

David's school staff demonstrated a similar attitude, as can be seen in the following observation:

During the meeting the staff identified several areas in which David's mom had not followed through on things she had agreed to do: She didn't get him to medical appointments, she didn't replace his glasses, and if he was out past 9 P.M. she locked him out for the night. Several teachers expressed anger and frustration. The staff agreed to 1) make sure good things are happening for him at school in terms of learning and keeping his behavior under control and 2) work on keeping him safe at home by continuing to communicate with his mom and helping her get resources.

Identifying Appropriate Expectations and Accommodations

Basing the school program on student goals helps focus the entire team on appropriate expectations for academic progress, social development, and school and community behavior. Long- and short-term goals function as reference points for making more immediate decisions about planning programs and acquiring resources. For example, a middle school language arts teacher will have different academic expectations for a student with ABI who intends to pursue a regular high school diploma than for another who will enter a vocational program in high school and is enrolled in language arts to work on communication skills and socialization. Likewise, knowing what a student's postsecondary plans are helps set expectations for performance in high school. For Jack, his goal of graduating with a diploma guided many of his team's decisions:

At the beginning of junior year the special education teacher reviewed Jack's goals in a team meeting. She pointed out, "American history is a really tough class. That book is terrible. It's written at a college reading level. If you want to get a regular diploma, we will work with the teacher to make accommodations, but you don't have to stay in that class. You

*can take American history with me in the resource room and get a mod-
ified diploma." Jack reconfirmed that he would like to try to go to college
someday and that he wants to earn a regular diploma so he can get better
jobs. The special education teacher then outlined a plan for holding Jack
to appropriate expectations. Because a pretest indicated that Jack could
master approximately 60% of the American history content presented in
several lessons, she suggested a criterion of 60% be set. The history
teacher would identify the 60% of information in each unit that was most
important, and Jack's tests and assignments would be designed to cover
this material. His grades would then be based on how well he demonstrated knowledge of this portion of the curriculum. Based on current
academic test scores and classroom observations, the special education
teacher suggested additional accommodations: help with note taking, a
book written at an eighth-grade level, a daily study period with the IA to
complete assignments, and additional time to complete tests.*

As this scenario illustrates, the development of appropriate
accommodations requires that general educators be active members
of the student's team. As noted previously, teachers tend to function
as entrepreneurs who set the standards and determine the criteria for
success in their classrooms (Little, 1982). Any accommodation for a
student who is not able to meet the standard criteria for success in
that classroom must therefore be developed in cooperation with the
teacher who is the authority on the subject matter and on what constitutes success in his or her classroom. The team discussions help
individual teachers see the role their subject area plays in the context of the student's current condition and long-term plans, making
it easier to identify portions of the curriculum that the student
should master.

It is important to note that the relationship between goals and
expectations is a two-way street. Students sometimes decide, with
their teams, to modify their goals after evaluating how well they are
meeting expectations for intermediate goals:

*Tia's and her mother's goal is for Tia to work in a video store. The school
staff has concerns about whether the expectations for reading, alphabetizing, and organizing on this job are higher than Tia can consistently
meet without putting herself under too much stress. They have also noted
that her vision problems seem to make this job difficult for her. At the
team meeting the staff showed Tia's mother a video of Tia working in the
video store, pointing out incidents that illustrated their concerns and
checking to see if Tia's mother interpreted the incidents in the same way
they did. They then discussed whether Tia should get more reading instruction, practice alphabetizing, and get another vision check-up, or try
some other jobs. The team, including Tia, decided to take a break from the*

video store and try jobs in a greenhouse and on a grounds crew during the spring and summer.

Supporting the student in attaining goals does not mean that school staff have to pretend that the student does not have cognitive and behavior problems that present challenges to meeting the goals. Rather, support involves understanding the origins of learning and behavior problems, but holding the student to high, appropriate expectations in these areas, with adequate support.

CONCLUSION

The educational challenges facing students with ABI and their teachers suggest strongly that there are interactions among educational environment, teacher capacity, and school–family communication that make it difficult for public schools to meet the needs of students with ABI. A promising approach to addressing all three factors is to design individual student programs using a student-centered, goal-based planning process. Other features of effective programs for students with ABI include frequent monitoring of progress toward goals; increasing teacher capacity through in-service training and consultation; frequent, respectful communication between home and school; and flexibility in school programming and individual accommodations.

Clearly, this approach is challenging. It requires educators to examine the way services are currently delivered to students with special needs, including those with ABI, and in many cases, to change the way they have been delivering special education services. It also requires emotional risk taking, in the form of parents and educators taking each others' perspectives and communicating honestly with each other. However, the rewards, as well as the challenges, are great, as Jack indicated in a letter describing the impact of such an approach on his junior year in high school:

My junior year has been my best one so far. I'm really pleased with the watch [the team decided on] because it has everything I could possibly need. I no longer have to ask the date or the time and I can keep my window-washing appointments more exact. Without [the team] support I wouldn't be where I am now or as happy. And also, I have been figuring out my life. Tonight at my house, while I was reading, I discovered that . . . I can read so fast I was shocked! I felt so happy, and I do almost all the time.

REFERENCES

Bannerman, D.J., Sheldon, J.B., Sherman, J.A., & Harchik, A.E. (1990). Balancing the right to habilitation with the right to personal liberties: The rights of people with developmental disabilities to eat too many doughnuts and take a nap. *Journal of Applied Behavior Analysis, 23*, 79–89.

Blosser, J.L., & DePompei, R. (1991). Preparing education professionals for meeting the needs of students with traumatic brain injury. *Journal of Head Trauma Rehabilitation, 6*(1), 73–82.

Blosser, J.L., & DePompei, R. (1994). Educational issues: Planning in advance for school reintegration. In J.L. Blosser & R. DePompei (Eds.), *Pediatric traumatic brain injury: Proactive intervention* (pp. 197–218). San Diego: Singular.

Bogdan, R.C. & Biklin, S.K. (1982). *Qualitative research for education: An introduction to theory and method.* Needham, MA: Allyn & Bacon.

Feeney, T.J., & Ylvisaker, M. (1995). Choice and routine: Antecedent behavioral interventions for adolescents with severe traumatic brain injury. *Journal of Head Trauma Rehabilitation, 10*(3), 67–86.

Filstead, J.W. (Ed.). (1979). *Qualitative methodology: First hand involvement with the social world.* Chicago: Markham.

Glang, A.E., Singer, G.H.S., Cooley, E.A., & Tish, N. (1992). Tailoring direct instruction techniques for use with students with brain injury. *Journal of Head Trauma Rehabilitation, 7*(4), 93–108.

Glang, A.E., & Todis, B. (1993–1994). [Model inservice training in traumatic brain injury: A regional team approach]. Unpublished raw data.

Glang, A.E., & Todis, B. (1994–1995). [Model inservice training in traumatic brain injury: A regional team approach]. Unpublished raw data.

Glang, A.E., & Todis, B. (1995–1996). [Model inservice training in traumatic brain injury: A regional team approach]. Unpublished raw data.

Glang, A.E., Todis, B., Sohlberg, M.M., & Reed, P.R. (1996). Helping parents negotiate the school system. In G.H.S. Singer, A. Glang, & J.M. Williams (Eds.), *Children with acquired brain injury: Educating and supporting families* (pp. 149–165). Baltimore: Paul H. Brookes Publishing Co.

Harchik, A.E., Sherman, J.A., & Bannerman, D.J. (1993). Choice and control: New opportunities for people with developmental disabilities. *Annals of Clinical Psychiatry, 5*, 151–162.

Individuals with Disabilities Education Act (IDEA) of 1990, PL 101-476, 20 U.S.C. § 1400 *et seq.*

Koegel, L.K., & Koegel, R.L. (1986). The effects of interspersed maintenance tasks on academic performance in a severe childhood stroke victim. *Journal of Applied Behavior Analysis, 19*, 425–430.

Lash, M., & Scarpino, C. (1993). School reintegration for children with traumatic brain injuries: Conflicts between medical and educational settings. *Neuro Rehabilitation, 3*(3), 13–25.

Light, R., Neumann, E., Lewis, R., Morecki-Oberg, C., Asarnow, R., & Satz, P. (1987). An evaluation of a neuropsychologically based reeducation project of the head-injured child. *Journal of Head Trauma Rehabilitation, 2*, 11–25.

Lincoln, Y.S., & Guba, E.G. (1985). *Naturalistic inquiry.* Beverly Hills: Sage Publications.

Little, J.W. (1982). Norms of collegiality and experimentation: Workplace conditions of school success. *American Educational Research Journal, 19*, 325–340.

Orenstein, A., & Budoff, M. (1986). *Mediating special education disputes.* Cambridge, MA: The Research Institute for Educational Problems.

Pearpoint, J., Forest, M., & Snow, J. (1992). *The inclusion papers: Strategies to make inclusion work (A collection of articles from the Centre for Integrated Education and Community).* Toronto, Ontario, Canada: Inclusion Press.

Reichardt, C., & Cook, T. (1979). Beyond qualitative versus quantitative methods. In T. Cook & C. Reichardt (Eds.), *Qualitative and quantitative methods in evaluation research* (pp. 7–32). Beverly Hills: Sage Publications.

Rosenshine, B., & Stevens, R. (1986). Teaching functions. In M.C. Wittrock (Ed.), *Handbook of research on teaching* (3rd ed., pp. 376–391). Chicago: Rand.

Salisbury, C.L., Gallucci, C., Palombaro, M., & Peck, C.A. (1995). Strategies that promote social relations among elementary students with and without severe disabilities in inclusive schools. *Exceptional Children, 62*(2), 125–138.

Savage, R.C. (1991). Identification, classification, and placement issues for students with traumatic brain injuries. *Journal of Head Trauma Rehabilitation, 6*(1),1–9.

Seidel, J., Friese, S., & Leonard, D.C. (1995). *The Ethnograph v4.0: A user's guide.* Amherst, MA: Qualis Research.

Shevin, M., & Klein, N.K. (1984). The importance of choice making for students with disabilities. *Journal of The Association for Persons with Severe Handicaps, 9*, 159–166.

Shurtleff, H.A., Massagli, T.L., Hays, R.M., Ross, B., & Sprunk-Greenfield, H. (1995). Screening children and adolescents with mild or moderate traumatic brain injury to assist school reentry. *Journal of Head Trauma Rehabilitation, 10*(5), 64–79.

Sohlberg, M.M., & Mateer, C.A. (1987). Effectiveness of an attention-training program. *Journal of Clinical and Experimental Neuropsychology, 9*(2), 117–130.

Sohlberg, M.M., & Mateer, C.A. (1989). Training use of compensatory memory books: A three stage behavioral approach. *Journal of Clinical and Experimental Neuropsychology, 11*, 871–891.

Sowers, J.A., Glang, A.E., Voss, J., & Cooley, E. (1996). Enhancing friendships and leisure involvement of students with traumatic brain injuries and other disabilities. In L.E. Powers, G.H.S. Singer, & J. Sowers (Eds.), *On the road to autonomy: Promoting self-competence in children and youth with disabilities* (pp. 347–371). Baltimore: Paul H. Brookes Publishing Co.

Stainback, S., & Stainback, W. (1984). Broadening the research perspective in special education. *Exceptional Children, 50*(5), 400–408.

Telzrow, C.F. (1991). The school psychologist's perspective on testing students with traumatic brain injury. *Journal of Head Trauma Rehabilitation, 6*(1), 23–34.

Vandercook, T., & York, J. (1990). A team approach to program development and support. In W. Stainback & S. Stainback (Eds.), *Support networks for inclusive schooling: Interdependent integrated education* (pp. 95–122). Baltimore: Paul H. Brookes Publishing Co.

Walker, B. (1989). Strategies for improving parent–professional cooperation. In G.H.S. Singer & L.K. Irvin (Eds.), *Support for caregiving families: Enabling positive adaptation to disability* (pp. 103–120). Baltimore: Paul H. Brookes Publishing Co.

Walker, B., & Singer, G.H.S. (1993). Improving collaborative communication between professionals and parents. In G.H.S. Singer & L.E. Powers (Eds.), *Families, disability, and empowerment: Active coping skills and strategies for family interventions* (pp. 285–315). Baltimore: Paul H. Brookes Publishing Co.

Wehmeyer, M., & Lawrence, M. (1995). Whose future is it, anyway?: Promoting student involvement in transition planning. *Career Development of Exceptional Individuals, 18,* 69–83.

Ylvisaker, M., Feeney, T., Maher-Maxwell, N., Meserve, N., Geary, P.J., & DeLorenzo, J.P. (1995). School reentry following severe traumatic brain injury: Guidelines for educational planning. *Journal of Head Trauma Rehabilitation, 10*(6), 25–41.

Ylvisaker, M., Feeney, T., & Mullins, K. (1995). School reentry following mild traumatic brain injury: A proposed hospital-to-school protocol. *Journal of Head Trauma Rehabilitation, 10*(6), 42–49.

Ylvisaker, M., Hartwick, P., Stevens, M. (1991). School reentry following head injury: Managing the transition from hospital to school. *Journal of Head Trauma Rehabilitation, 6*(1), 10–22.

chapter three

One Mother's Story
Including Her Son in Coma in a General Education First-Grade Class

Joanne Singer

I knew that this September, had he not been in the accident, I would be feeling like every mommy does seeing the bus drive up to take your youngest child to first grade. That first grade, I knew it was going to be tough. That is what got me thinking.

LESLIE STEVENS RECEIVED a telephone call from her husband, waking her from a nap one extremely cold winter afternoon, telling her that their 4-year-old son, Casey, was in the emergency room at the local hospital. She needed to come immediately. Her husband, Peter, was so upset that he was not able to tell her what had happened. Not until many hours later, after Casey had been taken to a major metropolitan, tertiary hospital in the neighboring state, did Leslie discover what had happened. Casey had been spending the afternoon, following preschool, with Peter in their video store. He was sitting on a stool next to his father, where he delighted in licking stamps and answering the telephone. Business was slow because of the cold, and Peter was gazing out the window, absorbed in his own thoughts. With no warning, Casey fell and hit his head on the carpet-covered cement floor. He has been unable to eat, speak, or breathe on his own since.

I had a research faculty appointment at a medical school 2 hours north of where the Stevens family lived. A colleague mentioned there was a child in the state who had been included in a general education classroom even though he was in a comatose state. Because this was the most unique story of inclusion I had ever heard, I was intrigued to learn more about how this came to pass. After receiving permission from Leslie, I arranged a visit with her and Casey in their home. I discussed the possibility of doing a study on how Casey came to attend Chandler Elementary School and what it was like for the staff and children.

This investigation utilized qualitative research methodology. In addition to repeated interviews with Leslie, all of the school professionals involved were interviewed and observed interacting with Casey. The professionals included the school principal, speech therapist, physical therapist, classroom teacher, nurse/aide, and a representative providing in-service training to the school staff on inclusion. I used participant observation with each of the professionals involved with Casey, observed the classroom on several occasions, and attended the annual individualized education program (IEP) meeting. The study was conducted approximately 1 year after Casey had returned home from the hospital.

THE HOSPITAL STAY

Casey underwent surgery as Leslie and Peter waited at the hospital, sleepless, through the night and the next day with no answers about what was happening with their son. They later learned that Casey had experienced a massive brain hemorrhage and had fallen into coma. He was put on a ventilator that breathed for him and was initially fed with an intravenous (IV) line and later via a gastrostomy tube (G-tube). Leslie and Peter Stevens were not included in the decision to put Casey on these life-support systems.

After spending the entire night and following day at the hospital, Leslie and Peter requested to speak with a doctor. A resident neurosurgeon, who appeared as though she had been crying and behaved in an angry and distant manner, complained about being called to come see them and said that it was too soon to know an outcome for Casey. She took them to a small, dark room to talk. When Leslie tried to turn on the lights, the neurosurgeon said she did not want the lights on. Leslie and Peter soon learned that the neurosurgeon had requested to be transferred away from Casey's care and that the head of pediatric neurology took over his care. Immediately thereafter, Leslie and Peter were told that the doctors believed that Casey was "brain dead," and that there probably was no hope of him awakening or recovering.

Leslie and Peter were told that Casey was in coma. The doctors did not know whether there was any chance for him to awaken or how aware he was of his surroundings. A test was performed to determine whether Casey was brain dead. During the exam, Casey's eyes dilated, an indication of brain activity. Casey spent 3 months at the tertiary hospital and then an additional 6 months at a hospital closer to the Stevens' home. Leslie was at his bedside every day, reading medical journals to learn more about his condition and advocating with the doctors for care that she believed would promote recovery. Peter came to the hospital every day during the first month. Being at Casey's bedside was emotionally difficult for Peter, but he would run errands, walk around the hospital, and be available if needed for meetings. Eventually, Peter had to go back to work, and Leslie came each day to the hospital by herself.

From the beginning, Leslie viewed her role as Casey's advocate and the one who would highlight Casey's unique individuality for the people who met him. She took on the responsibility of introducing her son to the world in a way that made others look at him as a beloved little boy, instead of a medical tragedy. She displayed family pictures of Casey on his bedside table and the walls of his room and brought his favorite stuffed animals to decorate his bed at the hospital. She would often use humor with people who were meeting Casey for the first time. When new residents or doctors would nervously approach, she would always good-naturedly greet them at the door.

❧

I would see them sit out in the hallway reading this long book [Casey's chart], they had an encyclopedia on him. They all looked worried. I would say, "Come on, Doctor, don't waste all your time reading that. Come on in and meet Casey. He is right here; *then* you can go read. He looks terrible on paper."

❧

After Peter went back to work, Leslie was repeatedly called into increasingly gloomy meetings with Casey's doctors, nurses, and social worker.

❧ ❧

The doctor would always begin these meetings by saying everything negative that could possibly happen to Casey. "He is never going to dress himself, he is never going to get up, never going to feed himself, never going to go to school, never going to this, this, this. . . ." He would go on for 10 or 15 minutes until I would start to cry. Then he would stop and tell me the agenda for the meeting. . . . I was frequently told that they would stop life supports on Casey if we wanted that to happen. Before leaving the tertiary hospital, we were told by the doctors and the social workers that we would not be prosecuted if we unplugged Casey's life supports.

❧ ❧

Leslie never expressed any uneasiness or disagreement with the decision to put Casey on life supports after his surgery. It is not possible to reconstruct how that decision was made. Several factors indicate that there may have been disagreement among the medical staff about the original decision to put him on life supports when the severity of his accident was so extreme. These factors include the apparent emotional upset of the resident neurosurgeon immediately following the surgery, the transfer of the case to the head of the department, and the active advocacy by the medical and social services staff to remove Casey from life supports.

Leslie and Peter decided they were willing to pull life supports from Casey if he did not pass the "brain dead" test. When he did pass the test, Leslie believed that Casey was giving them a message that he wanted to live and recover. Her job then became providing him with every possible opportunity to awaken. She would spend her days at the hospital reading Casey books that he had loved and repeating a variety of exercises to stimulate his senses. Leslie read significant meaning into the changes in Casey's skin tone, his quickening heartbeat when she played music, the blinking of his eyes, and a 12-hour period in which his lungs resumed working, only to tragically stop again. She believed that Casey was intellectually intact within a hurt body, trying to heal and return to his family.

MAKING THE TRANSITION FROM HOSPITAL TO HOME

When the time approached for Casey to be released from the hospital, the staff recommended that he live in a nursing home. Leslie and Peter could not imagine Casey living away from them and made the preparations to have him return home. Fortunately, they had excellent health insurance that covered the cost of around-the-clock nursing. The cost of Casey's hospital bills totaled approximately $750,000. Fortunately, their insurance covered the entire amount and most of the $20,000 it cost each month to have the nurses and equipment that were needed at the Stevens' home. Leslie and Peter did pay $33,000 to have a deck and a lift put on their house so that Casey would be able to be outside. Peter's business was affiliated with a national company that paid $10,000 toward the $15,000 cost of the van they purchased, but the wheelchair that Leslie could barely bring herself to buy was $5,000.

Leslie's faith in her son's potential recovery made her single-minded in her efforts to search out any opportunity or resource that might be advantageous to her son. Eventually, this faith and persistence led her to help Casey attend a general education first-grade readiness class at his neighborhood school.

The Stevens lived in a mixed rural and suburban area. Their two-story home was on a large lot with woods and a creek behind it, approximately half a mile from the school. The family dog was tied up in the yard, and the home looked like a typical 20- to 30-year-old suburban home, except for the large metal wheelchair lift going up the center of the house. On my first visit, Leslie answered my knock at the door wearing jeans and a pullover shirt. She was a short, trim woman with sandy hair, bright eyes, and a wide, quick smile. She immediately took me to meet Casey. I had expected to find him in an upstairs bedroom that would look like a room in an intensive care unit, overwhelmed with high-tech equipment. Instead, Leslie brought me to the downstairs dining room, next to the kitchen and the living room. As she walked, she explained that from the beginning she has wanted Casey to be part of the family, not locked off in an isolated room where there was no family activity. The ventilator and monitors were present, but they were not obvious in the brightly decorated room. Casey's blankets were bright-colored, and he had sheets with cartoon characters on them. The room was full of bright-colored pictures and stuffed lions (Casey's favorite animal) and mobiles. One wall had a large sliding-glass door that opened onto a screened porch, where Casey could go in his wheelchair in the summer. Another wall had windows, and the combination of decorations and light made for a delightful atmosphere. There was a nurse sitting next to his bed, reading a novel. Casey had dark blond hair and large eyes. They were open, and his head was turned to the side. He had on a bright sweater, and I immediately felt relieved when Leslie introduced him. His oxygen was connected to his trachea in his neck, and his face looked similar to some children with cerebral palsy who do not have good muscle tone. His head seemed slightly large for his body, but he was still an attractive child.

I had hoped that Peter would also participate in the study, but Leslie said that he was not there because it was too difficult for him to talk to anyone about the accident. "He has never spoken to anyone about how he feels about it, not even me. I think it would be good for him, but he can't do it." At the end of our first visit, Peter came home. He entered the front door, near where we were sitting in the living room. He was a gray-haired, attractive man of medium height. He nodded when he was introduced and quickly went into the kitchen without talking further. I went over the informed consent form, and Leslie agreed to let me observe Casey at home and at school and to interview the school staff and her sister. I proceeded to conduct the first of four lengthy interviews. All of the interviews were audiotaped, transcribed, and coded. Perceptions from observations and interviews were reviewed with Leslie and other participants.

Bringing Casey home from the hospital required more than physical adaptations to the Stevens' home. Except for 40 hours during the week, a shift taken on by Leslie, there was a nurse in their home 24 hours a day. To cover all of these hours, approximately four other nurses were required. Nurses would come and go, move on to other work, and new ones would arrive with varying degrees of medical and interpersonal skills. The Stevens began living their life in a "fish bowl" with strangers spending their days and nights in their home, caring for their son. I asked Leslie whether she was able to use the time when the nurses were there to do errands, go for walks, exercise, or visit friends. Leslie replied that the *only* time she would leave the house when a nurse was there was to go to the market. "I do not want them thinking I am a neglectful parent." Added to the other stress factors in Leslie's life was the perceived pressure that she needed to prove continually to strangers, in her own home, on a daily basis, that she was not a neglectful parent.

One afternoon when I was at the Stevens' house, Leslie asked me if I had traveled much since moving there. She began describing trips she and Peter had taken. Peter was in the other room and joined us in Casey's room. They both told wonderful stories of the fun they had traveling and camping, recommending where I should go with my family. I felt like they were showing me their life before Casey's accident, which was rich in enjoyment and adventure. I thoroughly enjoyed the conversation and felt great sadness for the impact Casey's accident must have had on their relationship. This was my one opportunity to speak with Peter.

Adding to the stress of the first "winter of discontent," as Leslie described it, was that Casey did not easily fit into any of the family support systems available in the community. The family lived in a state that had a state-funded strong family support system for children with developmental delays. The mandate for this system is to serve only children with developmental disabilities. Several of the regions, however, were more flexible and would find ways of helping families in which the child did not fit a rigid interpretation of the criteria. The family support coordinator in Casey's region, however, was not flexible and told Leslie that the family did not qualify for services because Casey's condition was the result of acquired brain injury (ABI). When Leslie called the program designated for people who had experienced brain injuries, she was told they had support groups and services *only* for families that had an adolescent child or an adult who had experienced ABI. The university-affiliated program in the state had a large federal grant to facilitate inclusion of children into their neighborhood schools in typical classrooms, but no one informed Leslie or linked her with these services.

Leslie never spoke with rancor or bitterness toward anyone involved with Casey's care, even when she was denied support services, had to argue to change treatments, and so forth. She seemed to take people at face value, realizing that most people would not understand what she was trying to do. She knew that some people would be resistant, but she did not allow initial resistance or defensiveness to deter her goals for Casey's inclusion in school. Leslie would always work on taking the next step toward improving opportunities for Casey, regardless of the reactions of those around her. She did not waste time in being upset with the behavior of others. When she described the pediatric neurosurgeon who insisted on talking to her and Peter in a dark room, she would say, "Well, she must have had some psych. problems, otherwise she wouldn't have behaved like that." After describing going to a family wedding at which she was virtually shunned by childhood friends, she tried to understand their behavior. "Old friends and some relatives are awkward and avoid me, because they do not know what to say. They forget that I am still the same person they grew up with." Or most frequently, "Well, we have to start somewhere." This meant that from wherever the professional was coming, that was only the starting point from which things could improve. Leslie did not have a Pollyanna view of her situation or of the people with whom she needed to interact with regard to Casey's life. She was aware when people were being resistive or unhelpful and aware when people were doing the best that they could. She just persisted in staying focused on what *might* be possible, instead of all that might be unrealizable.

MAKING THE TRANSITION TO SCHOOL

The impetus to have Casey attend school came from two directions. As quoted in the beginning of this chapter, the time when Casey would have typically gone off to first grade was looming large before Leslie. Seeing the school bus come pick Casey up for his first day of school was something that Leslie had imagined for years. Moreover, "It became very very hard to break his [Casey's] days up so they didn't look the same. I was very anxious to get to the warm weather, so we could get outside and have different environments." At around the time Leslie was thinking about finding stimulation for Casey, the occupational therapist, Susanna (who provided Casey with in-home therapy 4 days per week), mentioned that the neighborhood school was going to begin including children with disabilities in general education classes, and they were busy putting in ramps for wheelchair access. When Leslie was picking up her 8-year-old daughter, Michelle, at school the next day, she happened to see the principal, Mr. Erikson.

I stopped him to say I have a completely equipped handicapped van. You are going to have wheelchair kids next year. If you have any trouble I am 3 miles from school. If I can help you out in any way, I would be happy to. He asked if I wanted to do this for the town and get paid. I said, "No, I don't want a job; I'm just offering. You can put me down as a mommy with a handicapped van. If something happens and the school van isn't available or breaks down, you can call me. If I am free I can come get them and drive them home. Gladly!"

He took my name and that's what got me thinking about it. Now wait a minute. They have wheelchair access. Casey is in a wheelchair, and I had just gone through the "winter of discontent." One of the things I have had a very hard time with accepting is the future. I didn't like looking at the future.

The next time that Susanna came to work with Casey, Leslie broached the idea of Casey going to school.

I said, "Susanna, what do you think about Casey? He is going to be 6 next year. We just went through the winter being concerned about his days all looking the same. It has been tough. Do you think it would be possible to have him go to school a couple of days? One or two days a week and maybe using the mats in the gym. You can work him out there, do his physical therapy there."

Susanna replied with enthusiasm and discussed it with the other physical therapists in the district. She reported that they were all positive about giving it a try and that she would talk to Gwen, the special education preschool coordinator for the district. Gwen, although skeptical about the feasibility of the idea, agreed to meet with Leslie.

Leslie arrived at the meeting with Casey's birth certificate in hand. "I knew if there was going to be a stumbling block I was just going to say, 'Here is my ace of spades! He is going to be eligible for school as of September 1.'" Leslie did not speak with any other parents, advocates, or special education professionals. She simply believed that Casey's birth certificate guaranteed his legal entrance into school. In fact, there was a legal case in this state that went to the supreme court that established a child's right to a public school education, regardless of his or her learning ability. Leslie was unaware of this case.

Gwen copied the birth certificate and agreed to speak with the district special education director, Mike Wilkers. Eventually, a meeting was arranged with Mike, Gwen, the principal, the school nurse, and the three physical therapists. They were all curious about what Leslie wanted and expected. Leslie's response to them, right from the beginning, typifies her assumptions that they would all work together as a team. Her language was immediately inclusive.

Look, I don't have a lot of expectations. All I know is I spent last winter trying to figure out how to break up his day, not having them all look the same. He is school-age eligible this September, and I want to know, is it possible? Can "we" do this?

In order for it to work, it is going to have to be an open-communication thing. If it is not working I want to be able to come to you people and say it is not working. And, if you don't feel that it is working, or if there is a problem, I want you to be able to say that to me. I'm not going to get upset about it. "We" are going to sit down and talk it out and deal with whatever the problems are. If it is working, maybe we can go to a third day. I don't know; it has to be open. If there are certain days Casey can't make it in physically, we are not coming. I don't expect a report card. I don't know what I expect at this point. I don't know even if it is going to work. But, I want to at least try it.

Instead of someone at the meeting responding to Leslie in the same direct, inclusive manner, Mrs. North, the school nurse interrupted Leslie, telling her that what she was suggesting was impossible. Leslie described the nurse firing questions at her. She wanted to know who was going to take care of the equipment, how would Casey eat, how they could possibly change Casey, and so forth. Interspersed within these questions were repeated declarations, such as "This is impossible!" She could have easily asked Leslie to go through each of her concerns but instead immediately created the potential for an adversarial relationship. I tried unsuccessfully to interview Mrs. North. Mr. Erikson, the principal, told me that Mrs. North had difficulties being supportive of the team's effort and since the fall was no longer involved with Casey in any way. He did not want me to interview her. A few of the other staff members mentioned that the nurse was not supportive of their efforts and that it was best that she was not involved. Mrs. North may have believed that she would be liable for Casey's safety and was worried about that responsibility. The descriptions of her interactions with Leslie and the team, however, were consistently negative.

No one at the school realized how unflappable Leslie was or how willing she was to work with them. Leslie knew the nurse was creating obstacles, especially because it was already agreed that Casey would have a nurse/aide at all times who would be responsible for all of his care. Leslie continued to push forward.

Wait a minute, you don't understand. Before we left the hospital, Casey was made completely portable. Everything is portable. We go places. The hospital helped us make those decisions. He is totally portable. He has been on a pump, and those things would not be done at school. He wears a diaper and is changed like any child. None of those things are obstacles. All of them are doable.

The nurse then handed Leslie a large stack of papers to be filled out by her and by Casey's doctor. When she returned these to the nurse, she was given another stack of papers. When the doctor saw the second set of papers to fill out he declared, "Look, she wants blood. Tell her it's okay to do this."

The committee suggested that Casey attend the self-contained special education class at Chandler Elementary School. Because Leslie's purpose was to provide Casey with as much stimulation as possible, having him in a segregated class where all of the children had language delays made no sense to her. When the committee saw Leslie's disinterest in the special education class, they suggested a first-grade readiness class for immature 6-year-olds, and she agreed enthusiastically.

Arrangements were made for school staff to visit the Stevens' home during the summer to get to know Casey better. During the course of the summer, they had visits from Mr. Erikson, Mara Lozeau (Casey's designated nurse/aide), Mrs. North, Mike Wilkers (the special education director), and the classroom aide, and they had several visits from the designated teacher, Mrs. Waters. Leslie remained open and undaunted by the school professionals' hesitancy over the course of the summer. She could see where they were coming from but was unwilling to be thrown off course by their fears. When asked if the summer had provided everyone involved a chance to become more comfortable with Casey, Leslie nodded and replied, "I went through the process myself. It is a very intimidating one."

The Teacher

Debra Waters received a call during the summer that a "very medically fragile child" was coming to Chandler Elementary School and would be attending school in her classroom. At first she gave it little thought, because she had no choice or involvement in the decision or plans. As the day approached when she was scheduled to make her first home visit, Mrs. Waters tried to prepare herself for the worst. As I interviewed different members of the staff, I learned that everyone approached his or her first meeting with Casey with great trepidation, and everyone found meeting him easier than they had expected. Mrs. Waters described her first visit to me.

I was very nervous, and I was very apprehensive. When I did go, it wasn't nearly as severe as I thought it would be. I don't know what I expected, but I didn't feel [nervous] . . . Some people might feel a little squeamish because of the circumstances with the ventilator and that sort of stuff. It didn't really bother me at all, and I thought I would be because I am not somebody who's in any way prepared to go into the medical field.

I felt more . . . it just kind of hit you like a lump when you got home and you sort of said, "Thank God, count your blessings!" As difficult as your own kids can be sometimes, you really don't have it too bad when you see what the Stevens family was going through.

Casey was lying on the couch "watching" television with his nurse when Mrs. Waters arrived. Leslie immediately took Mrs. Waters to see Casey's bedroom and tried to show her a photo album with pictures of Casey before and after his accident, hoping that Mrs. Waters would share it with the children in her class. Mrs. Waters was so apprehensive about meeting Casey and adjusting to how he was in the present that she said she did not feel ready to think about how he used to be or how she was going to introduce him to her class. She admitted that she believed she was a little "standoffish" with Leslie during the first meeting.

I'm the kind of person who needs to take things slowly, one step at a time. And at that time [the first visit], I wasn't really ready for it.

In the fall, Leslie tried giving the photo album to Mrs. Waters again, and this time she looked through it carefully with her classroom aide. Mrs. Waters used it to introduce the aide to Casey before taking her to meet him. Eventually she used the album in her class with her students. She continued making visits during the summer, bringing the aide and the music teacher. Mrs. Waters hoped that if Casey was hearing anything, that the visits might make their voices familiar to him.

When I asked Leslie what she believed Mrs. Waters was feeling the first time she came to meet Casey she answered, "Scared."

They always are. They don't know whether to talk loud or to talk quietly. Just like you were going into anybody's sick room. I just looked at it like my job was to make them as comfortable as possible. I always tried to answer their questions. Just give them any information. Mrs. Waters became more comfortable each time she visited.

Mrs. Waters had never had a child with a disability included in her classroom. At first she felt like a "spectator," with everyone telling her what to do. Everyone at the school was telling her that it was going to be easy for her, because Casey was in coma and the nurse/aide would deal with him.

I couldn't envision at this point how I was going to teach my students and this person. What were they expecting of me? How much was I supposed to get him involved? Everybody kept saying, "Don't worry. He isn't going to be your problem; he is going to be there, but he is just going to be there."

She did not find these comments helpful. She believed that being his classroom teacher implied responsibilities to him and to her class as a whole.

When you are in the classroom and you have a child in your room, he is part of your class . . . somehow he has got to be part of your class. And I sort of felt the level of my kids, at the age level that they are, and having worked with the age level somewhat, I knew that having someone sort of be an outsider was not going to work. It can't. These kids have to have everyone part of the class. So that was kind of interesting.

Mrs. Waters and Leslie both believed that there was a need to find their own way of understanding how to proceed with including Casey in the class. They both resisted others telling them how to react to Casey and deciding what was best for Casey and them. During the early fall, Mrs. Waters attended some workshops on inclusion and visited classrooms in other schools in which children with disabilities were included in general education classrooms. She found a meeting with an inclusion specialist from the state's university-affiliated program to be supportive, but mostly it was her own early conviction that she had to find a way to make Casey a real part of her class that directed her efforts.

Delays

In spite of the school's agreement that Casey could come to school at the start of the school year in the fall, September and October had come and gone and the family was not given a starting date. First, there were delays until the school board approved funds for a nurse/aide to be with Casey at school. Leslie offered to provide transportation in her own van, which saved the school transportation expenses. Mrs. North, the school nurse, insisted on a current physical in early October. She gave Leslie a batch of papers before she left to drive the 2 hours to the tertiary hospital to meet with Casey's doctor. Although Casey was portable, getting him ready for a day at the hospital took a great deal of time and effort. When Leslie returned the next day, the nurse had another batch of papers for the doctor to fill out. Leslie made the trip back to the hospital without Casey; she refused to pack him up again. Having to contend with the negativity and obstacles from the school nurse gave rise to the only expressions of anger toward anyone from Leslie.

One day Leslie received a telephone call at 2:00 P.M. from Mrs. North, who asked whether Leslie was going to attend the parent/teacher meeting that evening. Leslie had the flu but said she would try to come. Mrs. North then announced,

"Well, we feel that you should bring Casey's wheelchair and his vent to the meeting tonight." I [Leslie] said, "Oh, really." Mrs. North replied, "Yes, a lot of parents have been talking about how they felt about Casey coming. I don't know how they found out," she said real quick. It was like, *Yeah, I bet you don't know how they found out.* I responded to her, "I have to tell you this, Mrs. North. I happen to be sick with the flu. I don't believe that I will be at the meeting tonight."

In retelling this event, Leslie was quick to explain how hard it is to think about dealing with a child on a ventilator for someone who has never done it before. She appreciated that sometimes it can be "touch and go" and that Mrs. North's license might be "on the line." Leslie also knew that at any time Mrs. North could have come to their home and observed how Casey's treatment was conducted, but she had not chosen to do so. Leslie was adamant that she was not going to allow Mrs. North to make a public show out of her or Casey.

She gave me no notice. I was glad I had the excuse of being sick. I figured that I am not going to buy into this. I am absolutely not going to buy into this. This is not going to become a side show. It's one thing to

be public, but I am not going to be the talk of the town. It is not fair to expect that or even ask that of me. I just did not like her attitude when she was speaking about it. When she said it, it sounded like, oh, gossips at work. So I decided I am not going to be a side show.

None of the staff members I interviewed mentioned *any* parents questioning or having concerns about Casey coming to school. In fact, Mrs. Waters and Mr. Erikson commented on different occasions how surprised they were by the parents' acceptance of Casey in public school. The principal said that he never received even one telephone call or comment from a parent of a child in Casey's class complaining about his presence.

Leslie began preparing so that Casey became accustomed to spending a lot of time in his wheelchair and so that all of the necessary equipment was inspected and safe. After completing the preparations, she had to deal with still more paperwork. Finally, she happened to see Mr. Erikson one day and said to him, "Mr. Erikson, is this going to happen?" He replied, "Of course, it's going to happen. Don't say that." Leslie told him how frightened she was that the coming winter was going to "shut them down" before Casey had a chance to start school. He called her soon after to come the next week to talk with the faculty and the children and to bring Casey's wheelchair for them to see. From then on Mrs. North was no longer directly involved with Casey or Leslie. When I came for my first school visit in February she was not part of the team. Mr. Erikson mentioned in my first interview with him that Mrs. North had difficulty with the decision to have Casey at school, and he thought it best that she was no longer on the team.

Mr. Erikson's early apprehension about having Casey at school was alleviated by the inclusion specialist, Barbara Bell. Barbara gave a generic speech about including children with disabilities in their neighborhood schools to the entire staff, which helped allay fears and reduce resistance from the faculty. She did not speak specifically, however, about children who had experienced ABI. Mr. Erikson appreciated that Leslie was open and grateful for anything the school was willing to do for Casey. He decided that they would "just take each issue as it arose and work on it," and he felt proud of Mrs. Waters' efforts and the work that other staff members had done to make it possible for Casey to come to school. He had worked to make sure there were contingency plans for any medical emergency that might occur.

In the fall, long before his actual arrival, Mrs. Waters began her efforts to introduce her class to Casey.

❧ ❧

Whenever we had activities involving getting to know each other, I would play the part of Casey. When they drew pictures of themselves and their families, I would draw a picture of Casey's family. I would tell about Casey's interests before his accident, and about being in a wheelchair, and getting help to breathe.

❧ ❧

The day before Casey was to begin school, Leslie came and spoke with the faculty and the students. Staff, especially Mrs. Waters and Mr. Erikson, were extremely apprehensive about how the children would react to Casey. Leslie never had a doubt that the children would accept him; adults were always the ones who had more difficulty with acceptance. Leslie reported that the faculty had typical adult questions, such as, "What do you expect from us?" and "What will we do in case of a fire?" Leslie loved the directness of the children's questions. For instance, after showing them Casey's wheelchair, ventilator, alarms, and other equipment, one boy asked, "Well, if you are here with his chair and his breathing machine, what's he breathing?" and "Can you take him on a plane?"

Casey in Class

The first day that Casey arrived, Mrs. Waters had the students sitting on the floor. As he was wheeled in and his ventilator plugged in, she told the children that if they wanted they could introduce themselves to Casey and shake his hand. She told them that she thought "he might like that." About 80% of the children introduced themselves. She then gave the children a chance to ask questions about Casey.

❧ ❧

The first question they had was about the tubes. They wanted to know about this business of the ventilator and stuff. The second question was about his eyes and his mouth. "Why is his mouth open and why are his eyes open if he is asleep? Can he see us? Can he hear us?" That sort of stuff. Leslie would answer the questions, and she did a real good job. She spoke very much at their level, without giving them too many specifics. They wanted to know about all the buttons on his back, so she pushed them all and showed what happened if they all went off. We

let them hear the beepers so they wouldn't be frightened when they
went off.

The next day the guidance counselor spent a half hour with the
class, letting them express their feelings about Casey being in their
class. A few children said that he scared them, but they could not
explain why. More children said that it was nice to meet Casey.

One day while the students were having their snacks, they
asked why Casey was not having a snack with them. Leslie explained how he ate, and one boy asked if they could see. Mrs. Waters
described how, much to her horror, Leslie pulled up Casey's shirt and
showed them where the catheter was located that was used to put
the tube in for him to feed.

And I thought, "Oh God, someone is going to be grossed out or something." Not a word, not a word. They just said, "Oh, that sounds okay."
On and on they went—fine. I was having a heart attack. I was positive
they were all going to freak out, but not a word from them. . . .

Leslie assumed that when she brought Casey to school, she
would be asked to help out in another classroom. After he was set up
on the first day, she went down to the office to find out what she
would be doing. When she arrived at the office, she was told to get
right back to Mrs. Waters' class. She was surprised but returned and
worked as an additional aide for the class when she was there with
Casey. When I observed her in the classroom, she was involved in
assisting the other children, who clearly enjoyed having her there.
She seemed to spend her time praising appropriate behavior and
efforts by children, redirecting them when they were off task, and
helping with special projects that needed extra preparations. Although she would regularly glance in Casey's direction, she did not
hover near him or interrupt what Mara Lozeau, the nurse/aide, was
doing with him. She did not want Mrs. Waters or Mara to feel intimidated by her presence, which was why she had wanted Mr. Erikson
to place her in another classroom.

When Mara started working as Casey's classroom nurse/aide,
she was quite nervous. Although she had experience with adults on
ventilators, those experiences had been in hospital settings in which
respiratory therapists dealt with any problems that might arise. She

regularly went to the Stevens' home to help Leslie move Casey to the car and then into the school, and she would also stay at the home for 1 hour after returning him after school. At first she did feel intimidated because Leslie was more knowledgeable about how to care for Casey than she. Leslie taught her how Casey's particular ventilator worked and gave Mara a helpful book to read. Quickly, she became grateful for Leslie's expertise, assistance, and presence.

Several emergencies occurred, including an incident in which Casey was stuck on the lift bringing him from the mezzanine entrance of his home down to the ground and incidents when different alarms would sound.

When you start a job like this, you prepare yourself for the worst scenario. You have to make an emergency plan, but in the back of your mind, you do not believe you will ever need it. But, these things happen all the time with Casey. One time the filter attached to the bottom of the ventilator developed a crack, and his pressures started going way up. His mother must be the strongest person in the world. Like one day he got stuck on the lift. Every time she takes him out of that house, she has such a risk involved.

She is great. She is very calm, and she just deals exactly with the issue at hand. She doesn't panic and say, "Oh my God!" She knows exactly what to do, and she does it. She knows to get the "ambu" (manual system for providing Casey with oxygen), she has been trained to get the bag and to put it on until we find out what the problem is. She knows at least she is getting air in. It's nice because you feel you have a back-up and she does know him so much better.

One time one of Casey's alarms went off and Mara and Leslie needed to remove him from the class to correct the problem. Mara and Mrs. Waters were impressed that Leslie insisted that she and Casey return to the class before going home, so that the children could see that Casey was fine. Mrs. Waters had been uneasy about having Leslie in the class but quickly grew to appreciate her involvement and help with the other students and felt reassured by having her expertise with Casey readily available.

Casey's Reactions to the World Around Him

Everyone I spoke with who worked directly with Casey seemed to spend quite a bit of time wondering whether he was reacting to anything in his environment. They also gave much thought regarding how they could interact with him in a way that made sense. On the one hand, they worried about being overly optimistic and reading meaning into unconscious physical reflexes. On the other hand, they were deeply concerned that they might mistakenly assume he was not perceiving anything when in fact he was. Mrs. Waters was dubious about claims from therapists who had worked with Casey at home, saying that they believed he reacted to some things. She thought it was wishful thinking on their part, until Casey was in her class.

I keep telling myself that I don't want to assume there is something there when there isn't, but sometimes I honestly feel that he has a reaction to the kids. Sometimes when he is feeling well, he seems very much alive in his own little sense, very alert.

I asked her to describe how she could tell this.

I don't know, a sparkle, his skin color, a sparkle in the eyes. He will move his eyes more, sort of in the direction of where things are happening. Casey can sometimes turn his head and upper body to the left. The kids always seem to approach him from that side. A couple times he turned toward them when they approached.

Mara spoke about believing that Casey might be reacting positively to music. Mara always would lean down and tell him what was going on in the class and anything she was about to do with him as well as help Casey participate in activities. When the music teacher would come to give lessons, Mara would often physically guide Casey's hands through clapping, beating a drum, or holding a baton and waving it in time with the music. She reported that Casey's hands, fingers, and arms were always relaxed and easy to move during music class. When she would try to physically prompt him to write with a crayon, however, his muscles were tense and he felt resistive to her. Mara took this resistance to mean that Casey did not like writing.

I have always had in mind that I have no idea if he can hear me or not or if he is processing anything. You have to go on the belief that he is. I always tell him what I am doing, and I always try to think that he is hearing what is going on and he is understanding. I am hoping that he is getting something, so I always try to keep in mind that whatever we are doing he is aware of it. I try to make him know ahead of time, because no one likes surprises. This is especially true for him, because he is in the predicament of being in the chair and can't do anything on his own.

Susanna, the occupational therapist, said that he seemed to dislike having his feet exposed to cold or tickling. He would frequently give a small kick when she did those things, and she believed the response was not just reflexive. When she provided any tactile stimulation to his face, Casey seemed to grow more relaxed. She also mentioned that he would sometimes turn to the left when she sat on that side, although the response was not reliable. Everyone mentioned that when Casey was first at school or he first encountered new people, he usually kept his eyes closed. Everyone spoke of being relieved to discover that most of the time his eyes were open, although they were extremely unclear about whether this meant he was conscious or aware.

I was able to observe all of Casey's reactions that others described to me, including keeping his eyes open and closed, appearing indescribably "alert," seeming completely not conscious, turning toward approaching students and his sister, and not turning toward approaching people. I also noticed changes in his skin color when he was in class, from pale to having more color (i.e., blotchy or redder). I would have liked to have seen someone carefully program stimulation to which they believed Casey reacted with a written data system to confirm whether there was any pattern in his responses. Watching him always left me wondering what was going on inside of him, imagining how to design systematic interventions that would test the randomness of his responses, and wondering whether it would be possible to build on the tiny behavioral repertoire he had. When I discussed how people working with Casey believed in the meaningfulness of his reactions, Barbara Bell, the inclusion specialist, talked about her belief in what she called "the least dangerous assumption."

Perhaps Casey was only having uncontrolled physical reactions. Because no one could say for certain, believing that his reactions might be meaningful caused no harm and avoided the danger of neglecting him if he was able to perceive.

Leslie believed that Casey's mind and soul were intact within his body. The doctors had serious doubts about whether Casey could see or hear, although no one who worked directly with him was completely certain in this matter. Except for Mrs. Waters and Mara, staff tended to believe that Leslie lived "in denial," that her optimism was a sign of not being willing to accept the tragic reality before her. Carefully listening to her, however, I never heard her make adamant claims about his abilities or his future. She always prefaced her statements with phrases such as, "This is what I believe," "This is a place to start," "I am operating this way because I find it best to assume he understands," and so forth. She did not make statements that indicated a denial of Casey's current status or future prospects, such as "Casey said this or that" or "Casey is going to come out of this coma and be fine." She often said, "I hate thinking about the future."

Leslie told me that she was trying a method of communication with Casey. If he blinked once following a question from her, she would decide that meant yes, and if he closed his eyes that meant no. The speech therapist mentioned thinking this was crazy because his blinking did not appear to be volitional, and Leslie was out on a limb claiming that he was communicating. However, Leslie never made this claim, except in jest. She would ask Casey things like, "Would you like to wear your green sweater or your blue one?" The questions were always questions about preferences, for which either choice would work fine. Leslie saw this as a way to try to shape a response if there was any understanding from Casey, which is a far cry from the staff's assumption that she was making claims that he was already communicating with volition through blinking. Both Mrs. Waters and Mara mentioned a few times that they often thought about how they might react if the same thing had happened to their child. They believed that others were too quick to judge Leslie.

Peer Perspective

What struck me first, and in every subsequent visit to Casey's class, was that the children did not seem to perceive boundaries between themselves and Casey. I have often seen adults and children approach someone in a wheelchair as if there were an invisible fence around the person. They typically maintain a distance of a couple of feet and never touch the person's chair. The children in Casey's class stayed clear of the back of his wheelchair where the oxygen was, but they would march right up to him, touching him and the chair. They would grab the armrests, the back handles, or touch his arms or hands. They did not seem wary of him at all. His wheelchair is smaller than most, with a sport design and parts that were bright Day-Glo pink. Leslie mentioned that she had gone to a great deal of trouble to order it. She thought it was worth the effort, however, because she did not want the other children to be afraid of his chair or of him.

Casey could be only in certain spots in the classroom because of the need to have access to electrical outlets for his ventilator. Students' desks were arranged in groups of four, and Casey's chair was next to a group of desks including one that was labeled with his name. When I came to observe the class on one occasion, the students were divided into different stations doing reading and writing activities. Casey was at one of the stations. Children would come to him and Mara and read the stories they had written. When Mrs. Waters gave instructions to the class, Mara would always lean down and whisper the instructions to Casey. If they were playing games, Mara would physically guide Casey to move the playing pieces on the board. I never saw him react when she did these things. Usually, when there were activity transitions, a few children would come see Casey and Mara before moving on to the next activity. They would touch his arm or face, say "hi," or ask Mara how Casey was doing.

One afternoon, grandparents of a student came to tell the class about their trip to Egypt. This activity characterized how students typically interacted with Casey in a large group. The students gathered as a group on the floor with Casey, in his chair, in the middle of the group. Five students (three girls and two boys) sat down next to or in front of Casey. A boy and girl rushed so that they would sit on either side of him. The boy, sitting on the left, kneeled and rested his arms on the arm of Casey's wheelchair. He would alternate between looking at the grandparents and at Casey. At one point during the presentation, Casey coughed. The boy instantly sat up on his knees, grabbed Casey's arm, and looked into his eyes. The boy looked alarmed. Several other students sitting near Casey also immediately looked up to see if Casey was all right. Mara leaned down and told them that Casey had just coughed and was okay. The boy's body relaxed, and he sat down, but for the next 5 minutes he kept looking up at Casey's face as though to make sure that he was still fine. He continued to hold Casey's arm for the rest of the presentation. The boy seemed proud of getting to sit next to Casey, showing no hesitancy or awkwardness.

The girl on Casey's right touched his cheek gently several times and stroked his arm. In addition, several times during the presentation, the girl would rest her hand on his arm for 2 or 3 minutes at a time. When the grandparents said anything that elicited laughter, raised hands, or responses from the children, the girl would either tap or stroke Casey's arm. I had the feeling that this was her way of sharing and including Casey in what she was experiencing. She did not seem to expect Casey to respond in any way, but somehow her tapping or stroking as she responded to the speakers seemed to be her way of responding "with" Casey.

After recess one afternoon, Mrs. Waters let me interview four students whom she believed felt most connected to Casey. Here is an excerpt from the interview that gives the flavor of how natural the students were in their responses to Casey and how much they viewed him as part of their class and community. I asked them what they thought about having Casey in their class.

Jessica: Our class is better than last year's class because Casey is in our class.

Kenny: I like having Casey in class, 'cause he's nice.

Josh: Casey is coming to school to learn with us.

Author: Can Casey tell what you are learning? Can he hear? [They all nodded and said emphatically, "Yes, sure!"]

Jessica: Casey is in a coma. He was on a stool, and he fell down.

Josh: He might get a little better.

Jessica: I saw someone on TV, on the news. He was in a coma, and he woke up and got better.

Author: Do you think that might happen with Casey? [They all nodded and said, "Yes!!"]

Adrienne: He fell backwards.

Jessica: My baby sitter sometimes babysits for Casey. She knows him. We drive by Casey's house and see it.

Adrienne: I drive by it, too. I can see his ramp for his wheelchair when I drive by.

The children view Casey as part of their class and part of their neighborhood. Instead of thinking it was strange that there was a large metal contraption in the front of Casey's home, they all seemed proud that they knew "all about" Casey.

I greatly enjoyed the following exchange.

Author: Kenny, I heard that you invited Casey to your birthday
           party. Was it your idea or your mom's?
Kenny: [Kenny screwed up his face and looked at me like I was
           crazy.] Why would my mom want to invite Casey to my
           birthday party? She doesn't know him! *I'm* the one who
           knows him; he's *my* friend! I invited him!

Kenny obviously did not think it was strange or unusual, in the
least, to invite someone who was in coma to his birthday party. He
thought I was crazy for suggesting that it might have been his
mother's idea. I was also amused speculating that there was a good
chance that he had not thought it necessary to mention to his
mother that Casey was in coma.

   Next, I asked what they thought Casey would say if he could
talk.

     Josh: Hi!
  Jessica: He would say that he likes the school playground.
Adrienne: He would say hello.
  Author: What do you do with Casey?
  Jessica: We hold hands.
Adrienne: Me too. And Mara helps me color with Casey.
     Josh: I sit next to Casey when we do stuff.
  Jessica: I got to do computer with him. [I asked how she did
             this.] I would do the pressing with him, to choose
             things.
  Author: Did you try to choose things that Casey likes or things
             that you like and know about?
  Jessica: I pressed things that Casey's mom told me that he liked.
             [She then paused and gave me a little smile, looking ab-
             solutely devilish before continuing.] Sometimes I press
             things that I like too . . .

In addition, they all mentioned that they knew Casey's mom, they
liked her because she was nice and she helped them in class, and
they knew where she lived.

   The children in Casey's class seemed to generalize their understanding and acceptance of Casey to other children with disabilities.
When Mrs. Waters' students saw another student in the school who
had only partial arms, they were curious about her prostheses but
seemed just to take it in stride. They showed no alarm and no aver-
sion to the child's condition. In the spring, Mrs. Waters' class received a new student. He was an adopted boy from Latvia who did
not speak any English. Once again Mrs. Waters was apprehensive

about her students' abilities to adjust to more differences. When they heard about him the only thing the class wanted to know was whether he had his own wheelchair also.

He just came in with the group and has been as much a part of the class as Casey has. [They act] the same way with him, very tolerant, very understanding. It is okay for him to scream out when the rest of them are not allowed to do that. They understand that he may go off and wander at different times. They are protective. They are insisting that we do something to help him learn English faster, because he doesn't understand. This is instead of being angry because they can't do the same sort of things. I did not expect this reaction.

The IEP Meeting

My last contact with the staff from Chandler Elementary School was the IEP meeting at the end of the spring term. School was dismissed for the summer immediately following this meeting, and I unfortunately did not have the release time from my other work responsibilities to meet with the staff during the summer to discuss what happened at this meeting. I expected this would be an occasion for sharing pleasure and pride in what they had accomplished that year. I was not prepared for what in reality transpired. In addition to Leslie and me, there were nine professionals at the table: Mike Wilkers, Mr. Erikson, Susanna, a physical therapist, Mrs. Waters, the assistant principal, and the music teacher. Mara and Casey's teacher for next year were not in attendance. Almost immediately it was obvious to me that the group had met prior to this meeting, without Leslie, and had decided on the goals and agenda for this meeting. No one in the group except for Mrs. Waters and me ever made eye contact with Leslie. Several rectangular desks were pushed together to make a very large table around which everyone sat. Leslie was there without her husband, a friend, or advocate. Everyone's voices were flat and professional sounding, and the format was that each person would read a description of Casey's current level of functioning and his or her predetermined goals for the upcoming year. At the end of each description, the person would perfunctorily ask Leslie, "Is that okay?" No one ever asked what Leslie's feelings were about what they were saying or if she had anything to suggest.

After the physical therapist's report, Leslie mentioned that she was planning to take Casey to get a better neck support during the summer. She had hoped to do it sooner but explained that they were very short of cash because of her husband's new business. The physical therapist replied in a pedantic manner that she should deal with it locally instead of going to the tertiary hospital and clearly implied that she would be remiss to wait. The physical therapist, as well as the other meeting participants, seemed to present herself as "the professional" and see her job as "giving directions and advice." She did not compliment or show any respect to Leslie for noticing that Casey needed the new neck support or for her willingness to take care of it without support from the school.

All through the meeting Leslie was the only one who used the pronoun "we" and was the only one who spoke as though they were all a team working together. Her only suggestion at the meeting was that the therapists might help give the nurses at home more to do with Casey. "We could be making better use of them." She said that she had a bulletin board over Casey's bed and that the therapists should feel free to write down therapies or activities that they would like the nurses to be doing with Casey each day. She offered to buy an erasable board if they would like that better. Susanna, who had always been so positive and supportive toward Leslie, replied, "You probably want to put it in the nurse's chart." The physical therapist added, "I believe the nurses are already doing range of motion." Neither of them said whether they were willing to do what Leslie was asking. All of the interactions continued in the same vein. I could not imagine what they were thinking about Leslie or what they had decided at their prior meeting that elicited such behavior. They had spent the year working very hard to be sympathetic and inclusive, and now, from my perspective, they were exhibiting the worst of bureaucratic insensitivity. Particularly insensitive was the assistant principal's pronouncement about how difficult it was to include Casey on their new computerized IEP goal system because he did not fit with any of the goals for any of the other children in the school. Finally, they found one goal, "The child will participate in the school day." The assistant principal was proud to report Casey could now be part of the new computerized IEP goal program. Leslie replied in a cheerful voice, "Well, we have to start somewhere." Before seeing her at this meeting, I had never heard the assistant principal mentioned by Leslie or any other staff members.

After everyone finished stating "their" goals, it became clear that there were issues with which the staff were uncomfortable, and Mr. Erikson was given the job to deliver the news to Leslie. His voice had tended to be loud and deep and now it was louder and harsher, as though volume would give him authority. He was delivering already-determined decisions. These staff seemed to have no idea how to conduct an IEP as a collaborative process *with* parents as full partners in decision making. First, Mr. Erikson announced that Casey would be going on to general education first grade instead of staying in the readiness class. Leslie looked surprised and said, "Really!" Mr. Erikson's face looked flushed, and his voice took on a defensive quality. He explained that they had decided on a teacher for next year who was not at the meeting, but they believed it was the best for Casey. He would not share the name of the teacher. Responding to Mr. Erikson's defensive manner, Leslie replied, "No, there's nothing wrong; I'm just surprised. I didn't know he would go up to the first grade. I just assumed that he would stay in readiness." Mrs. Waters chimed in, "Casey is the age for first grade and that's where he should go." Mr. Erikson concurred, "Yes, we were concerned about age appropriateness." Leslie said, "That's great! Age appropriateness, I never thought of that!" She went on to say that she had been worried that Casey would disrupt the first-grade class, because they had 31 children this year. Mr. Erikson, not expressing gratitude for her concern, just said the class was smaller this year.

Mr. Erikson then announced that Casey would come next year for 3½ days, instead of only 2. Leslie was quite happy about this, but again the news was delivered as though they expected her to object. Casey was not permitted to come to recess because of liability worries. Leslie wondered if he might be able to come to assemblies. She said she was thinking that other children in the school knew that Casey was there but had not had the chance to get "up close and personal" with him. "Kids think all kinds of things when they do not have the opportunity to come and see for themselves. It doesn't seem so strange once they meet him." Leslie's suggestion reflected her views of the school as part of her community and responsibility, and she viewed Casey as part of the "whole" school. Mr. Erikson agreed Casey could come to the assemblies, but once again there was no recognition or appreciation for what Leslie was trying to do.

The next announcement was that from that point on all the therapy would be done at school. Leslie was again surprised and a little taken aback by this. After the meeting Mr. Erikson passed by me and said that they just "had to wean that mom from the classroom and the therapy. She was way too overprotective." Susanna had been coming to the Stevens' house 4 days a week for 3 years, and the other therapist had come on the fifth day. Susanna is a friendly, talkative woman, and probably was providing some social support to Leslie. I was shocked that she allowed this decision to be delivered to Leslie in such a cold, impersonal, and public manner. Mr. Erikson's tone of voice implied there was something bad or wrong about Casey receiving therapy at home. No one there seemed to have any memory that the original spark for Casey coming to school was Leslie's idea that he could have his therapy at school, on the gym mats, instead of receiving it at home.

The last announcement I believed was delivered in the most cruel way. Mr. Erikson stated that Leslie would not be in Casey's class next year, because he and the staff believed that it would not be fair to the other children because they would want to know why their mother could not be in class. I wondered how many times adults call on imagined child injustices to hide their own inappropriate behavior. Leslie looked flushed, slightly confused, and hurt. Mr. Erikson immediately said, defensively, "We'll want your help somewhere else in the school. We don't know where. So, you will be there if anything goes wrong." Leslie replied, "Okay." No discussion was provided about having Leslie help with Casey making the transition to first grade when he arrived in the fall, what might make her feel most comfortable for the transition, or any other possible scenarios. After the meeting, Mrs. Waters came up and said that Leslie would continue to work in her classroom the following year. Leslie looked relieved and thanked her. Why Mrs. Waters could not have said that at the meeting remained a mystery.

At the conclusion of the meeting, Mike Wilkers gave a little speech about what a wonderful job the school had done, particularly Mrs. Waters. He said that it had worked so well because "she was a master person as well as a master teacher." No one had ever mentioned his name in connection with Casey being at school before, and I had never seen him at the school. With tears in her eyes, Mrs. Waters said that it had been a great challenge for her, but that it had proved a personally rewarding experience. Not a word of appreciation was expressed to Leslie for all of her efforts providing transportation for Casey, training Mara on how to care for him, helping the other children in Mrs. Waters' class, or working so cooperatively with the team. I had seen many school teams behave impersonally toward parents, but this was the worst example I had ever witnessed. The staff's teamwork throughout the school year was so at odds with their behavior during this meeting. I had the feeling that they believed that seriously engaging Leslie meant they had to pretend that Casey was not really in coma.

Later in the hallway, Mr. Erikson wanted me to tell them when they would be able to judge if "any of this" was actually benefiting Casey. No one in that room that morning seemed to give a moment's thought to what it would be like for them to be sitting in Leslie's seat for those 2 hours. The most unfortunate thing was that although there were positive outcomes to the meeting, such as Casey coming to school for an extra day, the staff feeling secure enough to have him in class without Leslie, a new teacher being ready to accept the challenge of having him in her class, Casey moving on with his classmates, and Mr. Erikson investigating full inclusion for other children with disabilities in the school; these were not presented in a positive way. Rather, the meeting was a negative way to end the term.

After the meeting, Leslie told me she was pleased that Casey would be moving up a grade with some of his classmates and happy that Casey had received a birthday invitation from a student in his class. She said that she had talked it over with Casey the night before, and he had said, "Ah, let's just get him a present." Then she laughed good heartedly. I laughed too and said that I thought it was really nice that he received the invitation. This kind of comment from Leslie is exactly what disturbs some of the school staff. They call it being "in denial" or being irrational about Casey. As I discussed previously, the only times I heard Leslie attribute direct communication to Casey was in the context of making a comment in jest. Leslie was so good humored and expressive when she made these comments, it always seemed to me that she was normalizing who Casey was and expressing her belief that she was still connected to her son in a very special way. I never felt that she was expecting me to believe that Casey somehow communicated exact words directly to her.

Final Words from Casey's Teacher

I asked Mrs. Waters, after her experiences with Casey, how she would respond to someone saying it was complete nonsense to have a child in coma in a class. Her own family doctor had told her that it was not fair to her other students. She said that she could sympathize with that attitude before she actually had the experience.

But I don't think that this is the case from having done this. I think a lot about how I tried to adjust to this. I tried to put myself into Leslie's shoes. I would say to myself, would I have done anything differently if this were my kid? I am sure I would not have. I would have done absolutely everything I could think of with the hope of maybe something that would bring him out of it. From that point I think it was beneficial to him. He has gotten used to being with other kids. It has given him some sort of a life instead of being bedridden or homebound. It has given him a life. I think there are going to be more and more of these kids. Children need to be prepared for that. I think that we, adults, are a lot more apprehensive than the children.

I have seen a lot of sensitivity and growth on the part of my kids. They really believe, I am convinced, he can do things. They never say to me, "Well, you did that for him." They don't, even if they believe it or think it, they don't respond by saying it. They think that Casey did it. They know that Mara does the drawing, but as far as they are concerned that is his participation and that's fine, that's okay. If nothing else they have learned that kids participate at different levels, which will make them more accepting of others. The speed with which they adjusted to the new Latvian child and figured out how to communicate with him has amazed me.

∝ ✎

Mrs. Waters also told me how her own family had grown more tolerant and accepting of differences in others as a result of hearing about Casey.

DISCUSSION

This story is rich on many levels. Leslie's efforts and experiences are not specific only to being the mother of a child in coma. Many parents of children with ABI and other disabilities face the same challenges in interacting with schools. The private, sincere efforts of many of the school team members, especially the teacher and the nurse/aide, were admirable. This study provided an opportunity to hear from staff and the mother what they were thinking as they moved through the process of trying to find a common path for effectively including Casey in Mrs. Waters' readiness class.

The extremity of Casey's brain injury is not the only reason that Leslie and Casey's story is special. Leslie had a strong sense of self-efficacy; a willingness to appreciate the perspective of staff; a willingness to work cooperatively with staff toward fulfilling her goal to have Casey attend school; and a remarkable ability to communicate her hopes and reasoning in a warm, positive, and straightforward manner. Her hopes and visions for her child, however, were not different from those of other parents of children with ABI or other disabilities. She wanted Casey to go to school in his own neighborhood and have exposure to children his own age. She hoped that he might benefit from the stimulation and peer interactions in a general education classroom. Leslie mentioned several times that she was willing to participate in this study and to be open to the school staff because she hoped that sharing her experiences would be of help to other children with disabilities and their families.

Whenever the staff described having direct interactions with Leslie at school or in her home, they all reported an appreciation for what Leslie had endured and what she wanted for her son. They were able to repeat what she had told them verbatim and reflect on her perspective as a parent. Several individuals mentioned that they imagined they would have done no less if it had been their own child in coma. I believe that this opportunity to hear and understand the parent's perspective was what allowed this mother and these staff to be satisfied and proud of their achievements with Casey. The early difficulties with the school nurse were an example of someone who was not able to "hear" or appreciate this mother's perspective. Everyone else on the staff seemed relieved when the school nurse was removed from the team, almost instinctively sensing that without the willingness to hear Leslie's perspective, they would be unable to create a collaborative team.

More effort needs to be made to understand what happens when the behavior of school teams serves to dehumanize parents and their children. This staff's lack of experience and training in how to develop and conduct IEP meetings was unfortunate. The decision to have a premeeting during which the "group" decided what Casey's goals would be and what new policies and decisions Leslie would be made to follow subverted the more open and inclusive manner staff had when they interacted directly with Leslie.

A starting point might be the realization that parents with a child who has complex health care needs have probably been through more before they come to the school setting than any staff person could imagine. Parents usually arrive with expertise on how to facilitate their child's safe entry into school. Using negative, clichéd ideas about parents such as "overprotective," "co-dependent," "needing weaning," and "dysfunctional" are insulting and indicate a lack of appreciation for the situation. When I asked Mara if she eventually became comfortable being with Casey, she replied, "Comfortable is not the word you use with someone who can stop breathing if you are not vigilant with his care." A typical, appropriate response to having a child in coma does not exist. Expecting parents to follow a professional's code of "normal" behavior is not fair. On no level was this a typical situation. For many families of children with ABI, expected norms for polite parent behavior is not supportive of the reality that parents are coping with each day.

A qualitative study, such as this one, always has the limitations of being one person's perceptions of an individual situation. Generalizing the experiences of this mother, her son, and the school staff would be difficult. However, by looking in detail at one family's story with an extreme example of having a child in coma included within his neighborhood school, successes and challenges to others working to include diverse children and families within our schools and communities are highlighted. The implications from this study are that truly collaborative efforts by schools and families can lead to the successful inclusion of a wide range of children who have experienced ABI. The study also highlights the benefits to other children of having a child with serious challenges included in their classroom. Over and over again, adults were frightened about the reactions they believed children would have. Over and over again, the children in this study showed their openness, kindness, and interest in being connected with Casey as best they could. They were also able to quickly adapt and accept another child who came with special needs to their classroom.

What was left as a mystery to me was the responses to Casey of the people who worked with him directly. Susanna, Mara, Mrs. Waters, a couple of the home nurses I met, and his classmates all spoke about him with feelings of connection, affection, and awareness of even the smallest responses that he made. My own college-age daughter, Jessie, came with me on a visit to his home one afternoon. We were on our way for a day of shopping in the large city an hour from the home, and I wanted to stop and observe how Casey was making the transition from home to school. On the way I mentioned to Jessie that Casey happened to be in coma and was included in a first-grade readiness class. Jessie looked at me as if I had lost my mind, declaring, "No way! Mom, you have gone over the edge this time! You can't tell me that someone in coma can go to school. You're nuts!" After a half hour at the home, meeting Leslie, Peter, Mara, and Casey, and watching them prepare Casey to go to school, she felt very differently when we returned to our car. She announced, "Casey is really sweet and cute. He's not like typical kids who are in coma! It's good that he's going to school."

I could never completely determine exactly what there was about Casey, himself, that elicited these responses from those who met him. However, I have seen, many times, that when children and adults actually have the opportunity to spend time with children with ABI or other disabilities in typical home, school, and community settings, they quickly begin talking about the child as though the child was the "exception" to whatever they imagined a person with such an injury would be like. Although Casey's condition was exceptional, being able to connect with the humanity of a child in unusual circumstances may not be such an exceptional response from children when they are given the opportunity. After the care the mother, principal, teacher, and nurse/aide took to introduce Casey to his classmates, the students were immediately able to accept the child from Latvia who joined their classroom. They accepted that here was another child with different needs, needing help learning to speak English and to settle into classroom behavioral expectations. Their experience with Casey did not teach them to be accepting only of children in comas.

Always present in my mind when I was with Leslie and Casey was something that a mother of another child with complex medical needs had told me. This mother said that after the first year she realized that her daughter had not just happened to her or to her family, but her daughter had "happened" to her block, her neighborhood, her school, and her community. Leslie believed that she and her son were part of the neighborhood, school, and community in which they lived, and she invited the rest of us to join in her vision.

Planning and Carrying Out Instruction

In recent years, the incidence of students with ABI in our high school resource program has grown at a dramatic rate. This appears to be the result of parent requests for placements that focus on academic, rather than life, skills. Students with ABI present real challenges to high school special educators. First, many of these students have fallen years behind their peers in both academic and social skills. Second, general education programs do not adequately meet the needs of these students. Third, there is a dearth of reliable information about recommended practices for students with ABI. Fourth, these students require a considerable amount of teacher time, and often the results appear insignificant. I am encouraged and excited to find how useful and practical the research in this book is to me and other special educators who are working with children with ABI. Applying proven teaching technology to this population will result in significant gains for students, their families, and the school community. I hope the authors continue to investigate questions that will allow students with ABI to make gains that increase the likelihood of quality independent living.

Larry Soberman, Special Education Teacher

chapter four

The Role of Neuropsychology in Educating Students with ABI

Robert T. Kurlychek, Thomas M. Boyd, and N. William Walker

BECAUSE OF THE complex medical aspects of acquired brain injury (ABI), children with ABI typically come in contact with a wider range of health care professionals than do most children with developmental disabilities. This contact can include specialists in clinical neuropsychology. Clinical neuropsychology applies the science of psychology to the study of brain–behavior relationships. Integrating knowledge of the expected effects of brain injuries or illnesses with the individual's performance on selected tests allows the neuropsychologist to make clinical judgments about a student's areas of strength, weakness, need, and potential. This information can be of benefit to teachers, counselors, parents, and, ultimately, the student as he or she reenters the school environment. This chapter describes this health care discipline, outlines the particular expertise these specialists bring to the educational planning process, and presents guidelines for educators who want to involve neuropsychologists with returning students who have experienced ABI.

OVERVIEW OF NEUROPSYCHOLOGY

The use of standardized tests and measures reflects the fact that neuropsychology has its roots in clinical and experimental psychology. Since the 1940s a number of techniques have been developed to assess various aspects of human neurobehavior. Furthermore, a number of test batteries have been developed to evaluate a wide range of functioning (Golden, Purisch, & Hammeke, 1985; Reitan & Wolfson, 1993). Abilities and functions typically examined by such a battery include the following areas: 1) general intellectual functioning, 2) attention and mental efficiency, 3) manual speed and dexterity, 4) sensory-perceptual functioning, 5) spatial-perceptual and perceptual-motor ability, 6) higher cognitive problem solving and concept formation, 7) learning and memory processes, and 8) psychological and emotional adjustment.

Although the fixed battery approach to neuropsychological testing is still widely used, since the mid-1970s there has been an increase in more individualized approaches to testing (Lezak, 1995). In the individualized approach, tests are selected according to the referral questions and the nature of the problems the student is experiencing. This can permit a more focused and efficient assessment.

A student who is finding it particularly difficult to plan and organize tasks (e.g., homework, term papers) may receive a group of tests weighted toward executive functions. Executive functions involve such organizing abilities as goal formation, planning, initiation, self-monitoring or self-awareness, and troubleshooting or error correction. Because ABI often affects the frontal areas of the brain in particular and the frontal areas appear pivotal to the executive functions, people with ABI often show poor organization and executive control. The executive functions are difficult to isolate from other skills and experience, and, therefore, formal measures are sometimes supplemented by more open-ended, real-world exercises such as path finding, trip planning, and telephone book searching. Understanding and treating executive function impairments is a major focus of research in the field of neuropsychology and one that has important implications for the classroom. Executive function difficulties become progressively more disruptive as students mature and are expected to take greater responsibility for managing their own studies rather than simply following directions and structures provided by a teacher.

Memory and learning represent other areas of functioning that are important to school success and are particularly susceptible to brain injury. The 1980s and 1990s have seen a number of advances in understanding how memory works (Squire & Zola-Morgan, 1991). Because the ability to remember information and skills is critical to all academic pursuits, a better grasp of how systems responsible for short- and long-term memory interact and of their relationship to different types of learning (e.g., procedural or skill learning) has useful applications in the classroom.

Personality and behavior measures similar to those used by a clinical psychologist can also be incorporated to assess emotional, psychological, and personality variables that contribute to the overall functional picture. Family members of children with ABI report that changes in personality and behavior are much more difficult to cope with than are cognitive impairments such as memory or attention problems (Oddy, Coughlan, Tyerman, & Jenkins, 1985). The information the neuropsychologist provides to teachers and families regarding emotional and behavioral features and the ways in which the coping process can be supported at times may be of greater value than information regarding cognitive strengths and weaknesses. Such input can be helpful to a teacher trying to differentiate between typical adolescent behavior and injury-related personality change.

APPLICATIONS OF NEUROPSYCHOLOGY

Although neuropsychologists are involved in a range of activities, the foundation for their work is clinical evaluation. Most neuropsychological testing addresses one or more of several basic issues. These include diagnosis, description, prediction, and prescription.

Diagnosis

Clinical neuropsychology began as a way of assisting in the diagnosis of neurological disorders. In certain situations this can still be the primary role for neuropsychological involvement. When the focus of the neuropsychological evaluation is diagnosis, the approach may be limited to the search for specific indicators of a particular illness or condition. The clinician may be asked to distinguish between psychological and neurological causes for symptoms or to specify which of several neurological conditions may be present.

Description

When the neurological condition is apparent, as is typically the case with ABI, the role of diagnostician takes on less importance and the focus turns more to planning remediation. Drawing on an array of behaviors, standardized test administration allows the neuropsychologist to draw out patterns of strengths and weaknesses. Test score patterns may help in determining the extent of damage to specific regions of the brain. Neuropsychological testing can also help to elaborate on the individual's capacity in each of a number of functional areas. This represents an important step between diagnosis and realistic educational planning.

Prediction

Utilizing such information as the nature of illness or injury, duration since onset, and test performance can allow the neuropsychologist to present an expected recovery pattern that can be helpful in intervention planning. For example, the same type of ABI will have different expected results if it happens to a 6-year-old student rather than to a 14-year-old student. A student attempting to return to school 6 weeks after a serious injury may have a different set of challenges from those experienced by another student returning 4 months later. Prediction also needs to take into account the ways in which disruption of brain function interacts with development. An injury to the frontal lobes may not pose obvious challenges to a 7-year-old because the school environment generally is very structured at the first- or second-grade level, requiring little organization and planning on the part of the child. A knowledge of ways that ABI affects the course of development helps the neuropsychologist look ahead to a time in middle and high school when the curriculum is less structured and when additional supports and training in executive skills may be needed.

When evaluating older adolescents, life skills as well as academic skills must be considered. A number of researchers have found that combinations of scores from neuropsychological assessments are useful in differentiating people with neurological involvement who can live independently from those who cannot (e.g., Heaton & Pendleton, 1981). A number of new tests have been designed specifically to sample real-world or functional skills more directly. This has occurred in such domains as memory (Wilson, Cockburn, & Baddeley, 1985); route or direction finding (Boyd & Sautter, 1993); and everyday competencies such as paying bills, reading store signs, and making decisions related to basic daily activities (Wang & Ennis, 1986).

Prescription

Neuropsychological evaluation plays an important role in transforming the knowledge of the injury or condition, demographic variables, and test results into recommendations for remediation and rehabilitation. In the hands of clinicians who have experience in rehabilitation and other treatment settings, neuropsychological test results can help in targeting areas of particular need and even in the selection of remedial techniques. Specific instances and excerpts from reports (in italics) are presented in the following portion of the chapter.

APPLICATIONS FOR CHILDREN AND ADOLESCENTS

Although the full range of applications for neuropsychological services is quite broad, the issue of school-related functioning is a major concern with children and adolescents. This issue represents the "real-life" experiences that these individuals must face. An effective neuropsychological evaluation considers the test results that are obtained from the assessment in light of any preexisting factors and current situational needs with the goal of assisting family members as well as those who will provide services to the child in the school setting. This includes the full range of individuals who typically interact with students with ABI—teachers, school psychologists, counselors, special educators, speech-language therapists, and occupational therapists. Effective consultation can accomplish a number of important objectives.

Clearly Explains the Effects of ABI

The neuropsychologist can be valuable in translating medical information and measured impairments for those who need to develop day-to-day intervention and instructional strategies. The neuropsychologist can explain the type and characteristics of ABI sustained by the child. In cases involving conditions other than traumatic brain injury (TBI) (e.g., brain tumors, encephalitis, anoxia), the neuropsychologist can explain medical terminology and procedures. He or she can describe and categorize the severity of brain damage, whether mild, moderate, or severe, and discuss the typical course of expected recovery at various points after the trauma.

The following report excerpt represents an example of how the neuropsychologist can relate assessment data to the student's level of cognitive function to better determine the degree of actual loss of abilities and implications for school programming:

C.L. (15-year-old male) will be reentering high school after an absence of approximately 6 months. He experienced very severe ABI that resulted in a comatose state for 36 hours, followed by posttraumatic amnesia (the period of time from trauma until the person has enduring memories for new events) lasting approximately 28 days. His condition was complicated by bleeding into the brain and several epileptic seizures. The CT (computed tomography) scan showed severe damage to both frontal lobe areas, and he continues to have a total absence of the ability to perceive odors (anosmia). On neuropsychological testing he showed significant impairments, primarily in regard to organization, planning and execution, self-monitoring, and impulse control. These objective measures correlate with descriptions from family members. Although we can expect that he will continue to improve in the next 12–18 months, it is important to consider his current problems in determining intervention and instructional strategies. He may be somewhat impulsive, repetitive, and unaware of his level of performance at times.

Delineates Neurobehavioral Strengths and Weaknesses

Although there are some common problems experienced by most students with ABI, there are often unique differences. Depending on a variety of factors, there can be a range of behavior patterns that can be described by the neuropsychologist. Because ABI most often occurs as a result of falls or car accidents, the ensuing injury associated with rapid change in speed of motion (acceleration–deceleration injury) is unique. With widespread tearing of the connections between neurons comes some fairly characteristic impairments, including slowed speed of processing, difficulty concentrating, and, in particular, impaired ability to retrieve recently learned information. Because of the bony prominence on the inside of the frontal and temporal areas of the brain, such injuries also tend to produce emotional and behavior changes as well. The tenor of such changes varies with the nature, extent, and location of the injury; with age, sex, physical condition, and educational background of the child; and with individual neuroanatomical and physiological differences. In addition, the student may have a preexisting history of academic problems that needs to be considered:

R.Z. shows some significant difficulties with attention, verbal memory, and fine motor dexterity. She fatigues quickly when performing written assignments and shows a limited learning capacity when information is presented in an auditory-verbal format. When she is required to keep track of several different sequences or concepts (complex attention), she quickly will be overwhelmed and lose information. She does show relative strengths in regard to her ability to learn information presented from a visual-spatial perspective and with perceptual-motor skills in general that do not require fine motor dexterity. Basic reading, calculation ability, and grammar appear preserved. Assistive devices such as an audiotape recorder, typewriter, or word processor might be incorporated usefully into her notetaking. Staff working with her will need to develop strategies that will impose structure and organization on her schoolwork. Setting up her environment to limit distractions and taking into consid-

eration the cognitive fatigue that can occur with this type of recovery process will be helpful. Other strengths include her high motivation, favorable orthopedic recovery, and very supportive family.

Describes the Psychological Effects of ABI

The determination of the pattern of strengths and weaknesses can assist the neuropsychologist in generating suggestions to the treatment team or to individuals working with the student with ABI. To develop a comprehensive program, it is important to consider not only test performance but also psychological adjustment and behavioral factors.

> *R.L. is a 9-year-old male attempting to return to school following extensive radiation and chemotherapy treatment for acute lymphoblastic leukemia (ALL). Neuropsychological assessment strongly suggests that he start back to school on a part-time basis. This would allow him to adequately deal with the fatigue brought on by almost any type of exertion. Also, it is important for those working with this child to look past the superficial appearance of well-being. Although he still possesses many of the basic skills and abilities he has demonstrated in the past, the challenge for those working with him will be to assist him in areas such as pacing, motivation, generalization, and follow through. Also, research on individuals with ALL has found there can be some delayed neurocognitive effects as a result of this medical treatment. Impairments in nonverbal areas such as visual-motor integration may appear first.*

Another important factor to consider in individuals with ABI is the individual's accuracy of self-awareness. It is not uncommon for students with ABI to be unaware of obvious cognitive and behavior impairments. This "denial" may be the direct result of damage to specific areas of the brain, or it may represent a coping mechanism (albeit often ineffective) that allows the individual to deal with the loss of abilities. This phenomenon may also be associated with the changes in reasoning and judgment that typically follow ABI. In fact, the term *denial* may be misleading, because in order to deny something one must first realize that it exists. A more accurate representation might be in terms of the student not being fully aware of his or her impairments. Regardless of the causes, the results are the same, and it is important for school staff to consider this factor in remedial planning.

Assists in Developing Intervention/Academic Strategies

Neuropsychological testing provides information regarding a wealth of behaviors indicating not only one's style of approach but also how a student monitors or evaluates and corrects errors. Such information proves particularly valuable in generating ideas for improving performance and compensating for lost skills that may not be regained.

With a growing emphasis on remediation and intervention, the neuropsychologist is in a good position to draw on research addressing cognitive rehabilitation (e.g., Sohlberg & Mateer, 1989).

M.J.K. continues to show left-side neglect, which is negatively affecting her ability to study and read. Studies have found it helpful to provide a left-sided target (e.g., a vertical line) as an anchoring point. The beginning and end of each line can be numbered sequentially to assist this student in locating the beginning and end of each sentence and learning not to skip lines. Phase out the use of the numbers and then phase out the anchoring line. Such an approach can not only make her more aware of this problem but also provide a reasonable solution.

Serves as a Baseline Measure

Tracking performance on measures sensitive to change can help educators monitor a student's progress in an objective fashion. This is especially important during the initial phases of recovery. Information from repeated testing can assist in the evaluation and readjustment of instructional strategies. It is important to remember that virtually all predictions about future performance are "carved in sand" in that they are inexact and subject to individual variability. Repeated evaluations can serve to better define the instructional needs of the student.

When the results of this testing are compared to those from 6 months ago, it is apparent that R.T. has shown significant improvement on tasks that require attention, concentration, and basic academic skills. The instructional format has contributed to improvements and it appears appropriate to continue in this direction. He fails to show significant gains on neuropsychological measures that require problem solving, concept formation, and abstract reasoning. I would recommend that the team reconvene to examine approaches to enhance his skills in these areas.

BECOMING A KNOWLEDGEABLE
CONSUMER OF NEUROPSYCHOLOGICAL SERVICES

Although neuropsychological services can be valuable, it is important for school personnel and parents to consider some basic issues when involving a neuropsychologist in a student's educational programming.

When to Seek Neuropsychological Services

In many instances, when a student with ABI is going back to school, neuropsychological testing may have already been carried out and the neuropsychologist's involvement with the team may be already underway. This may not always be the case, however. A student may have experienced a relatively mild brain injury without obvious consequences. Another student may have received medical treatment in an area in which such services are not available.

For students with a significant injury or medical condition, it is beneficial to seek neuropsychological consultation in the following situations:

1. When a child is reentering the school situation after a significant injury or medical condition known to affect central nervous system functioning
2. If behavior or academic problems become apparent when the child reenters the academic setting
3. At significant transition points when information about the student's current cognitive or behavioral status is needed to help in planning

How to Select a Neuropsychologist

Neuropsychology is a relatively young discipline, and there is not yet a consensus on how a neuropsychologist is legally defined. At least two certification boards have been established and there is a special division of the American Psychological Association devoted to neuropsychology. These groups have suggested guidelines for establishing basic and advanced competencies in the area of clinical neuropsychology (Lezak, 1995).

Although these guidelines may help in the selection of a neuropsychologist, parents, students, and educators need additional information regarding the training and experience necessary to provide neuropsychological consultation for the school-age child or adolescent. Educators seeking neuropsychological consultation should determine the neuropsychologist's experience with school-age students with ABI. Local advocacy groups (e.g., state chapters of the Brain Injury Association) may also be helpful in locating professionals who are qualified to consult on issues related to ABI.

Specify the Questions   When involving a consultant in any particular field, there is an understandable tendency to want answers, sometimes even before the questions have been asked. Lack of clarity regarding the specific information being sought is one of the greatest obstacles to a successful consultation with a neuropsychologist. This problem can be fairly easily avoided, particularly if the school team and consultant communicate early regarding what is being requested and what can be provided. One of the best ways for the school team to specify the questions is by working directly with the neuropsychologist to refine questions. Although it is the team's responsibility to provide an overall sense of what team members need from an evaluation, the neuropsychologist needs to assist in narrowing down and specifying questions.

Just as the lack of clarity of the referral question(s) constitutes a major limiting factor in the usefulness of a neuropsychological evaluation, clarifying the referral questions greatly enhances the opportunity for a meaningful consultation. One of the authors tested a student at the request of a team whose members had previously met with an advocate familiar with neuropsychological consultation. The team had generated a list of questions. The structure provided by these well-thought questions became the outline of the sections in the evaluation report addressing impression and, particularly, recommendations. These issues were also addressed in a subsequent meeting with the team and parent. This approach helped the team and family to "get to the same page" in regard to educational programs. (See Table 1 for a list of questions similar to the questions generated by the team.)

Seek to Overcome the Language Barrier   One of the most frequently encountered shortcomings in the use of neuropsychological consultation in the schools is that of troublesome communication or terminology. Neuropsychology, like so many specialized fields, has developed its own jargon that has often derived from the jargons of social sciences (e.g., "normative," "standardized"), psychology (e.g., "denial," "intelligence"), and neurology (e.g., "posttraumatic amnesia," "acceleration–deceleration injuries"). Likewise, education has its own set of terminology and a particular fondness for acronyms, such as using IEP for individualized education program

Table 1.   Sample questions generated by a multidisciplinary team to be addressed by the neuropsychologist

1. What are the student's specific weaknesses that will affect our educational approach? (Will these vary from class to class or subject to subject?)
2. Should we emphasize a vocational track, or is community college placement still possible?
3. Should we limit the length of the school day?
4. What kind of memory aid might we use?
5. What are some realistic short- and long-term goals based on the student's current strengths and weaknesses?
6. How can we improve the student's organizational skills?
7. What is the best way to teach the student new skills?

and MDT for multidisciplinary team. A goal for both educators and neuropsychologists is to clarify and understand what the other is saying. Such a barrier can be lowered by providing lists of terms and definitions frequently used, attempting consciously to use nontechnical language, and being willing to ask for a definition when an unfamiliar term is used.

Keep Contribution of Neuropsychological Consultation in Perspective   The authors strongly advocate for the benefits of involving neuropsychological assessment and consultation with individuals returning to school following ABI. It is important to avoid unrealistic expectations, however, and to guard against the possible negative aspects of such an involvement. Special educators and school psychologists should not abdicate their responsibilities for decision making and planning to any outside consultant. Such professionals need to keep in mind the particular skills and talents they bring to any planning team. It is rare for a neuropsychologist to have teaching experience at the elementary, middle, and high school level or to have formal training in instructional development. Most educators have developed a certain framework and theoretical orientation in the classroom. It is important to incorporate suggestions and information from the neuropsychological consultation to better enhance one's approach in working with a particular student.

There may be instances in which neuropsychological assessment is unnecessary or distracting. A neuropsychological consultation used in isolation and as a competing approach to other orientations will not serve the student or school personnel well. Sometimes school personnel would do well to avoid additional labels and focus on behavioral observation and analysis.

Neuropsychological consultation can be costly. If it is not provided as part of a medical consultation, the expense to the school system can be considerable. School psychologists skilled in testing can administer many of the basic tests that are part of a comprehensive neuropsychological assessment (e.g., Wechsler Intelligence Scale for Children–Third Edition [WISC–III] [Wechsler, 1991], Woodcock-Johnson Psycho-Educational Battery–Revised [Woodcock & Johnson, 1989]) and provide this information to the consulting neuropsychologist. This can serve not only to lessen the overall additional expense but also to provide information to the neuropsychologist to better enable assessment planning.

A new model that capitalizes on the strengths of both neuropsychology and school psychology is in operation in several states (Walker, Savage, Tyler, & Deaton, 1992). This system shows promise in meeting the needs of students with ABI in the school setting. The system begins with school psychologists completing comprehensive workshops that cover basic neuroanatomy, brain–behavior relationships, and an introduction to basic issues in ABI, including assessment and programming. This is followed by more advanced training in the use of some basic neuropsychological instruments that can be added to their present testing battery. These workshops are taught by experienced neuropsychologists. After this series of basic and advanced workshops, each school psychologist must complete a period of supervised practice under the guidance of an experienced neuropsychologist. School psychologists completing these requirements are recognized by the state and placed on a list of approved providers of psychological services to students with ABI. Although these school psychologists are not permitted to perform the evaluations that are used to initially determine if a student classifies as having ABI, they do the periodic, follow-up assessments and monitor and oversee the student's progress.

This program is cost effective and has the added advantage of using existing school personnel. The school psychologists are available to act as service coordinators for the student with ABI and to consult with school personnel regarding the unique aspects of ABI.

Neuropsychological Consultation as Outside Perspective

Because ABI can be such a formidable challenge to the student, family, and educators, the potential for conflicting points of view regarding the nature of problems encountered is great. For example, the same classroom behavior that may be seen by one individual as neurologically related may appear to another to reflect laziness or lack of interest. Because ABI affects emotions and behavior and tends to amplify existing personality characteristics rather than create them "out of the blue," it is even more difficult to determine what behavior is a result of the injury. There may be so much emotion stored up around these and other issues that meetings may be dominated by frustrations in communication rather than by teamwork in meeting the student's needs (see Chapter 11). Often it is not a matter of one participant being right and another being wrong so much as it is a matter of different but equally legitimate emphases. As a party relatively removed from the situation and with a complementary set of information on which to draw, the neuropsychologist can provide an outside perspective that may be useful in resolving issues or in helping to see solutions that might not otherwise be apparent. The capable neuropsychologist presents findings as objectively and with as much sensitivity to all parties as possible. The fact that many clinical neuropsychologists have received training in such areas as counseling, therapeutic communication, and conflict resolution can also be used to help the team find the middle path along which the "truth" most often travels.

CONCLUSION

A frequently encountered shortcoming of neuropsychological evaluations stemming from the traditional emphasis on neurodiagnosis is the tendency to report what is wrong with the student but not what can be done about the particular problem. It may be less important to assess comprehensively every possible domain of cognitive functioning when the cause of a set of impairments is known (e.g., ABI) than to provide ongoing assistance in tracking cognitive changes; tailoring a program for the student's individual needs; and providing support to the student, family, and educators at critical times of educational transition or emotional adjustment. Because every ABI affects an individual differently, it is impossible to develop a formula that will work with every student or in every situation. Despite the best intentions of educators and specialists, glitches will occur. It is well worth considering a follow-up consultation to help in troubleshooting problems when they inevitably occur. Educators may need to seek additional information from the consultant and become adept at using the neuropsychological information to supplement already established school system resources in better helping the child.

Historically, the neuropsychological report has been the major focus of the neuropsychologist. This convention evolves from a traditional emphasis on neuropsychological evaluation as an objective diagnostic tool used either to support or to counter the hypotheses of the requesting professional, most often from the medical field. This static, often one-time, involvement, although relatively objective and often practical for consultation with medical and legal fields, is less desirable when working with educational and rehabilitative issues. As important as it is for educators and parents to seek ways to become better consumers of neuropsychological consultation, it is equally important for neuropsychologists to develop the skills and experience needed for work with students with ABI.

Neuropsychologists can be valuable contributors to educational teams who are unfamiliar with the unique characteristics of students with ABI. A neuropsychologist can help by interpreting medical information; clearly describing the cognitive, behavioral, and emotional issues resulting from the student's brain injury; and assisting in planning and monitoring the student's educational program. As a liaison between medical and education professionals, the neuropsychologist can bridge the gap between these two fields to benefit the student, family, and the educators who serve them.

REFERENCES

Boyd, T.M., & Sautter, S.W. (1993). Route-Finding: A measure of everyday executive functioning in the head-injured adult. *Applied Cognitive Psychology, 7*, 171–181.

Golden, C.J., Purisch, A.D., & Hammeke, T.A. (1985). *Luria-Nebraska Neuropsychological Battery: Forms I and II*. Los Angeles: Western Psychological Services.

Heaton, R.K., & Pendleton, M.G. (1981). Use of neuropsychological tests to predict adult patients' everyday functioning. *Journal of Consulting and Clinical Psychology, 49*, 807–821.

Lezak, M.D. (1995). *Neuropsychological assessment* (3rd ed.). New York: Oxford University Press.

Oddy, M., Coughlan, T., Tyerman, A., & Jenkins, D. (1985). Social adjustment after closed head injury: A further follow-up seven years after injury. *Journal of Neurology, Neurosurgery, and Psychiatry, 48*, 564–568.

Reitan, R.M., & Wolfson, D. (1993). *The Halstead-Reitan Neuropsychological Test Battery: Theory and clinical interpretation*. Tucson, AZ: Neuropsychology Press.

Sohlberg, M.M., & Mateer, C.A. (1989). *Introduction to cognitive rehabilitation*. New York: Guilford Press.

Squire, L.R., & Zola-Morgan, S. (1991). The medial temporal lobe memory system. *Science, 253*, 1380–1386.

Walker, N.W., Savage, R., Tyler, J.S., & Deaton, A. (1992). *Recent legislation affecting the implementation of programming for traumatic brain injury (TBI) students*. Symposium presented at the 12th annual conference of the National Academy of Neuropsychology, Pittsburgh, PA.

Wang, P.L., & Ennis, K.E. (1986). *The Cognitive Competency Test*. Toronto, Ontario, Canada: Mt. Sinai Hospital, Neuropsychology Laboratory.

Wechsler, D. (1991). Wechsler Intelligence Scale for Children–Third edition (WISC–III). New York: Psychological Corporation.

Wilson, B.A., Cockburn, J., & Baddeley, A. (1985). *The Rivermead Behavioral Memory Test*. Gaylord, MI: National Rehabilitation Services.

Woodcock, R.W., & Johnson, M.B. (1989). Woodcock-Johnson Psycho-Educational Battery–Revised. Allen, TX: DLM.

chapter five

Effective Assessment and Instructional Practices for Students with ABI

Kathleen A. Madigan, Tracey E. Hall, and Ann Glang

WHEN A CHILD reenters the classroom following acquired brain injury (ABI), the teacher will usually have a range of emotions and thoughts. Most often teachers report that they feel unprepared and overwhelmed (Lash & Scarpino, 1993; see Chapter 13).

Each child, regardless of his or her ability, brings to the classroom a unique set of talents and challenges. Children who have incurred a brain injury, however, bring additional history that has developed as a function of their preinjury characteristics, the specific neurobehavioral changes resulting from their injuries, and their learning experiences since the injury. Families of children with ABI may also have a unique set of expectations created from their hospital experiences. Returning from a hospital environment in which intensive daily rehabilitation services were offered, families expect a similar level of services in the school setting (Lash & Scarpino, 1993; Savage & Carter, 1991). Working with the student and family to create an instructional program that addresses the student's unique history and the family's expectations presents a difficult challenge to the classroom teacher. Furthermore, accommodating the diverse perspectives of all of the different professionals who serve these students (e.g., physician, hospital- and school-based therapists, teachers, instructional assistants) compounds this complex picture.

Effective instruction for students with ABI must take into consideration the complexity of the challenges these students bring to the school setting. Students with ABI, like all students, will learn best in an educational setting that provides clear instruction, adequate practice, clear and consistent feedback, and ongoing assessment. This chapter first presents an instructional model that incorporates empirically validated assessment, instruction, and curriculum design practices. Second, the application of this model is illustrated through a series of case examples. Finally, a set of strategies is presented designed to address the unique academic challenges experienced by students with ABI in content area courses.

OVERMEDICALIZATION

Effective instructional practices that promote generalizable skills and strategies are key to successfully meeting the needs of children and adolescents with ABI in the general classroom setting. Although this statement may seem self-evident, the overmedicalization of the field of ABI has often misled educators to believe that teaching students with ABI is much different from teaching students with other types of disabilities (see Chapter 2). On the contrary, the few studies that have examined effective instructional strategies for this population suggest that many of the techniques found effective with other students with disabilities can also be helpful with students with ABI (Feeney & Ylvisaker, 1995; Glang, Singer, Cooley, & Tish, 1992; Koegel & Koegel, 1986). Suggestions from the medical field that understanding the length and severity of coma, length of posttraumatic amnesia, and type and location of brain damage will help to determine long-term outcomes and thus assist in designing plans for recovery (e.g., instruction) have not been adequately researched for children and adolescents with ABI. Recent qualitative studies by Todis and colleagues suggest that these predictors may not only be inadequate, but also can actually limit service delivery options (see Chapter 2).

A medical model—using a medical diagnosis to determine the student's pattern of cognitive strengths and weaknesses and then to plan instruction—is generally very difficult to apply in the school environment (Lash & Scarpino, 1993). A different assessment-instructional paradigm is needed to effectively teach students with ABI. In this next section a model of instruction and ongoing assessment is presented that allows the teacher to design an instructional program that is responsive to the unique cognitive challenges faced by students with ABI.

ASSESSMENT-INSTRUCTION CYCLE

Hudson, Lignugaris-Kraft, and Miller (1993) synthesized the work of several researchers and developed a dynamic model of instruction that can be adapted to effectively address the unique learning challenges faced by students with ABI. This cycle of effective teaching incorporates three components, but, because students with ABI enter the classroom with such unique and complex cognitive and behavior challenges, a fourth component is added. These four components, shown in Figure 1, are explained further in the following sections.

The components of the assessment-instruction cycle are supported by the work of many educational researchers: 1) plan instruction systematically (e.g., Berliner, 1984; Christenson, Ysseldyke, & Thurlow, 1989; Hoffmeister & Lubke, 1990); 2) teach new material using demonstrations, guided practice, and, when ready, independent practice using effective teaching procedures (e.g., Berliner, 1984; Ellis & Worthington, 1995; Englert, 1984; Rosenshine & Stevens, 1986); and 3) evaluate student progress (e.g., Berliner, 1984; Christenson et al., 1989; Hoffmeister & Lubke, 1990; Rosenshine & Stevens, 1986; Tindal & Marston, 1990).

Component 1: Initial Assessment

The first step in the assessment-instruction cycle is to complete an initial assessment. In addition to documenting the student's academic abilities, the initial assessment should also examine the differences between the child's pre- and postinjury abilities, the level and type of care expected by the family, and the student's learning history established in the hospital.

Academic Skills   Traditional assessment in schools consists of annual, standardized measures (Kameenui & Simmons, 1990). Although standardized tests (e.g., the California Achievement Tests/5 [CTB/Macmillan/McGraw-Hill, 1993]; the Iowa Test of Basic Skills [Hieronmus, Hoover, & Lindquist, 1986]; and the Wide Range Achievement Test–Revised [Wilkinson, 1993]) provide useful *summative* data for teachers (i.e., documentation of student performance at the end of the school year), these instruments do not assist the teacher with instructional planning, which is essential to effective instruction. Summative measures use a general index of performance in a subject area to inform teachers and parents as to *who* is failing in comparison to other students.

Other types of summative measures, such as a test on a science unit, are more effective in guiding instructional planning but still fall short of providing specific information about what students have and have not learned (Tindal & Marston, 1990). The typical model

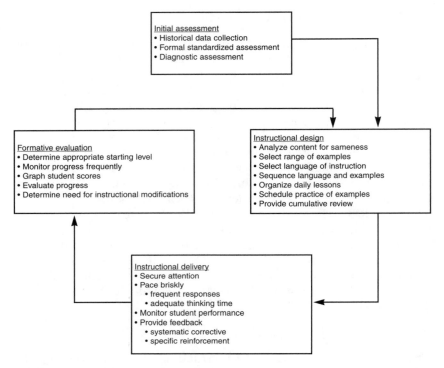

Figure 1.   An example of the assessment-instruction cycle.

of assessment in most public schools does not adequately inform teachers on what and how to teach students when they have difficulty in a subject area.

For students with ABI, more individualized assessment is recommended to guide instructional programming. This might include individually administered academic measures (e.g., the Key Math Diagnostic Arithmetic Test [Connolly, Nachtman, & Pritchett, 1971, 1976]; the Gray Oral Reading Test [Gray & Robinson, 1978; Wiederholt & Bryant, 1992]; and the Woodcock-Johnson Psycho-Educational Battery [Woodcock, 1989]). These measures help the teacher document strengths and/or weaknesses in specific academic areas. For example, the assessment may show that the student is able to decode words but has a poor understanding of what was read. For many students, a neuropsychological assessment can also provide a cognitive and behavior profile, which can be used to guide academic programming (Cohen, Joyce, Rhoades, & Welks, 1985; see Chapter 4).

Perhaps the most useful form of academic assessment is diagnostic assessment. These measures help the teacher evaluate student performance by examining the student's response to specific tasks within a new skill area. These data help teachers determine exactly what skills are currently in the student's repertoire and what skills are lacking in a particular subject area. Results from diagnostic measures provide the teacher with specific information about what needs to be taught. The teacher or school psychologist should administer diagnostic measures when the teacher needs to plan instruction in a new skill area. (See Appendix A of this chapter for a listing of recommended diagnostic assessments in reading, spelling, writing, and mathematics.)

Differences Between the Child's Pre- and Postinjury Status   In addition to gathering data about the student's academic abilities, the initial assessment can also provide information about the child's learning history. Most often children and adolescents with ABI are aware that their current performance is different from their performance before the injury (Lehr & Lantz, 1990; Shurtleff, Massageli, Hays, Ross, & Sprunk-Greenfield, 1995). Children with ABI can become frustrated with having to relearn once fluent skills. A thorough assessment of the child's pre- and postinjury abilities allows the teacher to incorporate this information into daily instruction. For example, if the teacher knows that the skill was at one time easy for the child to perform, then the teacher can design the learning task so that it looks different or acknowledge that the student was able to perform the skill prior to the injury and now needs to relearn it. If the child has significantly lost skills for which he or she was once acclaimed, then designing a reentry plan that takes this into consideration is critical. For example, the teacher might set up occasions so that the child does not have to publicly perform the "once-acclaimed skill" until fluency is regained.

Figure 2 presents questions that the teacher can ask parents, teachers, coaches, and other school staff to help determine the differences between pre- and postinjury performance. The students can be asked variations of these same questions to gain their perspective as well.

For students who were hospitalized as a result of their injury, it is helpful for the teacher to gather additional information about the types of services they received in the hospital and the learning history they developed as a result of the instruction provided by their first teachers—the hospital staff.

Level and Type of Care Expectation   Information regarding the duration and type of hospitalization may help teachers determine

Preinjury status

1. What things did the child like to do, find difficult, and avoid before the injury?

2. Were there things that the child did better than his or her classmates before the injury? If yes, what?

3. Were there things that the child did not do as well as his or her classmates before the injury? If yes, what?

4. What things did the child do about as well as his or her peers before the injury?

5. Were there some special traits or characteristics that people often remarked on about the child before the injury?

Postinjury status

1. What things does the child currently like to do, find difficult, and avoid?

2. Are there things that the child does better than his or her classmates since the injury? If yes, what?

3. Are there things that the child presently does not do as well as his or her classmates? If yes, what?

4. What are some things that the child does just as well as his or her peers since the injury?

5. During the recovery process, have there been special traits or characteristics that people often remarked on about the child?

6. What are the key differences between this student's pre- and postinjury abilities?

Figure 2. An example of a questionnaire to determine a student's pre- and postinjury status.

the level of care to which the child has become accustomed. By knowing whether the child was reinforced for independence or if the child was frequently "helped," the teacher can be prepared for the student's (and parents') expectations. If the child has learned to need a lot of "help," then the teacher can plan ways to increase independence. If the child has learned to be independent, then the teacher can reinforce independence. Figure 3 provides questions that the teacher can ask parents, therapists, doctors, and nurses that will help determine the expectations associated with the type and level of care the student received in the hospital setting.

Evaluate the Learning History Established in the Hospital   It is helpful for the teacher to know the student's history of success or failure with certain tasks, the typical number of repetitions needed to learn a new skill, and the types of prompting required for easy versus difficult tasks. With this information, the teacher is prepared to prompt when prompts are needed, provide adequate practice, and integrate difficult tasks with easy ones. Figure 4 is a brief questionnaire to evaluate a student's learning history after ABI.

Information from the initial assessment will help the teacher understand the needs and expectations of the family and the student. Using this information, the teacher and instructional team can develop the student's long- and short-term goals and an appropriate instructional plan. A child with ABI will most likely need an individualized education program (IEP). (See Appendix B at the end of this chapter for legal requirements associated with the development and documentation of the IEP.) Because recovery rates are different for every individual, the IEP for students with ABI must be a dynamic living document. The structure of the assessment-instruction cycle described in this chapter illustrates the teacher's need to formatively evaluate student performance and alter instruction and tasks depending on a student's success. The IEP should reflect these changes as alterations or additions are made to meet student needs.

Component 2: Instructional Design

The next step in the assessment-instruction cycle is to organize the instructional content using effective instructional design. To more fully understand this component of the cycle, this section provides a brief overview of studies that have shaped educational researchers' thinking about curriculum and instruction for youngsters with disabilities.

Direct Instruction   Prior to 1970, the model most frequently used in special education classrooms was a diagnostic-prescriptive model. The objective of the diagnostic-prescriptive model was to

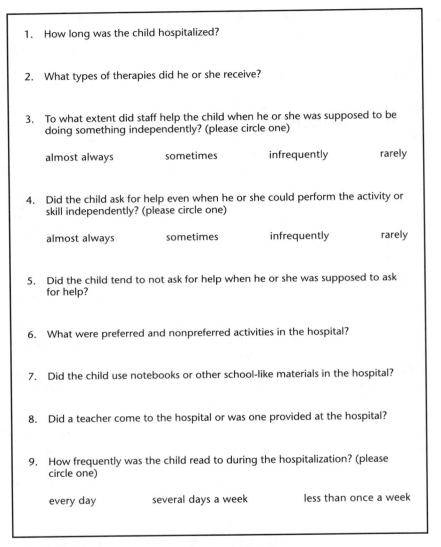

1. How long was the child hospitalized?

2. What types of therapies did he or she receive?

3. To what extent did staff help the child when he or she was supposed to be doing something independently? (please circle one)

   almost always   sometimes   infrequently   rarely

4. Did the child ask for help even when he or she could perform the activity or skill independently? (please circle one)

   almost always   sometimes   infrequently   rarely

5. Did the child tend to not ask for help when he or she was supposed to ask for help?

6. What were preferred and nonpreferred activities in the hospital?

7. Did the child use notebooks or other school-like materials in the hospital?

8. Did a teacher come to the hospital or was one provided at the hospital?

9. How frequently was the child read to during the hospitalization? (please circle one)

   every day   several days a week   less than once a week

Figure 3.   Assessment questions to determine a family's expectations of level and type of care.

determine 1) the cause of the learning disability for purposes of classification, 2) information about a child's learning style and psychological processes, and 3) the student's academic needs for instructional purposes (Swanson & Watson, 1982). The approach stressed the diagnosis of specific abilities that were said to be the building blocks of learning (e.g., auditory sequencing, visual-sequential memory). The model further suggested that instruction

1. How quickly did the child learn targeted therapy skills (number of trials to criterion)?

2. Which skills (physical/verbal) did the child learn most rapidly?

3. Which directions did the child follow without prompts or help?

Figure 4.   A brief questionnaire to determine a student's learning history after ABI.

that developed the specific "weak" ability or used the "strong" ability to compensate for the "weak" ability would improve academic functioning. Criticisms of the model surfaced in the 1970s. Ysseldyke (1973) reviewed 47 representative studies designed to demonstrate the effectiveness of the diagnostic-prescriptive model and concluded that there was no empirical support for the model. A research summary of several diagnostic-prescriptive models by Arter and Jenkins (1977) encouraged special educators to reevaluate the effectiveness of using the "underlying processes" model to formulate assessment constructs, develop curriculum, and define instructional methodologies. During the 1970s, special educators began to explore ways to design and deliver instruction that would be effective and efficient for diverse learners.

Direct Instruction, which initially grew out of the studies of Carl Bereiter and Siegfried Engelmann at the University of Illinois in the early 1960s and was later merged with behavior analysis through contact with Wesley Becker and Douglas Carnine, is regarded by many educators at the present time as the most systematic approach to design and deliver procedures for building and maintaining basic cognitive skills (Kameenui & Simmons, 1990). The visible features of Direct Instruction are small-group instruction with frequent responding by the students, as instructors follow precrafted programs in an active, participation-oriented classroom. The less obvious features are the core set of principles and assumptions that make up the details of the content and strategies that are being taught. These "invisible" features of Direct Instruction curricula are what make these uniquely suited to teaching students with ABI (Glang, Singer, Cooley, & Tish, 1992).

Engelmann and Carnine (1982) provided the educational community with instructional design and delivery practices that were empirically based (see Adams & Engelmann, 1996, for a review of research). These principles are based on the notion that by logically organizing the instructional content, the learner is more likely to generalize. That is, initial teaching sequences can be designed to promote generalized responding and prevent the learner from forming misrules (overgeneralizations or undergeneralization). The analysis assesses ways in which sets of stimuli (e.g., facts, concepts, skills, knowledge) are the same and how they are different (Becker, 1986; Kameenui & Simmons, 1990).

The universe of knowledge taught in schools can be classified into groups that can help educators design more effective instruction. Kameenui and Simmons (1990) developed a taxonomy of knowledge forms from simple to complex to help design lessons (i.e., verbal association, concepts, rule relationships, and cognitive strategies). The first level is verbal associations, consisting of simple facts (e.g., the student is asked, "How many days in a week?"), verbal chains (e.g., the student is asked to "Count by 5s"), and discriminations (e.g., the student is asked to identify symbols of the letter d, a, r, and m). The next level is concepts, defined as objects, events, actions, or situations that are part of a class (e.g., color, position, nouns, comparatives). Rule relationships are at the third level in the taxonomy. This is an instructional episode that specifies a connection between at least two facts, discriminations, or concepts (e.g., the harder you work, the more energy you need). The most complex category of knowledge, the fourth level, is cognitive strategies, which is defined as a series of multistep associations and procedures involving any or all of the other knowledge forms in the taxonomy (e.g., working multistep mathematics problems).

From the analysis of the learning task, the curriculum designer can then develop the strategies to be taught, create the wording used to explain the strategies, generate a range of examples used to illustrate the strategy's application, and sequence the information into daily lessons with appropriate lesson parts. The following seven principles guide this process of instructional design[1]:

1. It is impossible to teach a concept with a single example, because one instance of a concept can also be an instance of another concept. Suppose an educator wants to teach the child to identify the geometric shape of a square. If the child is shown a picture of a square that happens to be red, then the child might inappropriately generalize that if something is red it can be called a square. This one example belonged to another class of events, objects, or

---

[1]Adapted from Becker (1992).

actions (e.g., red) as well as square. Thus, *one needs a set of positive examples. Positive examples illustrate the relevant features of the concept.*

2.   The teaching sequence should produce generalization; the goal is for the learner to respond correctly to new examples not used in the initial teaching. *There must be a structural basis for this generalization in the sameness of the examples.* A "square," for example, has four equal sides with four 90-degree angles. To illustrate the concept of "square," one would vary the irrelevant features of "square" (e.g., color, size, texture of material) but maintain the relevant features (e.g., four equal sides with four 90-degree angles). Large squares, red squares, small squares, silk squares, burlap squares, and so forth, therefore, would be selected in order to illustrate the full range of sameness.

3.   It is impossible to teach a concept using *only* positive examples. In order to illustrate how skills and knowledge are the same, one must show how they are different. Thus, *one needs a set of negative examples. Negative examples illustrate that when one changes the relevant features of the concept it will be called something else.* To teach the concept of square, therefore, geometric shapes must be shown that vary the relevant features of "square." One would select examples that do not have four equal sides and four 90-degree angles.

4.   To minimize the number of examples needed to teach a concept, *one must show how the range of positive examples are the same and how the range of negative examples are different.* Thus, one must select negative examples that are minimally different from the positive examples. To teach the concept of square, one would need to select large rectangles, red rectangles, small trapezoids, silk trapezoids, burlap rectangles, and so forth.

5.   To minimize confusion and promote errorless acquisition of a concept, it is important to *use wording that is highly consistent.* To teach "square," one would create a script that labels those objects with four equal sides and four 90-degree angles as "square" and those objects without four equal sides and four 90-degree angles as "not square." If the "not square" objects were called "rectangle," for example, then it has not been illustrated to the learner that there is any connection between these objects. By using "not square" one has created a connection and has eased the requirements on the learner.

6.   *Systematically sequence examples* to show what is irrelevant and expand the range of applications. One would sequence the examples of "square" and "not square" in an unpredictable order

and still fully illustrate the sameness and difference of the concept.

7. After teaching a concept, one needs to *test with new examples*. The teaching sequence would include examples (positive and negative) that had not been previously used. The purpose of this principle is to assess whether the child has generalized the concept.

Figure 5 illustrates each of these design principles to teach the concept of "over." First, there is a simple set-up—just a ball and a table. By using only these items during the instruction, the learner will focus on the position of the objects that illustrates "over." (Note the use of positive and negative examples that are minimally different and the order in which the examples appear.)

To effectively teach new concepts, the teacher will need to develop daily lessons using well-designed instructional sequences. Daily lessons should have the following standard parts: initial introduction of the skill or strategy, guided practice, independent practice, and cumulative review.

Initial Introduction   Initial introduction of the skill or strategy usually involves careful modeling by the teacher. Viewing a systematic, dynamic model can increase the efficiency with which a student learns (Archer, Gleason, & Isaacson, 1995). When modeling, the teacher should demonstrate (show-and-tell) the new skill or strategy step by step. Even if the step requires a covert (thinking or internal) process, the teacher should orally describe the process. By labeling the covert process, the teacher is providing a valuable model for how thinking directly relates to the actions being performed. The teacher should use the precise wording, use positive and negative examples, and sequence each part of the initial introduction according to the design principles.

Guided and Independent Practice   Even though a new skill has been presented to the student using careful modeling and teacher presentation, it cannot be assumed that the skill will remain in the learner's repertoire. Research with children without learning impairments has shown the importance of providing sufficient practice on new skills to ensure mastery at each step in the learning process (Carnine, 1976). For students with ABI who have impaired memory and learning abilities, providing adequate practice on new skills and concepts is essential (Butters & Glisky, 1993).

Effective instructional design systematically provides for initial introduction of a new skill through modeling, followed by instruction in which sufficient practice is provided using *guided assistance*. When the teacher uses guided assistance, he or she gradually fades

An 11-step sequence that can be used in the initial teaching and testing of most any single-dimension basic concept will be illustrated. First the setup for presenting all 11 examples is designed. For example, to teach the concept OVER, the setup might be a table and a ball (a real table and ball):

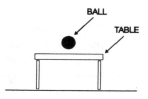

The first two examples are two negatives, with the second example designed to be minimally different from example 3.

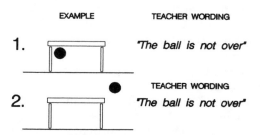

Next, show three positives which illustrate the possible range of positive examples, ending with a positive that is minimally different from a negative:

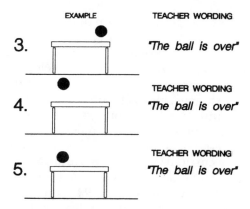

Next, show six random positive and negative examples (except that the first one is minimally different from example 5 and test the students.

Figure 5. An example of a sequence that guides the process of instructional design. First, there is a simple set-up—just a ball and a table. By using only these items during the instruction, the learner will focus on the position of the objects that illustrate "over." It is important to note the use of positive and negative examples that are minimally different and the order in which the examples appear. Reprinted with permission from Becker, W.C. [1992]. Direct instruction: A twenty year review. In R.P. West & L.A. Hamerlynck [Eds.], *Designs for excellence in education: The legacy of B.F. Skinner* [pp. 77–78]. Longmont, CO: Sopris West. All rights reserved.

the amount of guidance or the number of prompts to assist the student in using the strategy or skill with different examples. Using well-sequenced instruction, progressing from high levels of assistance to independence, the student has a greater probability of mastering the material being taught (Ellis & Worthington, 1995; Kameenui & Simmons, 1990).

Cumulative Review   If a skill is important enough to teach, then it must be systematically reviewed and practiced so that it is maintained. Cumulative review of material ensures integration of new skills with previously learned information (Rosenshine & Stevens, 1986). The procedures for designing review activities vary depending on the knowledge form. A skill can be reviewed either in isolation or as a part of a more complex knowledge form. For example, knowledge of simple math facts such as being able to multiply simple numbers (e.g., 7×5, 4×9, 3×9) is a preskill for working more complex math operations. In designing examples of multistep computation problems, the teacher can provide a review on previously taught math facts by using them in the example set (e.g., 374×59). In this way, those facts are being practiced within the more complex cognitive strategy of a multistep math problem. This promotes recall of the fact as well as generalization of the strategy across multiple examples.

The lesson design model that the Council for Exceptional Children's *Academy for Effective Instruction* developed (Archer et al., 1989) is particularly appropriate for use with students with ABI who are participating in general classroom experiences. This model divides the lesson into three components: opening, body, and close. Figure 6 presents an example of a lesson design format.

The principles of effective instructional design incorporated in Direct Instruction curricula have been empirically validated with students with a variety of ability levels (see Kameenui & Simmons, 1990, for a review). Furthermore, a 1992 study by Glang and colleagues showed that these same principles resulted in meaningful student progress when used with students with ABI.

Component 3: Delivery of Instruction

Although the design of the lesson is critical, it is also important that the teacher use delivery or presentation skills that increase the likelihood of the students' accurate and fluent responses. These include both management and delivery techniques. During the lesson, teachers should maintain a brisk instructional pace, require frequent student responses, provide adequate processing (thinking) time when student responses are requested, monitor student responses, and provide feedback to correct and incorrect responses.

	Description of component	Example wording
OPENING		
Attention	Gain the students' attention.	"Thank you. We are going to begin."
Review	Review prior knowledge necessary for today's lesson.	"In our last session, we..."
Expectations/ goals	State the expectations or goals for today's lesson.	"Today you will learn..."
BODY		
Model (teacher does it)	Demonstrate the skill or strategy for your students.	"Today you will learn..."
Prompt (teacher and student do it)	Assist the students in performing the skill simultaneously or by verbally prompting the students.	"Let's do this together."
Check (student does it)	Carefully observe the students as they perform the skill or strategy that was just modeled or prompted.	"It's your turn to..."
Guided practice (teacher does it)	Set up other examples that require the same skill or strategy. Prompt and check the practice by verbally or visually assisting or by setting up peer practice or group activity sessions.	"Let's do these together."
Independent practice	Assign seatwork or independent assignment.	"Now it's your turn to work by yourselves."
CLOSE		
Review	State the skill or strategy that was learned in today's session.	"Today we learned..."
Preview	Connect the skill or strategy to what will be learned in the next lesson.	"Tomorrow we will learn..."
Independent work	Assign homework that reviews skills from previous lessons.	"For homework you will..."

Figure 6.   An example of a daily lesson design. (From Archer, A., Isaacson, S., Adams, A., Ellis, E., Morehead, J.K., & Schiller, E.P. [1989]. *Academy for effective instruction: Working with mildly handicapped students.* Reston, VA: The Council for Exceptional Children; adapted by permission.)

Use Brisk Instructional Pace   When working with students with ABI, teachers may believe they should present information slowly. However, the opposite is true. When teachers present information with long delays between questions and answers, students with ABI are likely to lose attention and focus. After a question is presented and the student responds correctly, the teacher should present the next question without delay (Archer et al., 1995). Using a brisk pace when presenting a lesson helps the student pay attention to the instruction (Englert, 1984) and can increase the acquisition rate of new material (Carnine, 1976; Koegel, Dunlap, & Dyer, 1980).

Provide Adequate Processing Time   Presenting briskly, however, does not mean "rapid-fire" question-and-answer sessions. It is important for the teacher to provide adequate processing or thinking time. The complexity of the response required determines the amount of time needed. Inferential questions and questions requiring multiple covert (thinking) operations necessitate that the teacher wait a brief amount of time (usually just a few seconds) after asking the question and before requiring an answer. The teacher may also need to consider how quickly the child is able to produce the desired response. For example, if the child's speech has been affected by the injury and he or she has difficulty forming words, the teacher may need to give extra time.

Require Frequent Student Responses   When students actively participate in their learning, they achieve greater success (Ellis & Worthington, 1995). To ensure student success, the teacher must elicit student responses. True active participation goes beyond the occasional question-and-answer pattern found in many classrooms or group-oriented assignments. True active participation requires that the teacher and students have a highly developed *interaction*. This interaction should occur at high rates. That is, the teacher should ask the students to say, write, or do something several times each minute.

Monitor Student Responses   Watching and listening to the students' responses provides the teacher with essential instructional information. Teachers who monitor responses are able to make adjustments in the lesson *as* they are teaching. Teachers should be constantly scanning the classroom as the students are writing or orally responding.

Provide Feedback to Correct and Incorrect Responses   When learners make errors, it is important that they receive corrective feedback so that they can successfully complete the task when it is presented again (Carnine, 1980; Gersten, Carnine, & Williams, 1982). Students with ABI should receive immediate feedback to both correct and incorrect responses.

Teachers should provide feedback to incorrect responses in a businesslike manner. The feedback to incorrect responses should not be too "accommodating." That is, the teacher should not make excuses for the student's error by saying things such as, "Oh, that's okay. Don't worry about it. I know you really tried. It really isn't that important." When teachers react to errors in this way, they are unintentionally teaching students to be careless or that they do not need to pay attention to instruction. Nor should feedback be too "threatening." For example, when a child has made an error, the teacher may say, "We just went over this. Weren't you listening?" This type of feedback can have a negative effect on responding. Students may learn to stop answering questions or become withdrawn or noncompliant. When an error occurs, the teacher should just state the correct answer in a neutral tone, have the students make the correct response, go on to other questions, and then later in the lesson return to the questions that the students missed.

Providing feedback to students with ABI for correct responses is more challenging than just giving praise statements or points. When a child with ABI has made a correct response on a *new* skill, feedback needs to be immediate and quick. The feedback (e.g., praise, points, pats on the back) must not interfere with the timing of the next question/response interaction of the teacher and student. Feedback that is not quick or immediate can interrupt the teaching episode and disrupt the learner's ability to recall. In the following example, Tony is learning to say the answers to the following math facts printed on flash cards: $5 + 3 =$, $5 + 4 =$, $5 + 5 =$, and $5 + 6 =$. He will consistently make an error on $5 + 6 = 11$. Here is the interaction between Tony and his teacher:

Teacher: [Teacher is holding flash card for $5 + 3 =$.] Look at the card. Good job. Tell me the answer.

Tony: 8.

Teacher: Great. You are really learning these math facts. I knew you could do it. Let's try the next one. [Teacher is holding flash card for $5 + 4 =$.]

Tony: 9.

Teacher: YES! That's right. You know the answer. Let's try the next one. [Teacher is holding flash card for $5 + 5 =$.]

Tony: 10.

Teacher: I knew you could do it. You didn't even count on your fingers. You are really remembering these facts. Let's try the next one. [Teacher is holding flash card for $5 + 6 =$.]

Tony: 11.

Teacher: That's it! That's it! You got it! You got the hardest one. Good work. You are really getting good at these. I knew you could do it! Congratulations! Let's try the next one. [Teacher is holding up the same flash card for $5 + 6 =$.]

Tony: [pauses, counts on his fingers] 10.

Teacher: Oops. Let's look at the back of the card. Tony, read the fact for me.

Tony: $5 + 6 = 11$.

Teacher: Good reading the whole fact! You are really trying hard.

Although the teacher means well, she is actually interfering with Tony's ability to recall. By using so many praise statements after each correct response and before the next question, the teacher is providing unnecessary demands on his memory. Tony may like all the praise, but it does not help him to learn. For students with ABI, the teacher should acknowledge the correct response on new material quickly and immediately. One way to acknowledge correct responses is by repeating the answer. For Tony, after each correct answer the teacher could say, "Yes. 5 plus 6 does equal *11.*" That way, Tony hears it again and his response is confirmed.

Teachers should also be careful when they give praise for correct responses on already familiar or easy skills. This type of praise may slow the lesson pace and could detract from the value of the teacher's praise. For familiar or easy tasks, the teacher should require that the child make several correct responses prior to reinforcing. Thus, the child is expected to perform more for the same amount of reinforcement. Eventually, teachers should require that the student reinforce him- or herself for accurate performance. With a younger student, for example, the teacher might say, "Tell yourself that you are a good learner." Then the child must say, "I am a good learner." For older students the teacher might say, "Raise your hand if you think you did a good job just now." This form of internalization of praise is critical for students with ABI.

Component 4: Formative Evaluation

The final component in the assessment-instruction cycle is formative, or ongoing, assessment. Although both group- and individually administered summative measures (described previously) can provide teachers with information about students' progress at the end of an instructional period, more frequent formative assessment allows teachers to closely monitor acquisition and retention of instructional content. This is critical for students with ABI whose skill profiles have gaps and whose learning rates are variable. For these students, the teacher must have ongoing data about student performance so that instruction is tailored to the student's individual learning needs, and valuable instructional time is not wasted. Using formative assessment information, teachers can accurately evaluate student performance and make necessary instructional adjustments right away, not after the completion of a chapter, unit, or the entire school year.

A formative assessment procedure using performance-based measures known as Curriculum-Based Measurement (CBM) has been studied since the early 1980s (Deno, 1985; Deno, Marston, &

Tindal, 1985/1986; Fuchs, Fuchs, & Hamlett, 1989). In this chapter, CBM refers to a set of procedures for evaluating student progress in varying subject areas (e.g., reading, math, spelling, writing). These measurement procedures are technically adequate, easily administrable, and sensitive to student growth. Initially, teachers establish a performance goal or criterion. Using standard directions and procedures, they frequently measure student performance using the CBM and then chart their students' data. Teachers can literally see change or lack of change in student performance over time as they view the resulting graph. If student progress is inadequate, teachers may need to modify instruction. (See Appendix A at the end of this chapter for examples of student measures, teacher directions, scoring procedures, and sample charts.)

Summary

The assessment-instruction cycle offers a model of effective instruction that is empirically based and responsive to the changing cognitive profile of students with ABI. The initial assessment yields specific information about what the student knows and needs to learn. By using effective instructional design principles, the teacher can construct materials that are designed from the very first lesson to promote generalization of the content and/or skills. By employing empirically based, instructional delivery techniques, the teacher can ensure student mastery. Finally, the teacher can monitor the degree to which students are mastering the instructional content by using formative evaluation procedures. This last step is critical because it provides the teacher with information that helps guide refinement of the instruction so that it can be tailored to the individual student's learning needs.

APPLYING THE ASSESSMENT-INSTRUCTION CYCLE

In this section, the use of the assessment-instruction cycle for children with ABI is illustrated through a series of case studies. Case studies are presented in reading, language arts, and mathematics. To demonstrate the specific principles presented previously, the authors show how each teacher systematically answers the following questions:

- What does the student know now?
- What does the student need to learn?
- How do you teach what the student needs to learn?
- How do you know that the student has learned it?

Case Example A: Beginning Reading

Nicole was a typically developing 7-year-old when she was severely injured in a motor vehicle accident in the fall of her second-grade school year. She was riding in the back of her family's car when their vehicle was struck by another car traveling over 100 miles per hour. Medical records indicated that Nicole sustained ABI involving a linear skull fracture from the left frontal to the parietal-occipital region, with swelling in the left temporal region. She did not experience loss of consciousness. After several months of inpatient and outpatient rehabilitation, Nicole returned to school.

1.   Initial assessment: What does Nicole know now? *Nicole's parents reported that she had been a quick learner before her accident and that reading had been one of her favorite subjects. In the hospital, she had received daily occupational, speech, and physical therapy. On most days, her mother had also read to her from some of Nicole's favorite books. Nicole's parents and the hospital-based therapists believed that Nicole had learned to function as independently as possible. When Nicole went home from the hospital, however, she was still asking for help with some tasks that she was capable of doing alone.*

Because of the effects the injury had on her expressive language, it was difficult for the school psychologist to determine Nicole's cognitive and academic abilities. Test reports did show that Nicole had severe memory problems, difficulties with distractibility, problems with social judgment and reasoning, and mild difficulty with visual-spatial and perceptual-motor skills. On standardized academic assessment, Nicole scored at the kindergarten level in reading (K.8 grade equivalent [GE] or the eighth month of kindergarten), and the first-grade level in both math (1.2 GE) and written language (1.1 GE).

Although the GE score showed that Nicole's reading skills regressed following her injury—a typically developing 7-year-old would be reading above a K.8 GE—the teacher needed additional information to appropriately teach Nicole beginning reading skills. The school psychologist or teacher needed to administer a beginning-level diagnostic reading assessment (see Appendix A at the end of this chapter for a listing of recommended diagnostic reading assessments).

Figure 7 presents Nicole's diagnostic assessment of letter/sound identification. It reveals that Nicole could correctly identify 5 of the 26 lowercase letter names and sounds in the alphabet and the capital N, and that she knew the vowels a, i, and o. When Nicole heard a word said slowly, she could recognize and say the word at a typical speaking level. The assessment also revealed that Nicole could not say the sounds within a word (e.g., if she heard the word mat, *she could not say the letters or sounds in that word). Figures 8–10 illustrate diagnostic measure procedures to evaluate Nicole's beginning reading skills.*

2.   Instructional design: What does Nicole need to learn? *Research on beginning reading emphasizes the importance of phonemic awareness in establishing a firm foundation of reading skills (Chard, Simmons, & Kameenui, 1995). Based on the diagnostic information described previously, Nicole needs to work on several prereading skills to master reading decoding and comprehension. First, Nicole knew only five letters and sounds. She needs to learn the remaining letters, sounds, and sound combinations (e.g., "sh," "ch") to be a successful reader. She also needs instruction on hearing and saying words slowly and identifying the component sounds in a spoken word. These preskills prepare beginning readers like Nicole to sound out, blend, and recognize words in print.*

Because Nicole has severe memory and learning difficulties, one of the key strategies to be included in her instruction is review of previously taught material. Her teacher cannot assume that because she demonstrated some skills during the assessment that she will always remember them. The practice of continuous use and review of skills noted in research regarding effective teaching is of particular importance with students such as Nicole.

The five letters and sounds that Nicole recognized correctly during the diagnostic assessment must be reviewed. Concurrent to sounds review, new sounds can be gradually introduced one at a time. The teacher

a	+	d	-	u	-	v	-	q	-
m	-	r	-	c	+	p	-	z	-
t	-	o	+	b	-	y	-		
s	+	g	-	n	-	j	-		
i	+	l	-	k	-	x	-		
f	-	h	-	e	-	w	-		

D	-	E	-
A	-	B	-
R	-		
N	+		
G	-		

Figure 7.   A diagnostic assessment of letter/sound identification of a 7-year-old girl with ABI. (+ = correct; - = incorrect.)

Teacher says	Student response	Correct?	Sounds Correct
/t/ /a/ /n/	nap	-	~~1~~ ~~2~~ ~~3~~
/p/ /a/ /m/	mom	-	~~1~~ ~~2~~ 3
/f/ /i/ /b/	fake	-	1 ~~2~~ ~~3~~
/l/ /o/ /g/	log	+	1 2 3
/j/ /e/ /t/	t	-	~~1~~ ~~2~~ 3
/s/ /u/ /n/	sun	+	1 2 3
		Total Correct	8

Figure 8.   An example of a diagnostic assessment of auditory word recognition—telescoping of a 7-year-old girl with ABI. (+ = correct; - = incorrect.)

should model individual sounds for Nicole, practice saying them with her, and gradually have her say the sounds on her own. Once a new sound is mastered, Nicole should be taught to discriminate the new sound from other known sounds. This cycle of introduction, discrimination practice, and ongoing review should continue until all of the sounds are taught. Gradually, the teacher will build Nicole's knowledge of letters and sounds, which will become a part of her reading vocabulary.

Additional beginning reading skills should be taught and continually practiced using the effective instructional design principles described in the previous section. The auditory skills of saying words quickly after they are pronounced slowly (e.g., teacher says "sssaaaammm," and the student says "Sam") and saying the sounds within words must be taught and practiced to prepare for word reading using phonemic analysis. There are several beginning reading curricula that use the principles covered here to systematically teach beginning readers (see Appendix C at the end of this chapter).

3.   Instructional delivery: How do you teach what Nicole needs to learn? *Although instruction for Nicole could occur individually, it is most efficient for students to receive instruction with children who have similar skills (i.e., homogeneous grouping). The letters and sounds that Nicole needs to learn may be presented in different ways. To promote transfer, letters could be written on paper, the chalkboard, and/or flash cards.*

When teaching letters/sounds, the teacher should have Nicole and other students in the group practice the sounds orally (particularly the new sounds) many times each day. Sometimes the teacher may write the letters on the chalkboard and have the students practice saying the sounds for the letters four or five times. Later in the lesson and again later in the day, the teacher could use a flipchart or flash cards to give students more practice.

Students who have academic limitations, such as Nicole, must have frequent distributed skills practice. One period of learning and practic-

*ing reading skills is not sufficient. Students should have frequent re-
minders (practice) of the skills taught to correctly retain the information.
These same procedures of demonstrating, guiding practice, and moving
students toward independent practice of reading skills should be used for
the auditory preskills and again when students are prepared to read
words, sentences, and stories using phonetic analysis.*

4. **Formative assessment: How do you know that Nicole has
learned it?** *Nicole's teacher should consistently monitor knowledge and
retention of the skills taught. Students in beginning reading should be
monitored at least twice per week using CBM. For Nicole, reading pas-
sages (the most frequently seen CBM for reading) is not appropriate because passage reading is not yet in her repertoire. The measures used in
CBM must reflect the instructional goals. At this point, Nicole should be
monitored in letter/sounds knowledge and phonemic awareness. Because
the teacher established a goal for the students to quickly identify all 26
lowercase letters/sounds by the end of the school year, that is exactly what
should be evaluated. In the procedure for monitoring using CBM, the
teacher should develop 12–15 different pages with all 26 randomly written lowercase letters/sounds on each paper. Sample teacher directions,
student materials, scoring procedures, and graphs of student performance are provided in Appendix A at the end of this chapter.*

Case Example B: Language Arts

*Jason was 14 years old when he was injured while riding his dirt bike
without a helmet in a lot behind his home. He apparently lost control of
his bike and ran into a tree. His injuries included frontal basilar skull
fractures and right temporal contusions. Jason was in coma for approximately 1 week. He was hospitalized for a total of 7 weeks.*

1. **Initial assessment: What does Jason know now?** *Jason was a
below-average student prior to his injury. He attended school sporadi-
cally, earned poor grades, and was in trouble with the law. After his
injury, he had significant cognitive impairments, including difficulties*

Teacher Says	Student response	Correct?	Sounds Correct
fat	/a/ /t/	-	~~1~~ 2 3
bet	/b/	-	1 ~~2~~ ~~3~~
sill	/ll/	-	~~1~~ ~~2~~ 3
putt	no response	-	~~1~~ ~~2~~ ~~3~~
ton	no response	-	~~1~~ ~~2~~ ~~3~~
can	no response	-	~~1~~ ~~2~~ ~~3~~
		Total Correct	4

Figure 9.   An example of a diagnostic assessment of auditory word recognition—Segmenting of a 7-
year-old girl with ABI. (+ = correct; - = incorrect.)

it	-	cat		must		flag		stamp	
am	-	him		hats		step		strap	
if	-	hot		hand		drop		split	
sam	-	tag		last		skin		skunk	
mad	-								

Figure 10.   An example of a diagnostic assessment of word reading of a 7-year-old girl with ABI. (- = incorrect.) (Testing was stopped due to five consecutive errors, lack of success. The items are hierarchically ordered [easy to hard]. If the student cannot complete the easier tasks, the probability is he or she will be unable to complete the more difficult tasks.)

sustaining attention, severe memory problems, and a very limited ability to learn new information. In the hospital, Jason became easily frustrated and aggressive when asked to work on academic tasks. Hospital staff tended to avoid academic tasks that provoked aggressive behavior; therefore, most of his therapy focused on physical and daily living skills. Now a 16-year-old sophomore, Jason scores at the following grade levels on standardized assessments conducted by the school psychologist: reading: 5.2 GE; math: 6.9 GE; and written language: 3.4 GE.

The GE scores provided by the school psychologist give a general picture of Jason's academic skills. Jason's written language skills are especially low. It is difficult to determine whether Jason's low language skills are a result of his accident or his poor educational history. As with all students with disabilities, the cause of the impairment is less important than the remediation. The teacher must evaluate current performance and determine the best educational remedy. His teacher's first goal was to determine what additional areas should be diagnostically assessed.

The teacher administered several diagnostic assessments to specifically evaluate Jason's language arts skills. These included a spelling dictation measure that contained words representing several specific word types: phonetically regular words, high-frequency irregular words, and rule-based words (see Figure 11).

To measure functional expressive writing, the teacher asked Jason to write a note to his parents telling them where he went after school. Simultaneously, the teacher evaluated Jason's handwriting fluency to develop an instructional plan that would best address his specific needs (see Figure 11). Jason was timed for 14 minutes to complete writing this note.

Diagnostic test results indicated that Jason's spelling needed substantial remediation. He could spell some regular consonant-vowel-consonant (CVC) words (e.g., map, shot, pen), his name, and a few short high-frequency irregular words (e.g., some, many). However, the majority of words on the measure were spelled incorrectly. Based on these diagnostic measures, Jason demonstrated difficulty with the use of vowel sounds (both long and short), did not know many high-frequency (irreg-

Phonetically regular words		High-frequency words (Irregular)		Rule-based words	
Dictated word	Jason's response	Dictated word	Jason's response	Dictated word	Jason's response
run	run	*was*	whaz	*lake*	leck
m e	m i	*to*	tue	*lunch*	leontch
fat	feat	*said*	sd	*cent*	siendt
most	nushth	*you*	weww	*mean*	mnnien
seven	sifen	*friends*	verinzd	*tipped*	no response

Figure 11.   An example of a diagnostic assessment of Jason, a 16-year-old with ABI.

ular) words, and had great difficulty with any rule-based word. Although Jason's sentence structure was less than satisfactory, the primary reason his sentences were hard to read was his poor spelling.

From her experience with Jason in the classroom, Jason's teacher knew that he was unable to write cogent notes using complete sentences or understandable spelling. Jason labored over writing the simplest of notes (as seen in Figure 12). Although his notes were neat (legible), the sentence structure and spelling were so poor that even Jason was unable to read the message not long after writing it. Jason and his parents expressed this frustration to the teacher. In addition, the teacher discussed the functional writing skills students need at Jason's age. The priority skills identified by Jason, his teacher, and his parents included writing simple notes, completing application forms, and basic note taking. They decided that assessment and instruction in expressive writing (writing stories) were unnecessary for a student his age.

2.   Instructional design: What does Jason need to learn? *Well-designed diagnostic tests yield specific information that guides the design of efficient instruction. Results from Jason's diagnostic assessment showed that he had difficulty with basic spelling of phonetically regular and high-frequency words. Jason will also require frequent and continual practice of common irregular words (e.g., many, said, friend, was). Learning these irregular words is a memorization task. Jason must order the specific letters in words and recall the spelling, exactly. Each of these word types requires specific instructional planning. Finally, Jason should be taught some basic rules for word spelling (e.g., final e, words ending in y, doubling consonants with word endings).*

In the case of handwriting, the teacher determined that fluency practice would improve Jason's ability to communicate using written text. If Jason increases his handwriting rate and word spelling accuracy, his ability to write short letters, take class notes, and meet other basic writing tasks will significantly improve.

3.   Instructional delivery: How do you teach what Jason needs to learn? *Given Jason's skill limitations, age, and placement in middle*

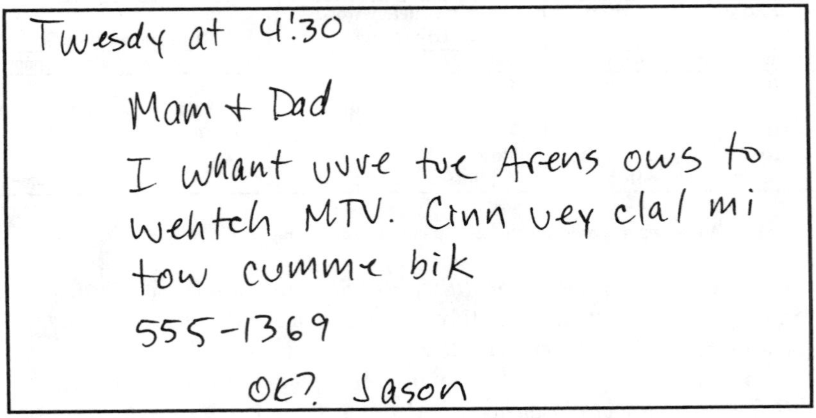
Twesdy at 4:30
Mam + Dad
I whant uvve tue Arens ows to wehtch MTV. Cinn vey clal mi tow cumme bik
555-1369
OK? Jason

Figure 12. An example of a fluency measure of Jason, a 16-year-old with ABI.

school, it is probably most appropriate to teach him in a tutorial rather than a group setting. Jason's goal is to be able to accurately and fluently write notes to his parents, teachers, and friends. He also wants to be able to complete forms (e.g., job applications) with correct spelling and in a reasonable amount of time. There are several critical skill areas that should be the focus of Jason's language arts instruction for him to be successful in and beyond school.

First, Jason needs to consistently write the correct symbols for the letters he hears in words, beginning with vowels and letters used frequently in his writing (e.g., a, m, s, e, d, r, f, o*). Instruction needs to systematically introduce letters, vowels, and consonants. Jason needs to state and write the letters for the sounds he hears dictated to him. For example, the teacher might say, "Listen, aaaa, write the letter for the sound aaa." [pause]. "What letter did you write? Here's a new sound, mmm. Write the letter for the sound mmm. [pause]. What letter did you write?" Jason should be allowed to hear the sound for the letter or the word dictated several times. Simultaneously, Jason should be taught to listen for letters in words to support the phonic spelling used in so many words (Dixon, 1993). This can be taught much like the exercise teaching auditory sounds for words described for Nicole previously.*

Once Jason is able to demonstrate consistent writing of letters dictated and can accurately hear and say the sounds in simple words, the teacher may begin word dictation, that is basic spelling. The teacher would then demonstrate and provide guided and independent practice for Jason with more complex, yet still frequently used words. There are several spelling programs using effective, explicit teaching practices recommended for students like Jason (see Appendix C at the end of this chapter for a list of recommended materials in spelling).

The teacher must also provide Jason with practice in written fluency. There are several options:

- *Have Jason write letters he knows how to write. He should not be pressured to write neatly or rapidly. The goal of this exercise is for Jason to write the same letter as many times as he can in an allotted time to build fluency.*
- *Write simple sentences multiple times on paper. Jason should copy each sentence as many times as he can without having to create sentences.*
- *Write a known word (i.e., a word spelled consistently and successfully) multiple times. This may be his name. Again, he should not be pressured to write neatly or rapidly. The goal is for Jason to write the same word as many times as he can in an allotted time.*

4. **Formative assessment: How do you know that Jason has learned it?** *The authors recommend progress monitoring using CBMs for students in language arts as well. The measures for such a diverse area of skills reflect the range of language arts tasks. For Jason, the instructional emphasis is on spelling and writing fluency. The measures to monitor his progress should reflect this instruction.*

In spelling, the teacher and Jason should determine what specific words and word types he should know at the end of the school year (or within some allocated time frame). These words should be randomly put into lists of 15 words each. During monitoring, the teacher will first dictate words and then allow Jason a set period of time to write the word, repeating the process until all 15 words have been dictated (see Appendix A at the end of this chapter for example measures, teacher directions, and scoring guidelines).

Any of the three fluency practice procedures described previously could be formalized with standard directions and a time allocation and be used to monitor progress in this area. The score would reflect the number of words or characters written in the time allowed. In addition, the teacher could establish rubrics to qualitatively evaluate handwriting legibility. The instructional interventions should be monitored bimonthly or weekly to provide the teacher with sufficient information to evaluate the effects of instruction and to make decisions about instruction using valid data. Writing narrative stories is not a goal for Jason. The traditional measure for progress monitoring in language arts is not appropriate. Nevertheless, there are fluency measures that can be administered to evaluate progress in Jason's legibility and written fluency (see Appendix A at the end of this chapter).

Case Example C: Mathematics

Sara, a 10-year-old fourth grader, was injured as an infant as a result of physical abuse. Her biological father shook her repeatedly when she was approximately 4 months old. Records of Sara's hospitalization are not available, but her mother reports that Sara was hospitalized twice before the age of 1.

1. Initial assessment: What does Sara know now? *Because Sara was injured as an infant, the initial assessment does not provide information about her hospitalization or pre- and postinjury status. Sara's development has been slow throughout childhood. She has visual impairments, difficulty in balance and gait, and poor fine motor coordination. Sara spends all day in the fourth-grade classroom and has a one-to-one instructional assistant who provides most of her instruction. Sara scored at the second-grade level in reading (2.1 GE) and at the first-grade level in both math (1.2 GE) and language (1.8 GE).*

Because math skills are diverse and complex, Sara's teacher and assistant need to have specific information about what she can and cannot accurately do. Diagnostic testing should include assessment in the following math skills: numeral identification, number value, rote and rationale counting, addition and subtraction facts, computation, and problem solving (see the "Component 2: Instructional Design" section in this chapter). Several examples of diagnostic assessments are provided in Appendix A at the end of this chapter, and Figure 13 provides an example of a beginning math diagnostic assessment that would be useful for Sara).

For all visual tasks in this case, the teacher should write in print large enough for Sara to see easily. The teacher should repeat all auditory tasks as often as necessary in order to test her academic skills, not her memory. As Sara reads each number, the teacher should note what she says rather than merely marking the number correct or incorrect. If Sara is able to complete with some success the above-mentioned tasks, the next area of diagnostic assessment would be facts and computation. Finally, problem-solving tasks using basic computation could be administered orally or in a written format.

2. Instructional design: What does Sara need to learn? *Based on the diagnostic assessment tests, it was known that Sara could count to 25 without error, but beyond 25 she was unable to make transitions (e.g., 29–30, 39–40). She also had some difficulty with keeping track of where she was in the counting scheme, occasionally cycling back through numbers she had already said. Sara demonstrated good rational counting skills for all single-digit numerals. She was able to write numerals for the*

Skill	Task	How to assess	Notes
Numeral identification	Randomly read single- and multiple-digit numerals.	Ask the student to read numerals and the teacher notes what the student said.	Attend to types of correct and incorrect responses, particularly for regular and irregular numbers (e.g., 15, we don't say five-teen; 20, we don't say two-ty).
Rote counting	Ask the student to start with 1 and count until you say stop.	Have a paper with the numbers 1–100 written on it. Slash any errors.	Listen particularly for transitions (e.g., 29–30, 40–50) and the pronunciation of irregular numbers (e.g., 11, 13).
Numeral writing	Dictate randomly. Include single- and mutliple-digit numerals.	Dictate each numeral twice and have the student repeat the numeral and then write it.	Score only correctly written numerals, no mirrored or inverted symbols.
Number value	Using known numerals, draw or clap the number of times necessary.	Teacher draws shapes, lines, or objects. Have the student count and write the numeral.	Use numerals the student can identify and write.
Rationale counting	Give the student objects to touch and count.	Observe the student closely to see if student touches and counts items correctly.	Consider correct only if student touches and counts correctly **and** ends up with the correct answer.
Addition and subtraction facts	Randomly place + and – facts on worksheet. Allow 2–5 minutes to complete.	Determine time allotment. Tell student to watch signs (+ or –), or separate the problem types and evaluate them at different times.	Rate and accuracy should be evaluated.
Addition and subtraction computation	Sequence easy to more difficult, multiple-digit + and – problems on worksheet. Allow 2–5 minutes to complete.	Determine time allotment. Tell student to watch signs (+ or –).	Rate and accuracy should be evaluated. Correct digits as well as correct answer can be evaluated.
Problem solving	Provide story problems either to read to the student or to have the student read and solve the problems on his or her own.	Provide paper with story problems. Include plenty of space between items for student to calculate and write response.	If the student has any difficulty reading, read to them to assess math skills. Also, ask the student to write his or her work and answers down for diagnosis.

Figure 13.   An example of a beginning math diagnostic assessment that would be useful for Sara, a 10-year-old with ABI.

digits 0–9 and write from dictation all single-digit numbers. Multiple-digit numerals were not accurately read or written.

In computation, Sara was able to add basic facts with good speed and accuracy. She was unable to correctly add any multiple-digit numerals (e.g., 24 + 3) or complete any type of subtraction problem. Sara was unable to complete any problem-solving tasks.

The diagnostic procedures listed previously for Sara are hierarchically organized. Thus, instructional implications are to begin teaching skills where gaps or incorrect answers appear in the assessment. In this case, Sara needs instruction in higher number rote counting, followed by higher numeral identification and writing. She also needs to learn strategies for computation and problem solving in addition and eventually subtraction. A scope and sequence for an introduction of mathematics skills is available in many basal math series. Recommended reading materials are listed in Appendix C at the end of this chapter.

3.   Instructional delivery: How do you teach what Sara needs to learn? *Students with ABI generally function well with strategy-based instruction that is both consistent and structured (Cohen, Joyce, Rhodes, & Welks, 1985). The content of math instruction lends itself particularly well to this type of structure. An instructional process that has been shown to be effective in teaching math to students with learning problems consists of five basic steps that follow (Good & Grouws, 1979):*

- **Daily review**   *The lesson begins with a "warm up" exercise that consists of previously taught skills.*

- **New skill introduction**   *Demonstrate new skill, focus on strategy to complete task, and provide systematic, controlled practice of the skill.*

- **Active practice**   *Student should actively practice skills, guided by teacher questions, to prompt use of the strategy.*

- **Systematic feedback**   *Systematic feedback (specific praise and corrective) should be provided, which helps reinforce the strategy for working versus merely providing students with the answer.*

- **Cumulative review**   *Cumulative review guided and independent practice should be demonstrated that is carefully monitored by the teacher for accuracy.*

4.   Formative assessment: How do you know that Sara has learned it? *In math, as with reading and language arts, frequent progress monitoring of student skills is also essential. For Sara, there are three basic areas to measure: rote and rationale counting skills, numeral identification, and math computation. Progress monitoring for these skills would be similar to the diagnostic test presented previously. A sam-*

ple assessment worksheet, teacher directions, and scoring procedures are included in Appendix A at the end of this chapter.

The teacher should measure student progress one to two times per week. Obtained scores should be graphed on a chart for Sara for each area assessed. If progress toward the goal is adequate, the teacher should continue instruction. If progress is higher than the goal, the teacher should design more challenging instruction. If progress is inadequate, the teacher should change instruction, teach math twice per day, provide extra practice, or modify instructional strategies.

Students with ABI, such as the ones described in these case examples, may be included in general education classes for some or all of their school day. Their instruction will include basic academic as well as content area subjects (e.g., science, social studies, health). In the following section, strategies that can help students with ABI have more successful experiences in these settings are presented.

CONTENT AREA INSTRUCTIONAL STRATEGIES

Students in elementary, middle, and high school grades are generally required to take certain content area classes, and students with ABI are often fully included in these classes. The student with ABI, however, may not have the necessary reading, math, language, or comprehension skills to participate fully or progress at the same rate as other students. Table 1 illustrates typical challenges faced by students with ABI in school settings and suggested modifications. In addition, teaching in the content areas may require that the teacher modify or adapt the material in order to meet the specific needs of the student with ABI. Some modifications demand that an entirely different approach to the material be developed. These types of modifications may be difficult to implement in the general education classroom. This section addresses ways to modify or adapt content area curriculum for implementation in the general education classroom. This does not imply, however, that these are the only ways to adapt curricula for students with ABI. The authors have selected strategies that have the greatest utility for implementation in the general education classroom.

Visual-Spatial Displays

The extent to which a learner understands an entire topic is directly related to how well he or she understands the individual facts and their relationship to the topic. Visual-spatial displays (also called graphic organizers, concept maps, and concept webs) provide a

Table 1.   Typical challenges faced by students with ABI in school settings.

Student challenge	Selected modification
Mary has difficulty remembering her assignments.	Use organization/memory notebook.
Kyle is easily fatigued during social studies. He likes social studies, but he just gets tired.	The teacher will meet with Kyle to discuss how long he can keep working at a particular task. From that information, the teacher and Kyle will develop a cuing system to indicate when Kyle should take a break. Shorter work periods that gradually increase may help reduce overall fatigue.
Karen is highly distractible. She glances around the classroom at regular intervals to "check-out" who is doing what.	The teacher should review seating arrangement. There may be a better location for her independent work station. The teacher could also increase interaction rates during instruction. A self-monitoring system could also be established to help Karen stay on task.
When asked a question for which Juan does not have an immediate answer, he will say "I don't know."	The teacher should prompt Juan to say, "I don't recall," instead of "I don't know." Then the teacher should establish a set of learning strategies that help Juan use recall aids (e.g., memory notebook, alphabet search, computer). Then when he says, "I don't recall," the phrase will prompt him to use his recall aids. Eventually, Juan will say, "I don't recall, but give me a minute."
Sara, who is in fifth grade, has learned that if she waits long enough, someone (e.g., teacher, friend, parent, classmate) will help her. For example, if she does not have a pencil, someone will get her a pencil. If she does not say the math fact, a classmate will tell her. If she does not get her lunchbox, her friend will get it for her. Sara is quite capable of performing these activities.	The teacher needs to talk with Sara about how she has learned to wait for other people to do her work. The teacher needs to teach Sara to say, "I want to do it for myself, please." Then the teacher needs to set up occasions for Sara to use her phrase and do the activity. For example, the teacher should pass out math worksheets to everyone but Sara. It is predictable that a classmate will tell the teacher that Sara needs a worksheet. Therefore, right after the classmate tells the teacher about Sara's need, the teacher should prompt (if necessary) Sara to say her phrase ("I want to do it for myself, please"). The teacher would merely ask, "What do you want, Sara?" to which Sara would reply, "A math worksheet." Other similar situations should be contrived. The teacher should not have to discuss the situations with the classmates. This way they are being taught by Sara that she is capable.

(continued)

Table 1. *(continued)*

Student challenge	Selected modification
Terry has the opposite problem from Sara. He thinks he can do all the same things that he could before. His actual performance levels, however, are very different from his preinjury levels. He used to be a very good math student. Terry was particularly good at doing mental calculations. He was in all of the advanced levels of math in his high school. Now, however, he needs to use a calculator to perform basic division problems. He refuses to use the calculator. Thus, he is failing his math class. He, however, thinks he is doing "just fine."	Terry needs to learn two things: the difference between his preinjury and postinjury status and how to ask for help. The teacher should set up a daily report card with a performance rating scale of 1, 2, 3, 4, 5. For each item, the teacher should rate Terry's performance and Terry should rate his own performance. If there is a match, then some tangible, highly sought after item should be awarded. If there is not a match, then Terry should be told why the ratings are different. An item might be: How well did you do on today's math quiz? If Terry rates himself high and the teacher rates him low, then the teacher needs to say, "You missed the math calculations because you didn't use your calculator." Terry needs to first recognize the poor math performance and then be told how he can improve. Terry is not making connections with his present performance. Once he begins noticing what he needs help with, his performance will improve. Next, he needs to learn to ask for help. Specific counseling or guidance is needed to help him learn to be comfortable with this skill. The teacher, however, should reinforce Terry each time he asks for help. The reinforcement may be very quiet but very sincere.

graphic framework for inducing this relationship. The spatial arrangement and shape of the cells that compose the graphic framework provide visual prompts to aid recall of the information. For students with ABI, the teacher should also carefully select key words that will assist the student in recalling the critical relationships and labeling each cell accordingly. Teachers create a script that accompanies the visual-spatial display and instruct the students to point to the elements of the display and say the exact words for each cell. After having been instructed with the visual-spatial display with exact words on the display, the students are asked to state the exact words for each cell from a version of the visual-spatial display that is missing the words. Once the students develop accuracy in recalling the information from a visual-spatial display without words, then they are asked questions about the topic by playing a cooperative learning game using the same blank cell version of the display.

Appendix D illustrates the use of a visual-spatial display to teach basic facts about landforms. Note the relationship of facts, teachers' scripted lesson, filled-cell to blank-cell chart, and game format.

Textbook Organizers

Shumaker and McKnight (1989) developed a routine referred to by the acronym TRIMS to help organize textbook materials. By using the organizational structure contained in the text (e.g., titles, headings, signal words), the teacher can help the students recall and understand complicated material. When the teacher introduces the text, chapter, or section, he or she should guide the students through identifying the key organizational elements or TRIMS: 1) **T**itle, 2) **R**elationships, 3) **I**ntroduction, 4) **M**ain parts, and 5) **S**ummary. The following steps illustrate the TRIMS instructional procedure using a chapter of a book:

1. Ask a student to read the title of the chapter.
2. Ask students to find the table of contents.
3. Using the table of contents, ask students to state the relationship among the previous chapter, the current chapter, and the next chapter.
4. Have the students read the introduction to the chapter and paraphrase what the introduction says.
5. Have students identify the major topics of the chapter. As students identify, the teacher should create an outline on the board depicting the organization of these topics.
6. Have the students identify key words or concepts associated with each major topic. Using the major topic outline on the board the teacher should write the information that the students identify.
7. Have students read the chapter summary and paraphrase what it says.

After using this procedure, the students should copy the outline from the board into their notebooks. If there is a reading assignment, the students should be encouraged to use their outlines and fill in more information.

Study Guides

Two types of study guides have been demonstrated to be effective with students who have ABI. Both types use a missing item format. The first type uses a guide with graphics or diagrams with parts of the picture or labels missing so that students can fill in the missing items. The second type uses questions from main concepts and vocabulary words so that the student must answer the questions or define the vocabulary words. Beregerud, Lovitt, and Horton (1988) found that either type works far better than self-study alone.

Peer-Tutoring or Peer-Assisted Assignment Completion

Research on the effects of students working together indicates that peers can greatly facilitate content learning (Lenz & Bulgren, 1995). Peer tutoring, peer assistance, cooperative learning groups, and student learning teams can be established to help teachers promote achievement for students with ABI. The key ingredient to the use of peers is training. If a peer is to be a tutor or an assistant, he or she needs to be fluent in the content material and understand the way to transmit the information. When using cooperative learning groups or student learning teams, the teacher must make clear that all students must participate in the activity. Cooperative learning or student learning teams should not be used to introduce content area, but instead should be used to expand and explore content that has already been introduced.

CONCLUSION

The overmedicalization of the field of ABI has in some ways prevented teachers from effectively teaching students with brain injuries. Focus on type, location, and severity of injury to determine student cognitive strengths and weaknesses has too often distracted educators from implementing instructional strategies that have been proven effective with students with ABI and other disabilities. This chapter and the appendices provide teachers with practical and proven strategies that promote learning for all students, including those with significant challenges such as those with ABI.

The assessment-instruction model illustrates the dynamic features involved in the learning processes. By performing an initial assessment, collecting ongoing information, designing effective instructional sequences and lessons, and employing empirically validated delivery techniques, the teacher will have the tools to make a difference for students with ABI.

Although this approach is highly effective for instruction in basic skills and concepts, students with ABI in content area courses often need other strategies to help them manage complex material. Visual-spatial displays, textbook organizers, study guides, and peer tutoring are some approaches that can help mediate memory and organizational challenges of students with ABI. However, just as the assessment-instruction model is a proven, effective approach to teaching all students, the content strategies discussed in this chapter can and should be available to all students, not just those who have disabilities. Teachers who use the assessment, instructional design, and instructional delivery principles presented here do so to the benefit of all learners in their classrooms.

REFERENCES

Adams, G., & Engelmann, S. (1996). *Research on direct instruction: 25 years beyond DISTAR.* Seattle, WA: Educational Achievement Systems.

Adams, R.L. (1993, October). *Creating thoughtful classrooms.* Paper presented at the Washington Organization for Reading Development Conference, Seattle.

Archer, A., Isaacson, S., Adams, A., Ellis, E., Morehead, J.K., & Schiller, E.P. (1989). *Academy for effective instruction: Working with mildly handicapped students.* Reston, VA: The Council for Exceptional Children.

Archer, A.L., Gleason, M.M., & Isaacson, S. (1995). Effective instructional delivery. In P.T. Cegelka & W.H. Berdine (Eds.), *Effective instruction for students with learning difficulties* (pp. 161–193). Needham, MA: Allyn & Bacon.

Arter, J.A., & Jenkins, J.R. (1977). Examining the benefits and prevalence of modality considerations in special education. *Journal of Special Education, 11,* 281–298.

Becker, W.C. (1986). *Applied psychology for teachers* (Rev. ed.). Chicago: Science Research Associates.

Becker, W.C. (1992). Direct instruction: A twenty year review. In R.P. West & L.A. Hamerlynck (Eds.), *Designs for excellence in education: The legacy of B.F. Skinner* (pp. 71–112). Longmont, CO: Sopris West.

Beregerud, D., Lovitt, T.C., & Horton, S. (1988). The effectiveness of textbook adaptations in life science for high school students with learning disabilities. *Journal of Learning Disabilities, 21*(2), 70–76.

Berliner, D.C. (1984). The half-full glass: A review of research on teaching. In P.L. Hosford (Ed.), *Using what we know about teaching* (pp. 51–77). Alexandria, VA: Association of Supervision and Curriculum Development.

Butters, M.S., & Glisky, E.L. (1993). Transfer of new learning in memory-impaired patients. *Journal of Clinical and Experimental Neuropsychology, 15*(2), 219–230.

Carnine, D.W. (1976). Effects of two teacher-presentation rates on off-task behavior, answering correctly, and participation. *Journal of Applied Behavior Anaylsis, 9*(2), 199–206.

Carnine, D.W. (1980). Three procedures for presenting minimally different positive and negative instances. *Journal of Educational Psychology, 72,* 452–456.

Carnine, D.W., Silbert, J., & Kameenui, E.J. (1990). *Direct instruction reading* (2nd ed.). Columbus, OH: Charles E. Merrill.

Cegelka, P.T., & W.H. Berdine, W.H. (Eds.). (1995). *Effective instruction for students with learning difficulties.* Needham, MA: Allyn & Bacon.

Chard, D.J., Simmons, D.C., & Kameenui, E.J. (1995). *Word recognition: Curricular and instructional implications for diverse learners.* Technical

Report No. 16, National Center to Improve the Tools of Educators: University of Oregon, Eugene.

Christenson, S.L., Ysseldyke, J.E., & Thurlow, M.L. (1989). Critical instructional factors for students with mild handicaps: An integrative review. *Remedial and Special Education, 10*(5), 21–31.

Cohen, S., Joyce, C., Rhoades, K., & Welks, D. (1985). Educational programming for head injured students. In M. Ylvisaker, (Ed.), *Head injury rehabilitation: Children and adolescents* (pp. 383–409). Austin, TX: PRO-ED.

Connolly, A. (1988). *Key Math–Revised: A diagnostic inventory of essential mathematics.* Circle Pines, MN: American Guidance Service.

Connolly, A., Nachtman, W.M., & Pritchett, E. (1971). *The Key Math Diagnostic Arithmetic Test.* Circle Pines, MN: American Guidance Service.

Connolly, A., Nachtman, W.M., & Pritchett, E. (1976). *Manual for the Key Math Diagnostic Arithmetic Test.* Circle Pines, MN: American Guidance Service.

CTB/Macmillan/McGraw-Hill. (1993). *California Achievement Tests/5.* Monterey, CA: Author.

Deno, S.L. (1985). Curriculum-based measurement: The emerging alternative. *Exceptional Children, 52*(3), 219–232.

Deno, S.L., Marston, D., & Tindal, G. (1985/1986). Direct and frequent curriculum-based measurement: An alternative for educational decision making. *Special Services in the Schools, 2*(2/3), 5–27.

Dixon, R.C. (1993).*The surefire way to better spelling.* New York: St. Martin's Press.

Ellis, E.S., & Worthington, L.A. (1995). *Research synthesis on effective teaching principles and the design of quality tools for education.* (Tech. Rep. No. 5). Eugene: University of Oregon, National Center to Improve the Tools of Educators.

Engelmann, S., & Carnine, D.W. (1982). *Theory of instruction: Principles and applications.* New York: Irvington.

Englert, C.S. (1984). Effective direct instruction practices in special education settings. *Remedial and Special Education, 5*(2), 38–47.

Feeney, T.J., & Ylvisaker, M. (1995). Choice and routine: Antecedent behavioral interventions for adolescents with severe traumatic brain injury. *Journal of Head Trauma Rehabilitation, 10*(3), 67–86.

Fuchs, L.S., Fuchs, D., & Hamlett, C. (1989). Effects of instrumental use of curriculum-based measurement to enhance instructional programs. *Remedial and Special Education, 19*(2), 43–52.

Gersten, R., Carnine, D., & Williams, P. (1982). Measuring implementation of a structured educational model in an urban setting: An observational approach. *Educational Evaluation and Policy Analysis, 4,* 67–79.

Glang, A., Singer, G., Cooley, E., & Tish, N. (1992). Tailoring direct instruction techniques for use with elementary students with brain injury. *Journal of Head Trauma Rehabilitation, 7*(4), 93–108.

Good, T.L., & Grouws, D.A. (1979). The Missouri mathematics effectiveness project: An experimental study in fourth-grade classrooms. *Journal of Educational Psychology, 71,* 355–362.

Gray, W.S., & Robinson, H.M. (1978). *Gray Oral Reading Test.* Indianapolis: Bobbs-Merrill.

Hieronmus, A.N., Hoover, H.D., & Lindquist, E.F. (1986). *Iowa Test of Basic Skills.* Chicago: Riverside.

Hoffmeister, A.M., & Lubke, M. (1990). *Research into practice: Implementing effective teaching strategies.* Needham, MA: Allyn & Bacon.

Hudson, P., Lignugaris-Kraft, B., & Miller, T. (1993). Using content enhancements to improve the performance of adolescents with learning disabilities in content classes. *Learning Disabilities Research and Practice, 8*(2) 106–126.

Kameenui, E.J., & Simmons, D.J. (1990). *Designing instructional strategies: The prevention of academic learning problems.* Columbus, OH: Charles E. Merrill.

Koegel, L.K., & Koegel, R.L. (1986). The effects of interspersed maintenance tasks on academic performance in a severe childhood stroke victim. *Journal of Applied Behavior Analysis, 19,* 425–430.

Koegel, R.L., Dunlap, G., & Dyer, D. (1980). Intertrial interval duration and learning in autistic children. *Journal of Applied Behavior Analysis, 13*(1), 91–99.

Lash, M., & Scarpino, C. (1993). School reintegration for children with traumatic brain injuries: Conflicts between medical education settings. *Neuro Rehabilitation, 3*(3), 13–25.

Lehr, E., & Lantz, J.A. (1990). Behavioral components. In E. Lehr (Ed.), *Psychological management of traumatic brain injuries in children and adolescents* (pp. 133–153). Rockville, MD: Aspen Publishers, Inc.

Lenz, B.K., & Bulgren, J.A. (1995). Promoting learning in content classes. In P.T. Cegelka & W.H. Berdine (Eds.), *Effective instruction for students with learning difficulties* (pp. 385–417). Needham, MA: Allyn & Bacon.

Rosenshine, B., & Stevens, R. (1986). Teaching functions. In M.C. Wittrock (Ed.), *Handbook of research on teaching* (3rd ed., pp. 376–391). Chicago: Rand.

Savage, R.C., & Carter, R.R. (1991). Family and return to school. In J.M. Williams & T. Kay (Eds.), *Head injury: A family matter* (pp. 203–216). Baltimore: Paul H. Brookes Publishing Co.

Shumaker, J.B., & McKnight, P. (1989). *Teaching routines to enhance the mainstream performance of adolescents with learning disabilities.* Final report submitted to the U.S. Department of Education, Special Education Services, Washington, DC.

Shurtleff, H.A., Massageli, T.S., Hays, R.M., Ross, B.R., & Sprunk-Greenfield, H. (1995). Screening children and adolescents with mild or moderate traumatic brain injury to assist school reentry. *Journal of Head Trauma Rehabilitation, 10*(5), 64–79.

Swanson, H.L., & Watson, B. (1982). *Educational and psychological assessment of exceptional children: Theories, strategies, and applications.* St. Louis: C.V. Mosby.

Tindal, G.A., & Marston, D.B. (1990). *Classroom-based assessment: Evaluating student outcomes.* Columbus, OH: Charles E. Merrill.

Wiederholt, L., & Bryant, B. (1992). *Examiner's manual: Gray Oral Reading Tests–3.* Austin, TX: PRO-ED.

Wilkinson, G. (1993). *Wide Range Achievement Test–Revised.* Wilmington, DE: Jastak Associates.

Woodcock, R.W. (1989). *Woodcock-Johnson Psycho-Educational Battery.* Hingham, MA: Teaching Resources.

Ysseldyke, J.E. (1973). Diagnostic prescriptive teaching: The search for aptitude-treatment interactions. In L. Mann & D. Sabatino (Eds.), *The first review of special education* (pp. 181–186). Philadelphia: JSE Press.

Recommended Diagnostic Assessments in Reading, Spelling, Writing, and Mathematics

READING

Sounds

Student protocol	Teacher directions	Scoring
a d f g k l w i x o p w r z t h u y e v m q x c n b e i w o q p c a s i t y o c x n y u	Tell me the sound each letter makes, if you don't know the letter say "I don't know" and go to the next one. It's okay if you don't know a letter, I will teach it to you later. Try to tell me as many sounds for the letters as you can and I will tell you when to stop. Stop the student after exactly 1 minute.	As the student says the sounds, circle the correct responses and slash the incorrect responses or the no responses. Count the number of each marking and chart.

Phonemic Awareness

Student protocol	Teacher directions	Scoring
Say it fast: Teacher Student ssaamm _____ (sam) llaasst _____ (last) sslleep _____ (sleep) **Say the sounds:** Teacher Student mat _____ (mmaat) pig _____ (piiig) rim _____ (rriimm)	**Say it fast:** When I say the sounds, like rraat, can you tell me the word? *If the student does not respond* say, "The sounds rraat blend together to say *rat.* Now, you try the next one." *If student responds correctly, say,* "Great, here are some more sounds. Tell me the words." **Say the sounds:** When I say sad, can you say each sound you hear in the word? *If the student does not respond* say, "the sounds in sad are /s/ /a/ and /d/. Now, you try the next one." *If the student responds correctly, say,* "Great. Here are some more words. Tell me the sounds you hear." There is *no* time limit on either measure for phonemic awareness.	**Say it fast:** There are two scores for this measure. 1. Count the number of words said correctly. 2. Count the number of sounds in the response that the student said correctly. **Say the sounds:** There are two scores for this measure. 1. Count the number of sounds said correctly in each word. 2. Count the number of total correct responses.

(continued)

Passage Reading

Student protocol

During the summer a	4
thick, green scum covers	8
part of a pond. This scum	14
is so thick, you cannot see	20
through it. Pond scum is	25
actually chains and chains	29
of plant-like cells. These	34
cells contain little green	38
bits called chloroplasts.	41
The chloroplasts are coil-	45
shaped. They give the	49
pond scum its distinctive	53
color and also help	57
generate food.	59

Teacher directions

When I say begin, start reading out loud at the top of this page. (Point to first word.) Show me your best reading. Keep on reading until I say stop. If you come to a word you don't know, I'll tell it to you. Remember to try your best. Do you have any questions? (Pause.) Begin.

Stop the student after exactly 1 minute.

Scoring

Follow along as the student reads. Slash any word reading error and word you tell the student.

Stop and thank the student after 1 minute.

Count the total number of words read. Count the number of errors. Subtract the errors (slashed words) from the total words read to obtain the score of correct words read per minute.

Student: *Sheri* Gr/Age: *2* Sch: *M* Tch: Area: *Oral Reading Fluency*

Number

100
90
80
70
60
50
40
30
20
10

Date	9/23	9/27	9/30	10/2	10/5	10/11
M		✓				
T				✓		
W						
Th	✓		✓			✓
F					✓	

Number of Words Read Correctly   x   Number of Error Words   O

164

SPELLING

Letter Dictation

Student protocol	Teacher directions	Scoring procedures
Paper with numbered boxes should be provided for student to write letters, including spaces for the name and date. Dictate letters that the student can identify by sound or name and ask the student to write it on his or her paper.	Listen as I say letters you know how to read. When I say the letter, you write it on your paper. I will say the letter three times and you will have time to write the letter on your paper. When I say a new letter you need to write that letter. I cannot go back to old letters, so listen carefully.

Dictate letters that the student can identify by sound or name. | Teacher would count correctly written letters as correct and no letter written, an incorrect letter, or a nonidentifiable letter as incorrect. The teacher should count the number of correctly written letters. Letters written as mirrors or upside down should be marked as incorrect. |

Word Dictation

Student protocol	Teacher directions	Scoring procedures
Student writes spelling words dictated from a preplanned list. Student should have a lined paper for writing the words. Sixteen to eighteen words are dictated.	The teacher should explain the dictation procedure. Each word is stated three times. First, the word is said, then the word is said in a phrase, and finally the word is said by itself again. The words are dictated every 8–10 seconds.	Rather than count a word as all correct or entirely incorrect, correct letter sequences (CLS) are counted. These are pairs of letters that are in the correct order. For example, if the student spells the word **myself** "miself," the correct letter sequence would be 5. Note the correct scoring marks below:

^m^y^s^e^l^f = 6CLS

^mis^e^l^f   = 5CLS |

Student: _Angie_   Gr/Age: _5_   Sch: _M_   Tch: Area: _Spelling_

Spelling Words

100
90
80
70
60
50
40
30
20
10

Date | 9/21 | 9/24 | 10/6 | 10/7 | 10/13 | 10/16 | 10/20

Correct Letter Sequences O   Correct Words ◆

166

WRITTEN EXPRESSION

For students who do have basic writing skills (i.e., can create and write sentences), a written expression measure for Curriculum-Based Measurement has been very useful for monitoring student progress in language arts.

Written Expression

Student protocol	Teacher directions	Scoring
For writing, student is given the starting sentence or part of a story. He or she is given a lined sheet of paper with the story starter at the top. Student is then asked to continue to write a story about what happened.	Student is told that he or she will write the rest of the story and tell what happened after the story starter. Students are told the story starter, allowed 1 minute to think or write notes about what he or she will write in the story, then given 5 minutes to write about what happened based on the story starter.	Scoring for written expression is based on spelling, grammar, and punctuation in what is called a correct word sequence (CWS). Two words that are correctly written and make sense equals a correct sequence. The number of words the student writes is also counted. Teacher may also score qualitatively based on creative and cohesive writing. Note correct word sequence scoring below: ^Susie^got^a^cute^ new^kitten^. = 7 CWS susie got^a qute knu kitten. = 2CWS

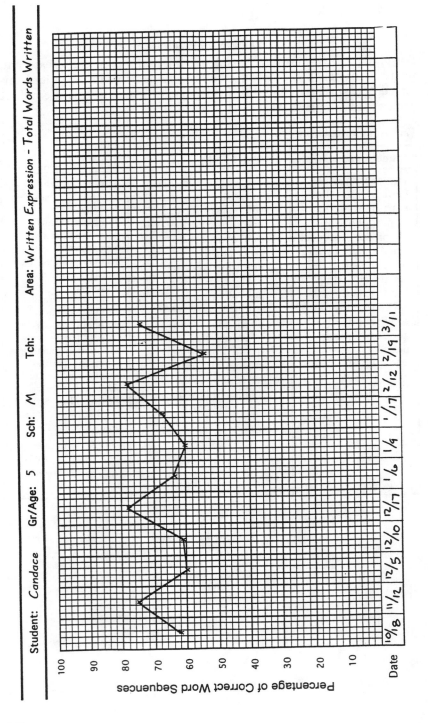

Student: _Candace_   Gr/Age: 5   Sch: M   Tch: Area: _Written Expression – Total Words Written_

Percentage of Correct Word Sequences

100
90
80
70
60
50
40
30
20
10

Date | ¹⁰/₁₈ | ¹¹/₁₂ | ¹²/₅ | ¹²/₁₀ | ¹²/₁₇ | ¹/₆ | ¹/₉ | ¹/₁₇ | ²/₁₂ | ²/₁₉ | ³/₁₁

MATHEMATICS

Math Computation

Student protocol	Teacher directions	Scoring
This measure includes different types of math problems depending on the grade and ability level of the student. On this measure, student works math computation problems from the operations included in classroom instruction. Problems may be mixed by operation.	Student is allocated a period of time to work as many problems as possible. There may be problems the student does not know how to do. In this case, student is told he or she may cross out unknown problems and continue. The student is asked to try each problem, do his or her best, and finish as much as possible.	Counting the number of digits in the correct place value is the procedure used for scoring math. Rather than counting the entire problem as correct or incorrect, all digits in the work shown by the student and the answer are counted as digits. Note the correct scoring examples below: $\begin{array}{r} 22 \\ \times\,43 \\ \hline 66 \\ +\,88 \\ \hline 946 \end{array}$ = 7 correct digits $\begin{array}{r} 25 \\ +\,16 \\ \hline 311 \end{array}$ = 1 correct digit

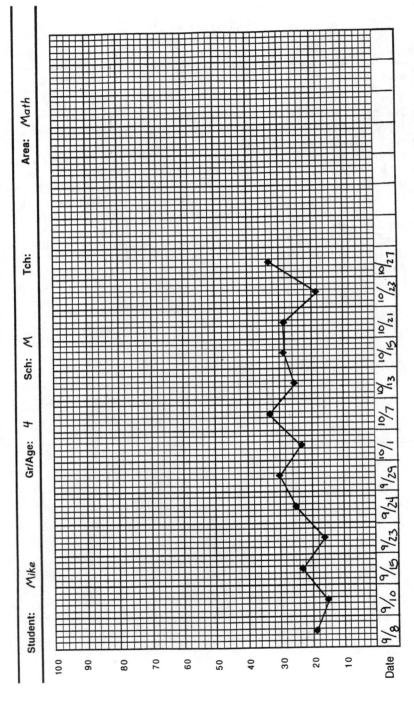

Individualized Education Program (IEP)
Background and Legal Requirements

SPECIAL EDUCATION IS defined as specially designed instruction intended to meet the unique needs of a child with a disability (Larsen & Poplin, 1980). The Education for All Handicapped Children Act of 1975, PL 94-142, amended the Education of the Handicapped Act (EHA) of 1970, PL 91-230. PL 94-142 required that a free, appropriate public education in the least restrictive environment be provided to all children with disabilities between the ages of 6 and 21. Since 1975, amendments (including the Education of the Handicapped Act Amendments of 1986, PL 99-457; the Individuals with Disabilities Education Act [IDEA] of 1990, PL 101-476; and the Individuals with Disabilities Education Act Amendments of 1991, PL 102-119) have extended this age range from birth to 21, clarified that students with traumatic brain injury and autism are to be included in the definition of children with disabilities; stated that therapeutic recreation, social services, and rehabilitation counseling are related services; and mandated that assistive technology services or devices must be provided by the state or local education agency when deemed appropriate on the child's individualized education program (IEP). In addition, IDEA made it clear that the intent of Congress is that no child with a disability be excluded from school and that all agencies follow a policy of zero reject (Turnbull, 1993). As a part of the zero-reject concept, IDEA further stipulates that neither the parent(s) nor the individual with the disability (nor the individual's insurance company) is required to pay for services to comply with IDEA (Turnbull, 1993).

The requirement that a child's public education be appropriate or suitable to his or her needs means that the education must be individualized. This policy of providing an appropriate education is achieved through an IEP. Section 1401(19) of IDEA states the following:

> The term "individualized education program" means a written statement for each disabled child developed in any meeting by a representative of the local education agency or an intermediate educational unit who shall be qualified to provide or supervise the provision of specially designed instruction to meet the unique needs of disabled children, the teacher, the parents or guardian of such child, and whenever appropriate, such child, which statement shall include: (A) a statement of the present levels of education performance for such child, (B) a statement of annual goals, including short-term instructional objectives, (C) a statement of the specific educational services to be provided to such child, and the extent to which such child will be able to participate in regular educational programs, (D) the projected date for initiation and anticipated duration of such services, and (E) appropriate objective criteria and evaluation procedures and schedules for determining, on at least an annual basis, whether instructional objectives are being achieved.

IDEA also stipulates that the following individuals be involved in the development of the IEP: a representative of the public agency (other than the child's teacher) who is qualified to provide or supervise the child's special education; the child's teacher, the child's parent(s); the child, when appropriate; and other individuals at the discretion of the parents or agency. Many steps, with associated timetables, are outlined in order to ensure parent participation in the planning of the child's IEP and timely service delivery.

Although each school district, county, province, or local education planning agency has developed its own set of forms to meet the requirements established by IDEA, the specific items mandated by the federal government stated previously must be included.

REFERENCES

Education for All Handicapped Children Act of 1975, PL 94-142, 20 U.S.C. § 1400 et seq.

Education of the Handicapped Act (EHA) of 1970, PL 91-230, 20 U.S.C. § 1400 et seq.

Education of the Handicapped Act Amendments of 1986, PL 99-457, 20 U.S.C. § 1400 et seq.

Larsen, S.C., & Poplin, M.S. (1980). *Methods for educating the handicapped: An individualized education program approach.* Needham, MA: Allyn & Bacon.

Individuals with Disabilities Education Act (IDEA) of 1990, PL 101-476, 20 U.S.C. § 1400 *et seq.*

Individuals with Disabilities Education Act Amendments of 1991, PL 102-119, 20 U.S.C. § 1400 *et seq.*

Turnbull, H.R. (1993). *Free appropriate public education: The law and children with disabilities.* Denver, CO: Love Publishing Co.

Curricula Incorporating Effective Instructional Assessment, Design, and Delivery Techniques

RECOMMENDED MATERIALS IN READING

Beginning Reading

Engelmann, S., & Bruner, E.C. (1995). *Reading mastery I* (Rainbow ed.). Chicago: Science Research Associates.

Engelmann, S., & Bruner, E.C. (1995). *Reading mastery II* (Rainbow ed.). Chicago: Science Research Associates.

Engelmann, S., Engelmann, O., & Seitz-Davis, K.L. (1997). *Horizons learning to read: Fast track A–B.* DeSoto, TX: SRA/McGraw-Hill.

Engelmann, S., Haddox, P., & Bruner, E. (1983). *Teach your child to read in 100 easy lessons.* New York: Fireside Books, Simon & Shuster.

Intermediate Reading

Engelmann, S., & Hanner, S. (1995). *Reading mastery III* (Rainbow ed.). DeSoto, TX: SRA/McGraw-Hill.

Engelmann, S., & Hanner, S. (1995). *Reading mastery IV* (Rainbow ed.). DeSoto, TX: SRA/McGraw-Hill.

Engelmann, S., Osborn, J., Osborn, S., & Zoref, L. (1995). *Reading mastery V* (Rainbow Edition). DeSoto, TX: SRA/McGraw-Hill.

Engelmann, S., Osborn, J., Osborn, S., & Zoref, L. (1995). *Reading mastery VI* (Rainbow ed.). DeSoto, TX: SRA/McGraw-Hill.

Remedial Reading

Engelmann, S., & Haddox, P. (1989). *Corrective reading program: Decoding A.* Chicago: Science Research Associates.

Engelmann, S., Hanner, S., & Johnson, G. (1989). *Corrective reading program: Decoding B-1.* Chicago: Science Research Associates.

Engelmann, S., Hanner, S., & Johnson, G. (1989). *Corrective reading program: Decoding B-2.* Chicago: Science Research Associates.

Engelmann, S., Hanner, S., & Johnson, G. (1989). *Corrective reading program: Decoding C.* Chicago: Science Research Associates.

Other Recommended Sources for Instruction in Reading

Carnine, D.W., Silbert, J., & Kameenui, E.J. (1990). *Direct instruction reading* (2nd ed.). Englewood Cliffs, NJ: Prentice Hall.

Celgeka, P.T., & Berdine, W.H. (1995). *Effective instruction for students with learning difficulties.* Needham, MA: Allyn & Bacon.

Mercer, C.D., & Mercer, A.R. (1993). *Teaching students with learning problems* (4th ed.). Englewood Cliffs, NJ: Prentice Hall.

RECOMMENDED MATERIALS IN MATHEMATICS

Beginning Mathematics

Engelmann, S., & Carnine, D.W. (1975). *Direct instruction strategies in teaching and remediation: Math. Levels 1 and 2.* Chicago: Science Research Associates.

Engelmann, S., & Carnine, D.W. (1992). *Connecting math concepts: Levels A & B.* DeSoto, TX: SRA/Macmillan/McGraw-Hill.

Intermediate Mathematics

Engelmann, S., & Kelly, B. (1994). *Connecting math concepts: Levels C and D.* DeSoto, TX: SRA/Macmillan/McGraw-Hill.

Engelmann, S., Kelly B., & Engelmann, O. (1994). *Connecting math concepts: Level E.* DeSoto, TX: SRA/Macmillan/McGraw-Hill.

Remedial Mathematics

Engelmann, S., & Carnine, D.W. (1982). *Corrective mathematics: Addition.* DeSoto, TX: SRA/Macmillan/McGraw-Hill.

Engelmann, S., & Carnine, D.W. (1982). *Corrective mathematics: Division.* DeSoto, TX: SRA/Macmillan/McGraw-Hill.

Engelmann, S., & Carnine, D.W. (1982). *Corrective mathematics: Multiplication.* DeSoto, TX: SRA/Macmillan/McGraw-Hill.

Engelmann, S., & Carnine, D.W. (1982). *Corrective mathematics: Subtraction.* DeSoto, TX: SRA/Macmillan/McGraw-Hill.

Other Recommended Sources for Instruction in Math

Celgeka, P.T., & Berdine, W.H. (1995). *Effective instruction for students with learning difficulties.* Needham, MA: Allyn & Bacon.

Silbert, J., Carnine, D.W., & Stein, M. (1990). *Direct instruction mathematics* (2nd ed.). Columbus, OH: Charles E. Merrill.

RECOMMENDED MATERIALS IN SPELLING

Spelling

Dixon, R., & Engelmann, S. (1990) *Spelling mastery: Levels A–F* (2nd ed.). DeSoto, TX: SRA/Macmillan/McGraw-Hill.

Remedial Spelling

Dixon, R., & Engelmann, S. (1990) *Corrective spelling through morphographs* (2nd ed.). DeSoto, TX: SRA/Macmillan/McGraw-Hill.

Other Recommended Sources for Instruction in Spelling

Celgeka, P.T., & Berdine, W.H. (1995). *Effective instruction for students with learning difficulties.* Needham, MA: Allyn & Bacon.

Dixon, R.C. (1991). The application of sameness analysis to spelling. *Journal of Learning Disabilities, 24*(5), 285–291.

Dixon, R.C. (1993). *The surefire way to better spelling.* New York: St. Martin's Press.

Mercer, C.D., & Mercer, A.R. (1993). *Teaching students with learning problems* (4th ed.). Englewood Cliffs, NJ: Prentice Hall.

RECOMMENDED MATERIALS IN WRITING

Language and Writing

Engelmann, S., & Seitz-Davis, K.L. (1991). *Reasoning and writing: Levels A–B. A direct instruction program.* DeSoto, TX: SRA/McGraw-Hill.

Engelmann, S., & Silbert, J. (1991). *Reasoning and writing: Levels C–E. A direct instruction program.* DeSoto, TX: SRA/McGraw-Hill.

Gleason, M., & Stults, C. (1986). *Capitalization and punctuation.* DeSoto, TX: SRA/McGraw-Hill.

**Other Recommended Sources for
Instruction in Language and Writing**

Celgeka, P.T., & Berdine, W.H. (1995). *Effective instruction for students with learning difficulties.* Needham, MA: Allyn & Bacon.

Mercer, C.D., & Mercer, A.R. (1993). *Teaching students with learning problems* (4th ed.). Englewood Cliffs, NJ: Prentice Hall.

Example of Direct Instruction with a Visual-Spatial Display

THE FOLLOWING CAN be used to teach basic facts about land forms through the use of a visual-spatial display. Teachers require students to respond orally to a filled-cell display (see Chart 3). Next, the teacher asks the students to state the exact words from Sheet 3). The teacher may need to repeat this step several times until students can accurately recall the words. Once fluent, the students play a cooperative learning game with Question Sheet 3. A scripted lesson is provided to aid teacher presentation.

From Englemann, S., Davis, K., & Davis, G. (1983). *Your world of facts II: Teacher's presentation book* (pp. 19–21) and *Your world of facts II: Student workbook* (pp. 3, 36). New York: SRA–McGraw-Hill Co.; reprinted by permission of the McGraw-Hill Company.

Chart 3

A.   Landforms

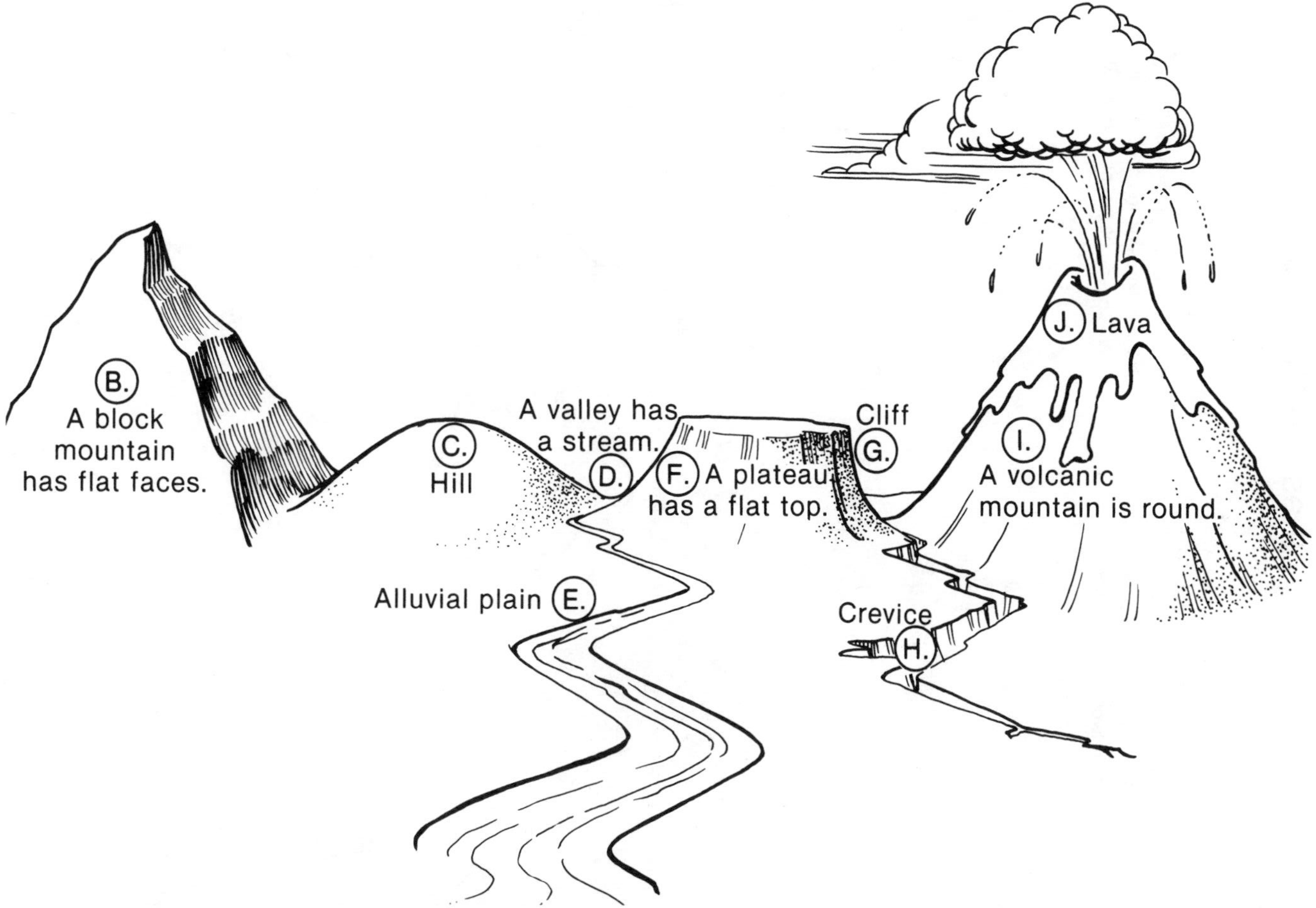

B. A block mountain has flat faces.

C. Hill

D. A valley has a stream.

E. Alluvial plain

F. A plateau has a flat top.

G. Cliff

H. Crevice

I. A volcanic mountain is round.

J. Lava

Question Sheet 3

2. What words go in space A?
3. What words go in space C?
4. What words go in space G?
5. What words go in space E?
6. What words go in space I?
7. What words go in space B?

8. What words go in space D?
9. What words go in space F?
10. What words go in space H?
11. What words go in space J?
12. Which type of mountain has flat faces?

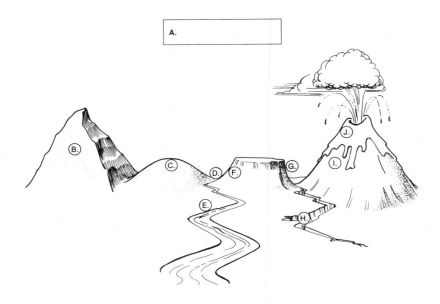

Lesson 2
Chart 3
3. Landforms—Introduce

Note: If students have gone
through Module 1, skip
script A and present
script B.

1. Everybody, open your student book to page 3.
(Check.)
Remember the exact word-
ing for each space.

2. Everybody, touch A.
(Wait.) Landforms. Say it.
(Signal.) **"Landforms."**
I'm going to tell you about
landforms. Landforms are
the different shapes that
you see on the earth.
Mountains, valleys, and
plains are landforms.
Remember: landforms.

3. Everybody, touch B. *(Wait.)*
A block mountain has flat
faces. Say it. *(Signal.)* **"A
block mountain has flat
faces."**
A block mountain has flat
faces because it is made
when huge rocks are
cracked off and tilted on
end. The biggest block
mountains are 10 kilome-
ters high.
Remember: a block moun-
tain has flat faces.

4. Everybody, touch C.
(Wait.) Hill. Say it. *(Signal.)* **"Hill."**

A hill is like a small
mountain with a rounded
top. It is usually not more
than 200 meters from top
to bottom.
Remember: hill.

5. Everybody, touch D.
(Wait.) A valley has a
stream. Say it. *(Signal.)* **"A
valley has a stream."**
A valley is a low place in
which a stream flows. A
valley is made by a stream
or ice wearing away the
earth and rock.
Remember: A valley has a
stream.

6. Everybody, touch E. *(Wait.)*
Alluvial plain. Say it. *(Signal.)* **"Alluvial plain."**
An alluvial plain is the flat
country below hills and
mountains. The soil in an
alluvial plain is very rich
because streams carry all
the rich soil from the
mountains and drop it in
the plain.
Remember: alluvial plain.

7. Everybody, touch F. *(Wait.)*
A plateau has a flat top.
Say it. *(Signal.)* **"A plateau
has a flat top."**
A plateau is like a hill or
mountain but it has a flat
top. Some plateaus have a
very big top. It may be 160
kilometers long. You know

when you come to the end of a plateau, because the sides are very steep.
Remember: a plateau has a flat top.

8. Everybody, touch G. *(Wait.)* Cliff. Say it. *(Signal.)* **"Cliff."**
The steep side of a mountain or plateau is called a cliff.
Remember: cliff.

9. Everybody, touch H. *(Wait.)* Crevice. Say it. *(Signal.)* **"Crevice."**
A crack like this is called a crevice. Crevices can be very dangerous for mountain climbers.
Remember: crevice.

10. Everybody, touch I. *(Wait.)* A volcanic mountain is round. Say it. *(Signal.)* **"A volcanic mountain is round."**
This mountain is volcanic. It is made when hot rock called lava comes from below the earth. Volcanic mountains are easy to recognize even if they are not making smoke or pouring out lava. They are round. They have no corners like block mountains.
Remember: a volcanic mountain is round.

11. Everybody, touch J. *(Wait.)* Lava. Say it. *(Signal.)* **"Lava."**
Lava is the hot rock that pours from a volcano.
Remember: lava.

12. Let's go over the facts about landforms one more time.

13. Everybody, touch A. *(Wait.)* Tell me the words. *(Signal.)* **Students respond.**

14. *Repeat step 13 with B, C, D, E, F, G, H, I, J.*

3. Landforms—Review B

1. Everybody, open your student book to page 3. *(Check.)*
Let's go over the facts about Landforms.

2. Everybody, touch A. *(Wait.)* Tell me the words. *(Signal.)* **Students respond.**

3. *Repeat step 2 with B, C, D, E, F, G, H, I, J.*

4. *Repeat the series no more than three times.*

3. Landforms—Firm-up

1. Everybody, open your student book to page 36. *(Check.)*
The spaces are empty on this chart. Get ready to tell me the exact words that go in each space.

2. Everybody, touch A. *(Wait.)* Tell me the words. *(Signal.)* **Students respond.**

3. *Repeat step 2 with B, C, D, E, F, G, H, I, J.*

```
┌─────────────────────────────────┐
│          Answer key:            │
│  A.  Landforms                  │
│  B.  A block mountain has       │
│      flat faces.                │
│  C.  Hill                       │
│  D.  A valley has a stream.     │
│  E.  Alluvial plain             │
│  F.  A plateau has a flat top.  │
│  G.  Cliff                      │
│  H.  Crevice                    │
│  I.  A volcanic mountain is     │
│      round.                     │
│  J.  Lava                       │
│  *To correct: Say the correct*  │
│  *words that go in each space.* │
│  *Have the students repeat the* │
│  *words. Repeat the series*     │
│  *from A.*                      │
└─────────────────────────────────┘
```

3. Landforms—Starter's Game Preparation

1. Now you're going to play the starter's game for Landforms.

2. I'll tell you who the monitors are for today.
    Identify a monitor for each group.

3. Monitors, open your student book to answer sheet 3 for Landforms on page 76. *(Check.)*

4. Monitors, give out a scorecard to each player, including yourself. *(Wait.)*

5. Write on the board:
    3. Landforms

6. Everybody, write your name and the name of this game at the top of your scorecard. *(Check.)*

7. *After all players are ready, tell the monitors to start the game. Note the time. The game is to continue for ten minutes.*

8. *At the end of the game, award points to the monitors. Award points for the table bonus.*

9. *Instruct the students to return their scorecard to their notebook or folder.*

chapter six

Successful Transition Planning and Services for Students with ABI

Sally Morgan Smith and Janet S. Tyler

THIS CHAPTER PROVIDES information on transition planning and services for students with acquired brain injury (ABI) that will enable the student, the family, and the school to identify long-range goals and design a school experience to ensure that the student gains the skills and establishes a community network necessary to achieve the goals. This chapter also presents a review of the factors that support the need for transition planning, the evolution of transition, and the federal mandates regarding transition. The role of transition assessment as an ongoing means of determining student strengths, needs, and preferences and the individualized education program (IEP) process are major highlights of this chapter, followed by a discussion of transition across the life span.

Transition is "life changes, adjustments, and cumulative experiences that occur in the lives of young adults as they move from school environments to more independent living and work environments" (Wehman, 1996, p. 7). As such, transition is not a single event but an ongoing process that relates to all roles in life. One aspect of transition—that of students with disabilities moving from school to postschool life—has been a growing concern because of the poor adult outcomes many of these young adults face. The need for improved services for secondary students is manifested in the high dropout rate among students with disabilities and the dismal employment prospects of young adults served in special education programs. Students with disabilities must have access to a broader array of options at the secondary level that address their needs, which range from academic support to community-based education focused on employment, including functional and independent living skills, personal and social content, and career awareness. These needs can be met only through comprehensive programs that provide a continuum of services that reflect the specific strengths of the individual student. Educators must understand the importance of vocational and transition planning for students with disabilities to provide a viable curriculum.

FACTORS THAT ILLUSTRATE THE NEED FOR TRANSITION PLANNING

With differing opinions about the state of educational reform, it is often asked if students are being prepared for a world that no longer exists. Answers to this question are of paramount importance to ensure effective transitions. For example, many secondary-level special education programs continue to focus on tutorials geared at success in general education classes or remedial programs without preparing students adequately for life after high school. Consequently, young adults with special needs experience 1) high dropout rates, 2) high rates of unemployment or underemployment and poor wages, 3) an inability to live independently, 4) dissatisfaction with quality of life, and 5) limited opportunities for making personal choices. These particular issues are problematic for students with ABI because the disability may be newly acquired and the students and their families may be forced to change long-held goals such as college attendance, professional career choices, or vocational decisions relying on technical or physical skills that have been lost as a result of the injury. To underscore the critical nature of transition planning and to illustrate the need for this planning, these five outcomes of poor transition planning are addressed; they are followed by recommendations for IEP development and implementation.

Limited data are available specifically regarding adult outcomes for students with ABI. This lack of data may be attributed to the fact that ABI is a relatively new classification of special education. Also, schools often do not "label" students as having ABI; instead they refer to them as having other health impairments (OHI) or as falling into some other classification. In addition, there are vast differences among people with brain injury, making it difficult to draw general-izations. For these reasons, outcome data are often addressed for special education students in general.

High Dropout Rate

Research shows that more than 30% of students served in secondary special education programs drop out of school. When compared by category of exceptionality, the numbers are more alarming. Specifically, the National Longitudinal Transition Study (Wagner, 1989) and Wehman (1996) indicate that the dropout rate for students with learning disabilities ranges from 27% to 54%, for students with behavior disorders from 39% to 47%, and for students with mental retardation from 20% to 25%. This high dropout rate implies that secondary-level special education fails to meet the needs of many students served in these programs. Because students with ABI are often included in programs for students with learning disabilities, behavior disorders, or mental retardation (Mira, Tucker, & Tyler, 1992), it is likely that these school programs do not meet their needs.

Unemployment or Underemployment and Poor Wages

Depending on the level and length of coma, people with ABI were reported in a study by Roessler, Schriner, and Price (1992) to have had postinjury unemployment rates that ranged from 52% to 97% compared with a preinjury unemployment rate of 14%. Furthermore, their return-to-work rate following ABI reportedly ranged from 23% to 30%. Clearly, these statistics show that employment is a problem for many people with ABI.

In addition to unemployment, the problem of underemployment is a major concern. Of those who were employed, 75% were employed only part time (Roessler et al., 1992). Furthermore, Edgar (1987) reported that although 60% of high school graduates with disabilities were employed, only 18% of them earned more than minimum wage. If students with learning disabilities and behavior disorders are not considered in this statistic, the percentage drops to 5%. The types of jobs obtained by graduates of special education programs tend to be entry-level jobs with low salaries, few or no benefits, and minimal opportunity for advancement (Edgar, 1988).

Fryer (1989) reviewed several studies that reported that cognitive impairments and related psychosocial issues are the greatest obstacles in making a successful transition into society, both vocationally and socially, after ABI. People with ABI indicated that their potential was not recognized and that their vocational preparation needs were not met. Therefore, if students with ABI are to be prepared for the work world, then specific skills must be identified in each of the previously mentioned areas and a delivery system must be developed to ensure relevant instruction and services.

Independent Living

Roessler et al. (1992) reported that 42% of the respondents with ABI surveyed reported living at home with their families. People with ABI find living independently to be challenging because of specific characteristics of ABI, including disruptive behavior, poor judgment, impulsivity, impaired memory, and poor social skills (Fryer, 1989). Therefore, school programs designed to address independent living and community survival skills must be provided to enable students to develop these skills.

Quality of Life

Quality of life is affected by the opportunity to develop social and interpersonal networks. Unfortunately, people with ABI often feel isolated from their peers (Kozloff, 1987). This isolation is the result not only of the changes imposed by the injury but also of rejection by peers because of the consequences (e.g., sexual disinhibition, inappropriate laughing, verbal and physical abusiveness) of these changes. It is imperative, therefore, that schools offer specific social skills training to combat these consequences.

Self-Determination

Quality of life is enhanced through self-determination, which provides the individual with disability the opportunity to make choices (Field & Hoffman, 1994). Greater importance must be placed on students learning to be more directive in their lives. This can be accomplished by giving students more opportunities to make choices and live with consequences as well as by teaching students to facilitate their own IEP meetings.

HISTORICAL PERSPECTIVE OF TRANSITION

To foster a better understanding of the evolution of transition, this section reviews the historical movements that involved the school as a foundation but extended to employment in the work/study model of the 1960s, the career education movement of the 1970s, and transition as it evolved from the mid-1980s through the mid-1990s. The following are brief descriptions of these models.

The Work/Study Program

The premise behind transition began in the early 1960s with work/study programs and the Vocational Educational Act of 1963, PL 88-210. Originally conceptualized as a cooperative program between the public schools and the local offices of state rehabilitation agencies, the main purpose of the work/study program was to create an inclusive academic, social, and vocational curriculum for students with mild disabilities accompanied by appropriate work experiences to prepare students for later community adjustment. PL 88-210 specified that people with disabilities had to be included in ongoing vocational education with peers without disabilities.

The Career Education Movement

When career education was declared a priority by the U.S. Office of Education in 1970, the general population of students was targeted. Soon, however, people with disabilities were also included, as stipulated in the Education for All Handicapped Children Act of 1975, PL 94-142. During this stage, career education was broadly structured and financed largely through federal money. The disadvantage of these programs was that students were trained for specific skills rather than in work habits that could be used in a variety of settings. As time passed, these limitations were lifted as the emphasis changed to training for generally acceptable employee behavior.

The Bridges Model of Transition

In the early 1980s, the transition movement emerged based on a rather limited premise that conceptualized transition was the "bridge between the security and structure offered by the school and the opportunities and risks of adult life" (Will, 1984, p. 1). Halpern (1992) described this early transition model as the Bridges Model, which allowed transition from school to work. The first bridge, transition without special services, was available to anyone. The second bridge, transition with time-limited services, provided access to short-term services. The third bridge, transition with ongoing services, was a small component used mainly in demonstration models. This transition model, which originally focused solely on employment, has evolved since the mid-1980s and now includes all aspects of adult life.

As discussed previously, since the early 1960s transition from school to adult living received a broad, life-career focus that included students, parents, school personnel, and adult services agencies working collaboratively to develop IEPs with adult outcomes. This change to a more global focus on the whole person is the guiding force behind developing appropriate IEPs and school programs that reflect transition-related outcomes.

LEGISLATION THAT AFFECTS TRANSITION

Legislation provides guidelines for federal mandates regarding planning and providing school programs that address postschool outcomes for students with disabilities. A better understanding of these regulations offers greater insight into transition planning. The Individuals with Disabilities Education Act (IDEA) of 1990, PL 101-476, mandates the participation of students in their own transition planning meetings. The Rehabilitation Act Amendments of 1992, PL 102-569, in turn, declares that people with disabilities have the right to self-determination just like their peers without disabilities. The following section specifically reviews IDEA; the Americans with Disabilities Act of 1990, PL 101-336; and the Rehabilitation Act Amendments of 1992.

The Individuals with Disabilities Education Act

IDEA requires that specific outcomes be identified based on students' needs, preferences, and interests and that educational programs for all students with disabilities 16 years of age and older "be supported by transition services language that would include instruction, community experiences, development of employment and other postschool adult living objectives, and if appropriate, the acquisition of daily living skills and functional vocational evaluation" (Section 300.18[b]).

Furthermore, IDEA recognizes a broad definition of transition:

> Transition services mean a coordinated set of activities for a student, designed within an outcome oriented process, which promotes movement from school to post-school activities, including post-secondary education, vocational training, integrated employment, including supported employment, continuing adult education, adult services independent living or community participation. (Section 300.18[a])

The Americans with Disabilities Act

The Americans with Disabilities Act (ADA) of 1990 offers more choices and options for people with disabilities. It is a form of civil rights legislation that prohibits discrimination against people with disabilities in employment, public accommodations, transportation, and telecommunications.

The Rehabilitation Act Amendments of 1992

According to the Rehabilitation Act Amendments,

> Disability is a natural part of the human experience and in no way diminishes the right of an individual to (a) live independently, (b) enjoy self-determination, (c) make choices, (d) contribute to society, (e) pursue meaningful careers, and (f) enjoy full inclusion and integration in the economic, political, social, cultural, and educational mainstream of American society. (p. 24)

Together, IDEA, the ADA, and the Rehabilitation Act Amendments of 1992 provide federal mandates that greatly affect people with disabilities. With these federal guidelines in place, the states have taken the initiative to develop their own state guidelines. The federal mandates and the ensuing state mandates hold school districts accountable for providing the transition services needed by each individual student.

THE DEFINITION OF TRANSITION

In 1994 the Division on Career Development and Transition (DCDT) of the Council for Exceptional Children adopted the following definition of transition:

> Transition refers to a change in status from behaving primarily as a student to assuming emergent adult roles in the community. The roles include employment, participating in postsecondary education, maintaining a home, becoming appropriately involved in the community, and experiencing satisfactory personal and social relationships. The process of enhancing transition involves the participation and coordination of school programs, adult agency services, and natural supports within the community. The foundation for transition should be laid during the elementary and middle school years, guided by the broad concept of career development. Transition planning should begin no later than age 14, and students should be encouraged, to the full extent of their capabilities, to assume a maximum amount of responsibility for such planning. (Halpern, 1994, p. 117)

This new, more inclusive definition of transition is the framework for the future of transition planning. The mandates of IDEA regarding transition, as well as the DCDT definition, provide a structure that is applicable for students with ABI as well as other disabilities. However, effective transition services are not yet in place in many schools throughout the United States. Special educators must take a more active and assertive role in the implementation of these transition issues in the development of IEPs and the program planning for their students.

Adjusting to change is an arduous experience for most people, but when a person faces the additional challenge of having ABI, it can be almost overwhelming. IDEA clearly places the initial responsibility for transition planning on the public schools. Thus, schools are responsible for providing appropriate transition programming and services. To be effective, therefore, transition planning must occur as a collaborative effort involving the student, family, school, rehabilitation counselor, adult services providers, and community members to develop and implement an IEP that will provide opportunities for the student with disabilities to acquire the skills necessary to successfully live and work in a complex society. Transition must extend beyond employment, also taking into consideration the quality of life and its impact on all aspects of adult adjustment. Identification of postschool outcomes must be the driving force behind developing long-range goals that enable students with ABI to achieve their dreams. In this regard, it is important that the process of transition planning involve making decisions *with* each individual student and his or her family, rather than *for* the individual with ABI. The steps of the transition planning process are outlined in Table 1.

There is no one single plan used for all students with a specific disability—a transition plan must be developed for each individual student. Several factors must be considered when working with a person with ABI, including the length of time since the accident, the severity of the injury, and the rehabilitative services he or she is receiving. Furthermore, student choice and preferences are also key factors in transition planning.

TRANSITION ASSESSMENT

The first step toward effective planning involves transition assessment to gain insight into a specific student's needs, preferences, interests, and present level of performance. Many states have not established procedures for needs assessment and transition planning. Without coordinated efforts, schools may not provide appropriate school programs or develop long-range goals with adult services agencies involvement to ensure continuation of services. Therefore, transition assessment includes a variety of procedures.

Assessment to determine transition needs must be multifaceted and ongoing. Transition is "a lifelong process that begins at birth and relates to all life roles, not just work" (Szymanski, 1994, p. 402).

Table 1.   Transition-planning process for students with ABI

Step 1	Meet with the student and his or her parents. Explain the transition-planning process and their roles in the process. Discuss their visions for the future. Obtain their input regarding assessment, appropriate adult outcomes, types of school programs and services needed, the student's vocational interests, and adult services providers to include in the IEP process.
Step 2	Review the student's records. Decide what additional assessment needs to be carried out. Conduct formal and informal assessments. Analyze assessment data. Develop a portfolio with the student. (Remember that assessment will be an ongoing process.)
Step 3	Provide the student with training so that he or she will be an active participant in the IEP meeting.
Step 4	Discuss assessment results with the student and his or her parents. Obtain their input regarding school programs and services and appropriate goals and objectives. Schedule the IEP meeting. After obtaining written permission from the student and his or her parents, invite adult services providers and the student's employer/supervisor (if employed) to the meeting.
Step 5	Hold the IEP meeting. Discuss visions for the future. Plan community experiences, including supervised work experiences. Develop goals and objectives reflecting adult outcomes.
Step 6	Implement the transition IEP.
Step 7	Monitor student progress.
Step 8	Reconvene the IEP team as needed to modify the IEP (at least yearly).

Therefore, transition assessment must also be a lifelong process that surveys all aspects of one's life.

Adult outcomes (e.g., independent living skills, personal and social adjustment, occupational adjustment) are the foundation for the development of transition assessments (Clark, 1995). That is, it must be the goal of the school to provide programs and school experiences that will enable all children to reach their fullest potential in all aspects of their lives. This includes enabling students to successfully make the transition from one stage of school life to another and, eventually, from school to the adult world. This process must include information from informal and formal means of assessment, including, when appropriate, some of the few commercially available transition assessment instruments.

It is imperative that transition assessment depicts a complete picture of the student. Effective transition assessment determines the student's present level of performance, as well as his or her needs, interests, and preferences. Such information may be collected from reviewing cumulative records; analyzing test information; administering additional assessments; interviewing the student; and gathering data from parents, school personnel, rehabilitation counselor, community members, and others who have an interest in assisting in planning for a student's future. The consolidation of the information gathered from various sources provides a global view of the student (see the section entitled "Portfolio Assessment").

Formal Assessment

Formal transition assessment includes 1) achievement tests, 2) aptitude tests, 3) interest inventories, 4) adaptive behavior scales, 5) transition planning assessment instruments (e.g., Transition Behavior Scale [McCarney, 1989], Life Centered Career Education (LCCE) Knowledge Battery [Brolin, 1992], Transition Planning Inventory [Patton & Clark, 1996]), 6) commercial work samples, and 7) medical evaluations.

Informal Assessment

Informal transition assessment includes 1) personal interviews with the student, parents, and teachers; 2) informal questionnaires and inventories with students, parents, and teachers (e.g., Enderle-Severson Transition Rating Scale [Enderle & Severson, 1991], LCCE Performance Battery, McGill Action Planning System [Vandercook & York, 1989]); 3) self-report checklists for students; 4) functional skills rating scales or checklists; and 5) interviews and questionnaires with the employer and job coach. Informal assessments provide information from a variety of people who directly know the student and can give their perspectives of the student's capabilities and level of preparedness. Specifically, questions should address a student's independent living skills, personal and social adjustment, ability to have access to the community, participation in recreation and leisure activities, academic and behavioral issues, dreams for the future, postsecondary training and education interests, and vocational interests. It is most helpful if the student and others are asked similar questions in order to get various perspectives on the same issues.

Functional Assessment

Functional assessment focuses on measuring an individual's daily living activities, skills, behavioral performances, environmental conditions, and needs. This type of assessment is conducted at home, at school, in the community, at the workplace, and in other environments in which the young adult lives and works. It is similar to the informal assessments but provides the opportunity to assess the student in the actual settings (e.g., providing on-the-job assessment of real work skills and habits, the student's ability to use public transportation).

Portfolio Assessment

Portfolio assessment consists of consolidating the assessments mentioned previously with additional information regarding the student. The development of a portfolio to follow the student throughout school is helpful, as it provides a complete profile of the student. In addition, it offers the opportunity to add new information so that it can be kept constantly updated. The student helps decide what information is included in the portfolio. This information may include 1) summaries of formal, informal, and functional assessments; 2) summaries of transition planning assessments; 3) videotapes of actual job performance; 4) interviews with employers and co-workers, friends, and family; 5) videotapes of participation in recreational and leisure activities; 6) videotapes of daily living and functional living skills performances; and 7) letters of reference from friends, school personnel, roommates, employers, and co-workers.

Portfolio assessment is ideal for students with ABI because it is an ongoing process that illustrates the growth, change, and abilities of the student. As the student develops through the years in school, his or her areas of strengths, concerns, and interests will change. Students with ABI are known to change initially and progress rapidly. Therefore, transition-related areas must continually be assessed and reassessed to provide adequate information pertaining to a specific student in order to plan and develop appropriate IEPs and modify the program to meet the student's changing needs. The importance of transition assessment cannot be overstated. It is the cornerstone for effective transition planning.

LIFE-SPAN APPROACH TO TRANSITION PLANNING FOR STUDENTS WITH ABI

Transition is viewed as a lifelong process that starts at birth and continues across the life span with emphasis being placed on the evolution of the whole person (Clark, Carlson, Fisher, Cook, & D'Alonzo, 1991; Repetto & Correa, 1996). The life-span approach to transition is based on the premise that transition is not a product but an ongoing process that begins at birth and continues throughout life (Szymanski, 1994), with career interests and aspirations evolving over time. Thus, transition affects students in a variety of ways as they become older and more independent. Schools, therefore, must provide programs that meet the specific needs of the individual student as the student grows and matures.

To encourage transition across the life span, students with disabilities need to participate in age-appropriate activities with same-age peers (students with and without disabilities). They also need to be contributing members of the community, participating in activities that are of interest to them. Schools must also help ensure that friendships develop that will grow into a support network throughout the community. In order for students to learn the skills necessary for a successful adult life, schools must provide a comprehensive program that includes academic support as well as community-based education focused on employment, independent living, and life skills. The following are examples of how such a program may be implemented throughout the school years.

Academic Support

Providing academic support, which is determined by the individual's age when the injury occurs, is vital for students with ABI. It is important to have the opportunity to play with peers with disabilities and to have age-appropriate responsibilities. During the preschool years students begin to develop an awareness of roles and responsibilities by observing others at work and by interacting with peers. In elementary and junior high school years, students develop work habits and interpersonal skills as they increase their social skills and career awareness. Most brain injuries occur during adolescence, which presents obstacles in terms of changing predetermined goals that may no longer be attainable as a result of the extent of the injury. In later school years, career interests and goals are developed as skills to live independently are acquired. Program planning and goals must be flexible in order to meet the individual's changing abilities and needs after a brain injury. A student who had previously planned to attend college may have to change the focus of his or her educational program to a vocational preparation program or something that better suits his or her postinjury abilities.

Community-Based Instruction

Given the intent of transition, a shift from traditional classroom-based education to community-based activities must occur. Community-based instruction provides opportunities for students with ABI to practice the skills they have learned in the actual settings in which the skills are naturally required. Because generalization is often a problem for people with ABI, the opportunity to practice life skills in the community permits students with ABI to understand how the skills pertain to their own lives and futures.

Students must realize their potential and be encouraged to work to attain their goals. Finding success in community work experiences, for example, may encourage some students to go on for further training or education after high school graduation. No matter what course of action a student decides to pursue after high school, the transition will be smoother if the foundation has been established during school. For example, connections with adult agencies should be made when the student is still in school so that the adult services provider has adequate time to put a plan of action in place, thereby avoiding a breakdown in services.

Paid Work Experiences

Paid work experience under the direction of the school offers students the opportunity to obtain employment during school with support from school personnel and to maintain employment after graduation. This not only provides a monetary incentive but also enables the student to experiment with a variety of occupations.

Community work experiences allow the student to participate in the community, to see firsthand what different jobs entail, and to develop relationships and friendships within the community. The opportunity to develop community ties also allows students with ABI to become an integral part of their community. For example, through such participation in community experiences, students' neighbors get to know them on a personal level that one hopes will lead to further acceptance and involvement.

Functional Skills Approach

Although different goals are developed depending on the individual student's needs and capabilities, a functional skills approach could be followed by all students. Functional skills for some students with more severe ABI might entail learning basic daily living skills such as brushing teeth and dressing independently. Other students with ABI might learn to plan a budget and use a checking account. Some students may need many trials and subsequent trips to the bank to achieve these goals, whereas others may grasp the concept of using a check register in the classroom. Finally, other students might be planning on attending college and consequently need to learn how to complete applications and follow deadlines for turning in paperwork.

No matter what outcomes have been chosen for a given student, successful transition from school to adult life requires effective planning, appropriate school experiences, and established connections with postschool resources such as 1) adult service providers (e.g., vocational rehabilitation, independent living centers, special transportation agencies), 2) vocational/technical school or college representatives (e.g., student services coordinators), and 3) community resources (e.g., recreational facilities, churches, organizations).

Developing the Transition-Related IEP

After careful analysis of the results of the transition assessment and input from the collaborative efforts of the student, family, school personnel, rehabilitation counselor, adult services providers, and interested community members, it is time to develop the IEP to ensure that the school will provide the appropriate programs and services to meet the needs of this individual student. Regardless of the student's age or level of disability, this process of IEP development is quite similar (see Chapter 5 for IEP requirements).

CONCLUSION

The student and family are the driving force in creating a vision for the future. What goals and dreams does the student have? What does the family envision for the student? Are these goals realistic? What school programs are needed to enable the student to attain the vision? These are all important questions. The student must assume responsibility for important life decisions and must gain a sense of empowerment with respect to transition planning. Long-range outcomes must be identified and goals and objectives developed to enable the student to reach those outcomes. Goals should be outcome driven and reflect the individual student's vision and capabilities. Furthermore, responsibilities must be identified for all parties involved. Delivery of transition must ensure that the instructional program is based on a student's needs, preferences, and interests and the inclusion of the student within the general education school program with community-based learning opportunities is provided. Ongoing evaluation of the transition-planning process allows all parties involved to monitor the progress and reconvene as needed. Changes will be made. Typically, as the student gets older, new visions and dreams take the spotlight and goals are modified to address the new vision. This is how life is for most people—changes occur and adjustments must be made to cope with these changes. Young adults with ABI can cope with the many transitions they will face if they have a strong sense of self-determination and an understanding of their capabilities. Transition planning will allow the student to develop both of these qualities and to acquire the skills needed to reach the vision.

REFERENCES

Americans with Disabilities Act (ADA) of 1990, PL 101-336, 42 U.S.C. § 12101 et seq.

Brolin, D.E. (1992). *Life Centered Career Education (LCCE) Knowledge and Performance Batteries*. Reston, VA: The Council for Exceptional Children.

Clark, G.M. (1995). *Transition planning assessment for students with learning disabilities.* A paper presented at the PRO-ED Symposium on Transition for Students with Learning Disabilities, University of Kansas, Florence.

Clark, G.M., Carlson, B., Fisher, S., Cook, I., & D'Alonzo, B. (1991). Career development for students with disabilities in elementary schools: A position statement of the Division on Career Development. *Career Development for Exceptional Individuals, 14*(2), 110–120.

Edgar, E. (1987). Secondary programs in special education: Are many of them justifiable? *Exceptional Children, 53,* 555–561.

Edgar, E. (1988). Transition from school to community. *Teaching Exceptional Children, 20*(2), 73–75.

Education for All Handicapped Children Act of 1975, PL 94-142, 20 U.S.C. § 1400 *et seq.*

Enderle, J., & Severson, S. (1991). *Enderle-Severson Transition Rating Scale.* Moorehead, MN: Practical Press.

Field, S., & Hoffman, A. (1994). Development of a model for self-determination. *Career Development for Exceptional Individuals, 17*(2), 159–169.

Fryer, J. (1989). Adolescent community integration. In P. Bach-y-Rita (Ed.), *Comprehensive neurologic rehabilitation* (Vol. 2, pp. 255–286). New York: Demos.

Halpern, A.S. (1992). Transition: Old wine in new bottles. *Exceptional Children, 58,* 202–211.

Halpern, A.S. (1994). The transition of youth with disabilities to adult life: A position statement of the Division on Career Development and Transition, Council for Exceptional Children. *Career Development for Exceptional Individuals, 17*(2), 115–124.

Individuals with Disabilities Education Act (IDEA) of 1990, PL 101-476, 20 U.S.C. § 1400 *et seq.*

Kozloff, R. (1987). Networks of social support and outcome from severe head injury. *Journal of Head Trauma, 2,* 14–23.

McCarney, S.B. (1989). *Transition Behavior Scale.* Columbia, MO: Hawthorne Educational Service.

Mira, M.P., Tucker, B.F., & Tyler, J.S. (1992). *Traumatic brain injury in children and adolescents: A sourcebook for schools.* Austin, TX: PRO-ED.

Patton, J.R., & Clark, G.M. (1996). *Transition Planning Inventory.* Austin, TX: PRO-ED.

Rehabilitation Act Amendments of 1992, PL 102-569, 29 U.S.C. § 701 *et seq.*

Repetto, J.B., & Correa, V.I. (1996). Expanding views on transition. *Exceptional Children, 62,* 551–563 .

Roessler, R.T., Schriner, K.F., & Price, P. (1992). Employment concerns of people with head injuries. *Journal of Rehabilitation, 58*(1), 17–22.

Szymanski, E.M. (1994). Transition: Life-span and life-space considerations for employment. *Exceptional Children, 60,* 402–410.

Vandercook, T., & York, J. (1989). The McGill Action Planning System (M.A.P.S.): A strategy for building vision. *Journal of The Association for Persons with Severe Handicaps, 14,* 205–215.

Vocational Educational Act of 1963, PL 88-210, 20 U.S.C. § 35 *et seq.*

Wagner, M. (1989, March). *The transition experiences of youth with disabilities: A report from the National Longitudinal Transition Study.*

Paper presented at the meeting of the Division of Research, Council for Exceptional Children, San Francisco.

Wehman, P. (1996). *Life beyond the classroom: Transition strategies for young people with disabilities* (2nd ed.). Baltimore: Paul H. Brookes Publishing Co.

Will, M. (1984). *OSERS programming for the transition of youth with disabilities: Bridges from school to working life*. Washington DC: Office of Special Education and Rehabilitative Services (OSERS), U.S. Department of Education.

Social and Behavioral Interventions

Many students with ABI who exhibit problematic or challenging behaviors in school are referred to private mental health providers like me and my colleagues. Often, by the time we see these students, behavior problems are deeply entrenched and difficult for us to address effectively in settings far removed from the school settings in which they occur.

The information included in this book is important for all educators working with these children and adolescents and their families. The emphasis in Chapters 7–10 on successful intervention strategies will be of great assistance to classroom teachers, counselors, school psychologists, and other on-line staff, allowing them to respond quickly to behavioral and social concerns before they become serious problems.

Jacqui Lichtenstein, Clinical Therapist

chapter seven

Understanding and Overcoming the Challenging Behaviors of Students with ABI

Ann V. Deaton

CHILDREN WITH ACQUIRED brain injury (ABI), whether mild or severe, tend to experience more behavior problems than their typically developing peers (Asarnow, Satz, Light, Lewis, & Neumann, 1991; Coster, Haley, & Baryza, 1994; Greenspan & MacKenzie, 1994; Jaffe, Polissar, Fay, & Liao, 1995; Parker, 1994). Long after the physical manifestations of an injury have diminished, ongoing maladaptive behaviors may continue to interfere with children's self-esteem, school performance, friendships, community functioning, and family interactions. For many, the most enduring and incapacitating effects of ABI are changes in behavior. Although no two children with ABI demonstrate precisely the same behaviors, some common patterns exist. Similar methods for intervention can be effective for a variety of individuals and behaviors. As noted in previous chapters, the cognitive effects of ABI (e.g., distractibility, cognitive inflexibility, poor memory) can contribute to behavior problems and interfere with school functioning. Adding to the difficulty are limitations in interpersonal skills such as poor anger control, attention-seeking behavior, inappropriate responses to others' social cues, and failure to monitor one's own behavior. When these behaviors are displayed by the student with ABI, they can lead to rejection by peers and, subsequently, to frustration and an escalation of behavior problems. This chapter describes the problem behaviors that may occur following ABI and behavior change strategies that can be helpful in improving the student's functioning and opportunities for success.

BEHAVIOR PROBLEMS IN THE STUDENT WITH ABI

Most research on ABI in children has focused on early outcomes, those achieved within the first months to a year after an injury. This focus on the short term may be appropriate for inpatient rehabilitation settings but is considerably less useful to schools and other postacute educational and treatment settings. The potential for recovering abilities long after ABI is the subject of controversy. Some studies have shown that there are continuing gains in abilities 3 or more years after injury in both children (e.g., Boyer & Edwards, 1991) and adults (e.g., Sbordone, Liter, & Pettler-Jennings, 1995). Others, such as a study of a cohort of children with ABI, have pointed out a plateauing effect after the first year of significant recovery (Fay et al., 1994; Jaffe et al., 1995). Despite the controversy, the most optimistic projections suggest that children can show improvement in cognitive, communicative, and psychosocial functioning for at least 3 years after injury. Given the right environment and programming, the likelihood of this projection may be increasingly certain. The opportunity for powerful intervention in the school is evident.

Complicating Factors

There are a number of complicating factors in identifying and treating behavior problems in the student with ABI. First, most of the same behavior problems also occur in children and adolescents who have not experienced ABI (Asarnow et al., 1991). Although ABI may worsen behavior problems or may cause the individual to be more resistant to change, challenging behaviors are partly a function of age and maturity level rather than solely a result of ABI. It is often difficult to separate age-appropriate maladaptive behaviors from injury-related behaviors. Both may require intervention, but differentiating between them allows for the most effective strategy to be chosen.

Environmental Circumstances   Many of the challenging behaviors observed after ABI have been caused not by the injury itself but by environmental circumstances following the injury. Some maladaptive behaviors are learned—sometimes to compensate for or cope with losses and sometimes because the acute hospital environment may reinforce behaviors (e.g., passivity) that are less than appropriate in community settings, such as the school. Parent, teacher, and peer protectiveness can also complicate or cause certain behaviors following ABI. These individuals may decrease the demands they make of the child with ABI, allowing behaviors or dependency that were not acceptable before the injury. Feelings of protectiveness occur because the child may appear physically vulnerable (e.g., lacking adequate balance or motor skills) and may result in others doing things for the child that he or she is capable of doing only with excessive effort. Health care providers may have warned not to stress the child due to fatigability and/or the risk of additional injury. Even when the child's skills have improved, the protective attitudes and behaviors of others may already be well established.

Missing School   The time a child misses from school after ABI can also cause or complicate behavior problems. Once the child returns to school, he or she is usually behind classmates in learning academic subject matter. Given decreased endurance and, most likely, lessened cognitive abilities in areas such as attention and processing speed, the child often experiences difficulty catching on and catching up with peers. The child's confusion and frustration can lead to behavior problems, either acting out behaviors (e.g., verbal or physical aggression) or internalizing behaviors (e.g., task avoidance). Peer teasing and lack of peer understanding of injury-related impairments can result in self-esteem problems that in turn can also result in an increase in problem behaviors (e.g., social withdrawal from peers, excessive reliance on adults for support, school avoidance). These behaviors increase the problems caused by school absences. Even transient problems can be enough for a child to be "labeled" as a problem. Peers may begin to see the student as "stupid" or as someone who does not listen. Others may see the student as a rude child, a child who is slow to catch on, a mean child, or one who just does not want to cooperate and do well. These "labels" can contribute to a cycle of worsening self-esteem, decreased motivation, and depressed performance that far outlasts the direct effects of the injury itself.

Communication Problems   Communication difficulties may be the source of behavior problems as well. Communication problems are common long after injury, particularly when the injury is severe (Boyer & Edwards, 1991). When children cannot communicate fluently, they often compensate by communicating in other ways. Specific communication impairments may cause the child considerable frustration. For example, the child who has difficulty finding his words or who often forgets what he is going to say may attempt to compensate by blurting out his thoughts as soon as they come to mind. This serves a positive function for the child in that he is able to let others know his thoughts and feelings. The poor timing of his communications, however, may result in others failing to listen, becoming irritated by the interruption, or attributing negative personality attributes (e.g., rudeness) to the child. Recognition of the communicative functions of some behaviors assists in developing strategies to improve them. Collaboration among speech-language therapists, psychologists, and educators can lead to an appropriate plan for intervention that specifically considers the communicative value of behaviors for the child (Feeney & Urbanczyk, 1994; Szekeres & Meserve, 1994; Ylvisaker & Feeney, 1994; see Chapter 8). In the case of more severe communication problems, an augmentative communication device also may be appropriate to increase the student's options for communicating.

Changing Behaviors

No matter how problematic a child's behavior may seem, it is important to remember that children almost invariably want to succeed. They typically do the best they can with the abilities they have. Behavior change programs seek to help shape behavior by developing positive, adaptive skills and decreasing problem behaviors. The ultimate goal of these programs is to enable the student to function as successfully and independently as possible, in the least restrictive environment. Improving adaptive skills is central to the child's self-esteem and quality of life. Decreasing maladaptive behaviors is typically necessary if the child is to remain in normative environments such as the home and the classroom.

Behavior modification theories and strategies have proliferated since the 1950s. Behavioral intervention is sometimes thought of as something that is "done to" or "carried out on" the student. However, ethical use of behavior change strategies, especially with children and individuals who have cognitive impairments, requires that the student with ABI and his or her parent(s) have an understanding of the procedure being implemented, the right to decide whether to accept this strategy, and the opportunity to participate in developing and monitoring the program (Jacobs, 1988). In general, the process of behavior change, much like the development of an individualized education program (IEP), should reflect collaboration, cooperation, and negotiation. All participants should agree on the behaviors that need to be changed and the procedures necessary to change them (Gelfand & Hartmann, 1984; see Chapter 8).

The ideal in behavior change is to have a situation in which the planned changes are perceived as beneficial by both the person with ABI and any other individuals who have initiated the change. An approach that acknowledges the need for all participants to have a say is more likely to meet the student's needs, ensure the student's cooperation, and, as a consequence, be successful (Feeney & Urbanczyk, 1994; Vredevoogd, 1986; see Chapter 8). The basic premise of behavioral approaches is that behavior has antecedents (i.e., events that elicit or precede behaviors) and consequences (i.e., events that follow behaviors). By changing these, the behavior can be changed. The following are steps that teachers and parents may take in developing an effective behavior change strategy.

Define the Problem Behavior   Develop a measurable and precise definition of the target behavior so that all can recognize and agree on its occurrence.

Identify the Function, Cause, and Rate of the Target Behavior Through careful observation and documentation, determine how often the behavior occurs, in what settings it occurs, what it accomplishes for the child, and what increases and decreases the behavior. Accurate baseline periods require that the demands made of the child during the baseline be typical of the usual classroom demands. During the baseline, no changes should be made in the classroom or in the methods used. The purpose is to accurately measure the problem behavior's occurrences. In one study of an adult with ABI, few problem behaviors were observed during baseline simply because staff had stopped making demands in order to minimize the risk of aggressive behavior (Davis, Turner, Rolider, & Cartwright, 1994).

At times, baseline data should be augmented by the use of a formal behavior rating scale. Rating scales are particularly useful for gathering objective data from several different team members (e.g., the student, teachers, parents). The choice of the scale depends on the type of information needed and time constraints of the rater. The ACTERS (Ullman, Sleador, & Sprague, 1988), for example, is a measure that includes scales that tap many problematic behaviors for youth with ABI. This scale has the advantage of ease of completion and comparison of input from many sources. These two advantages make it particularly useful at the middle school or high school level when students may have six or more teachers providing instruction. The Child Behavior Checklist (Achenbach, 1981) provides more detailed information, including scales assessing social withdrawal, depression, anxiety, hyperactivity, and physical or somatic complaints common after ABI. A useful aspect of this scale is the availability of parallel forms for teacher, parent, and youth self-report (ages 11–18). These comparisons provide the educator with important information, such as whether there are differences between the child's behavior in the classroom and at home.

Identify Resources for Behavioral Intervention   Resources may include 1) the student's assets, including his or her interests, memory, persistence, and ability to learn; 2) the professionals, including staff:student ratio, staff training, and staff individual traits (e.g., patience, sense of humor); 3) the student's family, including the ability to carry out programs at home, provision of relevant information about the child's skills, and ideas about preferred reinforcers; and 4) the setting, including natural reinforcers, other students, special equipment, and availability of time-out areas or quiet rooms (Deaton, 1987). Consider adding or developing resources if necessary.

Identify Strategies for Behavior Change   Choose the least intrusive procedure that will be effective. Altering antecedent conditions (i.e., environment) is one of the most effective and least intrusive ways to enable behavior change (see Chapter 8). This approach includes such strategies as preferential seating, written task instructions, frequent breaks, and a success-oriented curriculum. Problem behavior may seldom occur in such an environment as a result of the intensive cuing and the minimal frustration experienced by the child. At times, however, the child may need a more challenging environment in order to be prepared for other, less-structured settings. In this case, providing reinforcement for desirable behaviors may be an effective strategy. Reinforcers include rewards for task completion, praise, the opportunity to engage in a preferred activity, or additional privileges or attention.

Changing antecedent conditions or using reinforcers are preferred to punishment because they are more likely to lead to lasting changes in the behavior of the child with ABI (Eames & Wood, 1985) and to generalize to other settings (Zencius, Wesolowski, Burke, & McQuade, 1989). Punishment, however, may lead to depression, decreased initiative, and lower self-esteem (Malec, 1984). Punishment can sometimes be used, however, to extinguish a dangerous or disruptive behavior as long as an effort is made at the same time to reinforce a more appropriate behavior, particularly one that serves the same function as the maladaptive behavior (e.g., communicate frustration verbally instead of by hitting). Time-out, one form of punishment, is typically effective only if the environment is reinforcing and the child wants to return to it. Otherwise, a time-out can actually be a reinforcement (i.e., the child is rewarded for misbehavior by the reduction of demands) rather than a punishment.

Depending on the function of the behavior, its cause, and other characteristics of the student, any of these strategies (and others) may be appropriate. The best behavior management strategy for the student is one that uses "as few of your resources as possible, but as many as necessary, to achieve your goals" (Jacobs, 1987).

Implement Behavioral Intervention as Planned   Implement consistently across settings and individuals (Divack, Herrie, & Scott, 1985). Ensure that people in all settings focus on the same behaviors and respond similarly when they occur.

Evaluate, Modify, and Reimplement as Necessary   Evaluate effectiveness across a variety of relevant dimensions, including the frequency and duration of the target behavior and the child's apparent and self-reported self-esteem. For ineffective programs, identify the problem before modifying the program. Possible problems include poorly defined target behavior, premature evaluation (especially for long-standing behaviors), inadequate resources, or inconsistent implementation.

Maintain Change with Decreased Levels of Intervention if Possible   Maintenance of adaptive behaviors will be facilitated by gradual changes in the environmental contingencies. This is particularly true for students with ABI. Maintenance involves shifting the control for the behavior back to the student and away from external sources. The basic process is that of moving from primary (concrete) to secondary reinforcers, from artificial to natural rewards, from immediate to delayed feedback, and from continuous to less frequent reinforcement. In short, the movement is toward a type of reinforcement more often found in natural environments (Braunling-McMorrow, 1988; Divack et al., 1985). Some relapses should be expected as attempts are made to decrease the levels of reinforcement. If the relapse is severe or prolonged, however, it may be necessary to reestablish control over the behavior before again attempting to phase out the external controls, this time more gradually. With respect to changes in the antecedent conditions, it may not be necessary to fade these out unless they are unduly restrictive or intrusive. Use of a schedule, for example, is an acceptable strategy in a variety of settings and can usually be generalized to other settings without difficulty.

Generalize to Other Settings   Once desirable behaviors have been demonstrated in one setting, this change must be maintained in the original setting as well as generalized to other settings (e.g., other classrooms, the school bus, the home, the community). Plans for generalization should be made at the outset of the intervention.

These plans should take into account the environments in which the student will be expected to function and the characteristics of those settings. The likelihood of generalization can be enhanced by modifying the target behavior in a variety of settings and with a variety of different people. That is, the teaching of any skill will more likely generalize if it has been taught with a variety of stimuli and in a variety of environments. It may also be important to teach the student about situations to which he or she should not generalize (Horner & Albin, 1988). For example, although it is a good idea for a student to learn hand-raising behavior in a classroom setting, it is not desirable for the child to generalize this to the lunchroom, where he or she is interacting with peers at a table. Research shows that maintenance of learned skills and generalization to community settings can be successful following ABI, despite cognitive impairments (Lloyd & Cuvo, 1994). In cases in which generalization does not occur, the emphasis should move to teaching functional skills in each of the settings in which they are appropriate. Another strategy is to change the antecedent conditions by providing consistent cues in all environments (e.g., a watch with an alarm to cue self-monitoring or self-initiation on a regular basis).

SPECIFIC BEHAVIORS AND CHANGE STRATEGIES FOR THE STUDENT WITH ABI

Although the methods outlined previously have been applied to a number of different populations, much of the work with children and adolescents with ABI has consisted of case studies. The need for and potential value of behavioral approaches for people with brain injuries has been recognized since at least the mid-1980s (e.g., Eames & Wood, 1985; Zencius et al., 1989), and strategies have continued to develop and evolve. Children with ABI differ from the groups of individuals previously studied (e.g., children and adolescents with mental retardation, conduct disorders, hyperactivity) in regard to their learning histories (pre- and postinjury), their cognitive abilities, and their suddenly altered self-perceptions. These unique characteristics of children with ABI require that the effectiveness of behavior change strategies be reevaluated and modified to meet the needs of these children.

Common characteristics of students with ABI that affect behavior change strategies are their need for more repetition, more explicit expectations and contingencies, increased structure and cues, and specific programs to generalize behavior change to new settings. The abrupt loss in self-esteem and the need to establish a new sense of self also affect behavior programs. Increased support and reinforcement may be required. Maladaptive behaviors that have been inappropriately reinforced and thereby learned may persist even when the underlying cognitive impairments are no longer present (Malec, 1984). Challenging behaviors may include both the presence of maladaptive behaviors and the absence of adaptive ones. The following sample behaviors are arranged from the least to most intrusive. Although the least intrusive behaviors may be easiest to ignore, they are by no means the least costly and detrimental to a child with ABI. Perhaps because they are so easy to ignore, they are the most difficult to change.

Lack of Initiation

Children create many of their own opportunities for learning and socialization by initiating activities and interactions with others. As a result of the frontal lobe damage that frequently occurs with ABI, the ability to initiate is often compromised. Thus, children may be relatively passive, demonstrating neither intrusive problem behaviors nor positive behaviors (e.g., asking questions, starting a new activity after completing a previous one). It is particularly difficult to identify effective reinforcers for the student who lacks motivation and initiative as a result of frontal lobe damage (Grimm & Bleiberg, 1986). To increase initiation, a teacher may have to work very hard initially. The teacher first must decide on a behavior that he or she would like to see occur more often. The teacher should then let the child know what the target behavior is and be given the chance to give his or her agreement to work on this specific behavior. If the child expresses a preference for working on a different behavior first and it is one on which the teacher would also like to work, then that target behavior can be worked on first. After choosing a behavior, the teacher must work to consistently praise and reinforce that behavior every time it occurs. If necessary, the behavior can be shaped by reinforcing even close approximations or any component of the behavior. Both intentional and unintentional behaviors can be shaped into more complex and appropriate behaviors through rewards. For example, if the goal behavior for a particular child is that he spontaneously raises his hand to ask questions, the teacher would definitely reinforce this behavior every time it occurred. However, the teacher might also reinforce the child raising his hand for any reason (e.g., reinforcing the child raising his hand to scratch his head). Because the educator is trying to support the child's ability to initiate, spontaneous and appropriate ideas or activities must be reinforced whenever they occur. The question of how to reinforce a behavior depends on what is reinforcing for the individual child. In the simplest case, a child is reinforced by attention. Thus, if the child raises his hand, the teacher calls on him, and he feels successful, this behavior is likely to occur again. In other cases, the reward must be more concrete. For younger children, this may be a sticker on a chart each time they raise their hands to ask a question. For older children, praise alone may be effective or it may be necessary to work with each child and his or her family to identify rewards.

Somatic Complaints

Increases in somatic complaints are common following ABI in both children and adults. Complaints are variable but often include headaches, fatigue, dizziness, double vision, and problems with hearing. The difficulty in this behavior is that complaints of physical discomfort may prevent a child from focusing on and completing the task at hand. This behavior may also distance peers who grow tired of hearing the child's complaints no matter how legitimate they are. Somatic complaints should always be taken seriously and communicated back to the child's family to ensure that medical intervention is timely and effective in minimizing symptoms. It is also necessary, however, for children (like all of us) to learn coping strategies for dealing with discomfort without allowing minor irritations to interfere with daily activities. Again, a teacher's response to somatic complaints will vary depending on a number of factors, including the communicative function of the complaint. Because the verbal complaint may serve many different functions, teachers must become skilled in recognizing the individual child's way of communicating somatic complaints in each circumstance and respond accordingly. Table 1 provides a list of causes or functions of somatic complaints and possible responses the teacher can make.

Disinhibition

Disinhibition, behavior related to the loss of ability to self-monitor and control behavior, is frequently associated with ABI. The child may say (or do) nearly anything that occurs to him or her rather than "reading" the situation to decide what is appropriate. For example, a child may announce aloud that her parents fought the night before or that she likes a boy in her class. In the right setting (e.g., in a conversation with a close friend), these comments may be appropriate, but communicated to the entire class in the midst of a social studies lesson they are cause for laughter, shock, or ridicule. Disinhibition

Table 1.   Possible causes and functions as well as responses to somatic complaints

Cause or function of somatic complaint	Possible responses
The child is uncomfortable and needs help.	Refer the child to the school nurse or family doctor for medical care.
The child is attempting to avoid embarrassment in front of his or her peers.	Provide more frequent praise.
	Break the task into smaller parts for more frequent success.
The child is trying to get attention.	Ignore behavior until opportunity for giving positive attention occurs.
	Cue the child with a more appropriate way to get attention (e.g., "If you don't really have a headache but want me to talk to you, you can just raise your hand and I'll come as soon as I can").
The child is highly stressed by the task at hand and is having somatic symptoms as a result.	Provide a break.
	Decrease the time spent doing a task.
	Alternate easy and difficult tasks.
	Choose the child's best time of day for this task.
	Start with brief periods of doing the task and gradually increase time.
	Provide additional cues or supports to lessen the difficulty of the task.
	Provide a partner to assist with some aspects of the task.

can also manifest itself in inappropriate behaviors (e.g., lifting up one's shirt to scratch an itchy stomach; touching another person inappropriately, sometimes in a sexual manner). When environmental resources are significant, such as in a rehabilitation setting, staff can often be trained to respond to these behaviors in the same way each time. For example, each time an adolescent inappropriately touches a staff member, the staff member may say, "I don't like it when you do that" and briefly take the student to the time-out area. This strategy can work equally well in a classroom setting, but a problem may arise with peers implementing the strategy. Depending on the significance of the behavior, other students' maturity level and their willingness to help, and the self-awareness and motivation of the student with ABI to work on the behavior, classroom intervention can be effective. Alternatively, an aide can sometimes be used to help the student to monitor the behavior, to recognize and avoid situations in which the behavior may occur, and to cue the student with an alternative behavior as needed.

The following case study illustrates a possible approach to one child's difficulties that takes advantage of many of the school's resources in order to gradually increase the child's functioning and independence in the school setting.

Steven is a 9-year-old boy who sustained a brain injury in an automobile accident 6 months ago. Steven's motor and speech abilities were more affected by his injury than his cognitive abilities. During the acute stages of recovery, when he was still in the hospital, Steven was quite disinhibited and silly, using nonsense words and engaging in immature behaviors. These were reinforced by the immediate attention of those around him, as others were pleased by his increased verbalizations and responded immediately rather than identifying and rewarding more appropriate behaviors. When he returned to school, Steven found the work very difficult as a result of his physical and speech impairments (e.g., intentional tremor, left-side weakness, poor articulation). Steven's teacher recognized that she should not reward his silliness so she tried to ignore the behavior. However, Steven often cried if he was not able to get her attention. At this point, it was unclear whether these behaviors were a direct effect of his injury (a function of disinhibition) or learned behavior.

When Steven cried, his third-grade classmates teased him. Steven's self-esteem plummeted and his parents soon began to have difficulty getting him to attend school. Steven's parents met with school personnel to discuss the situation. They considered individualized home-based instruction but decided instead on a classroom aide to help Steven be more successful. This decision was made on the basis of both Steven's parents' and teachers' beliefs that a primary reason for Steven's behavior was that he wanted someone's attention. With the help of an aide, Steven's silliness in school decreased dramatically and he was able to focus on his work. He started to enjoy school again and did well on his assignments. Steven was allowed to use a word-processing program (with a keyboard guard) for written assignments and to take quizzes orally or on the computer to minimize the effect of his motor impairment. The aide's time with him was gradually decreased until she worked with Steven only during science and art classes, during which Steven's motor skills impairments still interfered with his ability to participate in classroom assignments. In these classes, she let Steven do as much as he could without getting frustrated and then would assist him in completing the task. One of Steven's friends was also paired with him in small-group activities, and the aide often made suggestions to his friend rather than actively helping Steven herself. When the aide left 2 months later, Steven's tremor had improved somewhat and his self-confidence had improved tremendously. He was able to ask for help directly, and the excessive silliness and crying had disappeared completely.

In Steven's case, the decision against home-based instruction was the right one. Reacquiring these skills in the school setting allowed Steven to continue to have positive contacts with his peers as well as a full day of academic programming. In addition, had he been placed in home-based instruction, he might have experienced problems generalizing skills to the school setting.

It should be noted that in this case, no "standard" behavior program was ever implemented to change Steven's behavior. Rather, the triggers for problem behaviors were addressed so that Steven was provided the resources he needed to be successful. He subsequently responded well to the natural reinforcement of academic success and mastery. His peers also proved to be excellent resources and support when they were provided with the necessary information and skills to deal with changes in Steven's abilities and emotional functioning. Finally, the collaborative and trusting relationship between Steven's parents and his school made it possible for his parents to allow Steven to face some challenges in the school setting rather than choosing the safe (but overly restrictive) option of home-based education. Although in many cases some period of home-based instruction is indicated, the use of this option may not always be beneficial.

Impulsivity

As many as one in four students have been described as impulsive following severe ABI (Edwards, 1987). Instead of waiting to respond to a question when called on, the child who is impulsive may blurt out his or her responses. The child may jump up from his or her seat for recess, momentarily forgetting about the balance problems that make sudden movement dangerous. This student may engage in dangerous or inappropriate behaviors because he or she does not reflect on behavior before acting. Although impulsive acts may not have led to injury or problems before, they may now cause problems because the child no longer has the same cognitive and physical capabilities as before the injury. Poor safety awareness and risk-taking behavior may thus lead to reinjury. Impulsivity in the child with ABI often has a cognitive basis, particularly impaired memory (e.g., the child acts impulsively because he or she does not want to miss the chance to act). Problems with attending to several salient aspects of a situation may also lead to impulsive behavior, as the child does not anticipate the consequences of the behavior. Strategies for intervening often focus on increasing the structure of the situation and changing the environment to provide additional cues for reflection and self-monitoring. The following case study illustrates potential intervention strategies.

Brian[1] is a 15 year old adolescent who had been struck by a bus while riding his skateboard nine months earlier. Brian had made an excellent physical recovery from his injury and remained an attractive and active adolescent. Unfortunately, he was far more impulsive than he had been prior to his injury and often made poor decisions, taking unnecessary risks to prove he was "cool". Brian returned to school and to his [general education] classroom two months after his injury. His school had no specific plan for his reentry and little information on the effects of brain injury. Due to the effects of his injury on his cognitive abilities, Brian was now unable to understand what was expected of him in the classroom and could not work independently on assignments. Brian reacted to these changes by impulsive refusals to do his work, clowning with his peers, and skipping classes. His behaviors seemed designed to preserve his self-esteem by avoiding situations where he might fail.

Testing by the school psychologist revealed that Brian had low average intellectual functioning and performed in the average range compared to peers on measures of academic achievement. This finding is not uncommon for a child soon after an injury before they have had a chance to fall behind peers in achievement (because of difficulties with new learning). An IEP was developed and it was determined that Brian's needs would best be met in a behavior disordered (BD) classroom. His parents agreed with this plan but remained bewildered by the sudden deterioration in Brian's behavior. Brian viewed the placement as a punishment and was angry to be separated from his old friends and primary sources of support and self-esteem. He became the "best at being bad" in his new classroom.

Evaluation and suggested plan: Defining the problem behaviors was relatively easy in this case, as the behaviors were overt and easily measured. The behaviors resulting in his BD placement included work refusal, clowning with his peers, and skipping classes. The cause of these behaviors was less clear. Brian had returned to school fully expecting to resume his typical routine, perhaps a bit of a hero after all he'd been through. Both he and his school were ill-prepared for the cognitive effects of his injury that made it difficult for him to complete his work adequately. It appeared that his misbehavior was designed both to get him out of doing work too difficult for him and to continue to maintain his status with his peers through his sense of humor and his clowning. How-

---

[1]This case study is reprinted from Deaton, A.V., & Waaland, P. (1994). Psychosocial effects of acquired brain injury. In R.C. Savage & G.F. Wolcott (Eds.), *Educational dimensions of acquired brain injury* (pp. 250–251). Austin, TX: PRO-ED; reprinted by permission.

ever, Brian's impulsivity and inability to succeed academically in the classroom resulted in feelings of frustration on Brian's part as he began to perceive himself as a failure. Because Brian denied [his] cognitive problems and perhaps was even unaware of them himself, Brian's parents and teachers initially attributed some of these difficulties to typical adolescent rebellion. However, the striking contrast between his preinjury and postinjury behavior convinced them he needed special assistance. They did not feel that his needs could be met in a [general education] classroom due to the limited resources available. Brian had distanced his peers and the frequency of his disruptive behavior made it unlikely that he could be effectively mainstreamed. Moreover, the severity of his new academic difficulties made it unclear whether and how Brian might be able to learn effectively once again. Based on this analysis of the problem and the available resources, recommendations for Brian included the following: (1) neuropsychological evaluation to identify injury-related cognitive impairments and to recommend an approach for remediation; (2) individual and family counseling to improve Brian's and his family's understanding of brain injury and to assist them in negotiating a plan whereby Brian could earn more independence and privileges by demonstrating agreed-upon behaviors; and (3) specific feedback on pragmatic skills (e.g., turn taking, interruptions, response to criticism) to improve Brian's competence and confidence in social situations. Additional recommendations were to be made pending the results of these interventions.

Poor Anger Control and Heightened Irritability

Heightened irritability and a "short fuse" are often noted following ABI. The cause of these may be the organic insult of the ABI itself, which affects structures in the brain that help mediate emotion (e.g., limbic system). Other causes may be more indirect (e.g., reactive anger as a result of frustration with achieving tasks that were easily accomplished before the injury). Heightened irritability may also occur because of changes in sensory perception and attention. For many children with ABI, heightened sensory experiences means that sounds of typical loudness are experienced as uncomfortably loud. For others, the difficulties with divided attention translate into frequent confusion when many things are going on simultaneously and the child is unable to effectively sort out the various pieces of information. One of the most effective ways of intervening with anger control problems is to reduce the triggers for anger. This means changing the conditions to which the child is exposed. For example, choosing a classroom with fewer students and less stimulation or altering the child's class schedule so that the most difficult subjects are presented at times when he or she is most able to handle frustration (often first in the day) both may reduce the triggers for anger. As the teacher gets to know an individual child, he or she will also be more able to recognize early signs of anger and to cue the child with a more acceptable response before the anger reaches a point at which it is difficult to control (e.g., "Why don't you take a quick break and get a drink of water before we continue"). Deescalating the behavior in this way helps the child to feel increased control and to be able to tolerate feelings of frustration without reaching the point at which he or she is likely to explode.

In the examples of behaviors noted previously, several commonalities in the intervention approach should be noted. First is the importance of collaboration with students and parents and the carry-over of behavior programs as appropriate. Second, salient and obvious rewards and reinforcement of behavior are initially provided rather than relying on incidental learning. Third, addressing cognitive and communication difficulties that underlie behavior problems is made a priority. Fourth, reasonable challenges and work load are important. Not all goals can be achieved simultaneously. Ensuring early successes is an excellent way to create additional resources in the form of the students' motivation and self-esteem, increasing the chances for further progress in developing adaptive behaviors.

For students with severe ABI and those in the early stages of recovery, a structured environment may be the treatment of choice for reducing or preventing behavior problems (Grimm & Bleiberg, 1986). Environments and programs can be designed to minimize difficulties and to maximize performance. Environmental modifications may reduce the need for new learning on the part of the student (Grimm & Bleiberg, 1986; Zencius et al., 1989). A routine daily schedule and a self-contained class, for example, can significantly reduce the amount of information a student has to remember and his or her confusion and anxiety about what to expect, thereby improving overall behavior and performance (Cohen, Joyce, Rhoades, & Welks, 1985). Communicating a positive attitude can provide the expectation that the student is going to be successful. Providing written lists and cues in some settings can also facilitate independent functioning, even when the child or adolescent has severe memory problems or difficulty continuing tasks to completion.

ALTERNATIVE INTERVENTIONS

Although this chapter focuses for the most part on change strategies that rely on resources available to the school and family, additional specific interventions may at times be necessary to address some of the more common behaviors occurring in students following ABI. These interventions include individual therapy, family support and counseling, peer-focused and group interventions, focused cognitive remediation, and pharmacological intervention. These strategies may also be necessary in cases in which the school's or family's available resources for consistent behavioral intervention are more limited. They are rarely a substitute, however, for school or home-based programming to meet a child's needs.

Individual Therapy

In situations in which behavior problems are a manifestation of emotional reactions to ABI and its effects, individual psychotherapy may be appropriate for dealing with the root cause of the behaviors. This is most effective with the student whose memory and insight are relatively intact and who has at least some awareness that his or her sadness and anger are related to ABI. Individual therapy interventions for the child or adolescent with ABI often need to be augmented by written and visual materials. For the child who has memory impairments but still seems to need individual intervention, making a memory journal with written summaries of sessions or pictures drawn to represent feelings and coping strategies may be useful. Videotapes are also helpful in circumventing cognitive impairments, enabling the child or adolescent to better understand how he or she appears to others. Serial videotapes of a child during various stages of his or her recovery can be valuable in providing the basis for insight into the severity of the injury as well as the significant progress already made. Because this type of counseling can differ greatly from traditional psychotherapy, it is best to seek out a practitioner who is accustomed to working with children and adolescents who have ABI.

Family Support and Counseling

Family support and information groups such as local chapters of the Brain Injury Association (previously known as the National Head Injury Foundation) can be invaluable in helping families to understand ABI, to recognize that they are not alone, and to deal with challenging behaviors resulting from ABI. Feelings of sadness, anger, exhaustion, resentment, and guilt are common. Family support may take the form of helping families to normalize some of the new experiences and may also help families to gain perspective. Information and support also enables families to advocate effectively for their children within the limitations of the school system, so that they may act as partners in the child's long-term recovery. When families continue to struggle with the effects of ABI even after receiving good support and information, they may benefit from family therapy to assist in adapting to a lifestyle that may differ greatly from that which they experienced before the injury. Therapy may focus on changing expectations, problem solving about specific issues, and/or securing additional resources that would improve the situation. Again, it is essential to choose a practitioner knowledgeable about the changes families experience as well as who is knowledgeable about the resources available to children with ABI and their families.

Peer-Focused and Group Interventions

Peer-focused interventions have the advantage of providing peer support, feedback, and modeling and may therefore be particularly appropriate for children and adolescents trying to reintegrate into their peer group when they return to school. Social skills impairments are a major barrier to successful school and community reentry (e.g., Flanagan, McDonald, & Togher, 1995). Following ABI, children are often less able to interpret others' emotions and the meanings of subtle nonverbal cues and, thus, are less appropriate in their social behaviors. The effect of this change in social competence is often severe when it comes to interactions with peers who may no longer view the child with ABI as the same person they knew before the injury (Pettersen, 1991). Peer-milieu and peer-group interventions may allow the child with ABI to feel less isolated and can facilitate social competence by providing practice in social settings. Peer-milieu interventions within the school setting may be particularly valuable because they occur in the natural school environment in which the child is expected to function. This is an important advantage because the ultimate goal of group interventions, as with any behavior change strategy, is to promote generalization. Clearly, one should not expect that merely having a child with ABI in a classroom setting with peers will enable him or her to improve social skills and develop friendships unless there is some formal intervention. In reviewing the literature on social skills in children with disabilities who attend general education classes, Gresham (1981, 1982) noted the need to make interventions explicit rather than expecting peer acceptance and modeling to occur spontaneously. With students who have ABI, the need for clearly communicated behavior expectations as well as cuing and initiation of appropriate social interactions by others appears to be critical. Therapeutic games (e.g.,

Never Say Never; Thinking, Feeling, Doing Game) and books are available to include in school curricula and to help structure the interactions of children in groups. These interventions may, in fact, be more effective than focusing on only changing the social skills of a child with ABI because they focus on peer acceptance and peer recognition of the child's competencies.

Formal support groups, often led by school psychologists or guidance counselors, can augment peer-milieu interventions by providing a degree of inoculation against teasing, peer insensitivity, and other stresses experienced by the child or adolescent with ABI (Barin, Hanchett, Jacob, & Scott, 1985). Examples of formal peer-group intervention include anger control, social skills, feelings management, and problem-solving groups. The setting, the individuals in the group, and the available resources will help determine the format. Initial studies indicate the effectiveness of groups in improving communication and social skills, especially when videotaped feedback and repeated practice are provided (Ben-Yishay, 1980; Helffenstein & Wechsler, 1982). Awareness of ABI-related impairments and residual assets can also be improved through formal group interventions for older children and adolescents who have sustained ABI (Deaton, 1986). Such groups are, however, more likely to occur in rehabilitation settings rather than schools. Although there are few documented applications of group interventions with younger children after ABI, there are a number of group formats developed to help children cope with other life-altering situations, such as life-threatening illness, divorce, and bereavement.

Focused Cognitive Remediation

In those situations in which problem behaviors are the result of cognitive impairments, cognitive remediation is often an effective route for addressing the cognitive impairments that cause or contribute to the behaviors. Individualized cognitive interventions may target impairment areas, capitalize on strengths, and teach compensation. These interventions allow the child to be less frustrated by the changes in his or her abilities and also enable the child to become more of a resource in his or her own academic program and overall recovery (Brown & Morgan, 1987). Cognitive remediation and neuropsychological evaluations can also be of value in ensuring that expectations of the student are realistic and that behavior problems are not a result of the student being asked to do tasks that are not within his or her capabilities. Although cognitive interventions are clearly the province of the classroom teacher, an altered approach to education may be necessary to meet the needs of the student with ABI (e.g., Ylvisaker, Urbanczyk, & Savage, 1995). For example, some students whose poor memory poses a major barrier to academic and social success can be taught to use a memory notebook to keep track of tasks, and, thereby, can be more successful in their completion.

Pharmacological Intervention

Professionals and family members often disagree on the use of medications to affect behaviors related to ABI. Wood (1984) has suggested that psychopharmacological interventions can sometimes be useful adjuncts to behavior management. The reported success of such interventions as aids to behavior change has been variable. Although little consistent data have been accumulated on the use of psychoactive medications in children with ABI, research data on this area continue to improve. Concern has been raised about the possible detrimental effects of medications on cognition, leading to a decrease in the student's ability to learn (Barin et al., 1985; Dean, 1986; Savage & Wolcott, 1988). However, medications have also been described as helpful in increasing attention (Dean, 1986; Kraus, 1995), decreasing agitation (Barin et al., 1985; Fowler, Hertzog, & Wagner, 1995), and reducing apathy (Marin, Fogel, Hawkins, Duffy, & Krupp, 1995), thereby facilitating learning and behavior change. A physician skilled in working with children with ABI and with using these medications post-ABI should be consulted before any pharmacological intervention is used. Such practitioners are often difficult to identify but may be located through a local chapter of the Brain Injury Association.

MAKING THE TRANSITION
TO A NEW SCHOOL OR TO A WORKSITE

Meeting the instructional (and other) needs of students with challenging behaviors as they move from one school to another or from a school to a work setting requires preparation. Although teachers', as well as the school's, responsibilities may officially end once the child or adolescent moves on to another setting, their ability to affect a student's success beyond the school setting is significant. Taking responsibility for the success of the transition will result in greater success on the part of the student and appreciation from the student, his or her family, and those who inherit the responsibility for his or her continuing development.

Although formal testing and reports can be helpful in preparing another setting to meet the needs of the child with ABI, practical strategies and detailed behavioral reports are needed to augment formal evaluations (Dymond, 1995). The following strategies (partially adapted from Dymond) will be helpful to the educator:

1. Invite the new teacher/employer to visit and observe the student in his or her current setting. If this is not possible, provide a videotape of the student's behaviors and strategies for assisting the student.
2. Give the student one or more opportunities to visit the new setting, initially accompanied by familiar others.
3. Use team members from both the old and new settings to develop a plan, whether it takes the form of an IEP, individualized transition plan (ITP), or work entry plan. Expect problem behaviors to occur and develop a plan for what to do (and not do) when the behavior occurs.
4. Involve the student in developing goals and strategies.
5. Build in regular opportunities for reevaluation and revision of the plan, possibly as soon as the end of the first week in the new setting.
6. Have realistic expectations. Do not expect perfection from either the student or from those teachers and employers new to working with him or her.
7. Include written documentation. This should include detailed descriptions of challenging behaviors, the apparent functions of or triggers for the behaviors, and a chronological list of strategies that have been used to prevent problem behaviors from occurring and to promote more positive behaviors. Include specific descriptions of strategies, length of time each strategy was tried, its results, and the rationale for changing strategies. Also include information about the student's likes and dislikes, strengths and weaknesses, any assistive devices, best methods of communicating with the student, and the student's preferred learning style.
8. Involve parents and peers in supporting desired behaviors in other settings.

By facilitating the transition to the next setting, the teacher is finishing the work he or she has done to improve the student's capabilities in the classroom and is providing tools that will be essential to the student's future success.

CONCLUSION

The effects of ABI can be dramatic, prolonged, and potentially devastating. The recognition and appropriate treatment of challenging behaviors is an essential part of helping the student with ABI to recover and function effectively, both in school and in the larger community. Whether behaviors are a direct result of ABI or have been caused or worsened by environmental conditions, many are capable of improvement. Standard behavioral methods provide the foundation for effective intervention, with modifications determined on the basis of unique aspects of ABI as well as the valuable resources provided by the school setting. The transition from one setting to the next, often overlooked, is an opportunity for maintenance and generalization of adaptive behaviors as the recurrence of maladaptive behaviors can be anticipated and minimized.

REFERENCES

Achenbach, T.M. (1981). *The Child Behavior Checklist.* Burlington: University of Vermont, Associates in Psychiatry.

Asarnow, R.F., Satz, P., Light, R., Lewis, R., & Neumann, E. (1991). Behavior problems and adaptive functioning in children with mild and severe closed head injury. *Journal of Pediatric Psychology, 16*(5), 543–555.

Barin, J.J., Hanchett, J.M., Jacob, W.L., & Scott, M.B. (1985). Counseling the head injured patient. In M. Ylvisaker (Ed.), *Head injury rehabilitation: Children and adolescents* (pp. 361–379). San Diego: College-Hill Press.

Ben-Yishay, Y. (Ed.). (1980). *Working approaches to remediation of cognitive deficits in brain damaged.* Supplement to the 8th Annual Workshop for Rehabilitation Professionals. New York: New York University.

Boyer, M.G., & Edwards, P. (1991). Outcome 1 to 3 years after severe traumatic brain injury in children and adolescents. *Injury: The British Journal of Accident Surgery, 22*(4), 315–320.

Braunling-McMorrow, D. (1988). Behavioral rehabilitation. In P.M. Deutsch & K.B. Fralish (Eds.), *Innovations in head injury rehabilitation* (pp. 8-1 to 8-52). New York: Matthew Bender & Co.

Brown, T.L., & Morgan, S.B. (1987). Cognitive training with brain-injured children: General issues and approaches. In J.M. Williams & C.J. Long (Eds.), *The rehabilitation of cognitive disabilities* (pp. 217–231). New York: Plenum.

Cohen, S.B., Joyce, C.M., Rhoades, K.W., & Welks, D.M. (1985). Educational programming for head injured students. In M. Ylvisaker (Ed.), *Head injury rehabilitation: Children and adolescents* (pp. 383–410). San Diego: College-Hill Press.

Coster, W.J., Haley, S., & Baryza, M.J. (1994). Functional performance of young children after traumatic brain injury: A 6–month follow-up study. *American Journal of Occupational Therapy, 48*(3), 211–218.

Davis, J.R., Turner, W., Rolider, A., & Cartwright, T. (1994). Natural and structured baselines in the treatment of aggression following brain injury. *Brain Injury, 8*(7), 589–597.

Dean, R.S. (1986). Neuropsychological aspects of psychiatric disorders. In J. Obrzut & G.W. Hynd (Eds.), *Child neuropsychology* (Vol. 2, pp. 83–112). New York: Academic Press.

Deaton, A.V. (1986, August). *Self assessment group: An intervention strategy for head injured adolescents.* Paper presented at the Annual Meeting of the American Psychological Association, Washington, DC.

Deaton, A.V. (1987). Behavioral change strategies for children and adolescents with traumatic brain injuries. *Journal of Learning Disabilities, 20*(8), 581–589.

Deaton, A.V., & Waaland, P. (1994). Psychosocial effects of acquired brain injury. In R.C. Savage & G.F. Wolcott (Eds.), *Educational dimensions of acquired brain injury* (pp. 239–256). Austin, TX: PRO-ED.

Divack, J.A., Herrie, J., & Scott, M.B. (1985). Behavior management. In M. Ylvisaker (Ed.), *Head injury rehabilitation: Children and adolescents* (pp. 347–360). San Diego: College-Hill Press.

Dymond, S. (1995, April). Behavioral strategies: Planning transitions for students with challenging behaviors: Documenting successful strategies. *Four Runner, 10*(7), 3. (Newsletter of the Severe Disabilities Technical Assistance Center, Virginia Commonwealth University, Richmond)

Eames, P., & Wood, R. (1985). Rehabilitation after severe brain injury: A special unit approach. *International Rehabilitation Medicine, 7*(3), 130–133.

Education for All Handicapped Children Act of 1975, PL 94-142, 20 U.S.C. § 1400 *et seq.*

Edwards, P.A. (1987). Rehabilitation outcomes in children with brain injury. *Rehabilitation Nursing, 12*(3), 125–127.

Fay, G.C., Jaffe, K.M., Polissar, N.L., Liao, S., Rivara, J.B., & Martin, K.M. (1994). Outcome of pediatric traumatic brain injury at three years: A cohort study. *Archives of Physical Medicine and Rehabilitation, 75*(7), 733–741.

Feeney, T.J., & Urbanczyk, B. (1994). Behavior as communication. In R.C. Savage & G.F. Wolcott (Eds.), *Educational dimensions of acquired brain injury* (pp. 277–302). Austin, TX: PRO-ED.

Flanagan, S., McDonald, S., & Togher, L. (1995). Evaluating social skills following traumatic brain injury: The BRISS as a clinical tool. *Brain Injury, 9*(4), 321–338.

Fowler, S.B., Hertzog, J., & Wagner, B.K. (1995). Pharmacological interventions for agitation in head-injured patients in the acute care setting. *Journal of Neuroscience Nursing, 27*(2), 119–123.

Gelfand, D.M., & Hartmann, D.P. (1984). *Child behavior analysis and therapy.* Elmsford, NY: Pergamon.

Greenspan, A.I., & MacKenzie, E.J. (1994). Functional outcome after pediatric head injury. *Pediatrics, 94*(4 Pt 1), 425–432.

Gresham, F.M. (1981). Social skills training with handicapped children: A review. *Review of Educational Research, 51*(1), 139–176.

Gresham, F.M. (1982). Misguided mainstreaming: The case for social skills training with handicapped children. *Exceptional Children, 48*(5), 422–433.

Grimm, B.H., & Bleiberg, J. (1986). Psychological rehabilitation in traumatic brain injury. In S. Filskov & T. Boll (Eds.), *Handbook of clinical neuropsychology* (pp. 495–560). New York: John Wiley & Sons.

Helffenstein, D.A., & Wechsler, F. (1982). The use of Interpersonal Process Recall (IPR) in the remediation of interpersonal and communication skill deficits in the newly brain injured. *Clinical Neuropsychology, 4*(3), 139–143.

Horner, R.H., & Albin, R.W. (1988). Research on general-case procedures for learners with severe disabilities. *Education and Treatment of Children, 11*(4), 375–388.

Jacobs, H. (1987, March). *Behavior problems.* Workshop presented at the National Head Injury Foundation Annual Conference, Crystal City, VA.

Jacobs, H. (1988). Yes, behavior analysis can help, but do you know how to harness it? *Brain Injury, 2*(4), 339–346.

Jaffe, K.M., Polissar, N.L., Fay, G.C., & Liao, S. (1995). Recovery trends over three years following pediatric traumatic brain injury. *Archives of Physical Medicine and Rehabilitation, 76*(1), 17–26.

Kraus, M.F. (1995). Neuropsychiatric sequelae of stroke and traumatic brain injury: The role of psychostimulants. *International Journal of Psychiatry in Medicine, 25*(1), 39–51.

Lloyd, L.F., & Cuvo, A.J. (1994). Maintenance and generalization of behaviors after treatment of persons with traumatic brain injury. *Brain Injury, 8*(6), 529–540.

Malec, J. (1984). Training the brain-injured client in behavioral self-management skills. In B.A. Edelstein & E.T. Couture (Eds.), *Behavioral assessment and rehabilitation of the traumatically brain damaged* (pp. 121–150). New York: Plenum.

Marin, R.S., Fogel, B.S., Hawkins, J., Duffy, J., & Krupp, B. (1995). Apathy: A treatable syndrome. *Journal of Neuropsychiatry and Clinical Neuroscience, 7*(1), 23–30.

Parker, R.S. (1994). Neurobehavioral outcome of children's mild traumatic brain injury. *Seminars in Neurology, 14*(1), 67–73.

Pettersen, L. (1991). Sensitivity to emotional cues and social behavior in children and adolescents after head injury. *Perceptual and Motor Skills, 73*(3 Pt. 2), 1139–1150.

Savage, R., & Wolcott, G. (Eds.). (1988). *An educator's manual: What educators need to know about students with traumatic brain injury.* Southborough, MA: National Head Injury Foundation, Task Force on Special Education.

Sbordone, R.J., Liter, J.C., & Pettler-Jennings, P. (1995). Recovery of function following severe traumatic brain injury: A retrospective 10 year follow up. *Brain Injury, 9*(3), 285–299.

Szekeres, S.F., & Meserve, N.F. (1994). Collaborative intervention in schools after traumatic brain injury. *Topics in Language Disorders, 15*(1), 21–36.

Ullman, R.T., Sleador, E.K., & Sprague, R.L. (1988). *The ACTERS.* Champaign, IL: MetriTech, Inc.

Vredevoogd, M.J. (1986, August/September). Suggestions for working with the difficult to handle closed head injured person. In *Ditty, Lynch, and Associates, A Newsletter/Updater.* (Available from Ditty, Lynch, and Associates, Inc., Bloomfield Medical Village, 6405 Telegraph Rd., Suite K, Birmingham, MI 48010)

Wood, R.L. (1984). Behavior disorders following severe brain injury: Their presentation and psychological management. In D.N. Brooks (Ed.), *Closed head injury: Psychological, social, and family consequences* (pp. 195–219). New York: Oxford University Press.

Ylvisaker, M., & Feeney, T.J. (1994). Communication and behavior: Collaboration between speech-language pathologists and behavioral psychologists. *Topics in Language Disorders, 15*(1), 37–54.

Ylvisaker, M., Urbanczyk, B., & Savage, R.C. (1995). Cognitive assessment and intervention. In R.C. Savage & G.F. Wolcott (Eds.), *An educator's manual: What educators need to know about students with brain injury* (pp. 61–79). Washington, DC: Brain Injury Association, Inc.

Zencius, A.H., Wesolowski, M.D., Burke, W.H., & McQuade, P. (1989). Antecedent control in the treatment of brain injured clients. *Brain Injury, 3*(2), 199–205.

chapter eight

A Positive, Communication-Based Approach to Challenging Behavior After ABI

Timothy J. Feeney and Mark Ylvisaker

PERSONALITY CHANGES AND CHALLENGING behavior are often the most troubling consequences of acquired brain injury (ABI) in children and adolescents. Teachers, family members, and others frequently report that they can understand and cope appropriately with physical, perceptual, and cognitive disability, but that the behavioral issues are both perplexing and difficult to manage. In this chapter, after a brief discussion of behavioral outcome, we attempt to articulate, explain, and illustrate seven intervention themes that have emerged as most critical in our attempts to support several hundred children and adolescents with ABI in their return to school and in their ongoing pursuit of academic and social success over the years after their injury.

BEHAVIORAL OUTCOME IN STUDENTS WITH ABI

ABI is a potentially misleading disability category. Unlike other educational disabilities, ABI classification does not support any inferences or assumptions about the functioning of the student. Some students with ABI experience remarkable recovery and succeed academically and socially with no special services or supports after the early acute phases of injury have passed. Others have profound and persistent disability across varied domains of functioning. Most have unique sets of strengths and weaknesses based on preinjury abilities, the nature and severity of the injury, postinjury care and intervention, psychological reactions of the student, and long-term supports. To add to the variety, many students with ABI were at risk for injury because of pretrauma cognitive, behavioral, or environmental concerns, which may play a larger role in outcome than do the direct effects of the injury itself (Asarnow, Satz, Light, & Neumann, 1991; Fletcher, Ewing-Cobbs, Miner, & Levin, 1990; Greenspan & MacKenzie, 1994). For all of these reasons, ABI classification identifies a varied population of students for whom it is highly inappropriate to prescribe a single intervention approach in behavioral or any other domains.

However, having frankly acknowledged the variability within the group, it is equally important to be sensitive to central tendencies, based in part on the disproportionate vulnerability of certain parts of the brain in closed brain injury. Armed with an understanding of common issues and typical patterns of long-term outcome, clinicians and teachers are in a better position to understand the student's behavior correctly, generate hypotheses regarding the student's needs, and anticipate possible long-term problems.

Pathophysiology and Behavioral Outcome

Pathophysiological studies of children and adults with closed brain injury invariably highlight the vulnerability of prefrontal cortex as well as medial/inferior temporal lobe structures (Diamond, 1991; Pang, 1985). From a behavioral perspective, the areas of prefrontal damage that have the greatest effect on social behavior are 1) orbital frontal injury, associated with transient or persistent disinhibition, impulsiveness, lability, reduced anger control, aggressiveness, sexual acting out, perseveration, and poor social judgment; 2) ventromedial prefrontal injury, associated with reduced ability to associate typical emotional states (i.e., "somatic markers") with memories for events, resulting in inefficient learning from consequences; and 3) mesial and dorsolateral prefrontal injury, associated with reduced initiation and apparent depression or lack of motivation (Benton, 1991; Damasio, 1994; Damasio, Tranel, & Damasio, 1990; Eslinger, Damasio, Damasio, & Grattan, 1989; Fuster, 1989; Saver & Damasio, 1991; Stuss & Benson, 1986). When these three possibilities are combined, what emerges is the clinical picture of a student whose physical, cognitive, and academic recovery may be adequate—or even excellent—but 1) who appears lazy and unmotivated when not directed by others; 2) who, when stressed or otherwise provoked, exhibits irritating or even explosive social behaviors that students who are neurologically intact manage to inhibit; and 3) who fails to change behavior patterns in response to the types of consequences and contingency contracts that may be effective in managing the behavior of peers. The literature on long-term outcome after prefrontal injury in children highlights exactly these themes (Ackerly, 1964; Benton, 1991; Eslinger, Grattan, Damasio, & Damasio, 1992; Grattan & Eslinger, 1991, 1992; Marlowe, 1992; Mateer & Williams, 1991; Price, Doffnre, Stowe, & Mesulum, 1990; Williams & Mateer, 1992), which are familiar to teachers and clinicians who have extensive experience with this population.

Cognition and Behavior

Challenging behavior after ABI is often related dynamically to cognitive weakness. Indeed, cognitive, behavior, and communication problems are often alternative descriptions of the same underlying reality. For example, what is labeled inappropriate social behavior may be a result of 1) confusion about what is expected; 2) difficulty in interpreting instructions, abstract or indirect language, or the nonverbal communication of others; 3) difficulty planning and organizing behavior around goals; 4) lack of insight into limitations; 5) failure to transfer learned behavior from one context to another; 6) forgetfulness; or 7) rigid adherence to rules and solutions that have worked in the past. Each of these cognitive symptoms is associated with prefrontal injury and may play a role in what is labeled a behavior problem. Furthermore, cognitive weakness predictably results in unsatisfactory performance in school, at least relative to pretrauma expectations, creating the foundation for increasing emotional and behavior problems associated with a growing sense of failure and frustration. Finally, if not well managed, challenging behaviors can easily become important components of the individual's communication repertoire (e.g., acting aggressively to escape a difficult task), making them doubly resistant to change.

Delayed Consequences

Researchers and clinicians alike have highlighted the frequency with which behavior problems increase over the years following frontal lobe injury in children and adolescents (Benton, 1991; Eslinger et al., 1989; Feeney & Ylvisaker, 1995; Grattan & Eslinger, 1992; Ylvisaker, 1993; Ylvisaker & Feeney, 1995). Although far from inevitable, this ominous phenomenon is sufficiently common to warrant careful monitoring of children with ABI and active attention to preventive

measures. Some investigators emphasize the neurobiological contributors to delayed onset of behavioral symptoms after frontal lobe
injury (Eslinger et al., 1989; Grattan & Eslinger, 1990, 1992; Marlowe,
1989, 1992; Mateer & Williams, 1991). According to this account, the
slow anatomical and physiological development of the frontal lobes
provides the biological foundation for maturation of executive or self-
regulatory functions—what is ordinarily thought of as personal and
social maturation—that continues through the adolescent years, possibly paralleling the ongoing biological development of prefrontal
neural systems during that period of development. Thus, it is possible for early damage to yield no observable consequences until the
function specifically associated with the injured part of the brain is
expected to mature. For example, a 3-year-old with prefrontal injury
who is impulsive, disinhibited, egocentric, labile, volatile, and concrete may be indistinguishable from typically developing peers. That
same child, however, may appear to have a serious disability at age
6 or 7 if adequate maturation in these areas of functioning has not
occurred in the intervening years. Ylvisaker and Feeney (1995)
described analogous delayed consequences when the injury occurs in
early adolescence.

In the authors' view, delayed behavioral consequences of frontal
lobe injury are rarely a biological inevitability. In all likelihood, delayed consequences are most often a result of vulnerability created
by the injury interacting with emotional responses to failure and
loss and with ineffective behavior management and cognitive supports. Successful efforts to reverse serious long-term behavior problems (Feeney & Ylvisaker, 1995) and to prevent them in children
who are known to be vulnerable (see the following section) support
this multifactorial explanation and give reason for optimism in relation to preventing behavior problems before they arise and to reversing downward behavioral spirals that are allowed to begin.

In summary, there are many possible contributors to behavior
problems in students with ABI. Therefore, even when staff are armed
with the best neurodiagnostic information available, there are no
alternatives to systematic, collaborative, and contextualized testing
of behavioral hypotheses as a basis for planning intervention and,
based on such creative and flexible assessment, a basis for implementation of customized programs of cognitive and behavioral support (Ylvisaker et al., 1995; Ylvisaker, Hartwick, & Stevens, 1991).
Furthermore, staff must continue indefinitely to be vigilant and flexible because of the unpredictability in ongoing development as a
child with brain injury faces increasing academic and social demands
in the years after the injury.

INTERVENTION PREMISES

This section describes seven intervention premises that compose the core of a positive, integrated, and communication-based approach to challenging behavior after ABI. This approach is sensitive to the neuropsychological realities associated with ABI in children and also to developments in behavioral intervention for students with other disabilities. In the final section of the chapter, these premises are illustrated and empirical support for their use is provided.

Premise 1: Behavioral Intervention
Begins with a Functional Analysis of the Behavior

The applied behavior analysis literature is rich with detailed descriptions of assessment approaches designed to identify the variables that elicit and maintain both desirable and problematic behaviors in individual cases. Assessment can be conducted by means of systematic manipulation of variables in experimental settings (e.g., Iwata, Dorsey, Silfer, Bauman, & Richman, 1982). Alternatively, many behavior analysts recommend direct observation of the individual's behavior in natural environments (e.g., Bijou, Peterson, & Ault, 1968; Durand, 1990; Lalli, Browder, Mace, & Brown, 1995) or indirect observation by means of a structured interview with people who have daily contact with the individual with challenging behavior (e.g., O'Neill, Horner, Albin, Storey, & Sprague, 1990). Increasingly, behavioral psychologists recommend approaching behavioral assessment within a communication framework (i.e., "What is the student communicating with this challenging behavior?" and "Is there a more desirable way for him to communicate the message?") (Carr & Durand, 1985; Carr, McConnachie, Levin, & Kemp, 1993; Durand, 1990; Durand & Carr, 1991; Feeney & Urbanczyk, 1994). Kern, Childs, Dunlap, Clarke, and Falk (1994) have illustrated creative procedures for systematically testing competing hypotheses regarding the purpose of challenging behavior in school settings.

The conceptual framework of applied behavior analysis and the assessment procedures developed within this framework are of great value in working with students with ABI. However, brain injury, particularly prefrontal injury, adds important complexity to the experimental analysis of behavior. For example, during the early stages of emergence from coma, difficult behaviors (e.g., random movement, resistance to restraints, unpredictable vocalization or lashing out at others) may be a direct result of neurological states or physiological events and have little relationship to observable environmental antecedents or consequences. Later in recovery, the child may appear to be alert but have minimal capacity to inhibit responses, resulting in behavior that is connected to internal and environmental antecedents but minimally related to consequences. In the chronic stages of recovery, it may be necessary to pay greater attention to internal setting events (see the following section) and to dramatically reduced neurologically based capacity to inhibit behavior, compared with students with behavior problems who are neurologically intact.

In most cases, challenging behavior is a complex mix of preinjury behavior patterns, physiological triggers, reduced initiation or inhibition, and newly learned behaviors. During hospitalization, sorting through these factors requires collaboration among the medical staff, family members, and all of the members of the rehabilitation team. Later in recovery, the set of collaborators expands to include school staff and the student. Because challenging behavior after ABI may begin as random or neurologically based but evolve into stable components of the student's communication system, it is critical to include an analysis of the communication competencies and behaviors of everyday communication partners in a comprehensive behavioral assessment. A valuable and often overlooked indirect consequence of collaboration in assessment is agreement regarding the reasons for the student's behavior and an associated increase in the consistency of intervention. Finally, behavioral assessment must be ongoing because neurological changes, situational changes, increasing demands of the academic and social curriculum, emotional reactions, and ongoing learning in response to consequences easily combine to change intervention needs and strategies during the months and years after the injury (Bailey & Pyles, 1989; Cooper, Wacker, Sasso, Reimers, & Donn, 1990; Dunlap, Kern-Dunlap, Clarke, & Robbins, 1991; Emery, Binkoff, Houts, & Carr, 1983; Halle, 1989).

Premise 2:   Effective Intervention for Children and Adolescents with ABI Focuses More on Antecedents than on Consequences

Traditional behavior management highlights manipulation of consequences of behavior (e.g., reinforcing the student for desirable behavior, either ignoring or punishing the student for undesirable behavior). Attention to consequences continues to be important after ABI. For reasons discussed previously (e.g., potentially reduced capacity for self-control or for modifying behavior in response to feedback), however, behavior management for students with frontal lobe injury must rely to a larger extent on the manipulation of antecedents. This principle is illustrated by typically developing toddlers and young preschoolers who are clearly capable of learning from consequences, but whose behavior is best managed by 1) "child proofing" the environment to eliminate triggers for challenging behavior, 2) establishing well-understood routines and scripts that help the child maintain appropriate behavior, 3) thoroughly preparing the child in advance for any deviation from routines, 4) making demands only when the child is in a psychological state to cope appropriately with the demands (e.g., not tired and hungry), 5) ensuring that demands placed on the child do not exceed his or her capacity to meet them, and 6) redirecting the child at the first sign of disruptive behavior. These procedures are particularly important in the early stages of neurological recovery after ABI but may remain necessary indefinitely for students with significant frontal lobe injury. Later, students with adequate cognitive recovery can be engaged in the important process of learning to manage their own antecedents (e.g., making plans in advance for coping with stressful situations, leaving stressful situations before they get out of control).

Setting Events Setting events, an important subcategory of antecedent conditions, has received increasing attention in the behavioral psychology literature (Colvin & Sugai, 1989; Michael, 1982, 1989; Vollmer & Iwata, 1991; Wahler & Fox, 1981). Setting events include 1) a variety of internal states of the individual, including neurological states (e.g., overactivation of the limbic regions), other physiological states (e.g., pain, illness), cognitive states (e.g., confusion), and emotional states (e.g., anger, depression, sense of loss); 2) task difficulty; 3) the presence or absence of specific people; and 4) other environmental stressors (e.g., ambient noise). Although neglected in the traditional behavioral literature on grounds that they are unobservable and beyond the reach of experimental manipulation, setting events must be considered critical in the management of students with ABI. In some cases, internal setting events can be *directly* manipulated (e.g., pharmacological treatment of temporal lobe rage behavior or of pain associated with heterotopic ossification). In other cases, internal setting events can be *indirectly* manipulated (e.g., reducing confusion by creating familiar routines; reducing frustration by ensuring that tasks can be completed successfully; reducing anger, resentment, and control battles by allowing the student to choose activities).

When difficult or unmotivating tasks are presented to students in the presence of a variety of negative setting events (e.g., physical pain, confusion, anxiety, frustration, depression), the predictable result is refusal, possibly accompanied by seriously challenging behavior. Alternatively, when such tasks are presented in the presence of positive setting events (e.g., relaxation, clear orientation to the task, understanding of routines, feeling of competence, sense of control), the likelihood of engagement in and successful completion of the activity increases. This important principle, illustrated in Figures 1 and 2, has been experimentally validated in the developmental disabilities literature (e.g., Davis, Brady, Hamilton, McEvoy, & Williams, 1994; Gardner, Cole, Davidson, & Karan, 1986; Harchik, Sherman, & Bannerman, 1993). A growing body of clinical research supports the application of this principle to students with ABI (e.g., Feeney & Ylvisaker, 1995; Ylvisaker & Feeney, 1995, in press). Because of the strong likelihood of persisting negative internal states and because it is easy for teachers and others to add to negative setting events by overestimating the student's ability and orientation to task (creating confusion and frustration), special attention must be paid to the generation of positive setting events before difficult tasks are introduced.

Behavioral Momentum   Closely related to the principle of positive and negative setting events, the principle of behavioral momentum states that positive and successful behavior increases the likelihood of subsequent positive and successful behavior, whereas negative and unsuccessful behavior increases the likelihood of subsequent negative and unsuccessful behavior (Mace et al., 1990; Mace, Page, Ivanck, & O'Brien, 1986; Nevin, 1988). In other words, individuals who face a challenging task from a background of successful completion of a large number of similar tasks are likely to accept the challenge, work hard, and succeed. In contrast, individuals who face a challenging task from a background of failure and frustration with similar—or nonsimilar—tasks are likely to reject the new task and to respond in an undesirable manner. Figure 3 uses a metaphor of a gas tank to illustrate this principle.

As with the principle of positive and negative setting events, the principle of behavioral momentum has special application to students with ABI because they generally have difficulty succeeding *in relation to their own standards for success, which were established by their preinjury profile of abilities.* That is, students naturally retain an understanding of who they were and what they could accomplish before the injury. With reduced abilities after the injury, they may succeed in the eyes of therapists, teachers, parents, and others but fail miserably in their own eyes. Therefore, what staff may label random explosive behavior in response to minimal provocation may rather be a natural response to an uninterrupted sequence of major failures in the student's eyes.

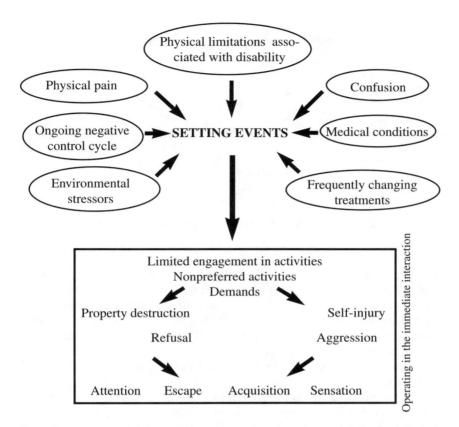

Figure 1.   Illustration of the relationship between negative setting events and challenging behavior.

Much of the experimental work involving this principle has been undertaken with individuals with developmental disabilities using highly artificial tasks to create behavioral momentum (Davis et al., 1994; Mace et al., 1988; Zarcone, Iwata, Mazaleski, & Smith, 1994). For example, it is popular to compare performance when tasks are presented with and without a successfully imitated sequence of simple gross motor movements. Although this procedure has some experimental support in work with individuals with developmental disabilities (Harchik & Putzier, 1990; Kennedy, Itoken, & Lindquist, 1995; Sanchez-Fort, Brady, & Davis, 1995), the authors' experience suggests that positive behavioral momentum is more effectively created when the tasks designed to establish a backlog of success bear topographical similarity to the presented task. That is, if problem behavior arises in response to social tasks, then every attempt should be made to create behavioral momentum with successful

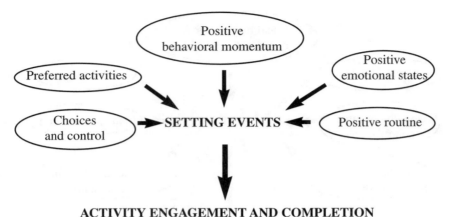

ACTIVITY ENGAGEMENT AND COMPLETION

Figure 2.   Illustration of the relationship between positive setting events and positive behavior.

performance on meaningful social tasks. Similarly, if problem behavior arises in response to academic tasks, then behavioral momentum should be created with meaningful academic tasks. Furthermore, success or failure must always be measured using the student's, rather than adults' criteria (Feeney & Ylvisaker, 1995; Ylvisaker & Feeney, 1994, in press).

Choice and Control   Harchik and colleagues (1993) reviewed more than 100 studies of the effects of choice making on positive engagement in tasks and reduction in challenging behavior in individuals with developmental disabilities. Despite expected conflicts in this literature, Harchik and colleagues concluded that there is solid evidence suggesting that opportunities for choice and control can increase the individual's level of participation, decrease the frequency of problem behaviors during participation, and improve subjective ratings of the activity. That is, when people with developmental disabilities are allowed to choose activities and control aspects of those activities, they tend to participate more willingly, behave more appropriately, and rate the activity as positive.

This principle of choice and control, like the principles of setting events and behavioral momentum, has special application to many students with ABI. Students, particularly adolescents, with the autonomy associated with typical development but who acquired disabilities after years of typical development are likely to react negatively to the pervasiveness of external control associated with disability (Zencius, Wesolowski, Burke, & McQuade, 1989). Life after brain injury is often dominated by externally imposed restrictions on physical and social activity, a protective posture by par-

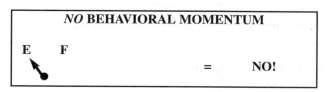

Figure 3.   The principle of behavioral momentum, as illustrated metaphorically with a gas tank.

ents and staff, and an overriding concern that the individual is incapable of making responsible decisions for him- or herself.

This concern easily becomes a self-fulfilling prophecy as students and adults are pulled into the classic negative cycle of control. That is, the adult imposes restrictions on the student's behavior that leads the student to react negatively to the restrictions. The adult in turn assumes greater control, causing the student to increase oppositional behavior, confirming the adult's perception that the student needs to be controlled externally. Therefore, controls are increased and the cycle is in full swing, which predictably results in explosive behavior (see Figure 4). This is a particularly common phenomenon after ABI because of the many restrictions that are believed to be necessary after the injury and because of the sense of protectiveness that adults naturally feel after a child is injured.

Premise 3:   Changing Negative Behaviors
After the Early Stages of Recovery Often Requires
Teaching Communication Alternatives to Those Behaviors

An important principle of applied behavior analysis is that behavior is rarely maladaptive. That is, there is typically an important purpose served by behavior, no matter how unusual or objectionable that behavior may appear. It is a short step from this principle to a communication interpretation of behavior problems; that is, challenging behaviors are components of the individual's communication system requiring parents and staff to routinely ask "What is this person trying to tell us with his [or her] unusual behavior?" (Carr & Durand, 1985; Carr et al., 1993; Durand, 1990; Durand & Carr, 1991;

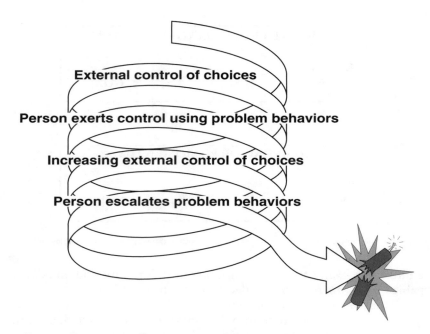

External control of choices

Person exerts control using problem behaviors

Increasing external control of choices

Person escalates problem behaviors

Figure 4.   An example of the negative cycle of control.

Feeney & Urbanczyk, 1994). Challenging behavior that is not initially communicative or intentional can easily achieve this status if
it is responded to by communication partners in a thoughtless manner. For example, early in recovery, behaviors like screaming and hitting may be neurologically driven or purely impulsive but, similar to
nonintentional behaviors of a young infant, can become part of the
child's communication system if they are unintentionally rewarded.
Challenging behavior often communicates one of the following messages: I need to *escape* (e.g., a demand, an activity, a person, a place);
I *want* something (e.g., a thing, an activity, a person, a place, the attention of others); or I need to *express a feeling* (e.g., frightened, surprised, excited, angry, happy).

A communication interpretation of challenging behavior dic-
tates that the goal of intervention is not simply to eliminate or extinguish the behavior, but rather to substitute a communicative
alternative that is at least as effective as the undesirable behavior, is
reasonably easy to produce, and is easier for others to live with (e.g.,
verbally requesting a break as an alternative to overturning the desk).
Teaching communication alternatives requires that staff and family
1) agree to situations in which escape or access communication can
be honored, 2) collaboratively select alternative communication be-

haviors to be prompted and rewarded, 3) create many natural opportunities for the alternative to be practiced and meaningfully rewarded, and 4) make every effort to prompt the alternative before the student engages in challenging behavior. Timing is critical. In effect, adults in the child's life must change their communication routines, thereby creating a large number of positive communication learning opportunities for the child. After the challenging behaviors have been largely replaced by positive communication alternatives, realistic demands on the child can be reintroduced, using the principles of positive setting events and behavioral momentum to ensure that when stressed the child does not revert to communication through challenging behavior.

Premise 4:   Effective Intervention Occurs in Social-Communicative Contexts and Is Designed to Influence Routines in Those Contexts

Partly because challenging behaviors are commonly components of a communication ecology and partly because people with frontal lobe injury tend to be concrete learners who have difficulty transferring learned behaviors from training context to application context, there is value in teaching alternative behaviors in the contexts in which the problems arise (Feeney & Ylvisaker, 1995; Ylvisaker, Feeney, & Urbanczyk, 1993). The most common alternative to this practice, namely teaching appropriate behavior and social skills in the context of social skills groups or pragmatics groups, may be especially unproductive for those students with ABI who have no difficulty remembering the rules of social behavior but who fail to guide their behavior with that knowledge because of the impulsiveness, lack of activation, misperception of social cues, and/or context dependency that are often associated with frontal lobe injury.

Furthermore, if everyday communication partners, including nursing staff, teachers, paraprofessionals, parents, and others, can be trained to become effective agents of behavior change, then the intensity of the intervention is dramatically increased. Most of the hours in a student's life, whether in a rehabilitation hospital or school, are spent with people other than specialists in behavior and communication. Efficiency of intervention requires that these day-to-day settings and interactions be made as therapeutic as possible, requiring that professionals get into real-world contexts and work closely with everyday people so that these interactions can become the contexts within which positive behaviors are learned. In the absence of this collaborative approach to intervention, consistency will be lost, with predictably negative consequences for the student's behavior.

Premise 5:   Behavior Problems and
Cognitive Problems Are Often Inseparable After ABI

Acting out may be an expression of frustration related to the cognitive difficulty of tasks, a means to escape tasks that are threatening, or a response to the cumulative effects of failure. Alternatively, inappropriate behavior may be associated with confusion, difficulty organizing behavior around complex tasks, inflexibility, misperception of social demands, difficulty monitoring behavior, and other types of cognitive weakness. In some cases, loss of knowledge of social rules, roles, and routines may result in behavior that is socially awkward.

In light of these and other possible interactions between cognitive and behavior difficulties, it is critical for professionals to integrate cognitive and behavioral perspectives in serving individuals with ABI. In particular, it is critical for family members and staff to understand the student's cognitive strengths and weaknesses so that appropriate cognitive supports are put in place without infantilizing the students or undershooting their ability to perform. An ongoing set of cognitive supports, adjusted as needed to fit the student's recovery, is probably the best prescription for preventing late-onset behavior problems.

Premise 6:   Crisis Management Is Not Behavior Management

Unfortunately, behavior problems after ABI are often allowed to evolve into high-risk issues before specific professional attention is sought. At that point, staff and family members primarily seek advice on managing crises. Although effective management of crises is needed to keep people safe and prevent further deterioration in behavior, it is important to recognize that a crisis is *not* the time to teach alternative behaviors. Rather, preventive or antecedent control procedures must be intensified to avoid crises so that genuine teaching, including teaching alternative behaviors to communication partners, can take place. Effective crisis management procedures are described by Colvin and Sugai (1989) and Willis, LaVigna, and Donnellan (1989).

Premise 7:   The Best Behavior Management After ABI
Is Prevention of Long-Term Behavioral Consequences

In the preceding discussion of behavioral outcome after ABI, the growing popularity of the view that behavioral issues after frontal lobe injury are largely biologically determined is discussed. It is unfortunately easy to move from a frank recognition of organic contributors to behavior to a pessimistic conclusion regarding the effectiveness of behavioral intervention. In our experience, this inference is wholly illegitimate. Indeed, intensive and intelligent management holds the potential to reverse the gradual evolution of seriously aggressive behavior after ABI in adolescents (Feeney & Ylvisaker, 1995). It is far wiser, however, to prevent challenging behavior from evolving with a combination of the teaching procedures and supports described in Premises 2–6. Children who live and receive instruction in positive environments rarely develop severe behavior problems. Positive environments are those in which 1) adults pay attention to positive setting events and positive behavioral momentum; 2) adults avoid control battles; 3) adults generously create opportunities for choice and honor the child's choices; 4) the child has a means to communicate intentions, and these communications, when reasonable, are routinely honored; 5) adults provide the child with needed cognitive support to be successful; and 6) adults remain calm in crises.

Taken together, these premises yield a functional and positive approach to behavior management that has received considerable experimental support in the developmental disabilities literature (Carr & Durand, 1985; Carr et al., 1993; Durand, 1990; Durand & Carr, 1991; Fowler, 1996; Gardner et al., 1986) and a growing body of support in the brain injury literature (Feeney & Ylvisaker, 1995; Hart & Jacobs, 1993; Jacobs, 1993; Ylvisaker & Feeney, 1994, 1996).

ILLUSTRATIONS OF INTERVENTION THEMES

The remainder of this chapter focuses on illustrating these intervention premises with case material. In the first illustration, effectiveness of the intervention is supported with frequency counts; in the second, with qualitative data from parent interviews; and, in the third, with ratings simultaneously completed by more than one member of the student's educational team. Elsewhere, we have explored each of these themes in greater detail (Feeney & Ylvisaker, 1995; Ylvisaker & Feeney, 1994, 1995, in press; Ylvisaker, Feeney, & Szekeres, in press; Ylvisaker, Feeney, & Urbanczyk, 1993; Ylvisaker, Urbanczyk, & Feeney, 1992). Each of the following cases illustrates the important principle (Premise 4) that effective intervention is delivered in everyday contexts and is designed to influence routines in those contexts.

Antecedent Behavioral Interventions, Including Cognitive Supports: Premises 2, 4, and 5

Feeney and Ylvisaker (1995) described a highly contextualized antecedent-focused intervention for three late adolescents whose behavior had deteriorated sharply over the years after frontal lobe injury in early adolescence. Two of the students had been expelled from high school because of aggressive behavior and averaged more than 20 episodes of aggression per day in their alternative educational settings. The third remained in high school with fewer episodes of aggression (5–10 per day), but he had received several suspensions. Conventional contingency management approaches had failed to improve their behavior.

Approximately 4–5 weeks of intervention, which included a combination of concrete advance organizers for academic and vocational tasks (i.e., cognitive support), active participation of the student in decision making, and positive behavioral momentum, resulted in nearly complete extinction of aggressive behavior with a corresponding increase in the amount of work completed. The focus of the intervention was a change in everyday routines (involving both staff and students) in the exact context in which the problems had evolved.

Before this intervention was implemented, the students' routines in school or in their vocational training program tended to have the following components: 1) the adult presented a task in a demanding manner, with no attention to the student's internal setting events and with no concrete organizational support to help the student complete the task; 2) the student either reacted negatively to the tone of the demand or began the task but stopped when it became too difficult; 3) the adult responded with verbal cues, which were interpreted by the student as nagging or infantilizing, or with reprimands; 4) conflict then escalated, resulting in verbal or physical aggression; and 5) the student was punished. These frequently repeated routines contributed to the adults' conviction that the students were unmanageable and had no realistic chance of succeeding in their educational setting.

Following observation and extended discussion and negotiation that included the students, professional and paraprofessional staff, and an ABI consultant, a decision was made to experiment with a change in these routine that included the following components:

- **Antecedents: Setting Events** Special efforts were made to ensure that the students were well oriented to their tasks (see below), that they knew that they could complete the task, that instructions were as much as possible self-instructions (to avoid the perception of "nagging"), and that they had effective "bail out" options that would be honored. These efforts helped to ensure that the setting events were as positive as possible.
- **Antecedents: Positive Behavioral Momentum** Staff worked hard to ensure that difficult, anxiety-producing, or nonpreferred

tasks were introduced only after a series of easier or preferred tasks was successfully completed. That is, staff and students worked together to generate positive behavioral momentum as a way of increasing the likelihood that the students would remain appropriately engaged in difficult or stressful tasks.

- **Antecedents: Advance Organizers** The students' need for concrete organizational support was frankly acknowledged. Phase 1 of the intervention included sequences of photographs to keep the students organized and oriented to the task. Photographs were used, not because the students could not read (they had no difficulty with reading), but rather because their degree of organizational weakness, combined with their long history of negative behavioral routines when faced with difficult tasks, necessitated extraordinary supports. During Phase 2, the photograph cues gave way to written task organizers.

- **Antecedents: Communicative Alternatives to Challenging Behavior** Staff, including paraprofessional staff, were trained to understand challenging behavior (e.g., swearing, throwing books, hitting) as communication (e.g., "Don't talk to me like that," "I can't do this, it's too hard," "I'm really frustrated, I need a break"). The students were routinely encouraged to use words rather than challenging behavior to communicate these messages (well *before* the onset of aggressive behavior) and their appropriate verbal requests or protests were honored.

- **Antecedents: Choice** Of fundamental importance to this program of intervention was the inclusion of the students in the decision-making process that led to the new program. Like many adolescent males, they were very oppositional human beings, more than happy to tell anyone willing to listen that they were not about to be compliant "good boys" just because adults told them to. More generally, presenting a task as a demand was by itself reason to resist doing it.

The positive outcomes for these boys are encouraging. Each graduated or received a diploma through examination, and each is now working with minimal or no vocational support. It is a serious indictment of the educational system, however, to recognize that their downward behavioral spirals that resulted in substantial costs (financial costs, emotional pain, physical pain) could very likely have been prevented with intelligent use of cognitive and social supports during the early years after their return to school. It is impossible to retrospectively make this claim with complete certainty. However, these case illustrations, and many more like them, challenge professionals to help students avoid these painful and personally damaging experiences by creatively helping them to succeed in their chosen environments with appropriate and creative cognitive and behavioral supports.

Choice, Routine, and Cognitive Flexibility: Premises 2, 3, and 5

This importance of choice, positive communication routines, and cognitive support is further illustrated by Jon, a 6-year-old boy who incurred a severe closed brain injury, with prefrontal focus, in a car accident at age 2. At age 6, his profile included mild motor disability, moderate visual-perceptual impairment, and cognitive disorganization. Of greatest concern to his parents and teachers, however, was his behavioral inflexibility. His difficulty accepting changes in his routine had come close to creating a situation in which his family members were prisoners of those routines. Violations of expectations were greeted with intense and protracted tantrum behavior.

At that time, an ABI consultant brainstormed with Jon's parents about the possibility of a routine to manage changes in routine. The parents decided to create a choice board on which several desirable activities were listed (negotiated with Jon). They explained to Jon that whenever it proved impossible to fulfill his expectations for routine (or nonroutine, but expected) activities, he would be invited to select an alternative from the board. After some practice, they implemented this new routine, which included needed cognitive support (i.e., a concrete way of representing a positive future for a child who was incapable of making this shift internally) and a positive communication alternative to challenging behavior (i.e., point to an option on the board rather than have a tantrum). Within 4 months, the tantrums, which had invariably accompanied deviations from important expectations, were eliminated and replaced by several seconds of sadness with the announcement that an expectation could not be met, followed by a selection of an alternative activity from the choice board. Significantly, the parents reported that they had become less worried about potential deviations from routines. Whereas previously they believed that they had to ensure that Jon's expectations would be met, now they had the luxury of letting their lives at home take a more normal course.

Prevention of Long-Term Behavioral Consequences Using Cognitive Supports: Premises 5 and 7

The concept of supported cognition and its role in preventing behavior problems is illustrated by Jim, who had a brain tumor removed in infancy. Surgery was followed by intracranial radiation and chemotherapy. His early outcome was characterized by moderate motor and cognitive disability. Academic delays grew over his grade school career as the curriculum grew increasingly abstract and complex. His teachers were most concerned, however, with a set of problems associated with executive system dysfunction. By fifth grade, Jim appeared almost incapable of successful classroom performance without a teacher or aide constantly at his side orienting and re-orienting him to task, focusing and refocusing his attention, organizing and monitoring his behavior, and solving his problems as they arose. His inattention was so extreme that by January of fifth grade, his teacher suggested that he may have been experiencing ongoing seizure activity (which proved not to be the case). More important, as an 11-year-old preadolescent, Jim was beginning to react negatively to the frequent adult cues and reminders that were part of his school life. Conflicts with his aide were beginning to escalate, and there was a concern that behavior problems would spiral out of control if Jim could not be helped to be more successful in school with less overt help from adults. That is, in Jim's case, one of the main goals of cognitive intervention from the outset was to prevent anticipated behavior problems.

At that time, an ABI consultant began to work with Jim's general and special education staff. Intervention had three major components. The first component was that Jim was given an executive system guide, which was a notebook that contained single sheets of paper (called task sheets) for each academic task. These task sheets included the following components: 1) *goal* (i.e., What am I trying to accomplish?), 2) *plan* (i.e., What are the steps that I need to go through to accomplish it?), 3) *evaluation* (i.e., How did I do? How do others think I did?), and 4) *review* (i.e., What worked for me? What didn't work for me?).

Before each demanding academic task, he or the teacher/aide wrote his goal and brainstormed about the steps for the plan, which were written by the teacher/aide. After the task, he rated his performance, the teacher or a peer rated his performance, and the teacher or a peer brainstormed with him about what worked and what did not work. That is, the executive components of his tasks were made explicit, concrete, and routine. This was a major component of his executive function support.

The second component was that prior to presenting each academic task, staff analyzed the task into its components (the *plan*) and, if the task was complex, created an organized flowsheet (advance organizer) that Jim could use to guide himself through the task. In some cases, the advance organizer was graphic (e.g., a picture-story grammar map to guide him through writing tasks). This was his organizational support (an aspect of executive system support).

The third component was that in order to reduce oppositional behavior, reminders to begin or to stay on task were provided by peers, rather than adults, as much as possible. That is, they tried hard to avoid adult nagging, an example of behavioral support.

By the end of fifth grade, 4 months after this supported executive system routine was initiated, Jim was largely independent in his work both in school and at home. Furthermore, his teacher, who 4 months earlier had argued that Jim ought not be in her classroom because he lacked the capacity to pay attention and learn in that setting, reported that his progress had been remarkable and that he should be promoted to middle school with the type of executive system support that had been implemented. Whereas in January she and the special educator had judged him to be at a kindergarten to first-grade level in most areas of executive functions (planning/organizing; initiating; inhibiting; orienting to task; self-monitoring and evaluating; strategic thinking; and general independence), in June they judged him to be at the fourth- to fifth-grade level in most of these areas. These ratings are presented in Table 1.

Jim's need for cues to return to task was reduced from an average of one per 5–10 minutes to at most one per 20–30 minutes, a decrease of about 75%. Furthermore, by June, when he had no task sheet, he either initiated a request for one or attempted to create one for himself. He had become extremely proud of his independence, and his teacher spoke confidently of his potential success in middle school. Jim's success in fifth grade was a result of implementing executive system routines in his real-world context with the amount of support that he needed at that time. His level of concreteness was such that out-of-context training in executive functions would likely have had no impact on his real-world performance.

This intervention was not intended to and did not reduce Jim's underlying and rather severe neurologically based cognitive and executive system impairment. His need for ongoing support was unfortunately demonstrated during the early months of sixth grade. Despite a comprehensive plan for support in middle school, the school district had failed to hire a consulting special educator to oversee Jim's program of supports. In addition, an aide was not hired until the first week of school in September and was provided with no training. Six weeks into the school year, the ABI consultant was invited to observe Jim and work with his new staff. At that time, executive system ratings (given by his general education teacher and aide) had nearly returned to the levels of the previous January (Table 1).

Table 1.   January to June (grade 5) improvements in executive functions with appropriate supports; deterioration by October of grade 6 without needed supports for a boy with ABI

	Fifth grade, January			Fifth grade, June			Sixth grade, October	
	CT	SE	M	CT	SE	M	CT	Aide
Planning/organizing	1[a]	1	1	4	4	4	K	K/1
Initiation	1	K/1	1	4	4	4	K	1/2
Inhibition	K	K/1	3	4	4	5	6	3
General independence	K	K/1	1	5	4/5	4	K	1/2
Orientation to task/ flexibility	1	2	1	5	5	4	K	1
Understanding of task difficulty	K	2	2	3	5	4	K	K/1
Self-monitoring/self-evaluating	K	K	2	3	3	4	K	K/1
Strategic behavior	K	2	2	3	5	4	K	K/1

[a]Actual grade level.

Abbreviations: CT = Classroom teacher; SE = Special educator; M = Mother; Aide = Classroom aide.

More ominous were the comments of the paraprofessional aide who said that Jim was becoming increasingly oppositional and antagonistic. This was the developmental course predicted for Jim in the absence of executive system support.

At the time this chapter was written, staff at Jim's middle school were working to implement the supports that had demonstrated their value the previous year. It is likely that Jim will require some degree of executive system support indefinitely, flexibly changing as his life circumstances change. For most rehabilitationists with traditional training, this represents failure. The goal of rehabilitation is said to be independence. In contrast to this commitment to independence, an appropriate cognitive rehabilitation goal for students like Jim is to identify and put in place whatever types of cognitive support they may need in order to achieve their goals in their chosen environments and activities. There are many people like Jim, who indefinitely require some degree of cognitive or executive system support from others. Furthermore, if they are young people, this support is critical to preventing the evolution of serious behavioral and emotional problems that are associated with the academic and social failures that predictably follow the absence of needed supports.

CONCLUSION

This chapter has outlined a positive approach to challenging behavior after ABI. This approach seeks first and foremost to prevent the evolution of behavior problems by providing students with a variety of cognitive and behavioral supports and by treating behavior as part of a communication ecology. Within this perspective the behavioral targets are positive communication acts (versus extinction of negative behaviors), teaching takes place largely in natural communication contexts, and the most critical deliverers of the service are everyday communication partners. Although ABI, and frontal lobe injury in particular, may substantially increase a student's behavioral vulnerability, creative application of the principles described and illustrated in this chapter holds the promise of preventing or reversing the downward behavioral spiral often observed after these injuries.

REFERENCES

Ackerly, S.S. (1964). A case of paranatal frontal lobe defect observed for thirty years. In J.M. Warren & K. Ackert (Eds.), *The frontal granular cortex and behavior* (pp. 192–218). New York: McGraw-Hill.

Asarnow, R.F., Satz, P., Light, R., & Neumann, E. (1991). Behavior problems and adaptive functioning in children with mild and severe closed head injury. *Journal of Pediatric Psychology, 16,* 534–555.

Bailey, J.S., & Pyles, D.A. (1989). Behavioral diagnostics. *Monographs of the American Association on Mental Retardation, 12,* 85–106.

Benton, A. (1991). Prefrontal injury and behavior in children. *Developmental Neuropsychology, 7,* 275–281.

Bijou, S.W., Peterson, R.F., & Ault, M.H. (1968). A method to integrate descriptive and experimental field studies at the level of data and empirical concepts. *Journal of Applied Behavior Analysis, 1,* 175–191.

Carr, E.G., & Durand, V.M. (1985). Reducing behavior problems through functional communication training. *Journal of Applied Behavior Analysis, 18,* 111–126.

Carr, E.G., McConnachie, G., Levin, L., & Kemp, D. (1993). Communication-based treatment of severe behavior problems. In R. VanHouten & S. Axelrod (Eds.), *Behavior analysis and treatment* (pp. 231–267). New York: Plenum.

Colvin, G., & Sugai, G. (1989). *Managing escalating behavior.* Eugene, OR: Behavior Associates.

Cooper, C.J., Wacker, D.P., Sasso, G.M., Reimers, T.M., & Donn, L.K. (1990). Using parents as therapists to evaluate the appropriate behavior of their children: Applications to a tertiary diagnostic clinic. *Journal of Applied Behavior Analysis, 23,* 285–296.

Damasio, A.R. (1994). *Descartes error.* New York: HarperCollins.

Damasio, A.R., Tranel, D., & Damasio, H. (1990). Individuals with sociopathic behavior caused by frontal lobe damage fail to respond automatically to socially charged stimuli. *Behavioral Brain Research, 14,* 81–94.

Davis, C.A., Brady, M.P., Hamilton, R., McEvoy, M.A., & Williams, R.E. (1994). Effects of high probability requests on the social interactions of young children with severe disabilities. *Journal of Applied Behavior Analysis, 27,* 619–637.

Diamond, A. (1991). Guidelines for the study of brain-behavior relationships during development. In H.S. Levin, H.M. Eisenberg, & A.L. Benton (Eds.), *Frontal lobe function and dysfunction* (pp. 339–378). New York: Oxford University Press.

Dunlap, G., Kern-Dunlap, L., Clarke, M., & Robbins, F.R. (1991). Functional assessment, curricular revisions, and severe behavior problems. *Journal of Applied Behavior Analysis, 24*, 387–397.

Durand, V.M. (1990). *Severe behavior problems: Communication based intervention.* New York: Guilford Press.

Durand, V.M., & Carr, E.G. (1991). Functional communication training to reduce challenging behavior: Maintenance and application to new settings. *Journal of Applied Behavior Analysis, 24*, 251–264.

Emery, R.E., Binkoff, J.A., Houts, A.C., & Carr, E.G. (1983). Children as independent variables: Some clinical implications of child effects. *Behavior Therapy, 14*, 398–412.

Eslinger, P.J., Damasio, A.R., Damasio, H., & Grattan, L.M. (1989). Developmental consequences of early frontal lobe damage. *Journal of Clinical and Experimental Neuropsychology, 11*, 50–62.

Eslinger, P.J., Grattan, L.M., Damasio, H., & Damasio, A.R. (1992). Developmental consequences of childhood frontal lobe damage. *Archives of Neurology, 49*, 764–769.

Feeney, T.J., & Urbanczyk, B. (1994). Behavior as communication. In R.C. Savage & G.F. Wolcott (Eds.), *Educational dimensions of acquired brain injury* (pp. 277–302). Austin, TX: PRO-ED.

Feeney, T.J., & Ylvisaker, M. (1995). Choice and routine: Antecedent behavioral interventions for adolescents with severe traumatic brain injury. *Journal of Head Trauma Rehabilitation, 10*, 67–86.

Fletcher, J.M., Ewing-Cobbs, L., Miner, M., & Levin, H.S. (1990). Behavioral changes after closed head injury in children. *Journal of Consulting and Clinical Psychology, 58*, 93–98.

Fowler, R. (1996). Supporting students with challenging behaviors in general education settings: A review of behavioral momentum techniques and guidelines for use. *The Oregon Conference Monograph, 8*, 137–155.

Fuster, J.M. (1989). *The prefrontal cortex: Anatomy, physiology, and neuropsychology of the frontal lobe* (2nd ed.). New York: Raven Press.

Gardner, W.I., Cole, C.L., Davidson, D.P., & Karan, O.C. (1986). Reducing aggression in individuals with developmental disabilities: An expanded stimulus control, assessment, and intervention model. *Education and Training of the Mentally Retarded, 21*, 3–12.

Grattan, L.M., & Eslinger, P.J. (1990). Influence of cerebral lesion site upon the onset and progression of interpersonal deficits following brain injury. *Journal of Clinical and Experimental Neuropsychology, 12*, 33–39.

Grattan, L.M., & Eslinger, P.J. (1991). Frontal lobe damage in children and adults: A comparative review. *Developmental Neuropsychology, 7*, 283–326.

Grattan, L.M., & Eslinger, P.J. (1992). Long-term psychological consequences of childhood frontal lobe lesion in patient DT. *Brain and Cognition, 20*, 185–195.

Greenspan, A.I., & MacKenzie, E.J. (1994). Functional outcome after pediatric head injury. *Pediatrics, 94*, 425–432.

Halle, J.W. (1989). Identifying stimuli in natural settings: An analysis of stimuli that acquire control during training. *Journal of Applied Behavior Analysis, 24,* 579–589.

Harchik, A.E., & Putzier, V.S. (1990). The use of high probability requests to increase compliance with instructions to take medication. *Journal of The Association for Persons with Severe Handicaps, 15,* 40–43.

Harchik, A.E., Sherman, J.A., & Bannerman, D.J. (1993). Choice and control: New opportunities for people with developmental disabilities. *Annals of Clinical Psychiatry, 5,* 151–162.

Hart, T., & Jacobs, H. (1993). Rehabilitation and management of behavior disturbances following frontal lobe injury. *Journal of Head Trauma Rehabilitation, 8,* 1–12.

Iwata, B.A., Dorsey, M.F., Silfer, K.I., Bauman, K.E., & Richman, G.S. (1982). Toward a functional analysis of self-injury. *Analysis and Intervention in Developmental Disabilities, 2,* 3–20.

Jacobs, H.E. (1993). *Behavior analysis guidelines and brain injury rehabilitation.* Rockville, MD: Aspen Publishers, Inc.

Kennedy, C.H., Itoken, T., & Lindquist, K. (1995). Comparing interspersed requests and social comments for increasing student compliance. *Journal of Applied Behavior Analysis, 28,* 97–98.

Kern, L., Childs, K.E., Dunlap, G., Clarke, S., & Falk, G.D. (1994). Using assessment-based curricular intervention to improve the classroom behavior of a student with emotional and behavioral challenges. *Journal of Applied Behavior Analysis, 27,* 7–19.

Lalli, J.S., Browder, D.M., Mace, F.C., & Brown, K. (1995). Teacher use of descriptive analysis data to implement interventions to decrease students' maladaptive behavior. *Journal of Applied Behavior Analysis, 28,* 135–163.

Mace, F.C., Hock, M.L., Lalli, J.S., West, B.J., Belifore, P., Pinter, E., & Brown, D.K. (1988). Behavioral momentum in the treatment of non-compliance. *Journal of Applied Behavior Analysis, 21,* 123–141.

Mace, F.C., Lalli, J.S., Shea, M.C., Lalli, E., West, R., Roberts, M.L., & Nevin, J.A. (1990). The momentum of human behavior in a natural setting. *Journal of the Experimental Analysis of Behavior, 54,* 163–172.

Mace, F.C., Page, T.J., Ivanck, M.T., & O'Brien, S. (1986). Analysis of environmental determinants of aggression and disruption in mentally retarded children. *Applied Research in Mental Retardation, 7,* 203–221.

Marlowe, W. (1989). Consequences of frontal lobe injury in the developing child. *Journal of Clinical and Experimental Neuropsychology, 12,* 105–112.

Marlowe, W. (1992). The impact of a right prefrontal lesion on the developing brain. *Brain and Cognition, 20,* 205–213.

Mateer, C.A., & Williams, D. (1991). Effects of frontal lobe injury in childhood. *Developmental Neuropsychology, 7,* 359–376.

Michael, J. (1982). Distinguishing between discriminative and motivational functions of stimuli. *Journal of the Experimental Analysis of Behavior, 37,* 149–155.

Michael, J. (1989). Motivation relations and establishing operations. In J. Michael (Ed.), *Verbal and non-verbal behavior: Concepts and principles* (pp. 40–53). Kalamazoo: Western Michigan University.

Nevin, J.A. (1988). Behavioral momentum and the partial reinforcement effect. *Psychological Bulletin, 103,* 44–56.

O'Neill, R.E., Horner, R.H., Albin, R.W., Storey, K., & Sprague, J.R. (1990). *Functional analysis of problem behavior: A practical assessment guide.* Sycamore, IL: Sycamore Publishing Co.

Pang, D. (1985). Pathophysiologic correlates of neurobehavioral syndromes following closed head injury. In M. Ylvisaker (Ed.), *Head injury rehabilitation: Children and adolescents* (pp. 3–70). Boston: College-Hill Press.

Price, B., Doffnre, K., Stowe, R., & Mesulum, M. (1990). The comportmental learning disabilities of early frontal lobe damage. *Brain, 113,* 1383–1393.

Sanchez-Fort, M.R., Brady, M.P., & Davis, C.A. (1995). Using high probability requests to increase low probability communication behavior in young children with severe disabilities. *Education and Training in Mental Retardation and Developmental Disabilities, 30,* 151–165.

Saver, J.L., & Damasio, A.R. (1991). Preserved access and processing of social knowledge in a patient with acquired sociopathy due to ventromedial frontal damage. *Neuropsychologia, 29,* 1241–1249.

Stuss, D.T., & Benson, D.F. (1986). *The frontal lobes.* New York: Raven Press.

Vollmer, T.R., & Iwata, B.A. (1991). Establishing operations and reinforcement effects. *Journal of Applied Behavior Analysis, 23,* 417–429.

Wahler, R.G., & Fox, R.M. (1981). Setting events in applied behavior analysis: Towards a conceptual and methodological expansion. *Journal of Applied Behavior Analysis, 14,* 327–338.

Williams, D., & Mateer, C.A. (1992). Developmental impact of frontal lobe injury in middle childhood. *Brain and Cognition, 20,* 196–204.

Willis, T.J., LaVigna, G.W., & Donnellan, A.M. (1989). *Behavior assessment guide.* Los Angeles: Institute for Applied Behavior Analysis.

Ylvisaker, M. (1993). Communication outcome in children and adolescents with traumatic brain injury. *Neuropsychological Rehabilitation, 3*(4), 367–387.

Ylvisaker, M., & Feeney, T. (1994). Communication and behavior: Collaboration between speech-language pathologists and behavioral psychologists. *Topics in Language Disorders, 15*(1), 37–54.

Ylvisaker, M., & Feeney, T. (1995). Traumatic brain injury in adolescence: Assessment and reintegration. *Seminars in Speech and Language, 16*(1), 32–44.

Ylvisaker, M., & Feeney, T. (1996). Executive functions: Supported cognition and self-advocacy after traumatic brain injury. *Seminars in Speech and Language 17,* 217–232.

Ylvisaker, M., Feeney, T., Maher-Maxwell, N., Meserve, N., Geary, P., & DeLorenzo, J. (1995). School reentry following severe traumatic brain injury: Guidelines for educational planning. *Journal of Head Trauma Rehabilitation, 10*(6), 25–41.

Ylvisaker, M., Feeney, T., & Szekeres, S. (in press). A social-environment approach to communication and behavior in children with TBI. In M. Ylvisaker (Ed.), *Head injury rehabilitation: Children and adolescents* (2nd ed.). Newton, MA: Butterworth-Heinemann.

Ylvisaker, M., Feeney, T., & Urbanczyk, B. (1993). A social-environmental approach to communication and behavior after traumatic brain injury. *Seminars in Speech and Language, 14*(1), 74–86.

Ylvisaker, M., Hartwick, P., & Stevens, M.B. (1991). School re-entry following head injury: Managing the transition from hospital to school. *Journal of Head Trauma Rehabilitation, 6*(1), 10–22.

Ylvisaker, M., Urbanczyk, B., & Feeney, T. (1992). Social skills following traumatic brain injury. *Seminars in Speech and Language, 13*(4), 308–321.

Zarcone, J.R., Iwata, B.A., Mazaleski, J.L., & Smith, R.G. (1994). Momentum and extinction effects on self-injurious escape behavior and non-compliance. *Journal of Applied Behavior Analysis, 27*, 649–658.

Zencius, A.H., Wesolowski, M.D., Burke, W.H., & McQuade, D. (1989). Antecedent control in the treatment of brain injured clients. *Brain Injury, 3*, 199–205.

chapter nine

Making Connections
Helping Children with ABI Build Friendships

Elizabeth A. Cooley, Ann Glang, and Judith Voss

I guess the biggest disappointment was when his friends found out it was more of a permanent situation, and they just kind of faded away from us. . . . They just stopped coming around, didn't see him anymore, and that was kind of heartbreaking.

Parent of a child with ABI (Singer & Nixon, 1996, p. 40)

ACQUIRED BRAIN INJURY AND SOCIAL ISOLATION

Children and youth who survive acquired brain injury (ABI) are often left with severe and lasting physical, cognitive, and emotional difficulties. Perhaps the most devastating of these changes for the student with ABI is the loss of friends and the decrease in social activity that typically accompany such an injury. Because of the frustration, anger, loneliness, and reduced self-esteem that these changes usually bring, the other problems and challenges associated with ABI are frequently compounded. Lacking a network of supportive friends, the child with ABI often loses confidence in his or her ability to succeed in school and the community.

Preparation of this chapter was supported in part by Grant #H086D10008 from the U.S. Department of Education. The views expressed in this chapter do not necessarily reflect those of the funding agency.

The causes of social isolation in students with ABI are many and interrelated. A brain injury brings with it emotional, behavior, and cognitive changes for the child. Some of these changes, which are a direct result of the injury itself, may in turn affect the way that other people react to and relate to the student, which consequently may contribute further to the child's difficulties. Following are some of the most common factors contributing to the social isolation frequently experienced by students with ABI.

Emotional Changes

ABI is an irreversible life change to which adjustment takes time and effort, and for many students with ABI, this adjustment is troublesome. As they realize that certain changes are permanent and that, in some ways, they will never be "themselves" again, students with ABI may become withdrawn or depressed (Garske & Thomas, 1992). Unfortunately, these very understandable emotional reactions may further isolate the student, making it difficult for him or her to develop and maintain the very friendships that could help him or her to cope more effectively with the stressful aftereffects of the injury.

Behavior Changes

Following a brain injury, the student's ability to handle social situations may dramatically decline. Ordinary interactions that once were easy may become much more difficult (Fletcher, Ewings-Cobbs, & Minor, 1991). He or she may begin to act differently, often displaying a lack of inhibition, decreased judgment, verbal aggression, an inability to read subtle social cues, insensitivity to others, and/or a lack of confidence (Dywan & Segalowitz, 1996). Peers may wonder, for example, what happened to their friend's sense of humor or why he or she uses embarrassing language. Because of the peers' confusion about or intolerance of these behaviors, the student may become ostracized. The ensuing social isolation can have an enormous impact on the self-esteem and psychological well-being of the student with ABI, who in turn may engage in even more negative behaviors in an attempt to get attention. Thus, in many cases, the child with ABI may find him- or herself virtually friendless and alone except for family members and paid service providers.

Cognitive Changes

The cognitive impairments associated with ABI may also negatively affect the student's social network. Some characteristic learning problems of students with ABI include problems with attention and concentration, poor memory skills, unpredictable and uneven learning progress, problems becoming and staying organized, difficulties with problem solving, and a tendency to become easily overloaded or fatigued (Vieth, Johnstone, & Dawson, 1996). A student's frustration with his or her cognitive abilities may lead to increased behavior problems in social situations. For example, a student who becomes frustrated with her inability to keep up with peers in a game might become aggressive when another student tells her to take her turn more quickly.

Other students may subtly or directly exclude a student who has problems keeping up with or tracking the flow of ideas in a conversation. Academic achievement may also decline, which may then lead to a more restrictive school placement in which opportunities for exposure to age-appropriate social situations are more limited.

Physical Changes

Many social activities (e.g., recreational sports) are physical in nature. A student's ability to participate in physical leisure or social activities may be limited by physical restrictions, fatigue, or depression-related apathy as a result of the injury. The student may then turn to more inactive, socially isolating pursuits (e.g., television, computer and video games), and social opportunities subsequently decrease.

Family Factors

In some cases, family members may unknowingly contribute to the child's social isolation. Following an injury, parents' attitudes toward and expectations for their child may change. Some parents may become more protective, emphasizing and fearing the potential dangers inherent in almost every activity (Sokol et al., 1996). And given that students who have already had one brain injury are indeed at greater risk for a second injury, parents' fears are not unfounded. Striking a balance between caution and acceptance of the everyday risks that are part of growing up can be very challenging for parents of children with ABI.

School-Related Factors

The school community may further contribute to the student's social isolation. Friends at school may be confused by the student's behavior and may even view the student's actions as offensive. The student's friends may be unsure of how to relate to the student following the injury. Without support for their own confusion and emotional reactions, these friends may eventually drift away. This problem is compounded by the fact that students with ABI have, in most instances, been absent from school for a lengthy period of time. In the meantime, friends may have moved ahead a grade, made new friends, or developed new interests. Consequently, the student with ABI then must face the prospect of reentering social and peer relationships that may have changed with the passage of time. Having lost many peer role models, the student's opportunities to relearn appropriate social behaviors from friends is diminished.

THE LACK OF SOCIAL SUPPORT AND INVOLVEMENT

The decrease in social support experienced by students with ABI is a very serious problem for several reasons. Most salient is the impact it has on the student's own well-being, but the decrease in social networks may also have a negative impact on the student's family. In addition, a decrease in a student's social support has implications for his or her school experience and degree of community involvement. Taken together, the problems associated with a dramatic decrease in a student's social network represent a potentially devastating blow to both the student's and the family's overall quality of life.

Effect on the Student

Many studies have indicated that social support is important, even crucial, to the psychological and physical well-being of adults (Cohen, 1988; Cohen & Wills, 1985). These studies have demonstrated that social support has both a *main effect* (i.e., a beneficial effect on individuals without life stressors) and an even greater *buffering effect* on individuals with life stressors. The same holds true for students. Numerous studies have reported this buffering effect of social support on students who have experienced severe life stressors (Cowen & Work, 1988; Garmezy, 1983; Sandler, Gersten, Reynolds, Kallgren, & Ramirez, 1989). Students who experience both the presence and perception of a supportive social network tend to have higher self-esteem and are able to cope more effectively with difficult situations than do students without such support (Belle, 1989; Rohrle & Sommer, 1994).

Conversely, the absence of or decrease in social support has been associated with a variety of difficulties in both adults and children, including depression and anxiety (Goethe & Levin, 1984; Wolchik, Beals, & Sandler, 1989), decreased self-esteem (Belle & Longfellow, 1983, 1984), a shift toward external locus of control (Belle & Longfellow, 1983, 1984), and conduct problems (Wolchik et al., 1989).

Social support, then, for students who have undergone stressful events, is especially important in that it may serve to shield them from some of the potentially harmful psychological and physical influences of those stressful events. Given the extreme stresses associated with ABI, the benefits derived from the presence of an adequate support network are especially crucial to the student's adjustment to a major life change. In a study of young males with ABI (Willer, Allen, Durnan, & Ferry, 1990), the presence of social support was identified by the young men as one of five primary coping strategies and was described as "the most essential element in overcoming the limitations imposed by their disabilities" (p. 170).

In addition to the critical role that social support plays in a student's ability to cope with the stresses of ABI, friendships are of key importance even to the typical development of children without disabilities. That is, students learn from one another many aspects of social functioning as well as other life skills (Meyer & Putnam, 1987). This is especially true in school environments in which students are expected to work together and learn from one another in a variety of ways. Students with ABI, who tend to have fewer friends and impoverished social networks, are less able to benefit from these kinds of learning experiences. In this sense, the decrease in friendships experienced by a student with ABI can impede the child's overall development.

Effect on the Family

In addition to the adverse effects of a decrease in social networks on children with ABI, a loss of social support negatively affects families as well. Parents of children with ABI and other disabilities may experience demoralization stemming from their child's impairment or from a lack of supportive relationships outside of the home (Acorn, 1993; Seaver-Reid, 1986; Singer & Nixon, 1996; Turnbull & Turnbull, 1986).

The child's difficulties in maintaining friendships also add to the practical demands of caregiving experienced by families (Singer & Nixon, 1996). As former friends fade away, family members may increasingly try to fill the gap. These family members may become the child's only source of social support or may take on the responsibility of orchestrating the child's social life. In the words of one parent,

> I try to make his life as normal as it can be and I saw him as being a very active outdoors type boy. So now I find myself helping like in Boy Scouts. I've been a den leader for Cub Scouts for three years . . . I've gotten him into baseball, basketball . . . I've been there to help with the coaches. (Singer & Nixon, 1996, p. 49)

As a consequence of this increase in responsibility, both parents and siblings may find it difficult to get away in order to spend time with other people or to engage in other activities, thus adding to their fatigue and strain. Siblings of young males with ABI identified the increase in caregiving responsibilities as a key problem, and some even described a feeling of having become "assistant parents" (Willer et al., 1990, p. 171).

Effect on the Child's School Experience

A decrease in social networks also has a negative impact on the quality of the student's school experience (Vieth et al., 1996). On returning to school, the student may be rejected by peers while lacking effective strategies for coping with that rejection. One parent described her son's way of dealing with the teasing he received from peers as perpetually looking at the ground "so I don't have to see the expressions on other people's faces when they look at me" (Singer & Nixon, 1996, p. 41).

In addition to the emotional consequences of peer rejection in school, a lack of social support can increase the likelihood of the student's placement in a more restricted environment (Kozlowski, Phipps, & Hitzing, 1983). That is, social isolation may lead to frustration, depression, and behavior problems that in turn contribute to the need for a more restrictive placement and a reduction in opportunities for social integration.

Furthermore, there is some evidence to suggest that the degree to which a student experiences (or lacks) adequate social support is directly related to educational outcomes because the presence of social support has been associated with students' higher academic achievement (Belle & Longfellow, 1984; Woods, 1972). Thus, a decrease in social support for a student with ABI may function to exacerbate the learning difficulties with which he or she must already contend.

Effect on the Child's Community Involvement

Being active and involved in a community is an essential element in anyone's quality of life, and the need for students with disabilities to be fully included in community activities and society as a whole has been frequently cited (e.g., Laski, 1991). The social isolation experienced by students with ABI often translates into a dramatic reduction in opportunities for participation in community leisure activities. Following the injury, students with ABI may often engage only in inactive, home-based activities such as watching television, reading, or playing with a computer (Lehr, 1990). These types of activities consequently reduce the likelihood of their becoming or remaining genuinely involved members of the community—a loss both to the individual and to the community as a whole.

APPROACHES TO INCREASE AND ENHANCE SOCIAL RELATIONSHIPS BETWEEN CHILDREN WITH AND WITHOUT DISABILITIES

Since the mid-1970s, a variety of approaches to increase or enhance social relationships and community involvement of people with disabilities have been developed (Cooper & McEvoy, 1996). Following is an overview of the major types of strategies that have been developed as well as the typical outcomes associated with each.

Pairing Individuals with and without Disabilities

One of the first organized and widely disseminated efforts to facilitate and enhance friendships between same-age peers with and without disabilities was developed by Voeltz and her colleagues (Voeltz, 1980, 1982). The Special Friends program recruited and matched elementary-age peers without disabilities to play with students with severe disabilities during recess, lunch, and activity times. School personnel encouraged and facilitated social interactions and play between the peers and were specifically instructed not to allow instruction or helping behaviors by the peer without disabilities. Positive attitudes toward students with disabilities and peer relationships among the students were found to increase as a result of participating in the project.

Other approaches have involved pairing students with disabilities with older students or adults without disabilities to increase friendship and involvement in community activities. The Fostering Friendships program (Cooley, 1989; Cooley, Singer, & Irvin, 1989), modeled loosely after the Big Brother/Big Sister program, paired university students with students with severe disabilities to take them out once a week for several hours to engage in community recreational activities. Participants indicated a high level of satisfaction with the program, the degree of participation in community activities increased for students with disabilities, and positive attitudes among the university students toward students with disabilities also increased.

Person-Centered Planning

Another type of approach to enhancing social inclusion entails involving the student and family more centrally in the educational or service delivery planning process. Examples of this strategy include the Circle of Friends approach (Forest & Lusthaus, 1989); Making Action Plans, or MAPs (Vandercook, York, & Forest, 1989) (formerly known as McGill Action Planning System [Lusthaus & Forest, 1987]); and Collaborative Problem Solving (Salisbury & Palombaro, 1992). Such approaches have resulted not only in enhanced friendship opportunities and support for individuals with disabilities but also in improved quality of service delivery to those individuals.

Community Bridge-Building

Another strategy employed has been to facilitate the involvement of individuals with disabilities in general community recreational activities or clubs. Termed Community Bridge-Building (Arsenault, 1990; Mount, Beeman, & Ducharme, 1988; O'Connell, 1988), this approach entails first identifying formal and informal opportunities available in the community for individuals to become acquainted with others with similar interests and then facilitating the inclusion of individuals with disabilities into these groups. A number of case studies have indicated that friendships between group members with and without disabilities developed as a result of this inclusion (Arsenault, 1990; Reidy, 1993; Strully & Strully, 1985).

Inclusion in General Education Classrooms

One key rationale underlying the growing trend toward including students with disabilities in the general education classroom is the need to increase opportunities for these students to interact socially with their peers without disabilities both in and out of class (Stainback & Stainback, 1990; Stainback, Stainback, & Jackson, 1992). Although it has been shown that some students with disabilities do increase their friendships by virtue of inclusion alone (Hall, 1994; Staub, Schwartz, Gallucci, & Peck, 1994), others require more active promotion efforts on the part of teachers or others to have a meaningful effect on social interactions and relationships with peers without disabilities (e.g., Cole, 1986; Meyer et al., 1987; Voeltz & Brennan, 1984). The cooperative learning strategies employed in many general education classrooms in the 1990s have been identified as promising in their potential effect on students with disabilities because of their tendency to enhance the social relationships among all students (Gartner & Lipsky, 1987; Stainback & Stainback, 1992).

Peer Tutoring

Yet another approach to promoting social inclusion efforts is peer tutoring (Haring, 1991; Odom & Strain, 1986), which focuses on recruiting and training students without disabilities to provide academic assistance to students with disabilities. Results of research on peer tutoring have shown an increase in positive social and academic skills by the students with disabilities as well as an increase in positive attitudes of the peer tutors toward individuals with disabilities (Gartner & Lipsky, 1990; Haring, 1991; Harper, Maheady, & Mallette, 1994). Peer tutoring has not been found, however, to have any effect on increasing friendships or involvement in social activities of students with disabilities. Moreover, the practice of placing students without disabilities in teaching or oversight roles vis-à-vis their peers with disabilities has been criticized because of the deleterious effect it can have on the formation of equal and reciprocal social relationships (Kishi & Meyer, 1994).

THE BUILDING FRIENDSHIPS PROJECT: AN UP-CLOSE LOOK AT ONE APPROACH

The Building Friendships approach was originally developed under a 3-year federally funded research grant from the U.S. Department of Education (Sowers, Glang, & Cooley, 1991). It focused on alleviating the social isolation that students with ABI experience by developing and enhancing school-based social networks. Research results from the study of this process (see Sowers, Glang, Voss, & Cooley, 1996) indicated that after being involved in the project, students, parents, and teachers reported that students with ABI increased their number of friends and also engaged more frequently in activities with their peers without disabilities. Parents and teachers also reported increases in their satisfaction with the students' social lives.

The Process

The Building Friendships process combines many of the features of MAPs (O'Brien, Forest, Snow, & Hasbury, 1989; Pearpoint, Forest, & Snow, 1992) and Circle of Friends (Perske, 1988; Snow, 1989) approaches. Like other person-centered planning strategies, this one strives to create an environment that encourages the student and family to direct as many aspects of the planning process as possible. Adaptations and modifications were made to the strategies previously developed in order to shorten the process, thus making it easier for people to participate as well as to place a greater emphasis on social network issues and follow-up activities.

The overarching goal of the Building Friendships process is to increase the quality of the student's social life through an ongoing, informal team process designed to bring together and mobilize important people in a student's life. The student, family, peers, and professionals participate in a four-phase process led by a facilitator. Brief descriptions of the four phases, which consist of gathering information, recruiting team members, conducting an initial team meeting, and holding regular follow-up meetings, follow. Specific how-to information is then provided.

Phase I: Gather Information Through Interviews with the Student, Parents, School Staff, and Peers   The facilitator, typically an educator located at the school, first interviews the important people in the student's life to identify opportunities within school and community settings to develop increased social opportunities and to enhance current friendships. Information gathered during this first phase is used as a basis for the initial team meeting.

Phase II: Recruit Family Members, School Staff, and Peers to Be Team Members   To develop broad-based support and to create a student- and peer-driven process, it is important to include a variety of team members at the initial team meeting. The student and family members play the primary role in determining which individuals to recruit as team members. In some cases this may include peers, extended family, and school staff whereas in other cases the initial meeting may involve a core group including the student, his or her parent(s), and several educators with whom the student has developed a close relationship. Team membership is fluid; new team members may be invited to participate at any time, and those team members who are unable to participate regularly may choose to attend meetings less frequently.

Phase III: Conduct an Initial Team Meeting to Share Information and to Create Visions for the Future   The team identifies individualized social goals and specific strategies to meet these goals.

Phase IV: Hold Regular Review Meetings   Every 2–3 weeks, team members meet to review progress, revise plans and strategies, and reevaluate team membership and responsibilities.

The Team Meeting

The Building Friendships process, like MAPs, is a dynamic and fluid person-centered planning strategy aimed at increasing the students' and families' abilities to arrive at their own solutions to problems of social isolation. It emphasizes the importance of including peers as team members as early in the process as possible.

The MAPs process uses the following seven questions to help guide efforts of team members in increasing the successful inclusion of students with disabilities (Vandercook, York, & Forest, 1989):

1. What is the individual's history?
2. What is your dream for the individual?

3. What is your nightmare?
4. Who is the individual?
5. What are the individual's strengths, gifts, and abilities?
6. What are the individual's needs?
7. What would the individual's ideal school day look like?

Whereas MAPs addresses a full range of student-centered issues, the Building Friendships process focuses solely on social issues and is thus of shorter duration and more narrowly targeted. Following are the questions/steps used in the Building Friendships team meeting.

Who Is [the Student]?   The facilitator asks team members to offer words and phrases to describe the positive qualities and attributes of the student. As participants share their thoughts, the facilitator records them with colorful markers on a large sheet of paper. This first question sets the tone for the rest of the meeting and for the entire Building Friendships program by focusing team members on the student's strengths and positive attributes. For some families, this can be an emotionally charged experience because it is the first time since their child's brain injury that they have heard professionals speak positively about their child.

Hopes and Dreams   Next, team members state their hopes and dreams for the student within the social domain. After the student has the opportunity to state his or her own hopes and dreams, the other team members offer their hopes and dreams for the student. The facilitator checks with the student frequently to make sure that the hopes and dreams offered by other team members are acceptable and deletes those that the student does not want recorded. As long as the student accepts the hopes and dreams offered by others, every response is recorded and nothing is censored. This brainstorming process serves both to empower the student and expand the team's notion of what is possible. In some cases, the most important goals emerge from hopes and dreams that initially appear unrealistic.

Circle of Friends   Based on the information previously gathered, the facilitator presents a prepared visual diagram representing the key people currently in the student's life. This diagram consists of four concentric circles with the student's name placed inside the innermost circle. Those closest to the student, trusted friends, acquaintances, and paid professionals are all listed on successive circles that extend outward from the student. The Circle of Friends diagram graphically depicts the nature of the student's social network (see Figure 1). In most cases, the diagram shows an abundance of acquaintances and paid professionals but few close friends. The goal of the Building Friendships process is to create opportunities for the student to make friends and expand his or her inner circle.

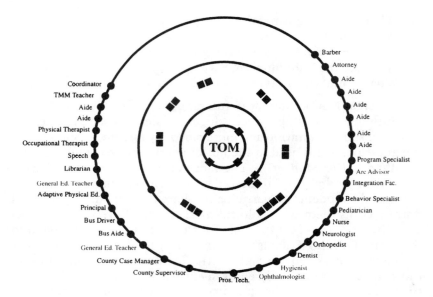

Figure 1.   An example of a Circle of Friends diagram for Tom, a student. (■ = family; ● = nonfamily) (From Schleien, S.J., Ray, M.T., & Green, F.P. [1997]. *Community recreation and people with disabilities: Strategies for inclusion* [2nd ed., p. 137]. Baltimore: Paul H. Brookes Publishing Co.; reprinted by permission.)

Goals   Next, the team identifies several goals toward which to begin working. These goals, derived from the hopes and dreams created previously by the team, are fluid; the team may add or change goals in future meetings. The student has the final say in determining whether chosen goals are acceptable.

Obstacles   The team next identifies obstacles to achieving the identified goals. Team members are asked to think of all the reasons it might be difficult for the student to reach the identified goals. Obstacles might involve financial constraints (e.g., Joey cannot afford to go to the video arcade), physical issues (e.g., Manuel's physical disabilities prevent him from playing soccer), or a school's approach to service delivery (e.g., Sarah's school has never had a student with disabilities participate fully in the second-grade class). This is the first opportunity during the meeting for team members to present "roadblocks" to meeting the goals set by the team.

Strategies   After identifying possible obstacles, the team then brainstorms specific strategies for overcoming them. It is the facilitator's job to help the group move beyond accepted practices and develop creative approaches and solutions. Although some strategies might take a concerted effort to implement (e.g., setting up a recess buddy system), others might be as simple as a schedule change to permit greater inclusion and opportunities with peers. The key to success at this stage is to encourage the team to adopt a "can do" attitude.

Action Plan   The last step in the process is for the team to prioritize goals and strategies and then develop a specific plan that details how team members will achieve their goals. The action plan specifies which team member will take responsibility for which task and when each task will be accomplished.

Menu of Strategies

Every student with ABI is unique. Therefore, the activities and strategies decided on will vary considerably from person to person. Following is a *menu of strategies* that might be included on a student's action plan, along with examples of each.

Schedule Changes: Modifying a Student's Schedule to Increase Social Opportunities in Inclusive Settings   One of the key obstacles identified by Sarah's team was her isolation from peers without disabilities. Sarah's team changed her schedule so that she spent lunch, recess, and several hours each afternoon with the other third-grade students.

Peer Education About ABI: Presenting Information About ABI to Peers with Specific Information About Their Peer's Experiences   In his middle school homeroom class, Richard and his mother presented a slide show about his rehabilitation from a severe brain injury several years earlier. The presentation included slides of Richard prior to his accident, during coma, and in various rehabilitation activities at the hospital. Richard's mother discussed the effects of the brain injury on Richard and their family. Richard and his mother then answered students' questions.

Organized Recreational Activities: Linking the Student to Typical Recreational Activities in the Community   Tom's team explored community-based social and recreational opportunities to find ways for him to become more involved with peers outside of school. As a result, he became involved in a church youth group and began going to the YMCA after school several times a week to play basketball. Jessica joined a Camp Fire club, Ralph and another young man started working out in a gym three times a week, and Alison volunteered once a week at a preschool for low-income families.

Friendship Clubs that Serve to Shift the Focus from One Targeted Individual to a Larger Group of Students   One instructional assistant began the Building Friendships process specifically for one of her students, Billy. As peer interest developed and grew, the focus gradually shifted away from an exclusive focus on Billy to a genuine concern for building a sense of community and belonging within the group as a whole. Soon Billy and his peers were meeting once a week to discuss concerns about friendships and were planning dances and other activities to engage in together.

Buddy System for Getting to and from Class and at Lunch and Recess   Initially, it can be helpful to ask peers to volunteer to assist and spend time with students with ABI at lunch and recess. For example, Helen's team facilitator arranged for several students in other classes to eat lunch with Helen and to play with her at recess. These formalized arrangements were helpful in bringing students together and in getting them acquainted with one another. After several months, the formal buddy systems were dropped in favor of the more naturally occurring routines that had evolved over time.

Cooperative Learning Activities: Structuring Classroom Activities so that Groups of Students Work Together Toward a Common Goal   Prior to his involvement in the Building Friendships process, Joey usually worked individually with the instructional assistant during most of math class. After the team meeting, Joey's math teacher created more opportunities for the students in Joey's class to work in cooperative groups.

Social Events Outside of School: Planning a Group Activity in the Community   Ramon's team planned an after-school ice-skating party. Most of the students were able to attend, and the experience gave everyone an opportunity to get to know one another in a different way outside the academic setting. Ramon's joking, usually viewed as inappropriate during class time, was well received and reciprocated in this recreational context.

Organizational Systems: Creating Compensatory Systems for Keeping Track of Important Information   Ted's team suggested that he use an audiotape recorder at school. This enabled him to record information for his classes (e.g., assignments, school schedule changes) and was a fun way for him to interact with other students as they taped messages for him. Each night he transferred the information into his memory log on his computer. Rachelle's team helped her create a book with pictures of her friends. Below each picture was the friend's name and telephone number. The idea was so popular among the group of friends that each one created his or her own photograph telephone book to aid in calling one another.

Informal Weekly Lunch Get-Togethers at School   Jack and the peers involved in his team decided to eat lunch together once a week. Each week they met in a reserved classroom, and they often took turns bringing special treats. After lunch the group played games and had organized discussions about topics of interest ranging from current events to the quality of cafeteria food.

Classwide Disability Awareness/Community-Building Activities As part of their involvement in the Building Friendships process, the facilitator for Billy's team coordinated a Brain Injury Awareness Week in the school gym. Each class spent their gym time rotating through various simulation exercises that were designed to provide students with the experience of having a number of different challenges associated with ABI. The facilitator for Michelle's team came to her health class several times and guided all of the students through some of the steps of the Building Friendships process. As each student talked about the importance of friends in his or her life, the focus of attention (and therefore, too, any pressure or embarrassment) was removed from Michelle.

Attending Extracurricular School Functions   Through the efforts of their respective teams, Shawn obtained a student identification card and attended several school dances with his brother, Cody started taking photographs for the school newspaper, and Mandy became her school's softball team's statistician.

CONCLUSION

Whether employing the Building Friendships process or any of the many other available strategies for increasing and enhancing friendship opportunities for students with ABI, there are several key features or guiding principles that are helpful to keep in mind:

1. **Every child is different; therefore, whatever approach is used must be tailored to meet that student's unique needs.**
    What works for one student may be inappropriate for another. Keeping the process creative, dynamic, and open to variation will further enhance its effectiveness. This flexibility is the essence of the Building Friendships process and others like it.
2. **Friendships involve reciprocity, so whenever possible, horizontal rather than vertical relationships should be emphasized.**
    Often, people tend to forget that the person with a disability has just as much to offer to a friendship as anyone else. Emphasizing this balance and stressing reciprocal relationships (as opposed to hierarchical or "helper–helpee" relationships) serves to maintain the dignity and contribute to the self-respect of the individual being singled out for assistance efforts.

3. **Although the commitment of at least one adult to serve in the facilitative role is vital, it is equally important to ensure that the process is as peer driven as possible.**

On the one hand, an adult's ongoing commitment will help to ensure that necessary follow-through will occur. On the other hand, a process that is entirely adult or professional driven may lack credibility with or attraction for students. Therefore, it is crucial to strike a balance between adult and peer involvement.

4. **Support from the school building administrator is critical.**

Approaches that strive to facilitate more social opportunities within school settings need, at a minimum, to have the awareness of and tacit support from the school principal. Even more helpful is the principal's active support and encouragement because it provides team members with an increased sense of freedom to think creatively and try new things.

5. **Sensitivity to family issues is essential.**

For some families, the child's loss of friends is a very difficult and sensitive issue. For example, one parent with whom the authors worked had initially been extremely reluctant to participate in the Building Friendships process. For the first time since her son's injury, she was confronted with the deep sadness she felt about her son's loss of friendships and loneliness. It took time for her to trust that this group of professionals and peers might actually be able to help her son reestablish important social connections.

Awareness of and sensitivity to the issues faced by family members is a critical aspect of the Building Friendships process. For some families, simply managing day-to-day stresses by necessity outweighs the desire to help their children develop friendships. It is thus necessary to let families define the level and extent of participation comfortable for them. In some cases, this may mean accepting only minimal family involvement and shifting the focus to the school setting to increase a student's social network.

6. **Social isolation is different from emotional isolation, and alleviating the latter is the ultimate goal.**

Weiss (1973) makes an important distinction between *social isolation* characterized by the absence of a peer network and *emotional isolation* that stems from a lack of deep, meaningful friendships. Many of the strategies discussed in this chapter are designed to address issues of social rather than emotional isolation. It is important to "keep one's eye on the ball" so to speak, however, by remembering the rationale and hope underlying the effort to increase social networks and opportunities. Ultimately, the aim of such efforts is to increase the quality of a child's life by ensuring the presence in that life of genuinely supportive and caring friendships—something needed and deserved by everyone.

REFERENCES

Acorn, S. (1993). An education/support program for families of survivors of head injury. *Canadian Journal of Rehabilitation, 7*(2), 149–151.

Arsenault, C. (1990). *Let's get together: A handbook in support of building relationships between individuals with developmental disabilities and their community.* Boulder, CO: Developmental Disabilities Center.

Belle, D. (1989). *Children's social networks and social supports.* New York: John Wiley & Sons.

Belle, D., & Longfellow, C. (1983). *Emotional support and children's well-being: An exploratory study of children's confidants.* Paper presented at the biennial meeting of the Society for Research in Child Development, Detroit, MI.

Belle, D., & Longfellow, C. (1984). *Turning to others: Children's use of confidants.* Paper presented at the meeting of the American Psychological Association, Toronto, Ontario, Canada.

Cohen, S. (1988). Psychosocial models of the role of social support in the etiology of physical disease. *Health Psychology, 7*(3), 269–297.

Cohen, S., & Wills, T.A. (1985). Stress, social support, and the buffering hypothesis. *Psychological Bulletin, 98*(2), 310–357.

Cole, D. (1986). Facilitating play in children's peer relationships: Are we having fun yet? *American Educational Research Journal, 23*, 201–215.

Cooley, E. (1989). Community support: The role of volunteers and voluntary associations. In G.H.S. Singer & L.K. Irvin (Eds.), *Support for caregiving families: Enabling positive adaptation to disability* (pp. 143–157). Baltimore: Paul H. Brookes Publishing Co.

Cooley, E., Singer, G., & Irvin, L. (1989). Volunteers as part of family support services for families of developmentally disabled members. *Education and Training in Mental Retardation, 24*(3), 207–218.

Cooper, S.S., & McEvoy, M.A. (1996). Group friendship activities. *Teaching Exceptional Children, 28*(3), 67–69.

Cowen, E.L., & Work, W.C. (1988). Resilient children, psychological and primary prevention. *American Journal of Community Psychology, 16*(4), 591–601.

Dywan, J., & Segalowitz, S.J. (1996). Self- and family ratings of adaptive behavior after traumatic brain injury: Psychometric scores and frontally generated ERPs. *Journal of Head Trauma Rehabilitation, 11*(2), 79–95.

Fletcher, J.M., Ewings-Cobbs, L., & Minor, M. (1991). Behavioral changes after closed head injury in children. *Journal of Consulting and Clinical Psychology, 58*(1), 93–98.

Forest, M., & Lusthaus, E. (1989). Promoting educational equality for all students: Circles and maps. In S. Stainback, W. Stainback, & M. Forest (Eds.), *Educating all students in the mainstream of regular education* (pp. 43–57). Baltimore: Paul H. Brookes Publishing Co.

Garmezy, N. (1983). Stressors of childhood. In N. Garmezy & M. Rutter (Eds.), *Stress, coping, and development in children* (pp. 43–85). New York: McGraw-Hill.

Garske, G.G., & Thomas, K.R. (1992). Self-reported self-esteem and depression: Indexes of psychosocial adjustment following severe traumatic brain injury. *Rehabilitation Counseling Bulletin, 36*(1), 44–52.

Gartner, A., & Lipsky, D.K. (1987). Beyond special education: Toward a quality system for all students. *Harvard Educational Review, 57*(4), 367–395.

Gartner, A., & Lipsky, D.K. (1990). Students as instructional agents. In W. Stainback & S. Stainback (Eds.), *Support networks for inclusive schooling: Interdependent integrated education* (pp. 81–93). Baltimore: Paul H. Brookes Publishing Co.

Goethe, K.E., & Levin, H.S. (1984). Behavioral manifestations during the early and long-term stages of recovery after closed head injury. *Psychiatric Annals, 14*(7), 540–546.

Hall, L. (1994). A descriptive assessment of social relationships in integrated classrooms. *Journal of The Association for Persons with Severe Handicaps, 19*(4), 277–289.

Haring, T.G. (1991). Social relationships. In L.H. Meyer, C.A. Peck, & L. Brown (Eds.), *Critical issues in the lives of people with severe disabilities* (pp. 195–217). Baltimore: Paul H. Brookes Publishing Co.

Harper, G.F., Maheady, L., & Mallette, B. (1994). The power of peer-mediated instruction: How and why it promotes academic success for all students. In J.S. Thousand, R.A. Villa, & A.I. Nevin (Eds.), *Creativity and collaborative learning: A practical guide to empowering students and teachers* (pp. 229–241). Baltimore: Paul H. Brookes Publishing Co.

Kishi, G., & Meyer, L. (1994). What children report and remember: A six-year follow-up of the effects of social contact between peers with and without severe disabilities. *Journal of The Association for Persons with Severe Handicaps, 19*(4), 277–289.

Kozlowski, R.E., Phipps, C., & Hitzing, W. (1983). *Promoting quality community living through formal support services and informal supports.* Columbus: Ohio State University, Herschel W. Nisonger Center. (ERIC Document Reproduction Service No. ED 250 900)

Laski, F.J. (1991). Achieving integration during the second revolution. In L.H. Meyer, C.A. Peck, & L. Brown (Eds.), *Critical issues in the lives of people with severe disabilities* (pp. 409–421). Baltimore: Paul H. Brookes Publishing Co.

Lehr, E. (1990). Psychosocial issues. In E. Lehr (Ed.), Psychological management of traumatic brain injuries in children and adolescents (pp. 155–184). Rockville, MD: Aspen Publishing, Inc.

Lusthaus, E., & Forest, M. (1987). The kaleidoscope: A challenge to the cascade. In M. Forest (Ed.), *More education integration* (pp. 1–17). Downsview, Ontario, Canada: G. Allen Roeher Institute.

Meyer, L., Fox, A., Schermer, A., Ketelson, D., Monton, N., Maley, K., & Cole, D. (1987). The effects of teacher intrusion on social play interactions between children with autism and their nonhandicapped peers. *Journal of Autism and Developmental Disorders, 17*, 315–332.

Meyer, L.H., & Putnam, J. (1987). Social integration. In V.B. Van Hasselt, P. Strain, & M. Hersen (Eds.), *Handbook of developmental and physical disabilities* (pp. 107–133). Elmsford, NY: Pergamon.

Mount, B., Beeman, P., & Ducharme, G. (1988). *What are we building? About bridge-building: A summary of a dialogue between people seeking to build community for people with disabilities.* Manchester, CT: Communities, Inc.

O'Brien, J., Forest, M., Snow, J., & Hasbury, T. (1989). *Action for inclusion: How to improve schools by welcoming children with special needs into regular classrooms.* Toronto, Ontario, Canada: Frontier College Press.

O'Connell, M. (1988). *Getting connected: How to find out about groups and organizations in your neighborhood.* Springfield, IL: Department of Rehabilitation Services.

Odom, S.L., & Strain, P.S. (1986). A comparison of peers: Initiation and teacher antecedent interventions for promoting reciprocal social interaction of autistic preschoolers. *Journal of Applied Behavior Analysis, 19,* 59–72.

Pearpoint, J., Forest, M., & Snow, J. (1992). *The inclusion papers.* Toronto, Ontario, Canada: Inclusion Press.

Perske, R. (1988). *Circles of friends: People with disabilities and their friends enrich the lives of one another.* Nashville, TN: Abingdon Press.

Reidy, D. (1993). Friendships and community associations. In A.N. Amado (Ed.), *Friendships and community connections between people with and without developmental disabilities* (pp. 351–371). Baltimore: Paul H. Brookes Publishing Co.

Rohrle, B., & Sommer, G. (1994). Social support and social competence: Some theoretical and empirical contributions to their relationship. In F. Nestmann & K. Hurrelmann (Eds.), *Social networks and social support in childhood and adolescence* (pp. 23–52). Berlin, Germany: de Gruyter.

Salisbury, C.L., Gallucci, C., Palombaro, M.M., & Peck, C.A. (1995). Strategies that promote social relations among elementary students with and without severe disabilities in inclusive schools. *Exceptional Children, 62*(2), 125–137.

Salisbury, C.L., & Palombaro, M.M. (1992). *Collaborative problem-solving: Peers and adults as advocates for inclusion.* Paper presented at the International Division for Early Childhood Conference on Children with Special Needs, Washington, DC.

Sandler, I.N., Gersten, J.C., Reynolds, K., Kallgren, C., & Ramirez, R. (1989). Using theory and data to plan support interventions: Design of a program for bereaved children. In B. Gottlieb (Ed.), *Marshalling social support: Formats, processes, and effects* (pp. 53–83). Beverly Hills: Sage Publications.

Schleien, S.J., Ray, M.T., & Green, F.P. (1997). *Community recreation and people with disabilities: Strategies for inclusion* (2nd ed.). Baltimore: Paul H. Brookes Publishing Co.

Seaver-Reid, M.E. (1986). *Preparation of trainers of volunteer parent service providers (including parents) for Vermont's school-age learners with severe developmental disabilities.* Final report of Vermont University at Burlington, Center for Developmental Disabilities.

Singer, G.H.S., & Nixon, C. (1996). A report on the concerns of parents of children with ABI. In G.H.S. Singer, A. Glang, & J.M. Williams (Eds.), *Children with acquired brain injury: Educating and supporting families* (pp. 23–52). Baltimore: Paul H. Brookes Publishing Co.

Snow, J.A. (1989). Systems of support: A new vision. In S. Stainback, W. Stainback, & M. Forest (Eds.), *Educating all students in the mainstream of regular education* (pp. 221–231). Baltimore: Paul H. Brookes Publishing Co.

Sokol, D.K., Ferguson, C.F., Pitcher, G.A., Huster, G.A., Fitzhugh-Bell, K., & Luerssen, T.G. (1996). Behavioral adjustment and parental stress associated with closed head injury in children. *Brain Injury, 10*(6), 439–451.

Sowers, J., Glang, A., & Cooley, E. (1991). Enhancing social support and integration for students with traumatic brain injury. (Grant # H086D10008). Washington, DC: U.S. Department of Education, Office of Special Education and Rehabilitative Services.

Sowers, J., Glang, A.E., Voss, J., & Cooley, E. (1996). Enhancing friendships and leisure involvement of students with traumatic brain injuries and other disabilities. In L.E. Powers, G.H.S. Singer, & J. Sowers (Eds.), *On the road to autonomy: Promoting self-competence in children and youth with disabilities* (pp. 347–371). Baltimore: Paul H. Brookes Publishing Co.

Stainback, S., Stainback, W., & Jackson, H.J. (1992). Toward inclusive classrooms. In S. Stainback & W. Stainback (Eds.), *Curriculum considerations in inclusive classrooms: Facilitating learning for all students* (pp. 3–17). Paul H. Brookes Publishing Co.

Stainback, W., & Stainback, S. (Eds.). (1990). *Support networks for inclusive schooling: Interdependent integrated education.* Baltimore: Paul H. Brookes Publishing Co.

Stainback, W., & Stainback, S. (Eds.). (1992). *Curriculum considerations in inclusive classrooms: Facilitating learning for all students.* Baltimore: Paul H. Brookes Publishing Co.

Staub, D., Schwartz, I., Gallucci, C., & Peck, C. (1994). Children's perceptions of fairness in classroom and interpersonal situations involving peers with severe disabilities. *Journal of The Association for Persons with Severe Handicaps, 19,* 326–332.

Stratton, M.C., & Gregory, R.J. (1994). After traumatic brain injury: A discussion of consequences. *Brain Injury, 8*(7), 631–645.

Strully, J., & Strully, C. (1985). Friendship and our children. *Journal of The Association for Persons with Severe Handicaps, 10*(4), 224–227.

Turnbull, A.P., & Turnbull, H.R. (1986). *Families, professionals, and exceptionality: A special partnership.* Columbus, OH: Charles E. Merrill.

Vandercook, T., York, J., & Forest, M. (1989). The McGill action planning system (MAPS): A strategy for building the vision. *Journal of The Association for Persons with Severe Handicaps, 14*(3), 205–215.

Vieth, A.Z., Johnstone, B., & Dawson, B. (1996). Extent of intellectual, cognitive, and academic decline in adolescent traumatic brain injury. *Brain Injury, 10*(6), 465–470.

Voeltz, L. (1980). Children's attitudes toward handicapped peers. *American Journal of Mental Deficiency, 84*(5), 455–464.

Voeltz, L. (1982). Effects of structured interaction with severe handicapped peers on children's attitudes. *American Journal of Mental Deficiency, 86,* 380–390.

Voeltz, L., & Brennan, J. (1984). Analysis of interactions between nonhandicapped and severely handicapped peers using multiple measures. In J. M. Berg (Ed.), *Perspectives and progress in mental retardation: Vol I. Social, psychological, and educational aspects* (pp. 61–72). Baltimore: University Park Press.

Weiss, R. (1973). *Loneliness: The experience of emotional and social isolation.* Cambridge, MA: MIT Press.

Willer, B., Allen, K., Durnan, M.C., & Ferry, A. (1990). Problems and coping strategies of mothers, siblings, and young adult males with traumatic brain injury. *Canadian Journal of Rehabilitation, 2*(3), 167–173.

Wolchik, S.A., Beals, J., & Sandler, I.N. (1989). Mapping children's support networks: Conceptual and methodological issues. In D. Belle (Ed.), *Children's social networks and social supports* (pp. 191–220). New York: John Wiley & Sons.

Woods, M. (1972). The unsupervised child of the working mother. *Developmental Psychology, 6*(1), 14–25.

chapter ten

Counseling Students with ABI

Ellen Lehr

COUNSELING FOR STUDENTS after brain injuries can be provided through a variety of agencies and settings, including hospitals, rehabilitation programs, community mental health centers, private mental health providers, and schools. Unfortunately, mental health professionals rarely receive specific training or experience in working with children and adolescents with acquired brain injury (ABI). In addition, mental health services are rarely provided in an organized manner over time. These services are instead often provided for brief periods as the family and child pass through each specific care setting with little continuity either of care or professionals. For example, the child's family may receive social work or chaplaincy support in the acute care hospital, then social work or psychological intervention during rehabilitation, and then community support and intervention as available over the years of recovery/improvement. Support services may be available through the local Brain Injury Association in the form of groups for families and survivors. It is unusual, however, for a family to have the experience of working with the same mental health providers from the time of their child's injury throughout the years of recovery/improvement.

School services can often provide more continuity to these students and their families than rehabilitation or community mental health services are able to provide. Although students change teachers and buildings, school staff continue to have daily contact with students throughout the school year, and the students remain in school programs for many years. In addition, there is often ongoing history and documentation of a student's functioning available through teachers' and counselors' records, special education records, and other school records.

Schools are the only agencies that are mandated by federal law to provide services for *all* children and adolescents. This is limited to educational services, however, and they are not mandated to provide counseling or mental health services unless these services are "educationally relevant." Therefore, schools are required to provide mental health services only if the student's mental health needs interfere with his or her functioning and performance in the school setting. Of course, many schools actually provide a range of counseling and mental health services within school buildings, by school staff, and sometimes on school time. It is also a fact of reality, however, that these services are often some of the first to be cut back when school funding is limited. Because community mental health service availability is also related to financial constraints, some schools and community mental health centers have begun to work together to provide services to children and adolescents (e.g., mental health staff coordinating with school staff to hold counseling groups in school buildings). In many areas of the country, schools are likely to be the primary community agency involved with children and adolescents. Mental health and medical/rehabilitation services may be geographically too far away or limited because of long waiting lists or financial constraints. Because of these caveats, school counseling staff members and school counseling services are often the most accessible ones for students with ABI.

The purpose of this chapter is to assist school counseling staff members in becoming more aware of the needs of students with ABI and more comfortable in providing school-based counseling services for them. In addition, one hopes that it will also be helpful in coordinating school and agency/rehabilitation management both in terms of assisting school personnel with appropriate referrals to community mental health services for these students and in collaborating with other professionals on their care.

THREE BROAD PSYCHOLOGICAL INTERVENTION AREAS

ABI often affects multiple areas of a child's functioning. Although a student may experience physical, motor, and sensory impairments after injury, this chapter examines those psychological factors that are critical for counseling intervention. The three broad areas of psychological functioning affected by ABI consist of behavioral, cognitive, and emotional factors. Disinhibition or loosening of behavioral controls is probably the most common behavior problem after injury and affects the student in a variety of ways (e.g., acting impulsively, making embarrassing comments). There are also many cognitive difficulties that can occur after injury, such as reduced memory, shortened attention and concentration, and processing delays and inefficiencies. Cognitive impairments affect not only the students' learning in academic areas but also their functioning in social and emotional areas. Cognitive limitations can reduce the speed and effectiveness of some behavioral strategies and approaches as a result of the students' difficulties in understanding and responding to behavioral cues. Emotional control can also be loosened, leading to emotional lability and irritability. In addition, after ABI students experience emotional reactions to trauma and to injury effects that can result from feeling different from their preinjury selves and from their peers.

All three factors are often present and interactive, but for any individual student, one of these factors may predominate and become the focus of intervention at any given point. Take, for example, a student who has lost most or all of his friends since injury and is engaging in very few social activities. If the primary reason for his lack of social interactions is his disinhibited behavior that embarrasses his friends, intervention can focus on helping him to better control his behavior and to work with his friends to reinforce controlled rather than disinhibited behaviors. If cognitive difficulties reduce his understanding of and contributions to group conversations and make him uncomfortable being with his friends, intervention aimed at the processing of and responding to fast-paced social interactions would be appropriate. If instead his increasing depression over the effects of his injury keeps him from his typical social activities, intervention specifically aimed at helping him to cope with these effects, manage his depression, and increase his social interaction would be an effective approach.

In general, the goals of intervention in these three areas can be summarized in terms of desired increases and decreases (see Table 1). In behavioral areas, the focus is on the decreased behavioral control demonstrated by many children and adolescents after they experience ABI. The goal of behavioral intervention after injury is to increase control through both external environmental structuring and self-control techniques. In cognitive areas, the focus is on the significant cognitive impairments that students with ABI often experience, including decreases in information processing and efficiency, decreases in memory and attention/concentration skills, and

Table 1.   Three areas for counseling intervention and their general goals

Areas	General goals
Behavioral	Increase control
	Decrease chaos
Cognitive	Increase competence
	Decrease confusion
Emotional	Increase confidence
	Decrease catastrophic reaction

changes in other cognitive abilities. The goal of cognitive intervention after injury is to decrease a student's sense of confusion and increase his or her own competence. Emotionally, the student may feel quite overwhelmed by his or her own feelings to the extent that sometimes the student becomes so overloaded that it leads to what has been called a "catastrophic reaction" (Prigatano, 1987). Because the student is not certain about being able to control his or her own emotions, the student begins to experience a compounding sense of loss of self-confidence. Goals for intervention in emotional areas are to decrease the student's feelings of being overwhelmed and to increase confidence in managing personal feelings appropriately.

EFFECT OF RECOVERY/IMPROVEMENT ON COUNSELING APPROACHES

One of the guiding principles of working with students after they experience ABI is that the specific interventions used must be tailored to the changing process of recovery/improvement (Lehr, 1990; Sbordone, 1990). As the student changes with recovery, the intervention approach also must be modified to address the unique aspects of each stage of improvement. If interventions are not tailored to the specific needs of the student, they will be less effective and will lead to frustration on the part of both the counselor and the student. This will tend to reduce the counselor's and student's willingness to engage in further intervention attempts because past attempts will have been perceived as not having been successful. It can also foster the impression that students with ABI are not good candidates for counseling intervention.

As an overall guide to some of the intervention techniques and changes that can be appropriately made throughout the often long period of recovery/improvement after injury, the model of a student who has sustained severe ABI and who has experienced steady progress over a period of a couple of years is used. Table 2 illustrates

Table 2.   Counseling interventions by student's stage of recovery/improvement

Stage	Intervention
Coma	Stimulation Family education about injury Family support
Agitation	Environmental stimulation control Safety Family education about injury Family support
Confusion	Cognitive orientation Basic daily routine teaching Family education about injury Family support
Cognitive	Individual education about injury Behavioral/environmental control Activity groups Peer support Family education about injury Family support
Psychosocial	Individual counseling about reaction to injury Group counseling focused on social skills, anger management, grief work, and substance abuse Family education about injury Family support Family counseling

the changes in intervention approaches that can be made depending on the student's level of recovery.

When students are in coma after ABI, they are usually in a hospital or other 24-hour care facility. Sensory stimulation to increase their level of consciousness is done by a variety of staff and family members. Schools may be asked to provide some hospital education services, especially if a student is slowly improving and will be in the facility for at least several months. The level of educational services provided, however, will consist of basic stimulation because of the reduced capacities of the student. Some students will return home with a very decreased functioning level, especially if they are quite young, and some may never significantly improve from this level of functioning. The primary counseling intervention that is appropriate at this stage consists of family education about ABI effects and management as well as support for family members. This is often provided by rehabilitation professionals and through Brain Injury Association support groups that consist of other family members with similar experiences.

As children with ABI progress out of coma, they often become agitated and confused as they begin to process some of the information from their environment, albeit at a reduced level as a result of the acuteness of their brain injuries. For children in rapid recovery/ improvement, they are likely to continue to be in hospital or rehabilitation settings during these periods. Those children in rural areas or who are very young, however, may well be sent home if they are medically stable. Intervention initially consists of managing and reducing the level of stimulation to which the children are exposed so that their level of agitation can be reduced. As they progress out of agitation, they are ready for reorientation to their daily routines and for basic information about what has happened to them. Although it can be very difficult and probably unwise for students in agitation to attend school programs, their decreased agitation signifies the beginning of their readiness to engage in schooling (or education). Orientation training and basic daily living skills are usually taught at this level, either at home or in individualized education settings (e.g., home teaching, special education programs). The counseling focus for students at these levels of recovery/improvement is again on the family but with an emphasis on planning for the students' return to more typical life activities. It is also a time for preparing the family for the next two stages that often extend over many months and sometimes years.

By the time confusion has resolved, the student is clearly ready again for involvement in academically related learning. As cognitive skills increase, the student is also ready to begin to understand the specifics of his or her own injury. Initially, this may be done in an educational, informative way through an approach of teaching the student what has happened and the effect it has had on his or her functioning. One of the reasons for educating the student about the injury is that during coma and early recovery, the student has little to no memory of his or her own experiences and needs to "fill in" this important gap in his or her life. Another reason, though, is to begin to teach the student about his or her own functioning after injury and to interpret the altered capacities in cognitive, behavioral, and emotional areas to help him or her regain control of them. School-based counseling staff may not believe that they are experienced enough or informed enough about the specifics of brain injury and its effects on the student to comfortably engage the student in learning about his or her injury. Assistance from rehabilitation staff, especially psychologists and social workers, may be quite helpful at this time. Involvement from people working with the local Brain Injury Association and support groups may be helpful as well.

More traditional school-based counseling is also often needed at this time. This counseling is likely to focus on helping the student begin to go through the school day in a more typical fashion through managing and altering the school environment. For example, the student may be able to tolerate being involved in general education classroom activities with the help of a classroom buddy or aide. The student may not yet be able to handle a full-day program without support or without a rest period in the middle of the day to lay down or to engage in quiet activities alone or with a few other students. Because of reduced behavioral controls and/or fatigue, an altered recess plan may be needed during which the student spends time in the nurse's area, resource room, or in the library rather than on the playground. These settings may also be used as time-out areas for the student if he or she cannot maintain control and/or attention in a large class setting. The student often needs assistance getting through the less-structured parts of the school day, such as recess, lunchtime, changing classes, and going to and from school. Planning for these times, by using either adult or peer support, can be essential services provided by the school counseling staff.

It is not until cognitive improvement has progressed that the student begins to emotionally understand and react to his or her injury. This can be a long, gradual process that may occur over many months to years after injury. Traditional school counseling services can be both appropriate and helpful in assisting students in coping with the trauma of injury as well as its effects on their learning, behavioral control, and emotional adjustment after injury. It is during this time that a student with ABI can usually be initially considered for direct involvement in individual counseling as well as participation in groups such as those focusing on social skills/friendship making, anger management, or grief work.

As can be seen from the preceding discussion, counseling interventions in the early stages of recovery/improvement are often focused on the family and on environmental control rather than on direct intervention with the student who has experienced the injury. This is due to the effects of the injury itself and the usual cognitive limitations, which often involve unawareness of injury and subsequent impairments. The focus of initial (or the early stages of) intervention is on family education and support with an anticipatory bias (i.e., teaching the family what to expect). In terms of timing, family support and intervention can occur frequently or at fairly long intervals of approximately 3–6 months, depending on the speed of the child's recovery/improvement and the specific behavioral challenges he or she presents.

Family education efforts can also be a way of directly or indirectly monitoring the individual student's recovery in order to determine when direct intervention may be appropriate with the student (Gronwall & Wrightson, 1990). Because of the often long-term nature of recovery/improvement as well as the changing focus of problem areas, intervention may be most efficient if it is timed to start when new problem areas just begin to emerge and then continues until stabilization has again occurred. In this way, short periods of brief intervention can be used rather than ongoing interventions. For the students who are experiencing the most significant behavior or emotional difficulties, however, intensive intervention involving a number of strategies and approaches may need to persist over long periods of time.

DEVELOPMENTAL ISSUES

Clearly, counseling approaches must acknowledge the developmental level of the child or adolescent after ABI (Lehr, 1990). Working with a 4-year-old preschooler will obviously be quite different from working with an 8-year-old school-age child, a young teenager, or an older adolescent. The developmental interests, needs, and concerns of students always must be taken into account. The student's functioning postinjury may not, however, reflect his or her preinjury developmental level. Intervention will need to be geared to his or her current postinjury level rather than necessarily to age or preinjury functioning.

As students get older after injury, they often understand what has happened to them in different and more complex ways. This can be thought of as a spiraling process with revisiting of previous issues throughout the various developmental stages. For example, soon after injury a young child may first experience depression and anger about changes, and later, as an adolescent, may again experience significant depression and loss over the adult he might have been had he not been injured. Emotional and behavioral issues often do not disappear but are redefined over time.

GENERAL GUIDELINES FOR
COUNSELING STUDENTS AFTER ABI

The basic guidelines for engaging students after ABI in counseling interventions include gaining their *cooperation, charting* their progress, and using *consistent* and *concrete* approaches so that they can more easily understand and make specific behavior changes.

Cooperation

When counseling students with ABI, it is essential to gain their cooperation. This is not as easy as it sounds, however, because students initially may not be aware of their impairments or the inappropriateness of their behavior. Later, they may become overwhelmed by injury effects and believe that little can be changed or improved. As with any other children or adolescents, the effectiveness of intervention is greatly increased with their own involvement. One way to engage students initially is to work on their self-defined goals even if they are not necessarily the most important goals in other people's opinions. Another way is to become the student's ally against the effects of injury. In this way, the injury or injury effects become the "bad guy" for the student and counselor to take on and even defeat. This is especially important in the early stages of awareness of the effects of injury, when the student is only beginning to perceive his or her impairments or changes as part of him- or herself and instead relies primarily on memories of preinjury functioning.

In order to engage students in counseling, a rationale must often be sought that makes sense to the students considering their altered perceptions and altered behaviors after injury. Sometimes the rationale that helps to ensure their cooperation is not one that makes logical sense to anyone who has not experienced ABI, but without it the students are likely to be resistant and see little to no purpose for intervention. Take, for example, a student who had severe initiation impairments after injury that interfered with her ability to complete any school assignments and limited her interest in social activities. She had very little awareness of the effect of her initiation impairments and would talk perseveratively about what she was going to do without taking action to actually do anything. It was determined that she should go to a physician to see if medical approaches could help, but she was initially very resistant and saw no reason to see a doctor. She was, however, able to be convinced that it was necessary for her school counselor to go with her and her mother to the doctor in order for the school counselor to complete her special education assessment. Because the student did have a good relationship with the counselor, she was willing to go to the doctor for the counselor even though she perceived no need to do so for herself.

Charting

Charting can involve typical methods for behavioral interventions that include taking baseline data to identify the specific behaviors that can be targeted for intervention, the circumstances under which they occur, and their frequency and intensity. For students with ABI, a visible record of behavior is also a very helpful way for them to become aware of specific changes in their behavior and functioning. They may not "believe" what other people tell them about such changes (e.g., the effects of disinhibited behavior or comments) until shown by data they either collect or agree to have other people observe and record. After seeing more explicitly what other people notice about them, it is often easier to engage students with ABI in actively attempting to alter their own behavior. Charting consequently becomes a way of documenting their attempts, successes, and even failures and can provide a visual record of their own recovery/improvement. Charting failures can be a way of engaging the students in redesigning intervention approaches that they will "buy into" and that they think will be more successful.

Charting can also be thought of as any visible record that the student is engaged in that documents his or her feelings or capacities as well as behavior. Journal writing, either separately or jointly with the counselor, is another way of keeping a record of the student's recovery/improvement for personal use as time passes. Although this initially may not seem to be very helpful, reviewing students' journal entries as they progress can be quite a powerful aid in assisting them to see the progress they have made in the context of their current goals.

Consistency

Counseling and behavior interventions often need to be simple and clear, with complex procedures broken down into small, well-defined steps and applied persistently and consistently. Because of the students' altered cognitive skills resulting in learning and memory problems, consistent use of the same basic intervention is more likely to be understood and lead to specific changes for these students. Interventions also need to be implemented repeatedly, with increased time for mastery and learning in order for students with ABI to be successful in altering their behaviors. This patient approach toward both behavioral interventions and counseling is likely to be quite rewarding for the students and the counselor.

Concreteness

Because of their cognitive difficulties, students with ABI usually need a very explicit, directive counseling approach (Deaton, Savage, Fryer, & Lehr, 1995). For counselors who have been trained in nondirective techniques, this can be somewhat uncomfortable and can be perceived as controlling. Very clear explanations of what the students are doing and how other people perceive them, though, actually help them to see and understand their own changed behavior. Directive counseling can also be done very sensitively with input from the students about their own perceptions and feelings. Helping the students to talk in a direct way about their feelings after injury, especially anger, frustration, and grief, can assist them in coping with these often overwhelming emotions in a verbal rather than behavioral way. Explaining how the students' sense of lessened control over their feelings and behaviors is related to their injury, as well as to how they can regain control can relieve the students and give them a sense of hope that they can reestablish self-confidence.

Although there are appropriate times to talk to and help a student better understand and cope with the effects of injury, specific behavior changes are probably best done in the situation in which they occur. Talking about how a student with ABI is *supposed* to behave in a specific setting is likely to be less successful than actually intervening in the situation itself. It also cannot be assumed that just because a student postinjury has mastered a behavioral control skill in one setting, he or she will be able to generalize this skill to a similar setting. Instead, generalization will also need to be specifically taught through intervention. This can often be done through verbal analogy, drawing the similarities directly to the student's attention and then providing support in the new setting for behavioral generalization.

COUNSELING APPROACHES

There are many traditional counseling approaches that can be effectively used for students who have experienced ABI, although some modifications must be made for their specific needs (see Table 3). The type of intervention that may be appropriate depends on the students' functional level and the individual problems being addressed.

Consultation/Monitoring

When a student initially returns to a school setting, consultation by the psychosocial rehabilitation staff can be particularly useful in helping school staff feel more comfortable with their understanding of ABI and how ABI has affected the particular student. If the school staff knew the student prior to injury, they will also have to cope with their own feelings about the injury, including their own sense of vulnerability, anger, loss, and grief over the changes the student has experienced. Hearing about how the student is doing from family and hospital staff can be quite different from having the responsibility of educating and interacting with him or her on a daily basis.

Table 3.   Types of counseling approaches

Consultation/monitoring
Behavior management
Individual counseling
Group counseling
Family counseling
Sibling support
ABI support groups

School staff are not the only people who need to prepare for the student's return to school. Other students need to be prepared as well. They need basic information about what to expect and some ideas for how to interact with the student. This is especially important if they have had little contact since the time of injury. Sometimes students who have been injured are able to talk to classroom peers about what happened to them, but often they are not yet capable of this on their initial return to a school program. After making the initial transition back to school, the responsibility for consulting with teachers and other students and monitoring the status of a student after injury usually falls on the school mental health staff. The importance of this consultation and monitoring role can be critical for the successful adjustment of the student in the school not only on initial return but over many years.

Behavior Management

Because of the prevalence and sometimes the severity of behavior problems in individuals postinjury, the application of behavior management approaches and techniques has been written about more widely than the application of other counseling or psychotherapy approaches (Deaton, 1987; Jacobs, 1993). The behavioral approaches can range from environmental manipulation to reinforcement techniques to self-management approaches. Because behavioral approaches proceed from direct observation and data collection, the adaptations needed for success with students following ABI often involve accurate selection of appropriate behavioral techniques and an extended time period for success. (See Chapters 7 and 8 for further information on behavior.)

Individual Counseling

Individual counseling approaches often focus on helping the students to understand what has happened to them as a result of injury and to better cope with its effects. Initial sessions may focus on going over the specifics of the student's injury. Because a student is usually unaware of much of what has happened, this information must be specifically told. Even after family members and friends have talked to the student about his or her injury, the student often may not have really understood the information. For example, one elementary student came into the counselor's office 6 months after injury and blurted out the question, "Did you know that I almost died?" After 6 months, he had finally really understood the implications of his severe injuries and the effect that they had almost had on his life. Students also often need specific information about the recovery/improvement course from the perspective of a person actually going through these changes. They benefit as well from explanations to the best of the counselor's professional knowledge of how and why the injuries affect them the way they do.

In addition to education about their own injuries, individual counseling is often a safe setting to explore and express feelings about having experienced the trauma and changes resulting from injury. It can take students months and even years to adjust to and cope with the effects of injury to the point of coming to terms with the injury and being able to go on with life.

The counselor may also have the role of helping students to regain a sense of control. Often students experience a loss of self-control that is directly related to neurological effects of ABI. Counseling can help them to understand this loss of control and consciously strive for increased control. Use of analogies such as the following example can concretize this process for students after injury. The reduction in control over behavior and emotions can be likened to a "gatekeeper" in the brain. The students have trained their gatekeeper over many years to watch what is going on and respond appropriately depending on the setting and who is around. For example, the gatekeeper learns not to swear in class or in front of most adults. After injury, however, the gatekeeper in the brain goes to sleep and for a period of time lets behaviors and emotions get out without monitoring them first. This is the period of confusion about which the students probably do not remember much. Family members and friends who were with the students at this time often have very striking and sometimes humorous stories to tell about the students' behavior. As the students recover, the gatekeeper again begins functioning but the students are not as quick or accurate as before. For example, a student may "let out" swear words but then apologize and say that he did not mean to swear. His apology is literally true because before injury he would have been able to stop swearing and avoid having it "come out" in inappropriate situations, and he does not realize he cannot do so effectively postinjury. The focus of counseling, then, can be put in terms of having students retrain their gatekeepers. Moving the focus of intervention to an analogy of their behavior can help the students recognize and cope with their disinhibited behaviors and emotions more directly without as much avoidance, embarrassment, or feelings of blame.

Role playing and videotaping of the students' behavior and alternative options can also be used in individual counseling sessions (Barin, Hanchett, Jacob, & Scott, 1985). Doing this with only one other person present can be much easier for the student to tolerate than in a group setting, especially initially.

Group Counseling

Students with ABI often experience increasing social isolation (Ylvisaker, Urbanczyk, & Feeney, 1992). Initially they may be able to participate in supervised social activity groups at school, although they may need increased supervision and cuing to maintain appropriate behavior in a group setting. As they become aware of injury-related changes, many students can also benefit from inclusion in the group counseling interventions typically offered in the school setting. Such intervention can be successful for these students without necessarily being specifically tailored to their injuries; rather they can be focused on more general problems that many students who have and have not sustained injuries may experience. Groups such as those focusing on social skills, friendship making, anger management, grief, and substance abuse may be appropriate, depending on the individual student's needs. Counseling programs such as peer counseling and developing a circle of friends may especially be helpful in avoiding and reducing the degree of social isolation for the students after injury.

In order for students to be able to participate effectively in group counseling after injury, they need to be at least somewhat aware of their own issues and problems, have the desire to interact with other students, and have their behavior under sufficient control not to disrupt the group. Involvement in school counseling groups can have the positive effect of helping students after ABI begin to recognize that other students also have problems, that they are more like other children and adolescents than different despite their unique experience of injury, and that they can help other students cope with problems that are similar or different from their own.

Family Counseling, Sibling Support, and ABI Support Groups

Support groups for families, siblings, and others affected by ABI are rarely provided directly through school mental health services. However, in order to make useful referrals, school staff need to be aware of the services and providers available in their own communities that are specifically geared toward working with families of children who have experienced ABI. The local and state chapters of the Brain Injury Association are excellent sources for information about family, sibling, and survivor support services that are available in their areas. Sibling support groups may be provided through a local children's hospital and often include siblings of students with a wide variety of chronic medical and neurological conditions.

CONCLUSION

In summary, children and adolescents who have sustained ABI often experience significant difficulties in social, behavioral, and emotional areas subsequent and related to their injuries. These psychological aspects of injury change over time depending on both the stage of injury recovery/improvement and the developmental stage of the child. Although psychological components of injury often interfere with functioning, many traditional counseling approaches and techniques can be modified and used effectively with students after ABI to aid in their recovery/improvement and their adjustment to injury effects.

REFERENCES

Barin, J., Hanchett, J., Jacob, W., & Scott, M. (1985). Counseling the head injured patient. In M. Ylvisaker (Ed.), *Head injury rehabilitation: Children and adolescents* (pp. 361–379). San Diego: College-Hill Press.

Deaton, A. (1987). Behavioral change strategies for children and adolescents with severe brain injury. *Journal of Learning Disabilities, 20*(10), 581–589.

Deaton, A., Savage, R., Fryer, J., & Lehr, E. (1995). Social/behavioral aspects of brain injury. In R. Savage & G. Wolcott (Eds.), *An educator's manual: What educators need to know about students with brain injury* (pp. 83–92). Washington, DC: Brain Injury Association, Inc.

Gronwall, D., & Wrightson, P. (1990). *Head injury: The facts. A guide for families and care-givers.* Oxford, England: Oxford University Press.

Jacobs, H. (1993). *Behavioral analysis guidelines and brain injury rehabilitation: People, principles, and programs.* Rockville, MD: Aspen Publishers, Inc.

Lehr, E. (1990). *Psychological management of traumatic brain injuries in children and adolescents.* Rockville, MD: Aspen Publishers, Inc.

Prigatano, G. (1987). Personality and psychosocial consequences after brain injury. In M. Meier, A. Benton, & L. Diller (Eds.), *Neuropsychological rehabilitation* (pp. 355–378). New York: Guilford Press.

Sbordone, R. (1990). Psychotherapeutic treatment of the client with traumatic brain injury: A conceptual model. In J. Kreutzer & P. Wehman (Eds.), *Community integration following traumatic brain injury* (pp. 139–153). Baltimore: Paul H. Brookes Publishing Co.

Ylvisaker, M., Urbanczyk, B., & Feeney, T. (1992). Social skills following traumatic brain injury. *Seminars in Speech and Language, 13,* 308–321.

Parents and Professionals Working Together

Parents, educators, and students often become so overwhelmed with the social, behavioral, physical, and cognitive effects of ABI that it becomes difficult to carry out a coordinated school program. The key is cooperation between parents and school staff. As a member of one of the ABI in-service teams discussed in Chapter 13, I had an opportunity to learn about effective team membership firsthand. Effective teams help the student identify and prioritize goals, and each team member contributes within his or her area of expertise to help the student take small, positive steps toward reaching those goals. Parent–professional partnerships make it possible to adopt a positive, solution-based model to build a foundation for the students' later successes.

The chapters in Section Four contain a wealth of helpful information on preparing for and accomplishing effective partnerships with other professionals and with parents of students with ABI. Given the complex challenges students with ABI face, their teachers and related services personnel have an obligation to learn how to work together and with parents to provide school programs that help students overcome those challenges to meet their daily, weekly, and long-term goals.

Jane Roberts, Physical Therapist

Creating Effective Educational Programs Through Parent–Professional Partnerships

Barbara R. Walker

FOR STUDENTS RETURNING to school settings following acquired brain injury (ABI), coordination among medical professionals, educators, and parents in the development of an individualized education program (IEP) is especially important to ensure a successful transition from the medical setting to school. To be most effective, IEPs must represent goals and values that can be sincerely endorsed by both parents and educators. Because parents and educators represent very different spheres of influence in the student's world, their perspectives and ideas about appropriate goals for the student may be very different.

Achieving mutually supported IEP goals can be a lengthy process and may require many parent–professional interactions before various parties can understand and combine their views and agendas. Parent–professional interactions during the negotiation of an IEP can be demanding, especially if they are fraught with interpersonal tension. Professionals and parents often struggle with their respective thoughts and feelings about the student's altered capabilities and the appropriate roles and responsibilities they are to have in planning and implementing a meaningful school experience for the individual student. Although the IEP process is usually quite structured and formal and can provide a supportive context, the fundamental quality of a parent–professional relationship is established in the more informal, day-to-day contacts that occur over the course of the school year, as additional or new information emerges from the student's responses to intervention efforts.

This chapter focuses on the importance of day-to-day relationship-building strategies that can enhance parent–professional partnerships. The dilemmas that occur in parent–professional relationships are discussed as well as strategies that professionals can adopt to resolve these dilemmas and enhance their success in collaborating with parents in effective parent–professional partnerships.

DILEMMAS IN FORGING
PARENT–PROFESSIONAL PARTNERSHIPS

Many of the dilemmas that confront parents and professionals trying to work together on IEP development and implementation have been described in the special education literature (Darling, 1983; Turnbull & Turnbull, 1985; Walker, Coyne, & Irvin, 1993; Walker & Erickson, 1991). These authors describe many of the barriers created by breakdowns in cooperation and communication between the home and school. These same dilemmas may occur for parents and educators who convene to plan and implement services for students returning to school following hospitalization from ABI.

Without knowing much about one another's expertise, point of view, values, or communication style, parents and professionals must work together to make decisions that are critical to the student's inclusion back into the school setting. Parent–professional interactions can be especially strained when there is a large discrepancy in attitudes and beliefs about the extent of the child's injury, the degree of recovery expected, the kind of intervention needed and its availability, and the appropriate role and responsibility of the various people involved. Parents' grief responses (Powers, 1993), emotional stress, and confusion can be acute and prolonged. Competition for control of the IEP agenda can emerge when parents and professionals are not able to agree on educational goals and use of resources. Expectations for high levels of involvement or support from one another for objectives that are not mutually endorsed may cause further strain in parent–professional relationships. Irregular and infrequent contact between parents and professionals further frustrates the development of a collaborative relationship. Lack of expertise in supportive and conflict-reducing communication skills may also prevent parents and professionals from successful navigation through difficult interpersonal exchanges. Use of jargon or evaluative, stereotyped, and overgeneralized language can undermine efforts at parent–professional collaboration. With careful attention to and use of collaboration strategies and communication skills, however, professionals can do much to foster effective parent–professional partnerships, constructively resolve conflicts, and engineer educational programs that represent the goals of all parties who are invested in optimal outcomes for the student.

STRATEGIES FOR CONSTRUCTIVE PARENT–PROFESSIONAL PARTNERSHIPS

Once professionals acknowledge and identify the dilemmas that occur in parent–professional relationships, they can learn and adopt strategies for resolving these dilemmas and preventing them from having a negative impact on the development of effective IEPs for students. There are many strategies professionals can pursue to enhance parent–professional partnerships and foster the rapport so critical to collaborative parent–professional alliances. Although parents' interaction and communication styles influence the quality of parent–professional relationships, professionals who insist on conducting themselves in a collaborative manner and on using constructive communication skills, regardless of parents' interaction styles, can enhance the quality of their interactions with parents and increase the likelihood of developing effective IEPs for students.

Developing a Constructive Mindset

Professional mindset plays a critical role in achieving constructive parent–professional interactions. Table 1 identifies and provides examples of the elements of a constructive professional mindset. With a constructive mindset, professionals can avoid many of the attitudinal pitfalls that sabotage parent–professional interactions. A constructive mindset enables professionals to achieve positive regard for parents and to set the stage for collaboration and productive interactions between parents and professionals. From there, they can more easily move on to handle strong emotions, value differences, and accept personal biases in ways that allow them to extend meaningful help to all parents, even to those with whom they experience considerable conflict.

Responding to Traumatic Stress Reactions in Parents

In addition to grief reactions, parents of students with ABI are likely to experience some form of traumatic stress reaction. During a stress reaction, parents vividly relive the events that are associated with

Table 1.   Elements of a constructive professional mindset

Element	Definition	Example
Genuine interest in parents'/family's experiences	Professional acknowledges limits of assessment and intervention strategies.	Professional asks parent, How has your child's injury affected members of your family? Tell me how you manage conversations with [child] at home when [child] gets frustrated.
Open mind	Professional avoids preconceived notions and judgmental posture on parents' behaviors, values, personality, and so forth.	Professional says to self, I am going to listen to how the parent wants to be understood. I am going to ignore rumors about how difficult this parent is and look for positive opportunities for us to work together.
Belief in parents' positive motivations	Professional acknowledges positive attributes in parents' caring, concern, and goals for the child.	Professional says to parent, I can see how committed you are to [child's] recovery. It takes a very committed parent to put in the kind of time you have with your child.
Look for resource in parents	Professional looks for and works with parents' expertise and knowledge.	Professional says to parent, I can see that you have read a great deal about brain injury and understand the medical picture far better than I do. Tell me what I need to know about [child's] previous math abilities.
Willingness to resolve interpersonal tensions	Professional acknowledges strain in parent–teacher interactions and addresses them in order to promote a strong working alliance with the parent.	Professional says to parent, I notice that you have not returned my calls this week. Is there something that is making it hard to talk with me? It is difficult for me to talk with you when you tell me how poorly I am doing with [child].

(continued)

Table 1.   *(continued)*

Element	Definition	Example
Willingness to risk mistakes, be corrected	Professional acknowledges limits of assessment strategies and professional expertise in presenting assessment information and recommendations for intervention.	Professional says to parents, As you know, we use [test name] to assess [child's] cognitive functioning. Tests are never perfect, but they do suggest . . . [test results]. I realize now that the behavior management approach I recommended has not been successful. Do you have any suggestions?
Ability to weather strong emotions	Professional acknowledges strong feelings and does not let them interfere with parent–professional working alliance.	Professional says to parent, I can see you are very discouraged today. Would it be better to discuss IEP revisions later this week? I am having a hard time concentrating when there is so much disagreement about IEP goals. I'll do a better job if we all cool down a little, think about the problems we are having making decisions, and come back together in a few days.
Freedom from preconceived expectations of parents	Professional recognizes that individual parents want to participate in ways that are most meaningful to them, rather than be assigned a function.	Professional asks parent, How would you like to be involved in [child's] school experience? How much information do you want about [child's] activities in the classroom?
Consideration of parents' values and beliefs	Professional incorporates parents' values and beliefs into own view of child's situation.	Professional says to parent, You say that you are offended by the instruction in evolution. Perhaps we can adapt [child's] biology program. You prefer not to use the medications prescribed for [child]. We will have to see if we can manage [child's] outbursts with a more structured behavior program.

(continued)

Table 1.   *(continued)*

Element	Definition	Example
Value placed on parent involvement	Professional validates parent's positive influence on the child's life and progress.	Professional says to parent, I always welcome your input because it ensures that I work in sync with what is important to you. Can you show me how you get [child] to manage flatware at home?
Sensitivity to parents' emotional pain	Professional demonstrates empathy and support for parents' feelings related to the child's injury.	Professional says to parent, I can see that [child's] injury has created an enormous sadness for you. Perhaps we should discuss [child's] language needs some other time. It must be hard to hear that [child] is not making the hoped-for gains in motor skills. Do you want to talk about it more?
Flexibility	Professional adjusts own agenda and schedule to include parents.	Professional says to parent, I had hoped to meet with you after school, but if you work swing shift, let's aim for early morning. I wanted to talk about motor control, but if you are more concerned about [child's] problems with classmates, let's talk about that first.
Ability to accommodate parental agendas	Professional incorporates parents' concerns into planning for the child.	Professional says to parent, So you are worried that we have too little time devoted to social activities. Let's see how we can fix that. You prefer that most of [child's] academic work be scheduled in the morning when [child] has more energy. Let's look at the teaching resources available in the mornings.
Commitment to collaboration	Professional demonstrates interest in working with parents.	Professional says to parent, It is very important to me that we work together on [child's] educational program. Together we can work this out.

their child's injury. The onset and intensity of this reaction will vary across individual parents and in some cases will meet criteria for acute stress disorder (ASD) or posttraumatic stress disorder (PTSD) (American Psychiatric Association, 1994). Stress reactions are triggered by stimuli that remind a parent of the traumatic event, including thoughts, feelings, conversations, activities, places, and people. Features of traumatic stress reactions often include intense fear, helplessness, horror, hyperreactivity, and physiological and psychological distress as well as numbing and decreased awareness of events. In instances of severe stress reactions, parents may become impaired in social, occupational, or other important areas of functioning. Professionals can be most helpful to parents experiencing a stress reaction by first acknowledging the strength of the observed reaction and its origin and then helping the parent to focus on the here and now. In instances in which parents cannot be calmed, assistance from a familiar supportive person or mental health professional may be needed. Table 2 lists some of the features of traumatic stress reactions, provides examples of behavioral manifestations, and suggests a positive response to a parent manifesting traumatic stress.

Sensitivity to parents in emotional pain often requires stamina and considerable self-control in order to override one's own distress at seeing people in pain. Professional intention in these situations should be focused on providing empathy and support to the parent in distress. By extending the same kind of consideration and compassion anyone recovering from a significant injury would be offered, professionals can assist parents in participating in their child's educational planning activities at levels that do not exacerbate their pain.

Focusing on Solutions to Resolve Conflict, Competition, and Polarization in Relationships

When conflict, competition, or polarization occurs in parent–professional interactions, it is important to guide the focus of planning discussions beyond problem-focused agendas to solution-focused agendas. With a constructive mindset in place and a commitment to working collaboratively with parents, professionals can more easily achieve a solution-focused perspective that includes both professional and parental concerns. So often resolution of relationship dilemmas is as easy as going a few steps beyond the initial step of describing the relationship problem. A guide to solution-focused resolutions is listed in Table 3. These solution-focused steps provide a guide for overcoming competition, conflict, and polarization in parent–professional relationships.

Table 2.   Traumatic stress reactions: Features and helpful responses

Feature	Behavioral manifestation	Helpful response
Flashbacks—an intrusive and distressing memory of the traumatic event, usually in the form of a thought or image triggered by a variety of innocuous stimuli: color, sound, movement, touch, smell, sight of similar objects, places, children of same age or characteristics, discussions about the event, child's injury, or treatment needs.	Parent may have a startled look or sudden onset of agitated motor and/or emotional distress. Hypervigilence, memory loss, reduction in awareness of surroundings, dazed look, avoidance of school and professionals, and/or vivid recounting of traumatic event. Level of distress is not proportionate to the immediate situation.	Professional maintains calm and might say, I notice that suddenly you seem [describe the sudden change in demeanor]. Did something strike a nerve in you? If parent does not reorient to time and place, the professional might say, [Parent's name], we are here in [child's] classroom and we are having a conversation.
Nightmares—recurring dreams of the traumatic event, or dreams of similar events affecting them or other people in their lives.	Parent may mention that he or she is having nightmares about the event.	Professional acknowledges the stress and might say, It must be very difficult to get thoughts of the [event] out of your mind. It sounds like the memory of the accident is haunting you even in your sleep. It must be a relief to wake up.
Obsessive thoughts and/ or compulsive behaviors designed to compensate for or ward off the repeat of the traumatic event. Sometimes behaviors are not productive. In calmer moments, parents may be willing to acknowledge that their anxieties are unfounded.	Parent may call school several times a day to see if his or her child is okay or may seem overly insistent about a detail that seems trivial, such as how objects are placed in a backpack.	Professional acknowledges parent's concern for the child and might say, You seem to be worried that something may go wrong. Can we talk about your worries and find ways to ensure [child's] safety to allow you to be less anxious?
Survivor guilt	Parent says he or she wished he or she had incurred the injury rather than the child.	Professional validates the thought and might say, You are a caring parent who would rather be injured yourself than have your child struggle with this problem.

For solution-focused strategies to work, professionals need to have a clear and accurate understanding of parents' perspectives, values, and desires for educational outcomes. At the same time, of course, professionals must be able to describe clearly and accurately their own ideas of a student's potential and precisely what the educational environment can and cannot provide. This process works best when written records describing problems and solutions are kept and made available to the parents and professionals involved. Written records provide reminders as well as a common plan for all to follow. Indeed, it would be a good practice to record goals and objectives for parent–professional contacts on the IEP document.

Managing Parent–Professional Contacts

Regular and frequent contact between parents and professionals is an important priority for a team working collaboratively on behalf of a student with ABI. Parent–professional contacts work to keep the communication lines open and allow partners to address various task and relationship needs as they arise. Initial contact allows parents and professionals to become acquainted or reacquainted with one another and provides opportunity for exploring concerns and expectations. A welcoming communication in the form of a telephone call or note prior to a more task-oriented meeting sends a clear invitation for parent input and participation. Subsequent contacts allow parents and professionals to complete the necessary tasks related to educational planning and attend to maintaining parent–professional relationships. Ongoing scheduled contacts between parents and professionals are valuable for information exchange, progress updates,

Table 3.   Solution-focused resolution of relationship dilemmas

1. Identify and describe the problem as a relationship dilemma. Use nonjudgmental terms and include how the problem is experienced by both the parent and professional.
2. Identify the change desired including the perspectives of both parent and professional. Again, use specific, nonjudgmental descriptors so that what is desired is not vague or open to too much interpretation.
3. List at least six possible solutions to the dilemma. At least half of the solutions should contain elements that address both parent and professional concerns and are supportive of both parent and professional expressed needs.
4. Evaluate each of the possible solutions. Avoid global evaluative comments. Evaluate in terms of relevance to IEP goals for the student, availability of resources, feasibility, and so forth.
5. Select one of the possible solutions that has emerged from the evaluation discussion as the most likely to satisfy IEP goals, parental preferences, and resource capacity.
6. Implement the strategy. Both parties need to have some responsibility and monitoring roles. Specify assignment of tasks, timelines, and criteria that will allow the parties involved to see whether objectives of the selected solution were achieved and whether the result was what was expected.
7. Evaluate the success of the solution at a predetermined date. Determine if the desired changes were achieved and describe the contribution of specific elements of each participant's efforts. If further effort is needed, repeat the steps above including modifications that participants agree will enhance the likelihood of achieving desired changes.

and problem solving as well as for working to decrease any tensions that occur over the course of time. In times of low tension, regular and constructive communication works to further develop rapport and trust among participants. Unlike formal IEP meetings in which the main purpose is to finalize intervention decisions and commit resources, scheduled contacts can be more informal and allow parents and professionals the opportunity to discuss important information and problems *before* final decisions need to be made. At the same time, scheduled contacts promote the development of trust and rapport that allow parents and professionals to work through the often stressful experiences of solving problems and making decisions. Careful management of parent–professional contacts ensures adequate communication at times convenient to both parents and professional.

There are a number of practical strategies individual professionals can adopt to promote regular contact with parents and demonstrate commitment to parent–professional partnership development (see Table 4 for particular strategies).

Depending on circumstances and parents' preferences, professionals can arrange a *preferred mode* for contacts with parents. These may include scheduled telephone calls, a note exchange system using a notebook that travels between home and school on a regular basis in a student's book bag, or face-to-face contact at regular intervals for specific lengths of time. One person can be designated as the *partnership coordinator.* This person can be in charge of monitoring the contact schedule to prompt the agreed-upon contact activities and monitor the climate of the parent–professional relationship. The partnership coordinator can also act as a liaison when contact is difficult to enhance the exchange of information between home and school and promote rapport among all team members. Parents and professionals can funnel questions or input to the partnership coordinator for consideration by the professional team.

Table 4.   Strategies for regular parent–professional contact

1.	Determine the preferred mode of regular contact: notes, telephone calls, drop-in meetings at school, and so forth.
2.	Designate a partnership coordinator to prompt contacts, meetings, and conversations and serve as conduit for information from parents and professionals.
3.	Establish work and relationship agendas with items of concern to parents and professionals alike.
4.	Monitor time and control of agenda to facilitate parents' participation in problem-solving processes.
5.	Promote communication that encourages parent participation in providing relevant information and sharing responsibility for decisions.

When necessary, the coordinator can activate a problem-solving or decision-making process for the team.

Agenda-Oriented Communications   The tasks involved in setting and revising work and relationship agendas are critical to coordinated educational planning. Collaborative agendas include topics of importance to both parents and professionals and can be achieved through regular contacts with the partnership coordinator. Without a procedure for managing the evolving agenda of important topics, a struggle for control of the topic priorities may develop. Professionals should take care to monitor the time and control of conversations with parents to allow adequate time for their own as well as parents' concerns. Adequate time and control will encourage parents to ease their way into the intervention-focused school environment. Communication that encourages parents' participation in agenda activities must devote a significant portion of the time allocated for the contact to hear parents' ideas and concerns, explore and attend to parent-initiated topics, and attend to parents' suggestions for solutions. This attention is important to the development of rapport and partnership with parents.

Initial agenda-oriented communications with parents can be expected to involve a greater proportion of exploration and topic identification, but adequate time for agenda-oriented communication is also important in later contacts because parents' and professionals' perceptions, concerns, and feelings about their relationship often vary over time. A professional can encourage parents to present their concerns or interests by regularly inquiring with questions such as "Are there topics that you wish we would talk about more?" or "What do you think we should talk about today or next time we talk?" Parents will benefit from ongoing professional interest and attention to their continuing efforts to focus on their child's educational needs as they struggle to make sense of their own traumatic reactions and feelings of loss.

Practicing Partnership Skills

Once professionals have mastered a constructive mindset and can effectively implement solution-focused strategies in their approach to parent–professional interactions, they can focus on more frequent use of the basic communication skills (Walker, Irvin, Coyne, & Bronson, 1995; Walker & Singer, 1993) and interpersonal skills (Bolton, 1979) that are essential to building and maintaining constructive relationships. Table 5 presents some key skills that facilitate effective parent–professional partnerships. Discussion and examples of how to implement each of these skills follow.

Table 5. Key partnership skills for parent–professional interactions

Exchange of descriptive information about home and school environment

Clarification of roles and perspectives

Use of basic communication skills

   Choosing language that works for parents

   Timing/pacing: Sensitivity to flow of conversation and parents' receptivity to professional information/recommendations

   Perception checking

   Perspective taking

   Listening: Eye contact and body language, reflecting, paraphrasing, summarizing, sensitive inquiry

   Appropriate empathy

   Validating parents' perspectives: Statements to let parents know that what they are saying is understandable and legitimate

   Reinforcing positives

   Constructive input: Referenced, concrete observations, suggestions, and opinions; choice of pronouns, adjectives, and verbs

Exchange of Descriptive Information About School and Home Environments   Information about the two or three environments in which the student spends most of his or her time is extremely helpful to both professionals and parents in the coordination of learning activities across all settings and is a relatively simple way to initiate give and take in a parent–professional relationship. This information can be sensitive when parents are worried about the purpose of professional inquiry, and it is wise to begin with an orienting comment such as "I'm interested in knowing as much as I can about Tommy's life outside of school so that I can make the things I'm thinking of doing for him worthwhile. I'd also like to give you as much information as you need about what his days in school are like. I believe that having accurate information about all of the places and people in his world will help you and me be more helpful to him." A professional can then offer the parents a choice of ways to provide information they believe to be relevant. For example, a teacher might say, "We can start by listing for each other things we would like to know, or I can answer your questions about school." If parents seem hesitant or unclear about what kind of information might be exchanged, a teacher could say, "I've made it a practice to give parents some facts about a typical day at school for their child. We could start with that." By going first the teacher may give examples of types of information that are useful and therefore may guide the parents' contribution. Of course, if a parent seems eager to describe the student's home life, it would be considerate to invite or support the parent's desire to start the exchange of information. If parents seem confused about the process of exchanging information, a teacher can encourage them by using open-ended questions that seek information such as "What are the things you would like most for me to know about your child? What are the similarities or differences you see between what your child is doing in school and out of school? What do you think I need to know about your child's life to be most useful to him or her?" Over time, parents will respond positively to professional efforts to exchange information if they see that professionals are actually attending to that information and making good use of it in their work with the child. As the working relationship grows, professionals and parents can ask one another to exchange observational information about key behaviors targeted in the student's intervention program. It is important that professionals provide information from the school environment that is of interest to parents in order to demonstrate active reinforcement of parents' status as team members with regard to measuring the student's progress in key areas of functioning. The exchange of information between home and school should occur on a regular basis and through a method established mutually by the professional and parent.

Clarifying Roles and Perspectives

By presenting their roles and perspectives to parents, professionals can convey an intent to work as partners. By choosing language that clearly describes a desire to work together with parents, professionals can set the stage for collaboration. Statements referring to professional expertise, opinions, and ideas can be clearly self-referenced to indicate that professional perspectives are offered as something to be considered on an equal basis with parents' expertise, opinions, and ideas. Collaborative, rather than directive, terminology further establishes a willingness and desire for partnership versus control. Specific examples of how the professional hopes to be beneficial to the team, rather than general statements about what will happen on the team, assist parents in understanding how the professional plans on helping the student. Table 6 offers contrasting examples of a collaborative versus directive presentation of professional expertise and help.

When professionals effectively take a collaborative rather than a directive role, present themselves as helpers with specific knowledge and expertise, and offer specific kinds of intervention, parents are more likely to see professionals as partners and collaborators instead of competitors or adversaries in planning a student's educational program.

Table 6. An example of collaborative versus directive professional role descriptions

Collaborative	Directive
I'm the occupational therapist who will be working with your son and you and the rest of the professional team [indicates collaborative intention] to come up with a meaningful physical rehabilitation program to put into practice in the classroom setting. If you would like, I can give you an idea of what occupational therapists typically look at in suggesting rehabilitation goals for students with brain injury [offers helpful information and collaboration] [pause for indication from parent about wanting more information and to address parents' requests]. I happen to have a particular interest [self-referenced perspective] in fine motor skills. By fine motor skills, I mean hand coordination. I believe [self-referenced opinion] that these skills help students perform activities like writing and handling flatware; that is, activities that are relevant to schoolwork and adaptive skills [specifics]. So you can expect me to suggest [indicates helpful intent, clarifying own bias without imposing it] exercises in that area. I'm also interested in finding out what is most important to you and Tommy [labeling personal bias as well as indicating collaborative intention].	I'm the occupational therapist who will be in charge [assumes directive role] of Tommy's rehabilitation program in the classroom and I'll make sure he gets what he needs [taking charge, vague]. I'm really big on stressing fine motor skills. They really are more important than other skills [imposes a generalized opinion]. So, I'll be sure [assumes directive role] there's a special emphasis on that in his program.

   Clear descriptions of professional roles help ensure that parents do not develop unrealistic expectations of professionals. When parental expectations of professional expertise seem unrealistic, clear reminders of the limits of professional abilities can further prevent misunderstandings about what professionals can accomplish. When a professional is unable to meet parental expectations, the professional should tell the parents and make it clear that although the parents' appeals are not unwarranted, he or she is simply unable to meet them. An explanation of the limitations of a professional's knowledge can be followed by a reminder of what the professional *can* offer that is most closely connected to what the parents want. In some cases this may mean that another professional or service resource may need to become involved. When professionals strive to clarify their roles and perspectives in concrete, self-referenced, and short-term language, they assist parents in understanding their ideas and at the same time make better use of the expertise they have to offer. Furthermore, clarity about professional training, experience, expertise, and biases helps reduce misconceptions about what professionals can and cannot provide. Table 7 contrasts a constructive versus a nonconstructive strategy for describing the limits of professional expertise.

Using Basic Communication Skills

Constructive communication skills are the tools necessary to convey professional intention to be collaborative. With effective communication tools, professionals are more likely to see the rewards in their efforts to engage parents in partnerships.

Choosing Language that Works for Parents   If professionals listen carefully as parents talk to them, they will discover the vocabulary and level of simplicity or communication patterns the parent typically uses. The professional should try as much as possible to match the parents' communication preferences in the language chosen to communicate to individual parents. For example, if a parent

Table 7.   An example of constructive versus nonconstructive descriptions of professional expertise

Constructive	Nonconstructive
I know you're hoping Tommy will someday regain his ability to complete essay tests at the same levels he did before his injury, Mrs. Brown, and I sense that you hope I can help make that happen. I'll be ecstatic if he does and if I can contribute to that happening [validates mother's wish for professional help]. At the same time, I have to be honest with you about my inability [clarifies limits of her ability] to guarantee or even give you the idea that this is possible. Based on the observations I've made of his current ability to answer essay questions, I've seen some gains in the past 2 months, but those have leveled off [offers concrete information based on recent observations of student's functioning]. That suggests to me that Tommy will not advance much further, at least not immediately, in expressive writing [self-referenced opinion linked to observations rather than long-term predictions]. However, I want to say that our knowledge about long-term recovery of preinjury abilities is far from perfect [acknowledges limits of professional knowledge] and we will keep working on this area as long as it's important to you and Tommy [validates parent's wish and indicates willingness to be helpful].	I know you want Tommy to be able to regain his ability to complete essay tests at the same levels he did before his injury, Mrs. Brown, but that's really not realistic [global opinion that is critical of parent's wishes]. You're expecting things that are just not going to happen [an unnecessarily negative global prognosis that exceeds available scientific knowledge about recovery from brain injury]. Nobody can accomplish what you're asking [unnecessary dismissal of parent's hopes].

uses a particular descriptor or a particular metaphor with reference to his or her child, a teacher can demonstrate desire to arrive at a common understanding by picking up on the language that is most congruent with the parent's manner of expressing him- or herself. For example, if a parent says "I know she gives everyone a lot of lip, but she's just trying to get a laugh from the other kids," a teacher might use those terms in later communication with the parent about this student. For example, "I'm seeing quite a bit less of that lip you mentioned this week and more willingness to let the other kids get the laughs." In another example, a parent might say "It's a regular zoo at our house," and the teacher might ask at a later time, "Are you still feeling like it's a zoo at home? I can understand that feeling. Some days it seems that way at school, too," as a way of accepting the parent's description of situations with children that are difficult to manage. Of course, care must be taken to mirror parents' language in a way that is friendly, not derogatory or critical. Indeed, care should be taken also to attend to tone of voice, body, and facial expressions to capture more sensitive feelings behind the words. A joke about one's child or household may be a cover for frustration, self-consciousness, or other vulnerable feelings. It is generally a good rule of thumb to accept at face value or adopt a demeanor of gentle curiosity about terms used by parents rather than to reframe them into our own preferred terms.

In addition, professionals should take care to avoid overusing technical terms and acronyms in their own language when talking with parents. If technical terms are essential to understanding the student's situation or are likely to be used frequently by professionals working with the student, then professionals should define those technical terms and if possible provide a written glossary of key terms for parents' use. Professionals should refrain from using terms such as "an ABI kid," and say instead "a child/student with acquired brain injury." In general, professionals can decrease misunderstandings and the impression that they are excluding parents from discussions by avoiding the use of acronyms.

In presenting technical information, professionals should be careful to reference information in ways that help parents identify the source of the information and understand how specific kinds of information shape a particular professional's perspective relative to an individual student's strengths and needs. In addition, professionals should avoid overly technical terms and language that imply infallibility of assessments based on technical methodologies. Such information can be more constructively presented if referenced in terms of its properties and usefulness to professionals in estimating the student's strengths and needs. Test scores can be presented as useful pieces of information that guide professionals' thinking in planning appropriate interventions rather than as an infallible truth about the student's abilities and limitations. Professionals, in presenting their perspectives, opinions, and ideas about appropriate intervention, can present themselves as approachable, receptive partners by labeling their input as useful information to combine with information parents may wish to contribute. Liberal use of self-referencing pronouns and adjectives helps to remind parents of the professionals' intent to offer help rather than to control decisions about intervention. For example, statements such as "I rely heavily on information from behavioral observations because it helps me look at . . . " or "I've found this particular test information helpful in understanding . . . " clearly indicate a professional preference for the information offered. At the same time, however, it is important to indicate an interest in and intent to use the information parents have found to be important and useful in understanding their child's strengths and needs with questions such as, "What have you observed that helps you understand Johnny's strengths and needs?" or "What indicators do you rely on to measure Johnny's recovery from this injury?" These types of questions invite parents to be equal partners in determining the focus of intervention planning.

By using self-referencing pronouns and adjectives, the professional should take particular care to avoid an "us versus them" orientation during presentations and during negotiations of educational plans. Professionals can use generous amounts of the pronouns "we" and "us," especially at the problem-solving, priority-setting, and decision-making steps of intervention planning, to convey partnership intentions. Statements such as "Let's see if we can resolve the issues related to . . . " or "We need to set some priorities and make some decisions that include all the important information we have gathered . . . " help to stress collaborative intention.

The choice of verbs and action modifiers is also critical in conveying intentions to collaborate with parents. Professionals can develop a repertoire of "can do" verbs and modifiers so that their messages to parents convey commitment to getting things done *with* parents rather than unilaterally. Statements such as "Together we can . . . ," "Let's work on a plan to . . . ," "How can we resolve . . . ?" and "Let's look at . . . " provide a collaborative tone to any parent–professional conversation.

Timing/Pacing   Mastery of timing and pacing in parent–professional conversations allows professionals to maximize the relationship-building and collaboration effects of their efforts to communicate constructively. Timing refers to decisions about when to listen to parents speak and when to speak to advocate professional ideas and issues. When professionals are trying to achieve a sense of rapport and partnership with parents, it is important for them to attend to what makes parents comfortable as they try to provide input. For example, when a parent who is obviously intense or emotional asks to speak to a professional, a professional can facilitate comfort and reassurance by finding time and a comfortable setting to encourage parents to speak openly. When a parent is expressing self-initiated concerns, it would be a poor time for the professional to interject his or her professional views or reactions. Instead, by providing ample time for the parent to finish, a professional can indicate respect and support and increase the chance that the parent will perceive the professional as interested and collaborative and, consequently, will be more receptive to what the professional has to say. By listening openly to a parent, the professional may actually enhance parental receptivity. Parental receptivity is especially important when professionals want to impart information that will be contrary to parental hopes and perceptions. In such cases, professionals can facilitate parental receptivity by inviting the parent to talk and allowing the parent to determine a preferred time and place. During the presentation, the professional should make every effort to provide privacy and to allow parents to indicate willingness to hear the difficult information, rather than simply take undue control of the interaction. In planning for these conversations, professionals' willingness to listen and their sensitivity to parents' reactions and questions assures parents that their thoughts and feelings are in fact important.

Pacing refers to the sequencing and rate of presenting information or other input. Parents vary in their reactivity to professional input. To ensure that important information and professional recommendations are heard, understood, and digested, professionals can check with parents about the order of receiving information and the rate at which to provide different kinds of input. In the cases of both timing and pacing, professionals are most successful when they are careful to take cues from parents' reactions to presentations of professional input and respond accordingly in ways that indicate respect and concern for parents' comfort and need to express their reactions.

Strategies such as timing and pacing are important in setting the stage for constructive conversations between parents and professionals. The basic communication behaviors used in conversations set and maintain the tone of these interactions and are the cornerstones for constructive parent–professional relationships.

Perception Checking   Perception checking is useful in achieving accurate understanding of a parent's point of view over time and across topics. Perception checking consists of frequent check-ins with parents using clarifying questions and reflecting statements to learn what they think and feel. The use of perception checking also helps maintain rapport by conveying to parents a sustained professional interest in what parents are thinking and feeling and decreases the likelihood of developing misperceptions and false assumptions from unclear messages. Useful perception checking might include questions such as, "Are you still happy with John's progress in language development?" "Do you think we are talking often enough?" or "Is our note exchange procedure working well for you?"

Perspective Taking   Perspective taking involves the professional imagining what it is like to be in a particular parent's shoes, to actually try to adopt the thoughts and feelings a parent expresses and be able to speak from that perspective. Perspective taking is a valuable skill in conveying empathy for points of view that are difficult for professionals to understand. If effective, the act of taking a parent's perspective enables a professional to speak accurately and compassionately on behalf of the parent in a manner that the parent would endorse. Examples of perspective-taking statements include, "This technical information must be confusing for you at times," "It must be difficult to hear Tommy talk about missing out on sports," or "You seem relieved that Kathy has made some progress with her motor skills." (Statements such as the last one can be made even if the professional speaking does not share the parent's belief.)

Listening   Effective listening is perhaps the most important communication skill for building rapport in parent–professional relationships. Listening is much more than being quiet while parents express themselves. Active listening includes a constellation of attending behaviors that enables professionals to suspend their own perspective in order to focus attentively on what a parent is communicating, including thoughts and feelings as well as descriptions of events and behaviors. Professionals who master listening skills are more able to develop accurate understanding and empathy for what parents are expressing, even when the professional does not like or agree with what is being expressed. Active listening includes nonthreatening demeanor and specific active listening behaviors (e.g., reflecting, paraphrasing, clarifying questions, summarizing statements). These behaviors work to develop rapport between parents and professionals and to ensure accurate understanding of what parents are saying. The outcome of effective listening is hearing from parents that they believe professionals are accurately understanding, properly acknowledging, and truly paying attention to their ideas and concerns. Effective listening enables professionals to pay full attention to what parents believe is important and indicate their intent to work effectively with the parents on behalf of students' needs.

Eye Contact and Body Language   Appropriate eye contact and body language are critical to setting the stage for comfortable parent–professional interactions. Making eye contact with parents allows professionals to demonstrate attentiveness and to observe nonverbal communication. It is important to remember that care should be taken to respond to "comfort" cues from parents when determining how much eye contact is desired. Some parents desire constant eye contact whereas others are uncomfortable with too much eye contact. Cultural differences play a role in the amount of eye contact that is comfortable, and attentive observers take care to be sensitive to individual parents' reactions to eye contact and make appropriate adjustments to enhance interaction comfort.

Body language includes posture, gestures, position of legs and arms, and facial expressions. As a general rule, body posture, movements, and facial expressions that convey openness and neutrality reflect an inviting, friendly, nonjudgmental demeanor and facilitate open communication and the development of rapport in parent–professional relationships. For example, arms that rest comfortably on a tabletop or in a professional's lap convey openness, whereas arms that are crossed or held tightly across a professional's chest communicate tension and guardedness. Likewise, having feet resting comfortably on the floor communicates openness, whereas having legs crossed or turned to one side communicates a more defensive posture. Rhythmic movements of legs or hands suggest tension and sometimes irritation. Nodding one's head indicates understanding and encouragement; whereas shaking the head, frowning, pursing the lips, and pulling back abruptly indicate disagreement or displeasure. Generally leaning forward indicates a friendly willingness to engage (so long as the professional does not invade the parents' personal comfort zone), whereas sitting back suggests withdrawal and distancing. Body and eye movements directed away from the parent or the mutual object of interest (e.g., an IEP document) communicate preoccupation with other things and may be interpreted as disinterest. Body and facial movements that are congruent with stated collaborative intentions enhance the effectiveness of collaborative efforts. Conversely, body and facial expressions that are incongruent can sabotage stated collaborative intentions as parents may attend more to nonverbal than verbal communication when there is a discrepancy.

Reflecting   Reflecting works to promote accurate understanding by using brief "mirroring" statements. Reflecting statements stay very close to the actual words and expressions used by parents and allow parents to know that a professional is attending to what the parent is communicating. For example, if a parent says, "I'm worried that Jane's friends are losing patience with her because she is slow to express herself verbally," a reflecting statement such as "You're worried that because Jane has trouble with verbal communication that her friends will lose patience with her" allows the parent to hear that the professional accurately received the intended message. Conversely, if the professional in this case said, "You're worried that Jane's speech is not progressing quickly enough," the parent could correct the professional's perception by saying, "I didn't say that. I'm really concerned about the impact her slowed speech has on her friendships." The professional could then reflect a more accurate understanding with a statement such as "Oh, you're more worried about the effect of Jane's speech problems on her relationships with her friends." Or, if a professional wants to understand the meaning of a parent's furrowed brow, a reflecting statement such as "I notice that your brow is furrowed" lets the parent know what the professional is noticing and provides an opportunity for the parent to explain that facial expression. If overused or used mechanically, reflecting statements can interrupt the normal flow of the parents' communication. Reflecting statements should avoid having a "parroting effect" and should be reserved to attend to key thoughts and feelings or messages that the professional wants to be sure he or she heard accurately. Reflecting not only reassures a parent that a professional is paying attention but also works to ensure that professionals arrive at an accurate understanding of what parents want to communicate. The more skillful a professional is in attending and providing reflecting statements the more quickly and surely he or she is to achieve accurate understanding of parents' intended message.

Paraphrasing   Paraphrasing involves a brief restatement of several messages in a more concise form using one's own words. Like reflecting, paraphrasing is intended to provide feedback and allow correction of misunderstanding. Regular use of paraphrasing demonstrates to a parent that the professional is interested in understanding the key points made by the parent in a series of messages. In addition, it allows a parent to hear what a professional has gathered from the communication. For example, a parent might say, "I think it's time we had a conference. There are a lot of things on my mind and I have a lot of concerns and questions about what's happening here at school. I just get the feeling that Bobby isn't getting what he needs, and I wonder if people really understand his problem." The professional then might say a paraphrasing statement such as "You have a number of things you'd like to discuss with me about what's happening for Bobby here at school" to concisely restate the parent's several statements. If the parent believes that the professional has missed a key point, the parent can then make any necessary corrections to ensure greater accuracy in the professional's understanding.

Summarizing   Summarizing is used to review the key points that all participants in a conversation have made before moving on to new topics or closing a conversation. Summarizing is useful to review key points of long interchanges between parents and professionals and at points in a discussion at which time it is appropriate to move on to another speaker or topic. At the conclusion of any parent–professional conversation, a simple summarizing statement can ensure that parties leave the interaction with a shared understanding of what has been discussed and/or decided. No matter how difficult the conversation has been, a statement that summarizes both professional and parental perspectives, the purpose of the conversation, and the commitment to collaboration can work constructively to maintain a working alliance between parents and professionals.

Asking Questions   Questions are also an important element of active listening but require more sensitivity in their use than paraphrasing, reflecting, and summarizing statements. Professionals have to be especially careful to avoid questioning parents in a manner that is construed as judgmental, demanding, or invasive. In general, a neutral tone of voice that clearly communicates a respectful interest and desire to benefit from parents' information is essential. Invitations to talk can be initiated by questions such as "What would you like me to know about [topic]?" or "Is there anything you want to be sure we talk about today?" Open-ended questions that begin with "Who," "What," "When," "How," and "Where" are generally less intrusive than pointed questions beginning with "Why" or a barrage of questions that require only one-word answers. In any case, a respectful facial expression and tone of voice are essential in conveying sensitivity and genuine interest when using questions in interactions with parents.

Appropriate Empathy   Conveying appropriate empathy in interactions with parents consists of expressing awareness of what the parent is feeling or trying to communicate in a specific situation. In showing empathy, professionals can acknowledge their perception of strong feelings such as happiness, relief, and gratitude as well as sadness, anger, frustration, and discouragement. Expressions of empathy should reflect closely what professionals are observing in the parent's behavior or spoken expressions. Care should be taken to gently acknowledge difficult thoughts and feelings and to avoid overspeculation about thoughts and feelings that are not readily evident. Likewise, care should be taken to avoid expressing pity or judgment regarding a parent's thoughts and feelings or giving unsolicited advice or suggestions when a parent is obviously caught up in strong opinions or feelings.

Validating Parents' Perspectives   Validation of parents' perspectives often occurs naturally with the expression of accurate and appropriate empathy. Validation tells parents they are believed and that their thoughts and feelings are legitimate and understandable, even when a professional does not agree with, endorse, or like hearing those thoughts and feelings. Validating a parent's perspective does not mean a professional will agree or cooperate with opinions and actions presented. It only means that a professional is indicating respect for the parent's right to hold opinions and express desires for certain outcomes based on his or her individual parental point of view.

Reinforcing Positives   In a solution-focused orientation, selective reflection, paraphrasing, and questions can be validating and, at the same time, reinforce positive coping or movement toward solutions. For example, in describing their situation at home, parents typically give examples of the student's progress or lack of progress and positive or negative emotional adjustment and engage in some kind of self-referenced commentary on how well they are coping with the situation. If professionals listen carefully, they can hear references or see signs of positive coping. For example, a parent's comment such as "We're managing somehow" or a smile on the parent's face both show signs of positive coping. These "nuggets" (Meichenbaum, 1995) can be mentioned later in an explicitly reinforcing way in a professional's active listening response. Timing of reinforcing statements is critical and should occur only after parents have been given adequate time to finish "their story." Otherwise, an interjection, even if meant to be reinforcing, may be perceived as a professional's unwillingness to hear the parents' perspectives. A well-timed professional response such as "I heard you say that you are managing somehow . . . ," "I noticed that you smiled . . . ," or "In spite of all you have had to contend with, where do you find the strength to do this?" lets the parents know that the professional sees something admirable in their ability to manage a difficult situation. A professional's attention to messages that indicate positive coping can be validating and help parents talk about, and thus focus more on, their strengths.

Another validating and reinforcing listening response involves a subtle reframing of a parent's self-defeating or self-blaming statements. For example, if a parent asks "I'm just a nuisance, aren't I?"

I will remember that collaboration means sharing control with parents in educational planning.

I will acknowledge the value of parents as primary decision makers in determining quality of life and intervention decisions on behalf of their child.

I will strive to establish and maintain rapport and trust in relationships with parents in order to negotiate family-centered decisions.

I will find a minimum of three positive influences each parent has on a student's quality of life.

I will work to use an assessment approach to a student's problems and needs that includes parent perspectives and values.

I will strive for educational programs that include equal proportions of parent and professional goals.

I will ensure that educational interventions will proceed only when parents have indicated understanding and endorsement of goals, even if endorsement is only provisional (with the exception of cases in which parental neglect or abuse necessitates the involvement of child-protective agents).

I will maintain regular contact with parents and work to devote half of our communication time to their concerns and input.

I will express interest in parental input on a regular basis.

I will learn and use constructive communication in my interactions with parents.

I will listen to parents and validate their perspectives.

I will strive to offer parents assistance that is meaningful to them.

I will present my professional perspective assertively (not aggressively or submissively) and accept the possibility that parents may not endorse the technical help I am able to offer.

I will remember that to experiment and err in interpersonal interactions is human and indicative of a willingness to engage in relationships.

I will work to resolve disagreements and interpersonal tension with parents.

I will learn and adopt solution-oriented strategies to resolve interpersonal problems between myself and parents.

I will learn to investigate the legitimate concerns behind aggressive, hostile, submissive, and emotional behaviors in parents.

I will work to mend rifts in parent–professional relationships in the belief that the process of mending can strengthen a relationship.

I will strive to develop respect for and become trustworthy to individual parents.

I will reward myself for efforts I make to improve my effectiveness in forming collaborative relationships with parents.

Figure 1.   An example of a professional creed for effective parent–professional partnerships.

a response such as "A nuisance? I see you more as a parent who cares and takes the time to let me know what bothers her" can be very supportive.

Constructive Input   To communicate effectively with parents, professionals need to present information and recommendations in a parent-friendly manner. As discussed previously, parents may become defensive when they perceive themselves as being discounted, lectured to, or overdirected by professionals. When parents are busy fending off unwanted messages, they pay minimal attention to the information professionals want them to hear. Constructive professional input is, therefore, a critical element in ensuring that professional points of view and recommendations are incorporated into education programs in ways that enable parents to endorse them.

Monitoring Partnership Skills

Professionals can develop or use an existing set of criteria to help them monitor and evaluate their use of partnership skills in their interactions with parents. Consistent self-appraisal using skill mastery criteria will enhance the likelihood that these skills will become an integrated part of a professional's relationship behavior with parents.

Sometimes professionals can find a "buddy" within their work environment who can help them establish and monitor evaluation criteria to measure their effectiveness in parent–professional partnerships. Supportive colleagues are essential to objective self-appraisal, especially during stressful parent–professional interactions. A supportive colleague can provide a constructive description of the problems as well as the positive areas in the partnership. Such a colleague can be useful in the effort to redirect one's thinking to constructive solutions for impasses in parent–professional relationships. Colleagues who simply reinforce negative appraisals of a parent are only adding to the negativity that undermines the likelihood of resolution and renewed effort to develop a collaborative relationship with the parent in question.

In some cases, the services of a communication expert or counselor can be essential in the identification of the features of a professional's interpersonal difficulties with a parent or particular interaction. Working with a counselor can lead to selection of key strategies to resolve attitudinal barriers and acquire the skills necessary to achieve more constructive parent–professional relationships.

CONCLUSION

The strategies for overcoming the dilemmas in parent–professional relationships and for facilitating the development of effective parent–professional partnerships involve skills that can be learned. To promote greater sensitivity and openness and to broaden their repertoire of collaborative behaviors in their interaction with parents, professionals can begin by including in their list of standards for professional excellence the principles and practices necessary to engineer constructive parent–professional partnerships. The professional creed in Figure 1 (on p. 318) is suggested as a list of reminders to guide this development of a collaborative approach to parent–professional partnerships.

This chapter has discussed the dilemmas facing professionals who hope to achieve collaborative relationships with a range of parents as well as offered some basic strategies and skills for including relationship-enhancing approaches to their interactions with parents. Professional commitment to increasing the effectiveness of parent–professional partnerships in planning meaningful educational programs for students with ABI begins with the observance of principles such as those listed previously. Mastery of the kinds of people skills and communication skills described in this chapter will facilitate the translation of these principles into behaviors that enhance professionals' ability to become agents for collaborative relationships and effective partnerships with parents as they work together to make a positive difference for students with ABI.

REFERENCES

American Psychiatric Association. (1994). *Diagnostic and statistical manual of mental disorders* (4th ed.). Washington, DC: Author.

Bolton, R. (1979). *People skills: How to assert yourself, listen to others, and resolve conflicts.* New York: Simon & Schuster.

Darling, R.B. (1983). Parent–professional interaction: The roots of misunderstanding. In M. Seligman (Ed.), *The family with a handicapped child: Understanding and treatment.* Orlando, FL: Grune & Stratton.

Meichenbaum, D. (1995, December). *Treating patients with post-traumatic stress disorder: A cognitive-behavioral approach.* Workshop presented by the Institute for Behavioral Healthcare, Vancouver, WA.

Powers, L.E. (1993). Disability and grief: From tragedy to challenge. In G.H.S. Singer & L.E. Powers (Eds.), *Families, disability, and empowerment: Active coping skills and strategies for family interventions* (pp. 119–149). Baltimore: Paul H. Brookes Publishing Co.

Turnbull, H.R., & Turnbull, A.P. (Eds.). (1985). *Parents speak out: Then and now.* Columbus, OH: Charles E. Merrill.

Walker, B.R., Coyne, P.A., & Irvin, L.K. (1993). *Family-focused collaboration in early intervention: Progress, problems, and dilemmas.* (Monograph of the 1993 Oregon Conference). Eugene: University of Oregon.

Walker, B.R., & Erickson, A.M. (1991). *Family focus in school/home collaboration.* (Monograph of the 1991 Oregon Conference). Eugene: University of Oregon.

Walker, B.R., Irvin, L.K., Coyne, P.A., & Bronson, M. (1995). *Family-centered collaboration: Training program toolkit.* Eugene, OR: Teaching Research.

Walker, B.R., & Singer, G.H.S. (1993). Improving collaborative communication between professionals and parents. In G.H.S. Singer & L.E. Powers (Eds.), *Families, disability, and empowerment: Active coping skills and strategies for family interventions* (pp. 285–316). Baltimore: Paul H. Brookes Publishing Co.

chapter twelve

Preparing Educators to Serve Children with ABI

Janet S. Tyler

STUDENTS WITH ACQUIRED brain injury (ABI) pose a unique challenge to educators. As a result of their injuries, these students demonstrate a variety of cognitive, behavior, and physical impairments that often require specialized educational programming. Unfortunately, even educators with special education backgrounds often have little or no knowledge about students with ABI. This lack of information is the result of a variety of factors. Teachers lack experience with students with ABI because only since the 1970s have advances in medical technology made it possible for many children with severe brain injuries to survive and return to school. Furthermore, information regarding ABI has not been routinely included in the curriculum of teacher preparation programs.

As a result of not having received training in ABI, educators may be unaware that children and youth with ABI are, in fact, in school. That is, the learning and behavior problems these students display may be mistaken for other disabilities. If these students are identified, educators are often ill prepared to meet their educational needs. Many school-related problems that students with ABI experience, however, can be addressed if education professionals are specifically prepared to work with them (Blosser & DePompei, 1991). As one educator wrote on an evaluation form after receiving training in ABI:

༚ ༝

I now realize that over the years I have served several students who had learning and behavior problems due to a brain injury. I feel badly that I didn't know that their problems were due to ABI. This explains why traditional programming methods often didn't work for these students. I now know I could have done so much more for these students.

༚ ༝

As the field of special education continues to move toward progressive inclusion, all teachers must be prepared to help accommodate students with special needs in general education classrooms. In addition, special education teachers need to be prepared for consulting and teaming functions as well as direct teaching functions (Reynolds, 1990). Because students with ABI often receive educational services in a variety of settings, *both* general education teachers and special education teachers need to be knowledgeable about ABI. Moreover, special education teachers need an in-depth understanding of all aspects of ABI to be prepared to provide consultation to general education teachers, related services personnel, and parents.

The following comment made by one special education teacher reflects the frustrations of many educators who lack training in ABI:

༚ ༝

When Nathan returned to school following a severe ABI, I was overwhelmed. Not only was I expected to provide direct service to this student, but also help his general education teachers, therapists, and parents understand his needs and help them program for him. I thought my educational training had prepared me to work with all students with special needs, but I never received any training to work with students who had brain injuries and I wasn't sure what to do.

༚ ༝

The purpose of this chapter is to suggest ways to provide preservice educators with a basis for developing and delivering training in ABI so that students with ABI will receive appropriate programming delivered by educators who are trained to meet their unique educational needs. Specifically, this chapter suggests ways to incorporate ABI training into preservice education programs at three levels: 1) an introductory training session that can be incorporated into existing special education classes to provide both general and special education teachers with an awareness of students with ABI, 2) a graduate-level course to train special education teachers in ABI, and 3) a field-based experience in ABI. This chapter ends with a look at the future directions of ABI training.

THE NEED FOR PRESERVICE TRAINING

It is generally agreed that specialized training is essential for meeting the needs of people with ABI (Becker, Harrell, & Keller, 1993). Unfortunately, very few general or special educators receive training specifically dealing with these students (Ylvisaker, Hartwick, & Stevens, 1991). Furthermore, other groups of professionals to whom educators may turn for advice on serving students with ABI, namely school psychologists and pediatricians, have not been trained about the long-term problems these children and youth encounter (Mira, Meck, & Tyler, 1988; Tyler, Mira, & Hollowell, 1989). Therefore, students with ABI are likely to be served by school personnel who lack knowledge about their educational needs. As one parent of a child with ABI stated,

The doctors told me my child had made a remarkable recovery and she was ready to return to school. I now realize they were talking about her physical recovery, not her overall recovery. When she returned to school she couldn't keep up with her classes and started acting out in school. Her teachers didn't seem to know what to do for her. When I talked with her teachers they told me they had never worked with a student with a brain injury. Aren't teachers supposed to be trained to teach all students?

Educators' Knowledge and Experience in the Area of ABI

Research has shown that educators lack basic information about ABI and report a lack of experience serving students with ABI. In a study conducted by Tyler (1995a), 853 educators enrolled in graduate-level special education courses from 1991 to 1995 completed a 12-item survey pertaining to basic information about ABI (e.g., incidence definition, causes, student characteristics). These educators were also asked to indicate if they had experience serving students with ABI. Results of this survey revealed that 57% of educators surveyed were unable to correctly answer 60% of the questions pertaining to basic information about ABI, and over one half of the educators reported having no experience serving students with ABI. In addition, Manier's 1991 survey of 120 special educators employed in public high schools revealed that 52% had never received information about ABI in their educational training and 56% reported never having served a student with ABI.

This reported lack of experience may be partly the result of the fact that many students with ABI have been inappropriately classified or have not been identified at all. As one school psychologist reported,

After receiving information on ABI, I went back to school and reviewed the records of a student who had many of the behavior and learning characteristics typical of a student with ABI. This student was having a great deal of difficulty in the general education classroom, but didn't qualify for the learning disabilities program and his IQ score was above the cutoff for receiving special services. I then went back and questioned the student's mother and discovered that this student had been hospitalized at age 3 for a severe brain injury. This student is now receiving services under the ABI classification and is making wonderful progress.

Of paramount importance is the fact that many educators have served, or are serving, students with ABI without a basic understanding of ABI. A general lack of knowledge about ABI, coupled with a lack of experience in serving students with ABI, causes many educators to question their ability to provide services for these students. This lack of confidence further decreases the educator's ability to provide appropriate learning experiences (Blosser & DePompei, 1994).

Review of Existing Preservice ABI Training

Few teacher-training programs address the needs of students with ABI and strategies for teaching these students (Janus, 1994). Information about ABI is generally not a part of the curriculum for educators. Indeed, the absence of teacher preparation programs in the area of ABI has been identified by state educational agencies as one of the major educational issues in the provision of services to such students (Janus, 1996).

The fact that ABI information is not incorporated in the curriculum of most teacher education programs is further evidenced by the scant information about ABI provided in most introductory special education texts. Although a 1988 survey of special education textbooks revealed that most did not cover the topic of ABI (R.C. Savage, personal communication, March 10, 1988, in Mira, Meck, &

Tyler, 1988), a review of special education textbooks published after 1990 (Tyler, 1995b) revealed that the majority do address the topic of ABI. Such coverage, however, is often limited to a brief overview of general information on ABI (usually not more than a paragraph), certainly not enough information for educators to gain an understanding of the unique needs of these students.

The combined absence of course content and written information suggests that if teacher-training programs are going to prepare professionals to adequately serve the needs of students with ABI, significant changes in academic content and experiences at the preservice level are required (Blosser & DePompei, 1991). In determining how to incorporate ABI training into existing preservice programs, it is helpful to examine how students with ABI are being served within the educational system.

PROVISION OF SERVICES TO STUDENTS WITH ABI

Because of the diverse nature of the cognitive, behavior, and physical impairments associated with ABI, these students are served in a variety of programs, including general education settings and programs for students with learning disabilities, emotional disturbances, physical impairments, and so forth. Furthermore, the unique needs of students with ABI may require services from a number of disciplines, such as occupational therapy, physical therapy, speech-language therapy, and psychology. Services begin with communication among school personnel and medical service providers at the time of injury and through the school reentry planning and continue with the need for individualized service (e.g., specialized assessment, programming, ongoing monitoring of the student) throughout the student's school years.

The Role of the General Education Teacher

Although a full range of placement options should be available, many students with ABI receive resource services (i.e., direct services from a special education teacher on a part-time basis) and are otherwise included in general education environments for the majority of their school day. Thus, with the movement in special education toward serving students in inclusive environments, general education teachers are increasingly required to provide direct services to a variety of students with special needs, including students with ABI.

The role of the general education teacher is one of not only providing direct instruction to students with ABI but also assisting the special education teacher in identifying such students, carrying out behavior management programs, collecting evidence that individual students are meeting individualized education program (IEP) objectives in the general education classroom, and monitoring student progress.

Research on effective teaching indicates that as schools try to meet the needs of more diverse populations of learners, the monitoring and decision-making skills of the teacher become more important (Hofmeister & Lubke, 1990). With respect to students with ABI, therefore, it is essential that general education teachers have an understanding of ABI. Furthermore, although not all students with ABI will require special education services, their unique learning profiles dictate that the general education teacher be prepared to address these unique needs (Bengali, 1992).

The following statement made by a teacher at an IEP meeting illustrates how general education teachers often believe that they are inadequately prepared to meet the needs of students with ABI:

I'd be happy to have this student in my class, but I don't know if I can give him what he needs. I don't have any training in working with students who have brain injuries and I have 30 other students in my class, so I don't see how I'll be able to give him much help. Shouldn't he be in a class for students with brain injuries?

The Role of the Special Education Teacher

With the emphasis on including children with disabilities in general education classrooms and the fact that many school districts are adopting inclusion models for service delivery, the role of the special education teacher has become one of serving not only as direct services provider but also as consultant and collaborator. Special education teachers need to be skilled in developing instructional strategies that meet the diverse needs of students with ABI as well as providing expert advice to general education teachers on how to meet the students' needs in inclusive environments. In addition, because students with ABI often require the support of a classroom aide or instructional assistant within general and special education settings, the role of the special educator also may include training and supervising such support personnel.

Furthermore, because of the multitude of professionals involved in the treatment of students with ABI, special educators must be able to collaboratively consult with a range of service providers, including medical personnel, related services therapists, faculty at postsecondary institutions, and people providing community resources (e.g., adult community service systems, independent living centers, vocational systems). According to Morsink, Thomas, and Correa (1991), collaboration among professionals serving students with disabilities will be a necessity in schools of the future. This is especially true for educators serving students with ABI.

The educational success of students with ABI served in general education settings is dependent on the availability of appropriately trained special educators who can provide consultation and support services to individuals who work directly with these students. The scarcity of trained personnel in this area does not bode well for these students' long-term success. It is imperative, therefore, that preservice teacher education programs incorporate ABI training into their curricula.

The following case study illustrates the complex role that the special education teacher must be prepared to assume when serving students with ABI:

> *Jason, a 14-year-old eighth-grade student experienced a severe ABI as a result of a car accident. He was comatose for 6 weeks and hospitalized for 3 months. When Jason returned to school on a part-time basis, he was still receiving outpatient services from a local rehabilitation center. It was determined by the school team that Jason would receive 1 hour of resource room services from the special education teacher, participate in two of his general education classes, and start receiving speech and occupational therapy services at school. In addition to providing direct services to Jason, the responsibilities of the special education teacher were as follows:*
>
> 1. *Assume the primary role in Jason successfully making the transition from hospital to school.*
> 2. *Interact with the rehabilitation center's personnel to determine Jason's current needs.*
> 3. *Coordinate the exchange of information among the therapists at the rehabilitation center and school.*
> 4. *Obtain diagnostic information from the hospital's neuropsychologist and school psychologist.*
> 5. *Provide Jason's general education teachers with information on Jason's current needs and help them to make necessary modifications.*
> 6. *Consult with the school social worker to obtain counseling to help Jason cope with the loss of his brother in the accident.*
> 7. *Collaborate with the district's transition specialist in developing a transition plan for Jason.*

8. *Consult with the district's technology team to determine if any assistive technology could be used to help Jason compensate for poor fine motor control.*

9. *Consult with the school nurse regarding Jason's seizures.*

10. *Communicate regularly with Jason's parents regarding Jason's school progress and receive information from parents regarding his medical needs.*

INCORPORATING ABI TRAINING INTO PRESERVICE PROGRAMS

Preservice training in ABI can be incorporated into existing teacher-preparation programs at three levels. First, at the minimum level, ABI *awareness training* should be provided to all general and special education teachers as well as related services personnel. At the second level, special educators who will be providing direct services to students with ABI, as well as providing consultation to general education teachers serving students with ABI, should receive more *in-depth information* through a course(s) devoted to ABI. Finally, at the third level, individuals who have taken courses in ABI and desire hands-on experience with students with ABI should participate in a *field-based experience.*

Specific instruction in ABI is, of course, only part of a thorough certification program to train educators to provide services to students with a variety of needs. Thus, preservice training must focus on establishing an essential knowledge base in legal and ethical principles, curricula, and educational theories and systems, including direct instruction, effective instruction, behavioral principles, classroom management, partnerships with parents, communication and consultation, assessment, technology, and so forth (Reynolds, 1990).

Because training educators to serve students with ABI is a relatively new endeavor, there is a lack of research on the specific competencies educators need to serve students with ABI. The basis for the awareness-level training objectives, competencies for special education teachers, and field-based skills that are presented in this chapter originally emerged on an empirical basis from early recommendations made by professionals engaged in training educators to serve children with ABI (e.g., National Head Injury Foundation Task Force, 1985; Nordlund, 1989). The following awareness-training objectives and competencies are the result of field-testing training materials in numerous ABI awareness sessions and graduate-level ABI courses delivered by the author over a 5-year period from 1991 to 1996.

Awareness-Level Training
for All General Education and Special Education Teachers

The majority of teacher preparation programs require that trainees take at least one course on educating students with disabilities to meet certification standards. Courses are generally listed under headings such as "Psychology of Exceptional Children" or "Educating Students with Special Needs." In these introductory courses, trainees receive an overview of the variety of disabilities students may have. It is within these courses that information on ABI could easily be incorporated.

The intent of awareness training is to provide educators with an overview of ABI. Training should focus on increasing the educators' awareness of the existence of this population of students through an understanding of the definition of ABI, the causes and mechanisms of brain injury, and the medical treatment and rehabilitation course of students with ABI. Because the impairments that result from ABI are often subtle, a portion of the training should focus on increasing the educator's awareness of the long-term cognitive, physical, and psychosocial impairments these children and youth may exhibit. Furthermore, because general education teachers are often called on to aid in the student's hospital-to-school reentry process and to provide educational modifications, the training must also focus on acquainting educators with school reentry techniques and programming strategies.

This training ultimately provides educators with an awareness of the variety of medical, rehabilitative, therapeutic, and educational interventions that students with ABI require, thereby alerting them to the fact that they will need to seek expertise from a variety of professional and literature sources to adequately serve these students.

Awareness-Level Training Objectives   The following are the objectives of an awareness-level training session. As a result of participating in an introductory ABI training session, trainees will have an opportunity to gain skills in the following areas:

1. Becoming familiar with federal and state definitions of ABI
2. Developing an understanding of the incidence and causes of ABI among children and youth
3. Gaining an awareness of the mechanisms of brain injury
4. Becoming aware of the recovery pattern of students with ABI
5. Developing an understanding of the immediate and long-term effects of ABI
6. Gaining an awareness of the medical, rehabilitative, and therapeutic interventions students with ABI require

7. Becoming familiar with techniques used to aid in the school reentry of students with ABI
8. Becoming familiar with educational modifications and instructional strategies used for students with ABI

Outline of Awareness-Level Training Session   The outline presented in Table 1 serves as the basis for developing a training session on ABI that can be incorporated into existing introductory special education courses. The model provided here is based on the assumption that the instructor has sufficient knowledge in the area of ABI to provide such training. If instructors do not believe that they possess the specialized knowledge needed to provide information about ABI, they can obtain access to prepared training materials (e.g., a prepared script, overheads), such as those developed by Tyler (1992), that contain everything needed to deliver an introductory ABI

Table 1.   Outline of acquired brain injury awareness-level training session

I.   Introduction
A.   Overview of training
B.   Explanation of why students with ABI have unique needs
II.   Demographic information
A.   Definition
B.   Incidence
C.   Causes
III.   Mechanisms of brain injury
A.   How brain injury occurs
B.   Primary effects
C.   Secondary effects
IV.   Immediate effects of ABI
A.   Coma
B.   Motor problems
C.   Alteration of affect
D.   Memory disorders
E.   Posttraumatic amnesia
V.   Sequelae (Effects of ABI)
A.   Physical
B.   Cognitive
C.   Psychosocial
VI.   Model ABI school reentry
A.   Traditional versus ideal school reentry
B.   Obtaining student information prior to school reentry
C.   Securing special education services
D.   Preparing for school reentry
VII.   Program modifications
A.   Scheduling
B.   Instructional strategies
C.   Curriculum modifications
VIII.   Conclusion
A.   Importance of long-term monitoring of student progress
B.   Summary and review of information presented

Adapted from Tyler (1992).

awareness-level training session, or they can arrange for a guest lecturer who has expertise in the area of ABI to deliver the training to their students.

Developing an In-Depth Graduate-Level Course in ABI

In addition to receiving awareness training, students completing graduate-level degrees in special education or related services areas (e.g., occupational therapy, speech-language therapy, school psychology) need more in-depth information about ABI. Because these educators will be providing direct services to students with ABI and serving as consultants to other educators who may work with these students in their classrooms, it is essential that they gain a thorough understanding of ABI.

A more in-depth understanding of ABI can be acquired through coursework that specifically focuses on ABI. Although ideal preservice training in ABI would consist of a series of courses devoted exclusively to the study of ABI, this discussion takes into consideration that the vast majority of teacher preparation programs do not offer even a single course devoted to ABI. Therefore, in light of past history as well as the limited resources and staff most teacher-preparation programs have available, a more reasonable and realistic starting point would be to develop a foundation course that provides students with an in-depth overview of ABI.

The intent of such a course is to allow special educators to acquire the competencies needed to serve students with ABI effectively. Therefore, such training focuses on providing educators with information and skills they can use in planning for students with ABI and in consulting with other educators who serve these students. This training recognizes that the special educator will also be required to collaborate with nonschool systems, including medicine, rehabilitation, psychology, and social services. Therefore, a portion of the course focuses on making educators knowledgeable about the services and expertise each system can provide, how to gain access to such services, and how to coordinate services and expertise to best serve students with ABI.

Competencies   After completing the ABI course, educators will demonstrate the following competencies:

1. They will have a basic understanding of the mechanisms of normal brain functioning.
2. They will know federal and state definitions of ABI.
3. They will have an understanding of the mechanisms of brain injury.

4. They will know the immediate and long-term physical, cognitive, and behavior characteristics of students with ABI.
5. They will have an understanding of rehabilitation procedures and the professionals involved at varying stages of ABI recovery.
6. They will be able to select, administer, and interpret appropriate evaluation techniques for students with ABI.
7. They will be able to determine which reentry procedures best facilitate the student's return to school.
8. They will be able to design and carry out appropriate educational programming that addresses the unique educational needs of the student with ABI.
9. They will be able to understand the family issues involved with ABI.
10. They will be knowledgeable about other agencies that provide services for children with ABI.
11. They will know how to plan for the student's long-term needs (e.g., transition planning, vocational/career planning).

Course Content A graduate-level course designed to provide trainees with the knowledge to provide services appropriately for students with ABI must introduce a variety of topics. A description of each of these major topics is provided here accompanied by suggested activities.

- **Overview of Normal Brain Functioning** Provide trainees with a brief overview of neuroanatomy to ensure that they have a basic understanding of normal brain functioning. Depending on the curriculum of individual teacher-preparation programs, this information may or may not be addressed in other courses.
  Activities Have trainees diagram the brain, noting which areas of the brain are responsible for specific functions. Provide trainees with written information that overviews normal brain functioning (see Savage, 1994, for an excellent overview of the brain and brain injury designed for educators).
- **Definition of ABI** Give trainees an overview of the advent of traumatic brain injury (TBI) as a separate category within the Individuals with Disabilities Education Act (IDEA) of 1990, PL 101-476; explain the evolution of the federal definition of TBI; and discuss the definition's inclusion of open and closed brain injuries versus other brain injuries (see Assistance to States for the Education of Children with Disabilities, 1992; and Savage & Wolcott, 1994, for an explanation of the definition of ABI).

Activities   Have trainees compare their state definition of ABI with the federal definition. Have trainees examine state guidelines for qualification of students with ABI.

- **Demographics of ABI**   Provide trainees with information about the incidence and causes of ABI.

  Activities   Have trainees research the incidence of other disabling conditions (e.g., spinal cord injury, multiple sclerosis, cerebral palsy) and compare those incidences with that of ABI.

- **Mechanisms of Brain Injury**   Explain how the brain is injured during an open or closed head injury. Discuss the primary (e.g., axonal shearing, bruising) and the secondary (e.g., intracranial pressure, hemorrhaging) effects of the injury.

  Activities   Have trainees compile a glossary of medical terms and definitions relating to the physical sequelae of ABI.

- **Acute Care Phase of ABI**   Discuss the medical management of children and youth with ABI, beginning with medical interventions provided in the emergency room and intensive care unit and continuing with rehabilitation services and long-term follow-up.

  Activities   Have a rehabilitation physician provide an overview of the medical management of children and youth with ABI, including emergency procedures, medical interventions, and rehabilitation procedures. Trainees could also gain an understanding of the medical interventions that take place by viewing a videotape chronicling a student's progression from hospital admission to discharge.

- **Related Services**   Explain the related services children with ABI receive when they are hospitalized. This includes the various types of therapies needed (e.g., occupational therapy, physical therapy, speech-language therapy) at varying stages of recovery.

  Activities   Have an occupational therapist, physical therapist, and/or speech-language therapist give an overview of the therapies students receive at each stage of recovery and discuss the interdisciplinary focus of the rehabilitation team. Have therapists point out how school personnel can interface with hospital therapists to ensure appropriate transition of therapies into the school setting.

- **Long-Term Characteristics**   Discuss the long-term characteristics associated with ABI. Review the research on the physical, cognitive, and psychosocial effects of ABI.

  Activities   Have trainees view a videotape providing case study examples of students several years postinjury (e.g., Tyler & Williams, 1992; Wilkerson & Tyler, 1994).

- **Age Effects**   Discuss the effects of injury at varying stages of the child's development. Discuss the relationship of age to speed of recovery, patterns of impairments, and extent of impairments in all areas of functioning.

     Activities   For a comprehensive review of age effects, have trainees read Lehr (1990).
- **Assessment**   Discuss why traditional IQ versus achievement assessments are not appropriate for students with ABI. Emphasize the importance of neuropsychological assessment and comprehensive educational evaluations.

     Activities   Have a neuropsychologist explain neuropsychological assessment, how it differs from traditional assessment, and how school personnel can use such assessment information in planning an educational program for the student with ABI.
- **School Reentry and Planning**   Discuss the importance of planning so that the student can successfully make the transition from the hospital to the school setting. Suggest how school personnel can communicate with hospital personnel in planning for school reentry. Emphasize the importance of providing in-service training to school personnel.

     Activities   Provide trainees with a case study of a student hospitalized with ABI. Have trainees develop a comprehensive school reentry plan for the student.
- **Behavior Management**   Explain how varying ecological factors affect the student's behavior. Discuss behavior management techniques that have been proven effective for students with ABI.

     Activities   Present case study examples of children and youth with ABI exhibiting problem behaviors. Have trainees assess environmental and situational variables and design interventions.
- **Families of Students with ABI**   Discuss how a child's ABI affects the whole family, and review the research on families of students with ABI. Provide suggestions for how to work with families during the varying stages of the student's recovery and educational course. Emphasize the importance of monitoring the siblings of students with ABI.

     Activities   Arrange a panel of family members who have a child with ABI to discuss the effects of ABI on families. Ask family members to provide educators with suggestions for how to assist family members at each stage of the child's recovery.
- **Programming Strategies**   Provide suggestions for developing an educational program for students with ABI, including how to modify the student's schedule and develop instructional strategies that address the student's unique needs. Also, explain how

the curriculum can be modified and adapted to meet the student's needs in general education settings.

Activities   Present specific impairments of children and youth with ABI and have trainees brainstorm about educational modifications to address each deficit area.

- **Transition to Adult Life**   Discuss the importance of planning for the student to make the transition to the community. Review the community services available for adults with ABI, including postsecondary programs that provide assistance to students with ABI, vocational programs, and independent living arrangements.

  Activities   Have trainees develop a resource list of telephone numbers and addresses of local community agencies that provide services for adults with ABI.

- **Mild Brain Injury**   Discuss the definition of mild brain injury and review the research related to the effects of mild brain injury. Provide trainees with guidelines for monitoring students who have experienced mild brain injuries (see Doronzo, 1990, for an overview of mild brain injury).

  Activities   Provide case studies of children and youth who have experienced mild brain injuries. Have trainees develop a plan for providing other educators with information about the possible effects of mild ABI and have them devise a plan for monitoring the educational progress of such children and youth.

- **Prevention of ABI**   Discuss prevention of ABI. Review the research relating to effective measures and programs to prevent ABI.

  Activities   Have trainees research and review prevention programs for students at various age levels and have them obtain information on how to start a prevention program for their own school.

FIELD-BASED EXPERIENCE IN ABI

It is a long-held practice that educators participate in a field-based experience working with the students whom they will ultimately serve. In addition to the knowledge base gained through coursework, trainees should have the opportunity to further refine their skills during a field-based experience. Such hands-on experiences in providing services for students with ABI will provide trainees an opportunity to practice what they have learned through coursework and to refine their teaching skills while under the supervision of an experienced teacher.

According to Buck, Morsink, Griffin, Hines, and Lenk (1992), a well-designed field-based experience for all special educators should include participation in an interdisciplinary, collaborative project in which trainees work with related services staff personnel to develop an intervention for a particular student or a group of students. As a result of the multitude of related services that students with ABI require, such activities will be a critical component of a field-based experience with students with ABI.

Objectives of Field-Based Experiences

During the field-based experience, trainees will have an opportunity to gain skills in the following areas:

1. Identifying the range of information available about a student
2. Determining the evaluation needs of the student
3. Developing an IEP for the student
4. Identifying appropriate services for the student
5. Aiding school personnel in implementing the IEP to meet the student's needs
6. Developing a plan to monitor the effectiveness of the individual student's program

FUTURE DIRECTIONS

ABI awareness-level training for all educators and an ABI foundation course and field-based experiences for special educators represent merely a minimal level of incorporating ABI training into teacher education programs.

Need for More In-Depth Preservice Training Programs in ABI

A master's degree program in ABI would represent a maximum level of training. Master's degree programs that provide training specifically in ABI are indeed rare; in fact, only one university, The George Washington University in Washington, D.C., has a history of offering a master's degree in ABI. Through a federal grant, the Department of Teacher Preparation and Special Education at The George Washington University offers an interdisciplinary-focused neuro-developmental model of ABI training that prepares educators to address the complex needs of students with ABI across a developmental continuum from birth through age 21 (T. Krankowski, personal communication, July 20, 1995).

Intensive training programs such as the master's program mentioned previously produce specialists that are uniquely qualified to provide services to students with ABI. Unfortunately, with many teacher-preparation programs moving toward programs that address mild, moderate, or severe disabilities as a whole versus master's degree programs in areas such as learning disabilities or emotional disturbance, it is unlikely that other universities will develop similar training programs.

As awareness of ABI increases, however, and as schools struggle to meet the educational demands of students with ABI, the need for specialized teacher training may become more fully realized. At that point, educators in charge of teacher training programs may come to understand the importance of providing a more comprehensive program of study in ABI. Although such training may not be in the form of a master's degree program in ABI, it may be in the form of providing a series of courses devoted to ABI or the infusion of ABI information into programs designed to prepare educators to work with students with a variety of mild, moderate, or severe disabilities.

Need for ABI In-Service Training to Supplement Preservice Training

Considering that teachers throughout the United States have an average of 15 years of classroom experience (Darling-Hammond, 1990), they clearly are not products of post-IDEA, preservice training programs. Therefore, in addition to preservice training, in-service training programs are necessary to bring about immediate effects that upgrade teacher skills in the area of ABI.

The need for in-service training of educators who will provide services to students reentering the school system after experiencing ABI has been emphasized by a number of professionals (Bengali, 1992; Blosser & DePompei, 1991; Gerring & Carney, 1992; Mira, Tucker, & Tyler, 1992; Savage & Carter, 1984). The need also exists for school systems to have in place a systematic means of delivering ABI in-service training to all school personnel, so that students with ABI who are already in the school system are appropriately identified and served (see Chapter 13).

CONCLUSION

All educators must have an understanding of the unique educational needs of students with ABI. In addition, special educators, who will be providing direct services to these students as well as serving as consultants to general education teachers and related services personnel, need in-depth knowledge of ABI and the necessary skills to provide effective educational programs for these students. Because of their diverse needs, students with ABI pose a challenge to all educators. The greatest challenge, however, may rest with educators at colleges and universities who are ultimately responsible for ensuring that teachers are prepared to serve students with ABI. This chapter has proposed an outline for incorporating ABI training into teacher-preparation programs. It is now up to university and college personnel to carry out such training so that students with ABI receive a quality education from professionals who are specifically trained to meet their unique educational needs.

REFERENCES

Assistance to states for the education of children with disabilities. (1992). *57 Fed. Reg.*, 44802, 44842–44843.

Becker, H., Harrell, W.T., & Keller, L. (1993). A survey of professional and paraprofessional training needs for traumatic brain injury rehabilitation. *Journal of Head Trauma Rehabilitation*, 8(1), 88–101.

Bengali, V. (1992). *Head injury in children and adolescents* (2nd ed.). Brandon, VT: Clinical Psychology Publishing.

Blosser, J.L., & DePompei, R. (1991). Preparing education professionals for meeting the needs of students with traumatic brain injury. *Journal of Head Trauma Rehabilitation*, 6(1), 73–82.

Blosser, J.L., & DePompei, R. (1994). *Pediatric traumatic brain injury: Proactive intervention.* San Diego: Singular.

Buck, G., Morsink, C., Griffin, C., Hines, T., & Lenk, L. (1992). Preservice training: The role of field-based experiences in the preparation of effective special educators. *Teacher Education and Special Education, 15*(2), 108–123.

Darling-Hammond, L. (1990). Teachers and teaching: Signs of a changing profession. In W.R. Houston (Ed.), & M. Haberman & J. Sikulal (Assoc. Eds.), *Handbook of research on teacher education* (pp. 267–290). New York: Macmillan.

Doronzo, J.F. (1990). Mild head injury. In E. Lehr (Ed.), *Psychological management of traumatic brain injury in children and adolescents* (pp. 207–224). Rockville, MD: Aspen Publishers, Inc.

Gerring, J.P., & Carney, J.M. (1992). *Head trauma: Strategies for educational reintegration.* San Diego: Singular.

Hofmeister, A., & Lubke, M. (1990). *Research into practice: Implementing effective teaching research.* Logan: Utah State University, College of Education.

Individuals with Disabilities Education Act (IDEA) of 1990, PL 101-476, 20 U.S.C. § 1400 *et seq.*

Janus, P.L. (1994). The role of school administration. In R.C. Savage & G.F. Wolcott (Eds.), *Educational dimensions of acquired brain injury* (pp. 475–488). Austin, TX: PRO-ED.

Janus, P.L. (1996). Educational issues in providing appropriate services for students with acquired brain injury. In A. Goldberg (Ed.), *Acquired brain injury in childhood and adolescence* (pp. 195–202). Springfield, IL: Charles C Thomas.

Lehr, E. (1990). A developmental perspective. In E. Lehr (Ed.), *Psychological management of traumatic brain injury in children and adolescents* (pp. 41–52). Rockville, MD: Aspen Publishers, Inc.

Manier, D.S. (1991). *Special educators' knowledge of traumatic brain injury.* Unpublished master's thesis, University of Wisconsin–Stout, Menomonie.

Mira, M.P., Meck, N.E., & Tyler, J.S. (1988). School psychologists' knowledge of traumatic head injury: Implications for training. *Diagnostique, 13*(2–4), 178–180.

Mira, M.P., Tucker, B.F., & Tyler, J.S. (1992). *Traumatic brain injury in children and adolescents: A sourcebook for schools.* Austin, TX: PRO-ED.

Morsink, C., Thomas, C., & Correa, V. (1991). *Interactive teaming: Consultation and collaboration in special programs.* New York: Merrill-Macmillian.

National Head Injury Foundation Task Force. (1985). *An educator's manual: What educators need to know about students with traumatic brain injuries.* Framingham, MA: National Head Injury Foundation.

Nordlund, M.R. (1989, December). *Enabling successful school re-entry of brain injured students: Educating educators about TBI.* Paper presented at the National Head Injury Foundation National Convention, Chicago.

Reynolds, M.C. (1990). Educating teachers for special education students. In W.R. Houston (Ed.), & M. Haberman & J. Sikulal (Assoc. Eds.), *Handbook of research on teacher education* (pp. 423–436). New York: Macmillan.

Savage, R.C. (1994). An educator's guide to the brain and brain injury. In R.C. Savage & G.F. Wolcott (Eds.), *Educational dimensions of acquired brain injury* (pp. 13–31). Austin, TX: PRO-ED.

Savage, R.C., & Carter, R. (1984). Re-entry: The head injured student returns to school. *Cognitive Rehabilitation, 2*(6), 28–33.

Savage, R.C., & Wolcott, G.F. (1994). Overview of acquired brain injury. In R.C. Savage & G.F. Wolcott (Eds.), *Educational dimensions of acquired brain injury* (pp. 3–12). Austin, TX: PRO-ED.

Tyler, J.S. (1992). *Traumatic brain injury preservice training module.* (Available from University of Kansas Medical Center, Department of Special Education, 3901 Rainbow Boulevard, Kansas City, KS 66160-7335)

Tyler, J.S. (1995a). [Educators' knowledge of traumatic brain injury in school-aged children]. Unpublished raw data.

Tyler, J.S. (1995b). [Review of special education textbooks]. Unpublished raw data.

Tyler, J.S., Mira, M.P., & Hollowell, J.G. (1989). Head injury training for pediatric residents. *American Journal of Diseases of Children, 143,* 930–932.

Tyler, J.S., & Williams, J. (Producers). (1992). *Perspectives on traumatic brain injury: Success in dealing with long-term challenges by students, families, teachers, and friends* [Videotape]. (Available from University of Kansas Medical Center, Department of Special Education, 3901 Rainbow Boulevard, Kansas City, KS 66160-7335)

Wilkerson, L., & Tyler, J.S. (Producers). (1994). *Never give up* [Videotape]. (Available from University of Kansas Medical Center, Department of Special Education, 3901 Rainbow Boulevard, Kansas City, KS 66160-7335).

Ylvisaker, M., Hartwick, P., & Stevens, M. (1991). School re-entry following head injury: Managing the transition from hospital to school. *Journal of Head Trauma Rehabilitation, 6*(1), 10–20.

chapter thirteen

Providing Ongoing Support to Educators Through Team-Based Consultation

Building Capacity to Serve Students with ABI in General Education Settings

Ann Glang and Bonnie Todis

THE PUBLIC SCHOOL system is by far the largest provider of services to students with acquired brain injury (ABI). Yet few educators have an understanding of the complex and unique issues faced by this growing population (Blosser & DePompei, 1991; Ylvisaker, Hartwick, & Stevens, 1991), and most are unprepared to meet their needs (Lash & Scarpino, 1993).

Results from two surveys in the 1990s show that special educators and classroom teachers score moderately low on measures of knowledge and rate themselves as unprepared to address these students' behavior, academic, social, and cognitive problems (Glang, Todis, Sohlberg, & Reed, 1996; see Chapter 12). These survey results

Preparation of this chapter was supported in part by Grant #H086R30029 from the U.S. Department of Education. The views expressed in this chapter do not necessarily reflect those of the funding agency.

are clarified by comments throughout the chapter from educators serving students with ABI.

~≈ ~

We are glad to get some help with Jack. He is a big problem for us, and we don't really know what to do with him. He is in my office three or four times a week venting his anger. He constantly seeks attention and is always complaining that he has no friends, which is true because nobody wants to be around him. He is socially inappropriate at times and is full of anger.

High School Counselor

I think the school [staff] has tried to do [their] best, but I also believe that [the educators are] not really sure what to do all the time. They try to do what they can, but there's a lot of areas where I can see what they're doing is lacking. It's a lack of knowledge of what you're supposed to do. But they all seem to care a whole lot.

Father of Student with ABI

I don't know what set off his behavior today. Maybe it was the assembly, the change in schedule. [Pause] I didn't have a practicum in this [behavior management for students with ABI].

High School Special Education Teacher

My first year of teaching, one of the kids with learning disabilities I was working with got hit by a car and experienced ABI and a lot of other complications. It was kind of a baptism by fire you might say. You start scrambling [and asking yourself questions such as] "What are we dealing with?" and I found out there wasn't any real good place I could just turn to and get some information.

Special Education Teacher

~≈ ~

ABI has a unique effect on a student's ability to learn and perform in cognitive, behavior, and social domains. Although many of the learning and behavior characteristics of students with ABI are similar to those of students with developmental disabilities, there are others that are specific to brain injury. For example, most teachers are unfamiliar with the uneven and unpredictable learning rates associated with ABI and with the disinhibition and social inappropriateness demonstrated by many students with ABI.

In the lab situation, what was right in front of him and the areas that he could do hands-on manipulations and stuff, he did okay. His lab reports weren't great, but you could tell he was understanding. When it came to remembering, when it came to the test, it was as if the material had never been presented to him before. It was as if he'd never seen it and he didn't have a clue. I just couldn't get to him.

Middle School Science Teacher

The questions I get the most relate to how these kids are in the class-room. I'm being asked questions [such as] "Why are they acting out?" "Why do they not remember?" "Why don't they seem to be tracking?" "Why are they so socially inappropriate?"

Itinerant Physical Therapist

Ironically, specialists such as occupational therapists, physical therapists, and speech-language pathologists may have had some pre-service training in the effects of ABI but lack the training in instructional strategies and behavior management that would enable them to serve as consultants to classroom teachers who have questions about how to teach students with ABI in their classrooms.

If you're going to be a therapist in schools, it almost seems like you should have some courses in education, because the most challenging part of this . . . is not necessarily a therapeutic problem. The things that teachers ask me about are not therapeutic but educational and behav-ioral, and somebody like me just has no background in that. You're coming into a domain of teachers and you're supposed to be a con-sulting person. But how can you consult about something you don't know anything about? You know, sure, the kid needs to learn how to walk, but if you don't know how to integrate [that training] into their natural school environment [that may not be the highest priority].

Itinerant Physical Therapist

The difficult job faced by educators serving students with ABI is complicated by the challenges of working in partnership with the students' families. Most parents have no experience with special education services and often find the system unwieldy. For parents whose children received rehabilitation following injury, the level of services provided by schools may be disappointing. In the hospital, children often receive daily physical, speech, and occupational therapies; but many schools can provide weekly therapies at best, and in some smaller districts in which therapists serve large geographic regions, even this level of service is not feasible. Perhaps most important is that parents are asked to work with the school to make difficult educational programming decisions for their child at a time when rehabilitation is still in progress and the outcomes are still unknown (Savage & Carter, 1991). The stressors faced by parents combined with the devastating changes in the student and the lack of knowledge on the part of educators make the process of planning the student's educational program extremely challenging, both professionally and interpersonally.

It's the kind of injury that you didn't grow up with. A lot of children who have congenital birth problems . . . their parents deal with those on a[n] ongoing basis. You're always looking for information. After a brain injury like this, where apparently he recovered and everything was fine, all of a sudden you are thrown into a world that you don't know anything about. And we're learning more and more and more and more. Probably other parents around the state right now, like me, are having to fight for anything that they get.

Parent of Student with ABI

The accident, basically, financially broke us . . . It's been hard physically and mentally to deal with this day after day. There's a lot of mornings for me, and I'm sure for [my wife], that it takes a lot to get up and just face the day. But we can't quit . . . It will be hard, there will be a lot of work to it. But I'm not going to give up, no matter what.

Father of Student with ABI

I had talked with Mike's mother earlier in the year and talked about expectations. To be real blunt, I thought I knew where she was coming from and she knew where I was coming from because we'd worked together the previous year. There was one particular conversation we had that she heard completely differently from the way I said it. That festered for months before I found out there was a problem, and by that point there was quite a wild build-up. I was on guard after that. I'm on guard about saying anything. I got real gun-shy after that.

Middle School Teacher

Every case is different. We've had some where parents are overly involved and wanting to do too much—they almost get in your way—to other cases where parents are totally lost to the point of not knowing what to ask for or if they should even ask for anything. In either of those cases, you can help them out and [eventually you can] find out the information that you need. In other cases the parents may deny that there even is a problem and basically don't want any involvement— they just pretend that everything is okay.

School Psychologist

The challenges associated with serving students with ABI and their families can appear overwhelming if educators are not provided with the support necessary to effectively meet these students' needs (Kauffman, 1993). Educators are being asked to teach increasing numbers of students with special needs with fewer resources and personnel (Bolick, 1991). In this educational climate, a classroom teacher who is responsible for 25 students may be resistant to the prospect of including a student with ABI who has academic, social, and behavior challenges in his or her classroom.

My big frustration was not so much his taking a long time to answer but the repetition. It just took more time to give him the information so he could adjust to it than I had in class. I don't know what kind of strategy to use to get around that.

Middle School Language Arts Teacher

Do you think we qualify for stress disability? I'm stressed. I never thought I'd say that in all my years. It's been a heck of a year. Besides the overcrowding, they raised the [general education] class size and the special education class size without giving more assistant time when we had more kids. The general education class teachers—like Jane's teacher, she has 31 kids. [There are] a lot of needy kids in that class besides Jane too.

Elementary Special Education Teacher

Unless teachers are provided with support, efforts to include students with ABI in general education classrooms may fall short of students', parents', and teachers' expectations.

ABI IN-SERVICE TRAINING MODEL

This section describes the first phase of a federally funded in-service training project in Oregon that provides support to teachers proactively through the use of consulting teams of "ABI experts." The intent of the model is to make available to schools throughout the state a group of well-trained consultants who can provide in-service and ongoing consultation in an effort to prevent many of the problems schools face in serving this growing population of students.

The research and development literature on effective practices for students with disabilities as well as the authors' efforts in adapting these practices for students with ABI (Glang, Singer, Cooley, & Tish, 1992; Sowers, Glang, Voss, & Cooley, 1996) provided the foundation for the ABI in-service model. This model is designed to support schools serving students with disabilities with whatever assistance is required to ensure successful outcomes (Brown et al., 1991; Stainback, Stainback, & Jackson, 1992). The key features of the model are its capacity-building and regional team approaches.

The capacity-building approach of the model avoids the problems with transfer associated with traditional training methods. Research in the field of staff development suggests that approaches that offer "one-shot" in-service training without follow-up are not effective in helping educators actually implement suggestions (Gersten, Carnine, Zoref, & Cronin, 1986; Sparks, 1983). On-site, situation-specific assistance greatly increases the likelihood that educators will transfer skills to their instructional situation (Gersten, Morvant, & Brengelman, 1995; Glang, Gersten, & Morvant, 1994; Showers, 1984; Ylvisaker, Feeney, & Urbanczyk, 1993).

The nature of ABI suggests a regional team approach. The incidence of ABI is sudden and unexpected, and its individual effects are unpredictable. Students with ABI who are reentering school present a host of challenges that may require the expertise of a variety of specialized educators. By working as a team, these educators can provide schools direct, immediate, and specific information and strategies for including students with ABI. Consultation from one specialist serving an entire state or region would restrict educators' access to the support they need.

The regional team structure combined with a capacity-building training approach provided a promising model for service delivery to students with ABI and the school personnel serving them. In order to refine procedures throughout the 3 years of the project, the project was implemented in three phases: a pilot test with a single team in Year 1, recruitment and training of two additional teams in Year 2, and training of the remaining three teams in Year 3. The following is an analysis of the data from the two teams trained during Year 2 that have been providing posttraining consultation for approximately 1 school year, as this chapter is written.

Team Members

The ABI in-service model's regional teams were composed of members of each of the disciplines from a particular area of the state who typically serve students with ABI (see Table 1). (Oregon is divided into six geographical and bureaucratic regions, each of which operates independently in providing services to students with disabilities.) This allows team members to address directly the issues facing individual disciplines when they consult with the districts. That is, when a speech-language therapist requests consultation on a new student with ABI on her caseload, she can meet directly with the regional team's speech-language therapist and get information that is relevant to her work with the student.

When recruiting team members, the goal of this model was to attract 1) school-based educators who had some experience working with students with ABI and 2) parents and survivors who could work well with a team in school settings. Hospital-based staff were purposely not recruited to become team members, largely because the context in which school personnel work is so different from the rehabilitation environment (Lash & Scarpino, 1993). Instead, community and hospital-based applicants were asked to become "adjunct team members" who could consult with team members on an as-needed basis.

Team members were recruited through the organizational structure set up by the state Department of Special Education. In the state of Oregon, special education services such as occupational therapy, physical therapy, and speech-language therapy are provided to students with low-incidence disabilities through regional programs. For the ABI In-Service Project, the most logical approach was to create a team of ABI consultants in each region.

Understanding that each region had its own political and organizational context and that for teams to be successful their activities would have to mesh with existing organizational structures, each region's administrators were asked for assistance in recruiting team members. It was believed that this approach would maximize local control of the in-service model and build on existing expertise and interest in ABI, both of which have been found to be important in creating in-service models (M. Ylvisaker, personal communication,

Table 1.   Composition of the ABI in-service model's regional teams

Parent	Physical therapist
ABI survivor	Occupational therapist
Local/regional administrator	Instructional assistant
Classroom teacher	School counselor
Special education teacher	School nurse
Speech-language specialist	School psychologist

March 17, 1994). As was expected, each administrator approached recruitment differently. Recruitment preferences were in some cases determined by the population distribution of the region and in other cases by the personnel who worked in the region and their job descriptions. For example, the regional director in the area in which the pilot team was recruited preferred to hand-pick team members to ensure success of the model.

ᢙᢛ ᢜᢖ

We know who the people are who can travel throughout the region and provide consultation as part of their jobs. We also know who has an interest in ABI.

Regional Director

ᢙᢛ ᢜᢖ

The director in the second region recognized the diversity of needs across the urban and rural areas of the region. After discussion with local special education directors, she chose to open recruitment to any school-based staff member who qualified. The third team combined these two approaches to recruit a team that represented all of the disciplines serving students with ABI and effectively covered its large, diverse, and primarily rural territory.

Applicants completed a brief application form that included information about their experience with students with ABI, a short essay describing why they were interested in being a team member, and a statement of support from their supervisors indicating that they would be relieved of their regular duties to attend trainings and provide consultation (a total of approximately 10 days of the school year). The authors met with the regional administrators to select the most qualified team members from the pool of applicants. Additional recruiting of team members was left to the individual teams; once they began to meet regularly, most of the teams sought out additional members to cover underrepresented geographic areas or disciplines.

Training for Consulting Team Members

The success of the ABI in-service model required substantial shifts in the roles and responsibilities of team members. Prior to their involvement with the team, the majority of the team members spent most of their time working directly with students and had little if any experience providing consultation or training. Because most classroom teachers have not been adequately prepared to work with students with disabilities, consulting team members needed to expand their roles to include assisting teachers through consultation. This shift is not a natural one. The authors believed that unless team members were provided with adequate training, they might not undertake the sensitive role of consultation (Gersten, Darch, Davis, & George, 1991; Glang et al., 1994; Morvant, 1984). The in-service model thus included training in effective consultation skills as well as information on ABI and strategies to address the social, behavioral, and academic needs of students with ABI. Figure 1 summarizes the changes in roles required by the model, the skills needed to implement these changes, and how the model addresses these needs.

The training consisted of two distinct phases: 1) team training workshops that provided training in the effects of ABI on the school

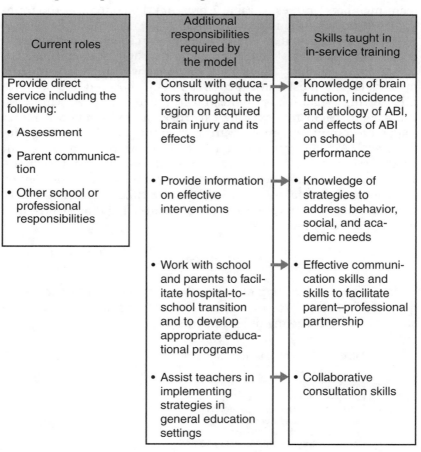

Figure 1.   A summary of the changes in roles required by the ABI in-service model, the skills needed to implement these changes, and how the model addresses the need for educators to shift roles.

experience; specific strategies for addressing these students' academic, social, and behavioral needs; and skill development in working collaboratively with parents and classroom teachers to provide educational services in general education settings; and 2) follow-up consultation to team members.

Phase I Training: Knowledge and Skill Acquisition   The goal of Phase I of the training was to provide team members with current information about the effects of ABI and strategies for working effectively with students, families, and teachers. Team members attended a total of 7 days of training workshops. Although a menu of topic areas was selected in advance from the literature on pediatric ABI, the specific training content was largely determined by the team members' interests. Table 2 presents the content of the training workshops for the two teams.

Workshop presenters were widely known speakers in their field of interest (e.g., special education, neuropsychology, cognitive rehabilitation, psychology). Each had experience working with students in schools, and most had experience in both hospital and community settings. The focus of the training workshops was more on using the participants' existing expertise and building on it rather than on retraining and restructuring programs to accommodate students with ABI. Suggestions for modifications were given to account for the unique cognitive profiles of students with ABI, but each presenter reassured team members that many of the effective academic, behavioral, and social interventions that are effective with other students are also effective with these students. This focus was well received by team members.

❧ ❧

[In the middle of a training on instructional strategies] a teacher raised her hand and asked "You mean I can correct Sara's mistakes? I've been afraid to treat her like my other students." The teacher went on to de-

Table 2.   Content of training workshops

Overview of ABI
Family effects
Parent–school communication
Behavior management strategies
Facilitating social interactions
Promoting academic success
Compensatory organizational systems
Collaborative consultation
Presenting an in-service training in ABI

scribe her confusion about how to provide instruction to a student with organically based learning problems. She assumed that unique instructional strategies would be required and was relieved to learn that the same strategies that were effective with other students with disabilities would be effective for the student with ABI.

Field Notes[1]

Following each workshop, team members were given assignments to apply the information they had learned. For example, following the presentation on the effects of ABI, team members were assigned an exercise in pinpointing problems. They were asked to observe a student with ABI in a variety of school settings (e.g., in the classroom, on the playground, during transition periods), interview the student's teacher and parent(s), and write detailed notes about their impressions of the issues involved in effectively serving the student.

Phase II: Skill Application   Phase II activities were designed to facilitate the maintenance and generalization of skills acquired during the workshop. Just as teachers learning new instructional techniques need support to apply new techniques in the classroom (Showers, 1984), novice consultants need on-site assistance to be effective resources for the schools they serve (Gersten et al., 1995; Glang et al., 1994). During Phase II of the training, the authors offered ongoing support to team members who were consulting with districts. These activities involved follow-up consultation, technical assistance, and support by project staff to the regional teams. For example, one team member requested assistance with preparing a brief in-service training for special education and related services personnel in her district.

[Two team members were asked by their supervisor to provide an in-service training on the effects of ABI for their colleagues (school psychologists, speech-language pathologists, and special education teachers). Apprehensive about how prepared they were to present on this topic, they approached me for assistance.] I met with them prior to the in-service training to assist in organizing and planning the presentation and to offer handouts and other materials they might use. On the

---

[1]The Field Notes throughout this chapter are taken from Glang and Todis (1991–1994, 1993–1996, 1995–1998). The research that generated these notes was funded by the U.S. Department of Education, Office of Special Research/Programs.

day of the presentation, I arrived early to provide support (both team members were quite nervous and were reassured knowing that I could be there). During the presentation I answered questions and provided clarification as needed. After the presentation, the team members and I met to review participants' evaluations and discuss possible changes in the presentation for next time.

Field Notes

Another team member not experienced with providing consultation in instructional situations asked for help observing a student and providing suggestions to the team of educators working with the student.

[The physical therapist on the team (Sean) was concerned about a sixth-grade student with a severe brain injury on his caseload. Unused to dealing in the academic realm, Sean asked for help in consulting with the instructional assistant (IA) and classroom teacher.] Sean and I observed today in the student's classroom. I was impressed with how perceptive Sean was. For example, at one point during the lesson, Sean leaned over and commented that the student was very isolated from her peers (she and her IA were seated in the corner of the room at a small table), and that the IA seemed to be "helping" much more than the student needed. A lot of what the IA did for the student, Sean noted, could be done by a peer. After the observation, we met briefly with the IA to compliment her on the positive aspects of her interactions with the student. We decided that the next step should be for Sean to convene the student's parents and school team to share the information from our observation and determine goals, strategies, and an action plan.

Field Notes

The components of this model (i.e., provision of knowledge to team members, follow-up support and consultation, and the capacity-building nature of a regional team model) were designed to provide the foundation of support needed for team members to take over responsibility for their teams once the federally funded project ended. The data described here provide an initial analysis of how successful the model has been in achieving the project goals.

EVALUATION OF THE ABI IN-SERVICE MODEL

Team members spent approximately 1 year participating in training activities and 1 year providing consultation and support in their respective regions. The evaluation plan called for both quantitative and qualitative analysis of training and of team members' interventions following training.

Quantitative Evaluation

Quantitative measures were designed to assess the frequency and effectiveness of team members' consulting activities as well as the social validity of the in-service model. Measures were administered throughout the 2-year period.

Activity Logs   Team members kept ongoing logs of their consulting activities throughout the second year of their involvement in the project. Table 3 summarizes team members' activities over the course of the 1995–1996 school year and reports mean ratings of team members' satisfaction with each activity.

Social Validation Ratings by Consumers of the Model   When team members conducted in-service trainings for regional audiences, they asked participants to rate the degree to which the training accomplished its primary goal (e.g., provided an overview of ABI, presented suggestions for academic or behavioral interventions, discussed effective compensatory techniques). Participants rated each workshop using a 4-point, Likert-type scale. Collapsed across re-

Table 3.   Frequency of team members' consultation in the 1995–1996 school year

	Team 1[a]			Team 2[b]		
Activity	Frequency	Team members' mean satisfaction rating[c]	SD	Frequency	Team members' mean satisfaction rating	SD
Meet with family member	25	4.32	.85	22	4.91	.43
Consultation						
Telephone	23	3.48	.90	3	3.00	1.73
On-site	95	4.69	.65	78	3.74	.54
In-service presentation	4	4.25	.50	19	3.68	.82
Provide written materials	4	4.25	.50	1	4.00	n/a
Attend meeting	12	3.92	1.00	5	3.60	.55

[a]n = 9.

[b]n = 11.

[c]1 = not at all satisfied; 2 = somewhat satisfied; 3 = neutral; 4 = very satisfied; 5 = extremely satisfied.

gions (N = 50), the average rating for the workshops was 3.50 (moderately to highly effective).

Individual Goal Attainment   At their initial training workshop, each team member identified several personal goals he or she wanted to accomplish as an in-service team member. Goals fell into the following six categories:

1. Goal: To increase knowledge of strategies (e.g., learn more about compensatory strategies to help students function more independently)
2. Goal: To increase skill level (e.g., increase skills in interpreting medical information for non-medical professionals)
3. Goal: To increase knowledge of resources (e.g., become more familiar with the Brain Injury Association of Oregon and services available)
4. Goal: To network with others (e.g., establish liaisons with medical facilities to improve communications between hospital and school staff)
5. Goal: To share information with others (e.g., present an in-service training for school psychologists in local district)
6. Goal: To develop systems for others to use (e.g., set up "red flag" system to help identify students with ABI so they and their families can have access to services)

Team members then developed their own criteria for measuring the extent to which they reached their goals and rated their progress toward attaining these goals at each subsequent team meeting. A comparison of ratings shows that team members' ratings gained an average of .65–1.61 points (on a 5-point, Likert-type scale) over a 16-month period (see Table 4). There was a significant difference in pre- and posttest ratings with the exception of Goal 5.

Measures of Team Effectiveness   To determine the model's impact, a measure of the team members' perceived competence to meet the needs of students with ABI was administered to all team members. The *team effectiveness rating* was designed to assess the degree to which in-service training prepared team members to be "experts" in effective interventions for students with ABI. Using a 5-point, Likert-type scale, the 20-item questionnaire asks respondents to rate how prepared they believe they are to meet the needs of students with ABI across four areas—physical, social/behavioral, cognitive, and academic. Team members completed the questionnaire prior to receiving training (pre) and at the conclusion of their year-long training (post). As shown in Table 5, t test analyses revealed pre- to post-

Table 4.   Mean pre- to posttest ratings on goal attainment scale

Goal	N	Mean rating at baseline (SD)	Mean rating at posttraining (SD)	t
1. To increase knowledge of strategies	15	3.33 (0.92)	4.33 (0.72)	-6.18[a]
2. To increase skill level	10	3.05 (1.16)	4.20 (0.79)	-3.85[b]
3. To increase knowledge of resources	9	2.83 (1.28)	4.00 (0.87)	-2.86[b]
4. To network with others	13	2.85 (0.90)	4.46 (0.52)	-5.58[a]
5. To share information with others	10	2.90 (0.70)	3.55 (1.01)	-1.74
6. To develop systems	12	2.75 (0.87)	3.88 (0.74)	-3.89[b]

[a]$p < .05$.
[b]$p < .01$.

test increases in mean ratings of perceived competence across all four goal areas. Each of the increases reached statistical significance.

A second questionnaire asked team members to rate their entire team's effectiveness in meeting the needs of educators serving students with ABI and to identify the aspects of the model that contributed to their team's effectiveness. The 15-item questionnaire uses a 5-point, Likert-type scale and asks the respondent to rate how effective the *team* is in providing the following: 1) in-service presentations in ABI, 2) written materials, 3) referrals for parents or teachers, 4) telephone consultation, 5) classroom observation/problem solving with teachers, 6) support/information for family members, and 7) assistance at the individualized education program (IEP) or other planning meetings.

This measure was given only once—after team members had been involved with the project for 2 full years. Mean ratings for the 2 teams ranged from 3.68 to 4.25 (1 = not at all effective, 5 = extremely effective). Team members rated being responsible for planning their own meetings, having their own budget, and having their own materials to distribute to interested educators as factors especially effective in assisting them to function as independent consultants. They also reported the support of project staff (availability for telephone consultation and copresentations) as extremely effective in helping the team to establish itself in their respective regions.

Qualitative Evaluation

Qualitative data from interviews and field notes were used formatively to refine the ABI in-service model and summatively to assess the impact the model had on educators, families, and students.

Table 5.   Pre- and posttest means of ABI in-service team effectiveness ratings on a 5-point Likert-type scale

Intervention Areas	Pretest			Posttest		
	n	M	SD	M	SD	t
Physical	17	3.28	1.29	3.81	1.22	-2.16[a]
Social/Behavioral	17	3.10	.75	3.87	.76	-4.34[b]
Cognitive	16	3.56	.79	4.08	.68	-3.28[b]
Academic	17	3.66	.73	4.26	.53	-3.77[b]

[a]$p < .05$.
[b]$p < .01$.

Open-ended, unstructured interviews were conducted with a total of 24 team members. The interview protocols were designed to encourage team members to discuss not only positive features of the training and support provided but also what could have been done better or more efficiently. For example, early interviews in the first year of the project revealed that trainees found it hard to sit still during trainings because most of them were accustomed to being very active in their classrooms or to traveling from school to school. Project staff therefore modified training formats to include more frequent breaks and more activities. Early interviews also indicated that teams needed additional time and support to develop a sense of team identity and plan how the team would function. Support for this was included in each subsequent meeting, and teams were encouraged to convene independent of project staff at least monthly during the second year of the project.

Typical positive comments focused on the following:

• Helpful aspects of training

The trainings have really changed my perspective on working with a couple of students. I've been able to do more than just the speech-language stuff with them. I've been able to coordinate with the teachers some different, broader types of programs.

Speech Therapist

When I went to Eugene and heard Tim Feeney [speak about behavioral interventions], I realized he was right. We've always focused on the consequences [to correct problem behavior]. I left there with this real focus on trying to dissect the antecedents instead of coming up with more consequences. That just kind of sat in my brain. It has really changed the way that I approach dealing with the youngsters.

Special Education Consultant

Everybody kept saying, "This kid is really weird. He has these things, and he doesn't have these things." That's all you could hear them say is "He's really weird, he's just so different from everybody else." Then I observed him diagnostically and when the parents came in to talk to me, because I wanted to do some more testing on my own, I asked them if there had ever been an incident [involving a brain injury] and they said yes. Prior to being on the team, I would have just assumed there is more going on than what I knew. Now I know how some of these kids present themselves; that helped. Before the training, no, I wouldn't have normally asked that question. Now I do ask it more.

Speech Therapist

⁓ ⁓

- Consulting with fellow team members

⁓ ⁓

[Team members] communicate back and forth. Networking helped a great deal. We pick up the phone and we'll call each other if there's a problem. I know that was intended [as an outcome of the project], and it worked really well.

Regional Nurse

Getting to know people on other teams has also been helpful. When I was going to start working with one young lady with ABI who was nonverbal, I was going to be doing her counseling, but I had never worked with a nonverbal student before. So I wasn't really sure where to begin or what to do. [Project staff] put me in touch with a woman who is actually on another team but does a lot of work like that. And that's been real helpful, and I was able to talk with her back and forth until I felt really comfortable.

School Psychologist

⁓ ⁓

- Being encouraged to implement training

⁓ ⁓

I learn what I know sometimes by doing in-services for others. Because when people ask you questions, I feel like that's when I really find out that, hey, I know this!

Special Education Teacher

The hands-on experience of actually conducting an in-service training is what finally made me feel ready to be in the "expert" role. Just
getting my feet wet and doing it was what I needed in order for me
to say, "Yeah, I can do this and do it well." But it's just until you do
something, you're not sure.

Speech-Language Therapist

Team members also reported on the positive impact their activities had on other educators, on students, and on parents of students
with ABI:

During the IEP meeting, I turned to [the mother of the student with ABI]
and said, "I'd just like to know whether you are noticing any differences
this year since we are doing things a little differently with [the student.]"
She looked very surprised and then said that this is the best year he has
ever had and that he's a completely different person at home—much
happier and more cooperative. After the meeting she told me no one
had ever asked her opinion in an IEP meeting before. She was very
touched.

Instructional Assistant

At one of my schools, a little girl was just discharged from the hospital
to her home with no information to the school or the family about the
effects of ABI. I gave the school and the student's grandmother some
information about ABI. [The grandmother] was very relieved to find out
that the behavior they were seeing was typical for this stage and that it
doesn't mean the family was doing something wrong.

Physical Therapist

Whenever possible, project staff interviewed parents, students,
or educators served directly by team members:

She's doing great, her self-esteem, everything about her is a lot better.
She has set higher goals for herself, and she's more confident that she'll
be able to make these goals that she set. I don't know if this is all attributed to you guys, but she's come a long way and it makes your heart
feel good to watch her, knowing where she was before and seeing how
she is now. She's getting more of the attitude of "I can do whatever I

want to do. It may take me a little longer, but I can do whatever I want
to do."

Mother of 11-Year-Old Girl with ABI

Summary of Outcomes

Results from both quantitative and qualitative evaluation data suggest that the ABI in-service model was effective in training teams
of educators to be consultants in pediatric ABI. As a result of their
involvement in the training effort, team members engaged in a variety of consulting activities in their respective regions, including
providing in-service trainings, sharing resources, and consulting in
classrooms on difficult cases. In general, the educators and parents
involved believed that their teams functioned efficiently and were
responsive to the needs of schools serving students with ABI. Most
important, the recipients of team members' efforts rated the in-
services and consultation provided by team members as highly valuable.

Discussion

The primary objective of the ABI in-service model was to create
teams of educators who can provide in-service and ongoing support
to schools that serve students with ABI. The preliminary findings
suggest that this objective has been met. As a result of the 3-year
project, six trained teams of educators have been established to provide support and consultation throughout the state of Oregon. The
teams are responsive to the needs of regional and local schools and
experienced in providing in-service and consultation services to educators and families.

The authors believe that the success of this model is the result
in large part of the extent of support it provides trainees to implement the training they receive so that it directly benefits students
with ABI. Others who have undertaken similar models (Tyler, 1994;
Ylvisaker et al., 1993) report that most trainees have difficulty
assuming the role of "expert" and providing consultation to other
educators or working directly with a student with ABI. The authors'
research reinforced the validity of this observation: Following trainings in ABI, educators rated themselves as less knowledgeable about
ABI than they were before they received the training (i.e., they
believed they were more knowledgeable until they learned about
ABI) (Glang et al., 1996). This may be because as educators attend
more training workshops they gain an appreciation of the complex-

ity of issues related to serving a student with ABI in schools. In other words, one function of training in ABI is that it makes educators aware of how much there is to know and how little most educators know about the topic.

Several features of the model were designed to help team members overcome their reluctance to consult. In addition, it was recognized that fostering the autonomy and self-sufficiency of teams at each stage was very important so that at the end of the 3-year project period, teams would be able to carry on their intervention and in-service activities without project support. The following are strategies for supporting implementation of training and team autonomy.

Establishing Local Control   Promoting local control and autonomy began with team recruitment when project staff followed regional administrators' recommendations for how to conduct recruitment in their respective regions. Once teams were formed and had received initial training, each team selected the additional training workshops they wanted and scheduled team meetings to accommodate their school calendars. During the final year of the project, teams were responsible for planning and running their own meetings.

Each team was given its own resource box containing articles, books, manuals, videotapes, overhead transparencies, and other materials to allow team members access to ample information as well as to offer them information that they could then provide to other individuals. The boxes were regularly updated as team members found and produced additional materials and made them available to their own team and to the other five teams in the state. Each team appointed a librarian to update the list of resource box contents and to mail or fax materials to team members as requested.

Team autonomy was also promoted by providing each team with a $2,000 budget for the school year. Funds were used for release time to permit team members to consult and provide in-service training, mileage for team members to get to these activities, books, other materials for the resource box, and photocopying and distributing of resource materials as they were requested by team members.

Follow-Up Training   Team members participated in 7 day–long training workshops over a 16-month period. This ongoing training approach avoided the problems with skill transfer associated with "one shot" in-service training (Gersten et al., 1986) by encouraging team members to try out the strategies they learned with students, family members, and teachers and report back to fellow team members about their experiences. At each training, participants discussed examples of how they applied their knowledge in the field and then problem-solved difficult situations in the group context. Team members were publicly acknowledged for their consultation efforts in team meetings and inter-team memos.

Although both teams received specific training in consultation skills, this training was not mentioned in interviews as a key factor in promoting team members' willingness to provide consultation. Team members did believe that learning effective strategies for working with students with ABI (e.g., compensatory strategies, strategies to increase students' social integration) was essential to feeling comfortable as "ABI experts."

Assignments   The assignments that accompanied each training session were identified by team members as one of the most effective ways of encouraging them to implement their skills and knowledge. In interviews, many team members commented on how valuable it was to "get their feet wet" by completing a structured assignment using what they had just learned. Although many team members expressed an initial sense that they were not ready, they found that their efforts were well received and helpful to other educators and to students. They also reported that completing assignments was extremely beneficial for building personal confidence and for establishing a sense of team identity.

Technical Assistance   In discussing assignments, team members also pointed to the support that was available from project staff as they tried putting their knowledge into practice. Project staff accompanied team members as they planned and conducted in-service trainings and consulted in classrooms. They were available to answer questions about specific situations related to students with ABI and to refer team members to specialized services in their regions. The opportunity to work closely with a more experienced ABI consultant allowed team members to use the skills they had learned in a supported situation in order for them to feel successful and confident when providing consultation independently.

In the end, being encouraged to function as an independent consultant was perhaps the most critical factor in team members' assumption of the consultant role.

∝ ∾

Until you're kind of put under the gun, you don't really start to go through the process of really setting up a presentation, things you would do if you really had a date to do it.

Special Education Teacher

∝ ∾

Challenges in Implementing the In-Service Model

Although preliminary findings suggest that this in-service model is an effective one, not all team members believed they were successful in their efforts to provide consultation to schools working with students with ABI. Perhaps the most frustrating experience for team members was when a family member or professional outside of the school requested the team's help with a particular student, but the school did not welcome the consultation.

David, a special education teacher on the team, is an active consultant who works with teachers serving students with learning disabilities in his rural region. However, when he was asked by a regional nurse to help one of the elementary schools in his region to develop a behavioral intervention for a student with ABI, David declined. He had worked with this school a lot over the past 2 years and knew that the staff wouldn't follow through with any strategies they came up with.

Field Notes

The mother of one of the students on Janice's (a team member) caseload was concerned about her daughter's math skills. The student was bringing home worksheets that she was unable to do without a lot of help. Janice told the mother that she would observe during math the next week and get back to her. During the observation, it became clear that the mother's concerns were justified. In the lesson, Janice observed that the student was struggling to do a worksheet with money-related word problems involving decimals. Janice suspected that the student didn't have much of a concept of money. When Janice showed her a group of coins, the student was unable to identify any of them. Janice mentioned her observations to the teacher during recess break. The teacher's response was surprising; she denied that the student was having any problems in math at all. According to the teacher, the student was very capable of working this kind of problem, and she was just not trying today in order to get attention. The next day, the teacher asked the special education teacher to tell the consulting team member to stay out of her classroom.

Field Notes

In some cases, team members found that educators wanted help, but had difficulty making any significant changes in their approach to working with the student. This situation usually occurred when an administrator contacted a team member, described the problems (usually behavior), and then seemed to ask the consultant to "fix it." This view of consultation fails to recognize that interventions must be tailored to the culture of the school in which they will be implemented and to the needs of the educators who will do the implementing. Part of the consultant's job is also to help educators figure out why the strategies they have agreed to try have not been implemented, or if they have been tried, why they have not been successful.

A team member was asked by a team of educators to help them come up with a behavioral plan to address their student's severe behavior problems (e.g., inappropriate touching of female students, swearing, noncompliance). After observing the student and gathering information from the student, his mother, and his teachers, the consultant spent a day with the team. She provided an in-service presentation on ABI, outlined some suggestions for an initial plan for decreasing the student's problem behaviors, and then facilitated a meeting with the student and staff. A specific action plan was generated and follow-up consultation was scheduled.

One week later, the consultant called the special education teacher to see how things were going. None of the specific strategies discussed at the meeting had been implemented. Three days after the meeting, the student had been suspended for a week; and although the teacher expressed an interest in implementing the action plan, there were no specific plans in place to do so.

Field Notes

The frustrating experiences of team members consulting in general education classrooms were anticipated. In general, the effects of consultation efforts to improve classroom teachers' practice to better meet the needs of students with disabilities have been less than satisfactory (Gersten et al., 1995; Jenkins & Leicester, 1992; Simmons, Fuchs, Fuchs, & Mathes, 1995). Unsuccessful experiences such as the ones reported here reflect the delicate nature of school-based consultation and the importance of tailoring the consultation process so that it is consistent with the school culture and meets the stated (or unstated) objectives of those seeking help (see Chapter 2).

Some team members were much more comfortable consulting than others. There are several possible explanations for this reluctance. The authors believe that from the beginning some team members may have just wanted to take advantage of the unique training opportunity offered by the project and had no intention of actually using the information they learned. These team members tended to be inconsistent in their attendance of team workshops and meetings and were less likely to complete assignments. Other team members wanted to consult but did not have their supervisor's permission to do so. Although all supervisors signed an initial application form indicating their support of the project, later some team members were directly told by their supervisors that they could not be relieved of their other job responsibilities so that they could perform team consultation duties. A third group of nonconsulting team members resisted crossing over the unspoken "discipline boundaries." These team members were uncomfortable providing suggestions in an area other than their primary area of expertise.

The majority of team members who willingly consulted in their regions were already experienced consultants in some other area (e.g., autism, augmentative communication, severe disabilities). They welcomed the opportunity to become a resource for parents and educators in a new, unrelated field. For team members such as these, becoming a consultant in ABI issues was challenging and kept them motivated in jobs that had many demands and few rewards.

Being involved in this project has been one of my only "perks" this year. It has been challenging to tackle a new area—I'm much more motivated than I was last year because of this project.

School Psychologist

CONCLUSION

The lack of awareness of ABI and its effects has led in many cases to a failure of the educational system to effectively meet these students' needs (Rosen & Gerring, 1986). The ABI in-service model described in this chapter provides a creative approach to informing educators of the unique characteristics and needs of students with ABI and their families. Preliminary findings suggest that with appropriate training and support, regional teams of educators can become effective consultants to schools and parents.

The success of the ABI in-service regional team model demonstrates the effectiveness of this approach in a state with both highly populated and remote rural areas and in which most educators had little or no training in ABI. The model has been shown to be adaptable and sensitive to local needs. It overcomes the problem identified by other team trainers (Ylvisaker et al., 1993) of trainee reluctance to apply training through consultation, and it results in direct benefit to students with ABI, their families, and the educators who serve them.

REFERENCES

Blosser, J.L., & DePompei, R. (1991). Preparing education professionals for meeting the needs of students with traumatic brain injury. *Journal of Head Trauma Rehabilitation, 6*(1), 73–82.

Bolick, N. (1991). School budget blues. *American School Board Journal, 178*(9), 34–36.

Brown, L., Schwarz, P., Udvari-Solner, A., Kampschroer, E.F., Johnson, F., Jorgensen, J., & Gruenewald, L. (1991). How much time should students with severe intellectual disabilities spend in regular education classrooms and elsewhere? *Journal of The Association for Persons with Severe Handicaps, 16*(1), 39–47.

Gersten, R., Carnine, D.W., Zoref, L., & Cronin, D. (1986). A multifaceted study of change in seven inner-city schools. *The Elementary School Journal, 86*(3), 1–20.

Gersten, R., Darch, C., Davis, G., & George, N. (1991). Apprenticeship and intensive training of consulting teachers: A naturalistic study. *Exceptional Children, 57*, 226–237.

Gersten, R., Morvant, M., & Brengelman, S. (1995). Close to the classroom is close to the bone: Coaching as a means to translate research into classroom practice. *Exceptional Children, 62*(1), 52–66.

Glang, A.E., Gersten, R., & Morvant, M. (1994). A directive approach toward the consultation process: A case study. *Learning Disabilities Research & Practice, 9*(4), 225–233.

Glang, A.E., Singer, G.H.S., Cooley, E.A., & Tish, N. (1992). Tailoring direct instruction techniques for use with students with brain injury. *Journal of Head Trauma Rehabilitation, 7*(4), 93–108.

Glang, A.E., & Todis, B. (1991–1994). [Enhancing social support and integration for students with TBI]. Unpublished raw data.

Glang, A.E., & Todis, B. (1995–1996). [Model inservice training in traumatic brain injury: A regional team approach]. Unpublished raw data.

Glang, A.E., & Todis, B. (1996–1998). [Improving education services for middle and high school students with TBI: Developing supports in inclusive settings]. Unpublished raw data.

Glang, A.E., Todis, B., Sohlberg, M., & Reed, P.R. (1996). Helping parents negotiate the system. In G.H.S. Singer, A. Glang, & J.M. Williams (Eds.), *Children with acquired brain injury: Educating and supporting families* (pp. 149–165). Baltimore: Paul H. Brookes Publishing Co..

Jenkins, J., & Leicester, N. (1992). Specialized instruction within general education: A case study of one elementary school. *Exceptional Children, 58*(6), 555–563.

Kauffman, J.M. (1993). How we might achieve the radical reform of special education. *Exceptional Children, 60*(1), 6–16.

Lash, M., & Scarpino, C. (1993). School reintegration for children with traumatic brain injuries: Conflicts between medical and educational settings. *Neuro Rehabilitation, 3*(3), 13–25.

Morvant, M. (1984). *The role of resource teachers in the elementary schools: Models and realities.* Unpublished doctoral dissertation. University of Oregon, College of Education, Eugene.

Rosen, C., & Gerring, J. (1986). *Journal of head trauma: Educational reintegration.* Boston: College-Hill Press.

Savage, R.C., & Carter, R.R. (1991). Family and return to school. In J.M. Williams & T. Kay (Eds.), *Head injury: A family matter* (pp. 203–216). Baltimore: Paul H. Brookes Publishing Co.

Showers, B. (1984). *Peer coaching and its effects on transfer of training.* Paper presented at the annual meeting of the American Educational Research Association, New Orleans.

Simmons, D.C., Fuchs, L., Fuchs, D., & Mathes, P. (1995). Effects of explicit teaching and peer tutoring on the reading achievement of learning disabled and low-performing students in general education. *Elementary School Journal, 95*(5), 387–408.

Sowers, J., Glang, A.E., Voss, J., & Cooley, E. (1996). Enhancing friendships and leisure involvement of students with traumatic brain injuries and other disabilities. In L.E. Powers, G.H.S. Singer, & J. Sowers (Eds.), *On the road to autonomy: Promoting self-competence in children and youth with disabilities* (pp. 347–371). Baltimore: Paul H. Brookes Publishing Co.

Sparks, G.M. (1983). Synthesis of research of staff development for effective teaching. *Educational Leadership, 41*(3), 65–72.

Stainback, S., Stainback, W., & Jackson, H.J. (1992). Toward inclusive classrooms. In S. Stainback & W. Stainback (Eds.), *Curriculum considerations in inclusive classrooms: Facilitating learning for all students* (pp. 3–17). Baltimore: Paul H. Brookes Publishing Co.

Tyler, J. (1994, November 6–9). *The traumatic brain injury project.* Paper presented at annual meeting of the National Head Injury Foundation, Chicago.

Ylvisaker, M., Feeney, T.J., & Urbanczyk, B. (1993). Developing a positive communication culture for rehabilitation: Communication training for staff and family members. In C.J. Durgin, N.D. Schmidt, & L.J. Fryer (Eds.), *Staff development and clinical intervention in brain injury rehabilitation* (pp. 57–85). Rockville, MD: Aspen Publishers, Inc.

Ylvisaker, M., Hartwick, P., & Stevens, M. (1991). School reentry following head injury: Managing the transition from hospital to school. *Journal of Head Trauma Rehabilitation, 6*(1), 10–22.

chapter fourteen

Common Questions When Serving Students with ABI

Ronald C. Savage and Sue Pearson

WITH THE IMPLEMENTATION of the Individuals with Disabilities Education Act (IDEA) of 1990, PL 101-476, the role of the classroom teacher changed significantly. Teachers have always been required to be knowledgeable and creative about curriculum issues, but today's teacher must also know how to effectively program for children with a range of disabilities. Children with acquired brain injury (ABI) pose a unique challenge to educators. Brain injuries result in sudden, often dramatic, unforeseen changes and challenges, leaving educators with the enormous task of acquiring medical information; coordinating meetings among medical facilities, the school, and the family; and learning how to educate a student with highly individual, complex needs. Teachers are faced with a number of questions as they adjust to the academic, social, and behavior changes they observe in the child with ABI who is returning to school. This chapter addresses some of the questions that teachers frequently ask about how to serve a student who has experienced a brain injury.

How can school personnel obtain general information about brain injury and specific information about the student who is making the transition back to school?

School personnel will find it helpful to speak with someone at the hospital or rehabilitation facility where the child has received treatment before the student makes the transition back to school. After contact has been made with the facility, a release form will need to be signed by the parents indicating that they are aware that communication is taking place and that they approve. Once the release form is signed, information about the student may be shared and communication can begin among the hospital, school, and family.

There are usually several professionals involved with the student at the medical facility and within the school system. Communication between medical and school teams will be better coordinated if a contact person is established for each team. All telephone and written correspondence should be channeled through this individual, who will disseminate information to the rest of the team. Having a contact person makes it easier for everyone to communicate and reduces the chance that information will be lost or forgotten.

In addition to providing specific information about the student, many hospitals and rehabilitation facilities are willing to provide general in-service training about brain injury to teachers and students. Brain injury associations at the state level are another good source of information. They will be able to provide a wealth of written information and resource material as well as possibly provide information about support groups throughout the state. Professionals who attend these meetings will learn firsthand about brain injury from parents, siblings, and spouses.

In their search for information about brain injury, school professionals may also find it helpful to contact their state Department of Education. Many states have developed manuals and other resource materials that address school issues related to brain injury. Other states have established networks of trained professionals who are available for consultation.

Individuals who have access to computers will find that the Internet and World Wide Web can provide information on brain injury in a variety of formats, including on-line discussion groups, resource materials, and medical information. With a little bit of technology, information is literally at an individual's fingertips.

Once resources are located, what is the best way for school personnel to share specific information about the student's brain injury with teachers and peers?

Teachers, students, and friends who are knowledgeable about brain injury can be instrumental in a student's successful return to school. As the team puts together a plan for reentry, the parents can indicate their preference for how information will be shared with teachers and peers. They may feel relieved that someone will address with the staff and students changes in their child since the injury, or they may object because of the additional attention that may be called to their child's problems.

Some families may want to be involved in the process of educating the students and teachers about brain injury. In some cases, families may want their child with ABI to be included in this process as well. In other cases, families may prefer that this is done on a day when the child is not present. In either situation, this is an opportunity for the team to work together. Although someone from the medical facility may have a wealth of information about brain injury, educators may have ideas about how the information will best be presented to children and teachers. Parents may be able to share information about changes in social behavior and personal interactions and will know more about the child's previous social relationships.

If the student has experienced physical impairments or changes since the injury, it might be helpful to have photographs or a videotape to help prepare the peers and teachers for these changes. In addition, although a student may have experienced some significant changes, it will be important to talk about the student's strengths, abilities, and preferences.

Jason was 12 years old and had just completed the fifth grade when he sustained a brain injury in a motor vehicle accident during the summer. Jason's fifth-grade teacher described him as an "average" student prior to the injury, but indicated that he had few friends and sometimes had difficulty getting along with other students.

In September, Jason's sixth-grade teacher telephoned the rehabilitation center and asked the social worker to initiate the necessary paperwork that would allow the school and hospital staff to begin communication. Jason's parents agreed to sign all the necessary releases and the school staff were invited to attend a routine staffing the next week. Jason was scheduled to be discharged from the hospital within the month.

At the staffing, the teacher provided information about Jason's previous skills and personality as the rehabilitation staff members and Jason's parents shared information about his current medical status and progress. Hospital staff were particularly concerned about Jason's physical safety. His impulsivity, lack of inhibition, and poor judgment put him at risk for reinjury. Fatigue was also a significant factor. Everyone present at the staffing, including Jason's parents, agreed that home-based instruction for a few hours a day would be an appropriate way to start the school re-entry process. After 3 weeks, he would return to school for half days and would be accompanied by an instructional assistant.

Jason's teacher believed it would be beneficial to have someone talk to the students in Jason's classroom and also requested that information be shared with the other students and teachers at the school. Jason's parents asked to be involved with the presentation so that they could answer any questions the students might have. The presentation occurred a few days before Jason was to return to school and included medical personnel who had been involved in Jason's rehabilitation, his parents, and a special education consultant. The students were provided with an overview about what can happen when a person experiences a brain injury. They also received specific information about what to expect when interacting with Jason and how to respond in difficult situations.

During the presentation, Jason's parents were able to share some of their personal experiences, which helped the teachers and students appreciate the effect this injury had on the entire family. The information they provided also allowed teachers and students to see the significant progress Jason had made in a fairly short period of time.

This orientation for the students and teachers proved helpful. When Jason returned to school, teachers and peers found that his personality had changed. His attention was poor and he had difficulty with academic work that had not previously been a problem. He frequently became argumentative with other students, making statements that hurt feelings or were embarrassing. Jason's teachers reported that the students handled themselves well and attributed this to the fact that they were prepared ahead of time for the changes in his personality and behavior.

Should a student returning to school from the hospital or from rehabilitation resume a full-day school schedule?

It depends. Observation of the student at home or in the medical setting will provide the information needed to answer this question. A student who still requires frequent naps or rest periods during the day will probably not tolerate a full-day schedule at school. There is often an increased need for sleep following brain injury that may be related to fatigue or general level of arousal. The increased need for sleep may last for a few months or may continue for several years.

Some individuals may find that it takes more energy to focus their attention on academic tasks following a brain injury, which may cause them to become fatigued more quickly. Physical impairments can also increase fatigue because of the exertion required for typical activity.

Because there are medical and safety issues involved, it is probably best to be conservative when deciding on the number of hours that a student should attend school following an injury. If the student tends to have more difficulty with fatigue in the afternoon, then it would be best to start with one or two easy classes in the morning. If the student experiences low arousal in the morning, then afternoon classes might work better. If the student does well with the abbreviated schedule, classes can be added as appropriate. Length of the school day and complexity of coursework should be increased based on the student's progress and tolerance.

What about extended year or summer programming for a student who is recovering from a brain injury?

Although individuals recovering from brain injuries may continue to improve for many years after their injury, the most rapid recovery will probably occur within 1–2 years postinjury (Wolcott, Lash, & Pearson, 1995). Recovery, however, should not be confused with "the student has accomplished all he or she can accomplish." Students with brain injuries need structure and continuity if their educational programming is going to help them make the transition between academic years. Providing summer programming, tutoring, or extended year programming may greatly enhance the retention of skills previously learned and the development of the transition supports that will help the student begin the new school year.

Is there anything special to consider when a child moves from elementary to middle school or from middle school to high school?

Transitions in general are difficult for students with brain injuries. Consistency, structure, and routine help students to predict what comes next and to feel more secure. Unfortunately, students with brain injuries will experience many transitions: hospital to school, grade to grade, school to school, and school to community (Wolcott et al., 1995). Thus, it is critical for teachers to proactively plan for these transitions and prepare the student prior to any new change.

When any student makes these transitions in school, expectations change. Usually these transitions involve increased responsibility, organization, and more independent thinking and planning. For a student with a brain injury, this may be especially difficult. The frontal lobes of the brain that help with executive functions (e.g., organizing, initiating, planning, staying focused) are very vulnerable to injury. Therefore, parents and teachers can predict that a student will have increased difficulty when making these transitions. The best way to help the student is to provide practice in making the transition as well as participate in the planning process. For example, over the summer and prior to the first day of school, students who will be making grade-to-grade transitions can visit their new classroom and meet their new teacher. Or, for school-to-school transitions, students can visit the new school and practice moving about the hallways, locating the lockers and cafeteria, and reviewing their new textbooks before school starts.

During the spring of fifth grade, Manuel participated in the Building Friendships project (see Chapter 9). In preparation for the transition from elementary school to middle school, Manuel's friendship facilitator and his father conducted informal question-and-answer sessions in individual classrooms to give students and teachers information about brain injury. Two weeks before the end of the school year, the friendship facilitator and the middle school counselor scheduled a meeting at the middle school for Manuel, his friendship group from the elementary school, and fifth-grade students from other elementary schools who would also be entering the middle school the following year. These students had received information about the meeting from their fifth-grade teachers. The meeting was informal and refreshments were served. The counselor answered questions about middle school, and the friendship group told the middle school students about the Building Friendships project, which the counselor would facilitate the following year. Manuel's father attended the meeting and talked about how Manuel had enjoyed being with friends before his injury and why it was harder for him to make new friends now. The group talked about how to help each other, including Manuel, make new friends and find their way around at the new school. They set a date for their first meeting in the fall.

The following week, Manuel's class, along with other fifth-grade classes from other schools, attended a half-day orientation at the middle school. Each fifth grader was paired with a sixth-grade buddy. The sixth graders showed their buddies around the school, demonstrated how to use the lockers, and took them to a couple of classes. Manuel interacted with several students who had attended the Building Friendships meeting throughout the orientation.

Before school started in the fall, Manuel's special education teacher at the middle school repeated the school tour. She and the counselor also convened the students who had attended the spring transition meeting. The students worked out a schedule for accompanying Manuel from class to class for the first couple of weeks of school.

Should a student who has had a brain injury participate in physical education or other sports activities?

Contact sports (e.g., basketball, football, soccer, baseball, wrestling) are not usually recommended after someone experiences a brain injury. During the initial recovery stages, the student's physician may not want the student to participate in physical education or any other physical activity. Parents and educators should always check with the physician before allowing a student to resume these activities. Experience and research have shown that repeated concussions/brain injuries (especially through professional sports), even mild ones, can have a cumulative effect that may cause permanent damage (Kelly, 1995). Individuals who have already experienced one brain injury are at increased risk for another—and the next one could have devastating effects. The teaching of safety skills and strategies to prevent a second brain injury is necessary for each student.

> *Erin sustained a severe brain injury in a car/pedestrian accident when she was 7 years old. She was in a coma for 2 weeks and hospitalized for 2 months. When she returned to school, numerous modifications were made to assist her during the school day.*
>
> *Over the next year, Erin made a good physical recovery and performed well enough academically that special education support was not needed. Her team (medical staff, educational staff, parents) recommended, however, that documentation of her brain injury be included in her cumulative record on her individual health plan. Included with this documentation was information about the risk for reinjury and the need to avoid contact sports. School personnel were encouraged to contact Erin's physician at the hospital if they had questions about specific activities.*
>
> *This information served as an important reminder to staff when Erin reached junior high school, where few of the teachers knew about her injury. It allowed the physical education teacher to make informed decisions about appropriate activities for Erin and also provided guidance for everyone when Erin indicated an interest in playing basketball on the junior high school team. The individual health plan prompted important communication among Erin's parents, the school, and medical professionals regarding safe participation in activities.*

What about driver's education and obtaining a driver's license?

The answer to this question will vary from person to person. Anyone who is attempting to acquire a driver's license should be able to demonstrate the necessary cognitive and physical skills that are required in driving. Individuals who have experienced a brain injury may have visual-perceptual problems (e.g., field cuts or other vision impairments) that do not allow them to see or perceive things accurately. There may also be problems with judgment or reasoning, especially in emergency situations. Driving simulators can be used to assess a person's ability to react quickly, responsibly, and accurately in an emergency. Individuals with seizure disorders may obtain a driver's license if their seizures have been under control for an amount of time specified by each state. The student's physician and a qualified motor vehicle instructor should determine whether a student can safely drive or resume driving.

How do I know if a student is having problems with his or her medication?

The student's primary care physician and the school nurse should have information about any medications a student may be taking (e.g., for behavior management, seizures, attention improvement). Teachers working with any student taking medication should educate themselves about what the medication is, what its uses are, and what the possible side effects may be. This information can be obtained from the school nurse, medical personnel who have worked with the student, or from other resource materials that provide information about many common medications. Familiarity with the medications will help a teacher be more alert to problems, should they arise.

> David's brain injury occurred when he was involved in a motor vehicle accident during the month of May. At the time, he was just finishing ninth grade and his teachers described him as an above-average student.
>
> David was released from the hospital in June, and although his physical recovery appeared to be complete, he immediately began having difficulty with tenth-grade academic work. He denied having any learning problems despite testing that indicated otherwise, and he refused special education assistance.
>
> David's behavior deteriorated rapidly. He became argumentative and defiant at school, and his parents reported an increase in aggressive behavior at home. He frequently refused to complete school assignments, and over time his teachers were too intimidated to challenge him. Family life became so disrupted that his parents began to talk about an out-of-home placement for David.
>
> David was referred to a clinic that specialized in the treatment of brain injury. During his evaluation, staff members observed several staring episodes. His parents reported that these had been common at home and at school and thought that these episodes were just symptoms of poor attention. Although his previous EEG (electroencephalogram) had been within typical limits, the physician recommended a trial of Tegretol, anticipating that it might reduce the staring spells and David's aggressive behavior. A telephone call was made to school personnel asking them to document any changes in behavior they might see over the next several weeks.
>
> A few weeks after David started taking the medication, his teachers and family observed a significant improvement in his behavior and fewer staring episodes but noted that he seemed excessively fatigued and often fell asleep in class. His parents noticed that he would doze off while watching television and that he fell asleep earlier in the evening than usual. This was reported to David's physician, who reduced the dosage.

A few weeks later, David appeared more alert and seemed to have better control of his behavior.

How can we help students be successful?

Team planning will allow the educator to see the student from many different perspectives and will make it easier to set appropriate expectations. Too often students with brain injuries are assessed through only one set of eyes—the physician's eyes, the teacher's eyes, the psychologist's eyes, *or* the parents' eyes. For students with brain injuries to have continued success, a team with 360-degree vision of the student must be created, and this vision must look forward 5, 10, and even 20 years into the future. The key is to manage the environment as well as teach the student new skills and strategies.

If the student seems to have difficulty with a particular type of task or assignment, careful observation will help determine which parts of the task are most problematic. It should not be assumed that a student is apathetic or lazy when assignments are not completed. The real reason could be that the assignment may require skills that the student has either lost or never learned, the student may not have understood or may have forgotten the assignment, the student may not be able to work fast enough to complete the work, or the student may not know how to get started.

Once the problem has been identified, the supports that the student needs to complete the task successfully must be provided. Supports to address skill impairments may include remediation in specific skill areas, assistance from special education personnel, or materials at a more appropriate reading level. In some cases, the student's team may determine that this particular class is not appropriate and the student may need to be in a different setting in order to be successful while working toward academic goals. General and special education staff can work together to determine appropriate supports and accommodations to address problems with initiation, memory and organization, and work load. Systematic posting of assignments, a quick check-in to be sure the student has started the assignment, periodic examination of the student's work progress during each class period, and agreements about which portion of each assignment the student should complete are all common accommodations teachers employ to address the needs of students with brain injury. It is important to remember that planning an appropriate curriculum with adequate supports is not an exact science and it may take a few attempts to get it right.

In their desire to help students be successful, educators sometimes provide too much assistance or place students in settings in which they are successful but not challenged. Students who have experienced a brain injury have the right to try and to take risks just like anyone else. There has probably been a time in everyone's life when he or she wanted to try something but was discouraged from doing so because no one else believed it could be done. Sometimes failure resulted—and sometimes determination and passion led to success. When a student succeeds in completing a new or difficult task, assistance may be needed to examine the strategies used and determining what worked. Too often students hear only what did not work or what they did wrong. The use of metacognitive strategies, which help students develop plans before trying something new and identify strategies that worked when they do something well, build on the students' successes. In summary, student failure can often be avoided when team members are versatile, flexible, and positive in their approach to problem solving.

What if the student denies or seems unaware of changes resulting from the brain injury?

Some students with brain injury, particularly adolescents, do not seem to have an accurate perception of their own strengths and weaknesses. This lack of awareness can be frustrating to educators because it means students may not be willing to try special accommodations or compensatory strategies. Frustrated educators may believe that a student is stubbornly denying problems that are clearly obvious. In some cases, older students may suppress or deny evidence suggesting they have problems in order to avoid or delay the pain of recognizing the changes that have occurred. This type of psychological "denial" may be the student's primary coping strategy. In many cases, lack of awareness is directly related to the specific areas of the brain that have been injured (i.e., those areas involved with awareness and thinking processes). Sometimes a student with a recent injury who believes he or she is fully recovered simply has not had an opportunity to experience changes in his or her abilities to perform a variety of tasks.

When working with students who exhibit a lack of awareness, educators must use communication techniques that minimize arguing and give the student an opportunity to assess his or her own abilities (Sohlberg, Johansen, Hoornbeek, & Geyer, 1994). Sohlberg and others recommend the following approaches for educators:

- *Work together with the student.* Trying to confront a student about shortcomings is likely to provoke an argument and entrench the student in the mindset that there is no problem. To avoid polarizing the teacher's and the student's views, use collaborative, supportive language stressing that the goal is to work together to figure out how the student can be most successful. Rather than discourage activities because of impairments that the student denies, the student's attempts to try challenging activities and to function independently should be praised. Supports should also be offered to help with these attempts.

- *Allow the student to experience impairments and strengths in a supportive atmosphere.* Structure tasks that the student can complete successfully followed by others that reveal impairments. Then discuss the student's impressions of the performance. The goal is not to prove to the student that there are problems but to provide an opportunity to try a variety of activities and draw conclusions about what kinds of supports the student may need that were not necessary before the injury.

- *Learn the art of questioning (Sohlberg et al., 1994).* Ask questions in a way that accentuates strengths and allows students to preserve self-esteem. Instead of asking what kinds of problems are present as a result of the injury, discuss the student's recovery in general, beginning with things that have gotten better since the student was injured. This gives the student an opportunity to focus on strengths and perhaps compare recovered skills with preinjury abilities with an answer such as "My memory is better but not as good as it was." General questions give the student a chance to look at both what has been regained and what is still difficult.

Lisa and her mother had been arguing for weeks about whether Lisa could get a driver's license. These arguments were highly emotional, with Lisa accusing her mother of using the brain injury as an excuse to keep her from engaging in typical adolescent activities like driving around with friends and dating. In an attempt to get Lisa to see her point of view, her mother repeatedly listed all of the reasons it would be unsafe for her to drive (e.g., mild physical impairments, slowed reaction time, impaired judgment, impulsivity).

The school counselor gave Lisa's mother information about lack of awareness that helped her see Lisa's behavior as a result of ABI rather than as an attitude problem. He offered some suggestions to improve communication and increase Lisa's awareness of the effects of her brain injury that might make driving unsafe. The counselor also facilitated a conversation in which Lisa's mother began by saying, "I want you to know that I would like nothing more than for you to get your driver's license, and I hope that it will be possible. I would like to have it be a goal that we work toward together. I know it must be hard to hear that you can't just go get your license tomorrow." At that point Lisa began to cry quietly. Her mother continued, "But let's talk about what we can do right now to help you get your license." Lisa and her mother, with the help of the counselor, came up with a plan to set up a driving evaluation to determine which skills Lisa would need to work on to be ready for a driver's training class.

How can parents and teachers distinguish between typical adolescent behavior and behavior that is related to brain injury?

A student injured in adolescence may exhibit new, problematic behaviors postinjury and may, in fact, be described by parents and teachers as "acting like a different person." Often these behaviors include risk taking, acting out in class, being disruptive in other areas of the school, skipping classes, and other activities that challenge and test the limits of adult authority. Because adolescence is a time when many students engage in similar behaviors, teachers and parents may wonder if the student's behavior is part of typical development or due to cognitive impairments and disinhibition resulting from the brain injury.

This is not an easy question to answer, but when there has been a documented brain injury, parents and teachers might want to ask themselves the following questions. If the answer to most of these questions is "yes," it is likely that the student's problems may be related more to brain injury than to adolescence. Careful observation of the student's performance at home and at school may provide further insight into the origin of behaviors.

- *Is the student's behavior now qualitatively and quantitatively different from how it was before the injury?* That is, is the student engaging in more inappropriate behaviors and have the inappropriate behaviors escalated from minor pranks to more serious offenses? For example, preinjury a student may have skipped a class to hang out with friends on a nice day. Postinjury, the same student might take off from school as soon as the bus drops him off, missing the entire day.
- *Is the student's behavior qualitatively and quantitatively different from that of other adolescents you know?* Students with brain injuries sometimes appear to lack the subtle timing and judgment other adolescents call on to "get away" with playing pranks, taking minor risks, and defying rules. The student with a brain injury may not know when to stop or may not discriminate that the teacher who easily excused disruptive behavior yesterday is in a bad mood today.

- *Does the student seem frustrated or embarrassed with his own performance?* A student may act out in class in order to divert attention from his or her inability to answer questions or complete assignments. In other cases, a student who continues to try to do work that is confusing, or too difficult, may explode in frustration.
- *Do problems occur in all environments, as opposed to only one or two?* Problem behaviors that occur in only certain settings may be related to problems (e.g., frustration, embarrassment) specific to those settings. Observation may reveal supports or guidelines that are available in the nonproblematic settings and could be instituted in the areas in which problem behaviors do occur.
- *Do many of the problems seem to be related to memory, attention, initiation, and organization, in addition to impulsiveness and poor judgment?* Adolescent problem behaviors are often attributed to poor judgment and lack of self-control or impulsiveness. Adolescents with ABI may be more likely to exhibit problems in these areas and, as discussed previously, their problems may be more severe than those experienced by their peers. Careful observation of the antecedents of challenging behaviors, however, may reveal other factors related to the brain injury that contribute to the problem. Problems with memory, attention, initiation, and organization can contribute to frustration, leading to either avoidant or acting-out behavior. A student who consistently forgets the behavioral requirements of a classroom, materials, or assignments; has trouble starting tasks; seems to tune out; or appears hyperactive may appear to the teacher to be noncompliant or engaging in passive resistance. Helping the teacher identify supports for students with problems in these areas may help these students avoid more extreme behaviors and concentrate on classroom activities.

What about long-term developmental needs? Do children and adolescents "grow out" of their injuries?

Children and adolescents are best described as "works in progress." Neuroscientists and other experts are challenging the notion that "the younger you are, the better you'll do" after a brain injury (Allison, 1992; Lehr & Savage, 1992). Thus, the concept of neuroplasticity and brain injury is far more complicated than previously believed. For example, infants or toddlers who sustain an injury to their frontal lobes may not demonstrate effects from that injury until much later in their development (e.g., beginning adolescence).

Or injury to the areas of the brain that represent a young child's language centers may not appear significant until the child is required to comprehend at higher levels of abstraction (Savage, 1995). Although many children are certainly resilient enough to survive even severe trauma to their brains, they are just as vulnerable as adults to the long-term effects of trauma. Sometimes, it just takes longer for the effects of the injury to their brains to be seen. New research utilizing advanced scanning technology and statistical analysis of EEGs have better identified how a child's brain matures from birth through adolescence (Allison, 1992). Hence, it is critical to monitor growth and development as a student continues to progress through school. Schools can then set up preventive measures to plan for possible problems around the student's typical developmental milestones before little problems turn into serious psychological issues.

CONCLUSION

As these 12 common questions indicate, the challenges educators must face when serving children with brain injuries are complex and diverse. Getting answers to these and other questions can be just as challenging as the questions themselves when few educators or even special educators receive preservice or in-service training specific to students with brain injury. Teamwork and communication among systems in medicine, education, and the community can help teachers answer some of the questions in this chapter. But getting answers to the questions is only part of the task. Once educators know how to address the needs of students with ABI, schools must provide enough resources and flexibility to carry out the recommended approaches, many of which require observation, individualization, and communication to a degree that is difficult to maintain in a public school setting. Other chapters in this volume contain more specific suggestions for implementing school-based practices that address the problems posed in these questions.

REFERENCES

Allison, M. (1992, October/November). The effects of neurologic injury on the maturing brain. *Headlines*, 2–10.

Individuals with Disabilities Education Act (IDEA) of 1990, PL 101-476, 20 U.S.C. § 1400 *et seq.*

Kelly, J.P. (1995, Winter). Education, awareness and prevention of brain injuries in sports. *TBI Challenge*, 3(1), 3–7.

Lehr, E., & Savage, R.C. (1992). Community and school integration from a developmental perspective. In J. Keutzer (Ed.), *Community integration following traumatic brain injury* (pp. 301–310). Baltimore: Paul H. Brookes Publishing Co.

Savage, R.C. (1995). An educator's guide to the brain and brain injury. In R.C. Savage & G. Wolcott (Eds.), *Educational dimensions of acquired brain injury* (pp. 13–31). Austin, TX: PRO-ED.

Sohlberg, M.M., Johansen, A., Hoornbeek, S., & Geyer, S. (1994). *Training the use of compensatory memory systems*. Puyallup, WA: Association for Neuropsychological Research and Development.

Wolcott, G., Lash, M., & Pearson, S. (Eds.). (1995). *Signs and strategies for educating students with brain injuries*. Houston, TX: HDI Publishers.

Index

Page numbers followed by *t* or *f* indicate tables or figures, respectively.